The University and the Teachers

The University and the Teachers
France, the United States, England

Harry Judge
Michel Lemosse
Lynn Paine & Michael Sedlak

Oxford Studies in
Comparative Education,
Volume 4(1/2)

General Editor: David Phillips

Triangle Books

Triangle Books
PO Box 65, Wallingford, Oxfordshire OX10 0YG, United Kingdom
Triangle Books is a division of Triangle Journals Ltd

Published in the United Kingdom, 1994
© Triangle Journals Ltd

ISBN 1 873927 08 8

**This publication is also available on a subscription basis
as Volume 4(1/2) of** *Oxford Studies in Comparative Education*
(ISSN 0961-2149).

Typeset in Monotype Plantin by Triangle Journals Ltd
Printed and bound in the United Kingdom by Cambridge University Press

Contents

Preface 7

Introduction 9

1 **France: 1963**
The Decision 15
The System 20
The Teachers 25

2 **France: before 1963**
Continuities 37
The Agrégation 40
The University 47
The Ecole Normale 55

3 **France: since 1963**
The Crisis of 1968 65
Holding the Line:
    the Right and the seventies 76
Pressures for Change:
    the Left and the eighties 83
An Uncertain Outcome? 90

4 **The United States: 1963**
Towards 1963 95
Normal Schools and Universities 100
1963: Two books 109

5 **The United States: since 1963** 121
A Non-System? 123
The Uncertain Profession 133
Heart versus Head 141
Responses 147

6 **England: towards 1963**
1963 155
The Rise of the Teacher
    Apprentice, 1789-1902 160
The Triumph of Academic
    Credentials, 1902-1963 169

7 **England: after 1963** 183

8 **England: towards 1994**   199

                    Towards 1994   202
                    The Story within Teacher Education:
                        centralisation of control   203
                    Anti-Professionalism: resurrecting
                        the teacher   apprentice   221
                    Competition in a
                        Destabilised Environment   229
                    Concluding the Era: surprise   238

9 **Reflections**   1963 Again: the University   241
                    1963 Again: the Teachers   246
                    The Dynamics of Change   251
                    After 1995   258

Bibliography: France, United States, England, General   265

Preface

We wish to dedicate this volume to the memory of Lawrence Cremin, historian and educator, who died in 1990.

The writing of this book was made possible by the generous support of the Spencer Foundation of Chicago and by the willingness of many people in the three countries studied to share with us their time and their experience. Some acknowledgment of this debt is made in the following pages.

More personally, Lynn Paine and Michael Sedlak thank their spouses, Brian DeLany and Rhonda Sherwin, who contributed to the success of every phase of the work, and their new daughters, Macon DeLany Paine and Aleksa Sedlak, whose arrival during the study complicated and enriched all aspects of the project.

Oxford Studies in Comparative Education, Vol. 4(1/2), 1994

Introduction

This is on the surface a book about the role of the university in the education and professional preparation of teachers. It examines that relationship in a cross-national perspective, and in a way which we hope will be illuminating and believe to be original. The central argument is that describing the ways in which, within these three countries, universities regard school teachers and their professional education will serve to expose a whole range of embedded attitudes about education, of cultural assumptions, and of political habits. The three countries – France, the United States and England – were chosen precisely in order to throw such differences into sharp relief. This book therefore is, no doubt to the disappointment of some, about differences rather than similarities: its style is contrastive rather than comparative. It does not suggest that easy "lessons" are to be learnt, or that supposedly good practices can be whisked from one side to the other of the Channel or of the Atlantic.

If the countries were chosen with such purposes in mind, so was the subject. Teacher education, treated in artificial isolation, can indeed be a dull and unrewarding subject; so can the institutional behaviour of universities. The geometry of the following chapters is derived from the axiom that to understand teacher education, above all in a cross-national framework, is to understand much more than teacher education. How teachers are educated, and where and by whom, reflect beliefs about what teachers are for and why society employs them. Any examination of such beliefs must unpack underlying theories of the purposes of an education provided by the State. Such theories in turn can be shown to be part of a rich texture of national habits and assumptions (as well as controversies) about the nature of the State, the actual and desirable shape of society, the duties and autonomy of the citizen, the relationship between education and the economy, and the character of that culture which it is one of the purposes of the schools to transmit.

The methods of analysis and discussion adopted here are, therefore, in no sense peculiar to a study of teacher education, or indeed to a wider study of schooling. A similar case could be made for a contrastive study of transport in the three countries embraced by this study. French, American and British railway systems are as they are because of sharply differing assumptions and beliefs about the role of competition or the distinction between private and public. They are at the same time marked by differences in geography and demography, in political history and economic conditions. So much is obvious. AMTRAK has almost nothing in common with the SNCF and

British Rail is about to be dismantled (at the very moment when it is being connected to the French system by a tunnel). Parallel arguments could be deployed for a contrastive study of the civil service in these three countries. This book is therefore in its essence an essay in cross-national studies rather than a technical study of teacher education and the universities.

The theme is chosen because (obviously) it is one in which all the authors have a particular interest, and a peculiar qualification. That qualification is the paradoxical one of expert ignorance. The studies reported in this book were undertaken by partners from France, the United States and Britain. Each of us, for good or ill, has been engaged for many years in the study and practice of teacher education in her or his own country. But the design of this work has required each of us to learn and to think about an experience quite foreign to our own. Each of us has struggled to maintain a distance, to observe from the outside, to interpret what we see in terms intelligible to those who for the moment are as ignorant as we were. The triangular nature of the study is therefore integral to its character. For example, the French partner in this enterprise, who brought to his task an extensive appreciation of the English as well as of the French educational world, is required to interpret the American experience (previously unfamiliar to him) in ways which make it intelligible to his British partner and which at the same time – but now in the judgment of his American partner – do not violate the facts. We have tried, carefully but not always successfully, not to influence one another's opinions.

This study elects to concentrate on a small number of countries, namely three. This is because the authors preferred to work in depth rather than to employ more generalized survey methods. The reasons for this choice must be by now obvious. The thrust of the whole work is to clarify how one narrowly focused issue – the relationship of the universities to teacher education – can be illuminated by what is essentially a contextual and historical approach. This has entailed for the authors an extended study of the general workings of the educational system in the country under study. Examples will abound in the following pages. Wider surveys of course have their own advantages and uses, but do not permit a descent into the finer grain of reality. They must also seek to synthesize, to amalgamate, to homogenize: in a word to be comparative rather than contrastive. The choice to be narrow has therefore been consciously made.

A similar preference underlies the choice of these three countries, rather than of any others. Our belief is that there need to be enough comparable features to render contrast meaningful. Even if we ourselves had the necessary linguistic and other skills, we would all remain sceptical of the value of a study of the kind attempted here but focusing upon, say, Japan, Norway and the Ukraine. Two of our countries share a common language; all three of them enjoy, even if in one case the assertion has itself become contentious, continuity with a deeply rooted tradition of western civilization. Yet in education, as for example in law, the differences appear to be as fundamental as the similarities. Consider the use of one of the two key terms of this study: "Universities". A French university has something, but not much, in common with an American university; the term "an American university" is itself almost devoid of meaning, given the rich variety of institutions covered by that one term; some British universities are more like the French grandes écoles, while others could be more readily likened to liberal arts colleges in the States. And so on. It is this mixture of propinquity and distance that makes our particular triad so rewarding a subject of study.

Harry Judge has been responsible for the work on France, as for the overall design of the project and of this book. He wrote (in addition to this Introduction) the first three chapters, as well as chapter 9. Chapters 4 and 5 are from the pen of Michel Lemosse. Lynn Paine and Michael Sedlak worked together on chapters 6, 7 and 8.

Harry Judge was until 1988 Director of the Oxford University Department of Educational Studies, where he had worked since 1973. He has been a Fellow of Brasenose College since the same year. Before that he was Principal of Banbury School in Oxfordshire and during that period was a member of the James Committee (reporting in 1972) on the reform of teacher education. His disciplinary background is in history and his graduate work in London was on early modern French history, which is the field of his earlier published work. During the 1980s he was increasingly active in discussions on teacher education in the United States, and in 1982 published for the Ford Foundation *American Graduate Schools of Education : A View from Abroad.* Two years later, Oxford University Press published his *A Generation of Schooling : English Secondary Schools since 1944.* He has served as Visiting Professor at several American universities, and for the first five years after his retirement from the Oxford directorship enjoyed a part-time appointment at Michigan State University, teaching a course in comparative education. He has published many articles and contributed chapters to collective works in recent years.

Michel Lemosse is a Professor at the University of Nice, where he teaches British Civilization, and in particular the political and social history of Britain since the seventeenth century. He is a product of the classically French école normale who went on to study for the agrégation at the Sorbonne. He has taught in both anglophone and francophone Africa. He has published many articles on education and on white-collar unions: his work for the Doctorat d'Etat was on teacher unions in Britain and his *Education in England and Wales* was published by Longman in 1992.

Lynn Paine is an Associate Professor in the College of Education at Michigan State University. Her own undergraduate work was in East Asian Studies at Princeton, while her graduate studies in sociology and education were completed at Stanford. Her research interests include the relationship between teacher education policy and practice, the links between teacher education and teaching, and the connections between educational reform and social change. She has conducted extensive field research in China and published journal articles and book chapters on teacher education policy, the educational policy process, and teaching in Chinese classrooms. As a senior researcher with the National Center for Research on Teacher Learning she is currently participating in a cross-national comparative study of novice teacher learning with and from mentors.

Michael Sedlak is Professor of the History of Education and Associate Dean of Academic Affairs in the College of Education at Michigan State University. His undergraduate work in history was completed at the University of Washington and his graduate work at Northwestern University. He has worked with the Rand Corporation on an array of projects related to history and to policy, and has directed two large-scale historical projects funded by the US Department of Education. He has published widely on the history of professions and of professional education, on high school reform and on public policies and services for adolescents. He is the author of a score of articles and of four books, including *Education in the United States : An Interpretive History* (1976), with Robert Church, and *Selling Students Short : Classroom Bargains and Academic Reform in the American High School* (1986).

Our work is based upon the published sources cited in the text and brought together in the bibliography at the end of this volume, and upon an extensive series of visits and interviews across a period of four years. In several of the cities and regions listed below interviews were conducted in more than one institution of higher education, as well as in primary and secondary schools, and with educational administrators, civil servants, politicians, and senior officials in private as well as public agencies. In all cases a commitment to protecting anonymity has been observed, and in some cases more detailed information is given in the notes at the end of relevant chapters.

Interviews were conducted:

- in France: in Paris, Lyon, Grenoble, Limoges, Rouen, Nice and Caen
- in the United States: in Massachusetts, Virginia, Louisiana, Michigan, Connecticut, California and Washington, DC.
- in England: in London, Exeter, Staffordshire, Leeds, Cambridge, Reading, Oxford, Coventry and Bristol

The reader will have noted the reference to "England" rather than to Great Britain or to the United Kingdom. This is of course deliberate. There are significant differences between Scotland and England, in education as in law and not least in matters relating to the training of teachers. We chose to concentrate on England as a case study. Although most of the comments made will also apply to Wales, and many to Northern Ireland, it would have been cumbersome to keep adding such special references. The context will make it clear when the references are to Britain as a whole.

The dominant method of this study is historical, although unfortunately history has not stopped while we have been working. "The university" may be resumed as the key example. The use and definition of that term were radically changed in Britain in 1992, when institutions that had in the 1960s been baptised as Polytechnics changed overnight not only their names but also their relationship to the apparatus of the State. In France in 1991, new university institutions were created (again overnight) to provide novel forms of teacher education. Things, for good reason, may not happen so abruptly in the United States but the years during which this study was conducted have seen changes of deep if often contradictory importance in the interaction between universities and teacher education.

It soon became clear to each of us, writing of a foreign country, that nothing in the present scene could possibly be explained without a constant and regressive appeal to the explanatory power of history. Even in France there is no such thing as pure rationality. It became equally clear that to explain the 1990s in terms of all the necessary history of (at least) the past century produced no explanation at all: only a bewildering account of successive changes, described from a contemporary angle. Hence our dilemma: history alone could explain everything but only by making it unintelligible. Circumstances differ widely in all three countries, but for all of them it can be argued that the mid-1960s represented a time of dramatic and fundamental change. For reasons that are given in the body of the text, 1963 is an appropriate year to take as a starting point for each of our expositions.

Each of the three studies therefore begins with an overview of the situation in that year. An analysis is then offered of how the prevailing relationship between the university and the training of teachers had by 1963 been generated. Some degree of stability and clarity having been established, the evolution of that relationship since 1963 is examined and, it is hoped, explained. History is usually written forwards and sometimes backwards: in these pages, it is written outwards, from the middle.

In order to focus attention on this aspect of our work, the first chapter is written in the present tense, so that the reader is invited to adopt the perspective of 1963 and (for the moment) to leave out of account all that has happened since. And so to France.

Oxford Studies in Comparative Education, Vol. 4(1/2), 1994

CHAPTER 1

France: 1963

The Decision

On 3 August the Government promulgated a decree incorporating an uncompromising decision to modify the shape of secondary education in France. The full effects upon the lives of teachers and on their education have yet to be assessed. Some weeks earlier, President de Gaulle called a special meeting with a small group of his ministers at the Elysée, the presidential palace.[1] Georges Pompidou, who was in attendance and has been Prime Minister since 1958, was disconcerted to learn that a major change of educational policy had already been decided. His Minister of Education, Christian Fouchet, shared both his surprise and his displeasure.[2] The years of hesitation are at last ending: the interests of France require that there now be created a new form of educational institution, a "College" of General Education (Collège d'Enseignement Général, or CEG) to provide four years of comprehensive education for all pupils leaving the primary school at the age of about eleven. France requires such a change if it is to maintain its proud place among the world's leading democracies, if it is to recruit an élite from a base wider than in the past, and if it is to maintain its noble traditions in higher secondary education. By one clear statement of intention, the President has brusquely initiated a series of changes designed to ensure that the best traditions of French education are not fractured, and that those traditions are by explicit government order adapted to meet the changing needs of the nation in the later twentieth century.

This decisive event captures much of the essence both of contemporary French politics and of French education. It will take two decades for the implications of what is now prescribed to work their way through the world of teaching and ultimately into the professional education of teachers. It is the President who determines this structural change in policy, for this is the Fifth Republic, founded only five years ago. The Algerian crisis of 1958 brought to an end the short and troubled life of the Fourth Republic, inaugurated after the liberation of France in 1945: de Gaulle was summoned to return to power from his retreat at Colombey-les-Deux-Eglises. In his self-imposed exile, de

Gaulle had lost none of his haughty contempt for professional politicians and their shabby ways, and was determined to be a statesman with real powers, and not simply a constitutionally convenient decoration. The powers attributed to his office in 1958 were last year strengthened further when, after the necessary referendum, the constitution was amended to require the election of the President by direct universal suffrage. The President can now plausibly claim to be an expression of the will of the whole French people, and not merely that of the political classes. Since 1958, he has more than once used the referendum to strengthen his own authority and that of the office he holds. He is therefore confident of his own right to direct educational policy, and his intervention now proves to be decisive. As so often in the past, the means and purposes of educational change are in 1963 tightly connected to the world of contemporary politics.

It is also notable that, even if the Ministers of de Gaulle's Fifth republic enjoy less power than many of their predecessors, they share the Presidential axiom that it is for the State to determine for the whole of France the nature of the educational system and to control its structures and operation. Whether he follows the orders of the President in the Elysée or the Prime Minister in Matignon, the Minister of Education controls from the rue de Grenelle the whole apparatus of education. He is surrounded by those advisers whom he has appointed to his Cabinet, and who will depart from power with him. He is served by a strong bureaucracy organised systematically to apply State policies in each corner of the educational world. He is advised by a strong central Inspectorate, made up of some one hundred and forty scholarly experts, most of them specializing in a particular subject area (such as mathematics, or philosophy). These General Inspectors (Inspecteurs Généraux, IGs) exercise strategic control over the careers of teachers, over the curriculum as it is taught in schools, over the preparation of the texts which govern much of the detail of education in France.

Paris, in 1963 as in 1863 and for centuries before that, asserts the strongest of claims to dominate France. But no longer does it lack (as it often had in the more distant past) the practical means of extending its power into the remotest corners of "the Hexagon".

In education, as in all branches of civil government, the machinery for the local application of national policy is in place and well tested. Metropolitan France is divided, on principles clearly established in the earliest years after the Revolution of 1789, into less than one hundred Departments, each of them of manageable size and each under the administrative tutelage of a Prefect who represents the authority of all the Ministries and not simply that of the Interior. His dignity is registered in the respect with which he is received and the elaborate uniform which in 1963 he still wears on ceremonial occasions. He is, moreover, a highly educated, and in most cases highly competent, public official. The Departments in turn are grouped for purposes of educational administration into over twenty Academies, and these emanations of the power and will of Paris have a wide range of duties delegated to them. It will be the duty of the Academies to apply locally over the coming years the general policy for secondary schooling which the President has just proclaimed, together with the meticulously detailed regulations which as a consequence of that decree will pour down upon them from the Ministry in the rue de Grenelle. Responsibility for each Academy lies with a Rector, who is appointed by the Minister for a limited period of years and who must by law be a senior member of one of the university Faculties, dispersed throughout France but dominated by Paris. The Rector is the agent of the Minister, responsible only to him and removable by him.

Each Rector is supported by a hierarchy of professional assistants, who in total greatly outnumber the civil servants employed in the work of the Ministry in Paris itself. The duties of the financial and of some administrative officers are well-defined, but in most cases there is no clear line to be drawn between administration and pedagogy. Much of the supervisory work in each of the Departments composing an Academy is undertaken by the Academy Inspector (Inspecteur d'Académie, IA), who has especially wide powers over primary education. He in turn directs a team of less prestigious Departmental Inspectors (Inspecteurs Départementaux de l'Education Nationale, IDENs) each of whom manages a group of primary schools. More important for the secondary schools are the Regional Pedagogical Inspectors (Inspecteurs Pédagogiques Régionaux, IPRs): these are for the most part specialists in a particular subject matter, Latin and Greek for example, who work with and monitor the teachers of those subjects in the lycée, the French secondary school. They have responsibilities to the IGs, as well as to the Rector, and it is from their select number that most of the General Inspectors are recruited by a subtle process of cooptation.

Universities as such enjoy in 1963 only a shadowy existence, and (yet again) Paris lies at the very heart of the academic universe. The chief official responsible within each region (that is, an Academy) for the functioning of higher education is, to be sure, the Rector. But universities do not have Presidents, whether elected or appointed, and they have few elected committees or councils and, perhaps most significant of all, no proper budgets. Provision for higher education is an integral part of a national responsibility towards education at all levels, and the notion of "the Faculty" is more familiar than that of a local or regional university. "Faculty" refers not, as in the United States, to the totality of academics within one institution but to an organizational unit based on a family of disciplines or a learned profession: Letters, Science, Medicine, Law. Where, as in several major provincial cities, universities are – often for historic reasons – perceived as existing, they are in practice little more than loose groupings of largely autonomous Faculties, each with its own Dean and each regarding cognate Faculties elsewhere (rather than other Faculties happening to reside in the same city) as the primary constituency of reference. Behind these shadowy institutional arrangements broods the dominant ghost of The University of France, alive and well in spite of having been abolished in the middle of the last century, standing as surrogate for and sponsor of all educational provision at all levels throughout the nation. From that conception of THE University is derived the rationale for and the historical explanation of the special position of the Rector, a professional university scholar nominated to assume responsibility for the provision by the State of education at all levels within his Academy – pre-school, primary, secondary, higher. Students in 1963 do not themselves speak in terms of "going to University": they cycle or take the bus to "the fac". Researchers and teachers in higher education seek to advance their standing and careers by seeking an appointment in Paris; or, if those hopes are frustrated, they prefer to live in Paris and commute for a few days each week during term time to the city where they hold an appointment in a Faculty. Degrees and diplomas are national awards, their quality and parity being guaranteed by the State which confers them. Nowhere is the special character of the French system in 1963 more striking than in higher education.

There is, moreover, an important sense in which parts at least of secondary education in France are entangled with higher education: it is not just a quaint anomaly that teachers in the lycée proudly exercise their right to the title of professeur, and that many of the most academically able among them prefer to teach in a lycée in the capital rather than in a provincial Faculty. The ranks of the secondary school teachers are graded in terms of their academic quality and degree of specialization: the most prestigious among them luxuriate in the title of agrégé. The professeur derives comfort and pleasure, and not just a sense of security, from his respected status as a civil servant. Professionally, he may cultivate a relationship with his IPR, with whom he shares many scholarly values, and through him with the IGs and the whole network of subject teachers. None of this is inconsistent with active membership of a teacher's union. For many, this will be the SNES (the *Syndicat National des Enseignements du Second Degré*), a constituent since 1948 of the FEN (*Fédération d'Education Nationale*). To the active secondary school teacher, nothing is more important than career mobility, and especially if that involves finding an appointment in Paris itself. Many of the decisions about such transfers (mutations) are taken by joint committees representing both the officials of the Ministry and the union – the SNES or one of its rivals – to which teachers belong.

The baccalauréat, for many the keystone of the whole educational system, is conferred on students aged about eighteen at the end of a successful secondary schooling and yet is – in every sense of the term – a university degree. That is precisely what it is meant to be, and why it has for so long been stoutly defended. Its importance has grown steadily in recent years: the number of successful candidates has trebled in the thirteen years since 1950 (Croissandeau 1993, p.190). The most successful and ambitious among the students even remain in the lycée for at least two further years after the bac, either to follow advanced technical courses or to prepare to compete for admission to high quality courses in national institutions of a specialised character (the grandes écoles). For students in sciences and especially in the humanities the fac has little to offer; the situation is very different for those wishing to study medicine or law. From those remaining in the lycée for the two extra years of intensive preparation exceptional standards of academic performance are demanded. It is not the case in France that higher education dominates secondary education; rather, for many years and still in 1963, it is secondary education as given distinctive shape in the lycée which is the dominant partner. Much of this may soon change.

There is perhaps no other developed country where in 1963 the distinction between primary and secondary schooling is so sharp, and so deeply rooted in principle and in history, as it is here in France. Some of the reasons for the traditional clarity of this distinction will be explored in the next chapter. The primary school of the Fifth Republic still has its own ideology, its own hierarchies, its own terminology, its own unions, its own teacher training system. It has not been designed to provide in any sense a preparation for the secondary school, the traditional lycée, but seeks to offer instead an alternative based on different principles. Its roots strike down into the école maternelle, the nursery school in English and the kindergarten in American terms, which is already attended by a surprising number of young children. In 1960, 91.4% of five year olds and 62.4% of four year olds were already attending schools of this type (Durand-Prinborgne 1991, p. 10). In the years between the two World Wars, many lycées had their own preparatory departments, which were favoured by the children of the more prosperous classes and which often in effect guaranteed a place at the partner secondary school. Although fees in secondary schools were abolished three decades ago, access to these schools is still heavily biased towards the middle classes. An examination for entry can be and is taken by eleven year olds in the primary schools, but the nature of that examination and the emphasis still placed upon Latin in the lycée have long discouraged from the competition many of the children coming from less prosperous families. One of the most powerful reasons underlying the shift in government policy announced this year lies, however, in the growing pressure from ever larger numbers of pupils to secure access to a full secondary education. The point of most acute tension in the system now lies at the frontier between the primary and the secondary school, traditionally more or less sealed, more recently opened to a deserving minority of children coming from the primary schools, and now being openly challenged.

Champions of the primary school argue that it has long and successfully met the needs of those for whom a traditional secondary education, dominated by mathematics and Latin, has been inappropriate or inaccessible (Briand, 1992). Its teachers, most of whom have in the past been men, are dedicated to providing opportunities for those who are least well served by an orthodox secondary education. They have instilled, and continue to espouse, the civic virtues of republicanism and have emphasised the useful rather than the decorative in education. They guard the title of instituteur, a term for which no adequate English translation can be found, and are expert in instilling basic knowledge in a range of necessary subjects. They have no wish to emulate the subject-mindedness of their secondary colleagues. But the primary schools, as a self-contained system, have energetically developed educational opportunities for older pupils who wish to pursue their schooling beyond the school leaving age of fourteen. A long tradition of providing upper or senior primary schools (the *école primaire supérieure*, EPS) was officially endorsed in 1959 when the Minister of Education of the day, Jean Berthoin, rebaptised such schools and associated programmes of study as *Collèges d'Enseignement Général*, CEGs. Moreover, for the past four years these collèges have been required to offer courses which to some degree parallel those offered in the lycées, so that in appropriate cases transfers from the one institution to the other can be arranged after the first two years. The Government has of course now decided that in principle these various forms of higher primary/lower secondary schooling should be amalgamated in the four years of the unified CES. Only experience will show how this will work out in practice, but it is already clear that the troubled frontier between secondary and primary now has to be manipulated to make room for a new kind of institution, neither primary nor secondary in the traditional senses of those terms, with new kinds of teachers.

Meanwhile, the instituteur remains very much at the centre of the scene. His work is supervised by an IDEN, the local agent of the Rector, representing the Minister in Paris. He is appointed to the service of the Department, being paid by the State and accorded the status of a civil servant. He belongs to the SNI (*Syndicat National des Instituteurs*, affiliated like the SNES, to the all-powerful FEN) which represents his interests, locally and nationally, in all matters related to his status and career, and which also connects him to an impressive network of services – insurance, travel, house purchase, mail order agencies (Auber 1985). In many rural areas he remains so much a part of the public system of government that he acts as assistant to the Mayor and carries out a range of administrative duties.

The System

As an English observer appreciates these dominant features of French education in 1963, what might strike him as most distinctively "French", as most contrastive with what he knows of Britain and the United States? And how are those most salient features reflected in the patterns of teacher education and training as they currently exist in France?

Of course, the portrait just outlined is over-simplified, and for that reason may also appear idealized (in at least two senses). If that is so, then the balance will be corrected in the following chapters. Yet the contrasts remain impressive and instructive. The most obvious and most frequently remarked characteristic of the French system is the intensity of central control (Nique, 1990b). Governments in Paris may do things well or ill, but nobody contests their right to prescribe. Parliamentary debates are not unlike stage performances, marked by rhetoric rather than by detailed analysis or by an effort to adjust and seek consensus. The decisions which matter are taken in the rue de Grenelle (unless imposed by yet higher central authority) and on the advice of experts in a professional cabinet of experts who are not elected, and depend entirely on the favour of the Minister of the day. The General Inspectors regulate the content of what is taught, especially but not only in the secondary sector, and the heads of the various administrative services labour mightily to express in the densely packed pages of the Bulletin Officiel the detail which cascades from the policy decisions taken by the Minister for the whole of France. Teachers and other personnel in the education service, from the highest to the lowest, are moved from place to place and post to post in an effort to ensure that a consistently high service is delivered. Since France is not a military dictatorship, such movements have to be carefully negotiated with powerful unions, which exist to defend their own members and press both their individual and their corporate interests. The power of the unions, and especially of the loosely articulated FEN, parallels that of a centralised administration, and has been growing steadily for most of the past twenty years (Toulemonde, 1988).

The instructions and exhortations of the central administration are not issued into an empty space. They are repeated and amplified through a network of hierarchies, based throughout France on a uniform pattern. There are no structural variations in the system: whether the area of the country affected is urban or rural, whether it is densely or thinly populated, whether it is rich or poor, whether it is near to the centre or distant – the pattern of administrative and pedagogical control is uniform, and all lines lead back to Paris. In administrative as in cultural and intellectual life, Paris is where all important things happen: opposed to Paris is "the desert" (the rest of France), and that which is not in Paris is "down there" (là-bas). Academies are of unequal size, in area as in population, but in each of them there presides a Rector, an established academic chosen for his present office by the Minister himself, and assisted by a variety of administrators and Inspectors. His territory is divided for educational as for other purposes into its constituent Departments, and each Department (for the purposes of primary school administration) into smaller areas under the direct supervision of Inspectors. The Prefect, as an all-purpose representative of central government within his territory, has in the past enjoyed much direct authority over primary schools, but his task now is to work closely with the Rectorate and its officials in integrating educational with other policies (housing, transport and health, for example). Subject-based Inspectors exert continuing and direct influence upon the work of secondary schools and their teachers, reporting not only to the Rectorate but also directly to the presiding General Inspectors in Paris. At no stage in this process of disseminating the orders and wishes of central administration is there any space for control by or consultation with locally accountable or elected bodies. Local administrators are responsible only to the officials in Paris, and through them to the Minister and so to the nationally elected authorities who have appointed him.

French education is in 1963 a centralised service having at its command a meticulously designed and carefully managed machine for disseminating orders and for distributing resources, as well as (at least in principle) for harvesting advice and comment. Critics naturally object that it is better at ordering than at listening and that the overwhelming size of the apparatus makes it cumbersome, insensitive and unresponsive (Crozier, 1970). It is on the other hand argued that uniformity is a precondition of equity: since all French citizens have the right to an education of the same quality, local variations whether of content or resources are unacceptable. Centralization in the Parisian manner is therefore a necessary condition for the effective and equitable operation of a great public service, which is precisely how national education should be perceived. Teachers and others working within the education service wish therefore to be and to be accepted as public servants, *fonctionnaires,* whereas in other political cultures the term "civil servant" if applied to a teacher would carry many unwelcome connotations. But not in France, where – in spite of the strains and pressures of recent years – the teacher, professeur or instituteur, occupies a decent and even an envied role in society. Primary and secondary teachers have since the 1940s been formally incorporated in the nationally defined scales of salaries for all types of civil servants.

This historically important celebration of education as one of the great public services of the Nation has in the past often been hotly contested as an unwelcome monopoly. The central argument in the republican tradition is that one of the basic tasks of education is to nurture loyal republicans, able to resist the blandishments of Catholic priests and monarchist propaganda. Education must for those who embrace this argument be non-denominational and secular, *laïque* in the evocative French term. On the other hand, those who reject this argument have fought across the years for a more pluralist system, for (in their terms) freedom in education, for the rights of parents rather than the duties of citizens. Roman Catholic schools in particular have for long existed alongside the public schools of France, and (as will appear in the next chapter) have frequently enjoyed a considerable measure of support from the State, not least in financial terms. At other times, ferocious political pressure has secured the formal and absolute separation of Church and State so that (as in the United States but not as in Britain) it has been forbidden by law to provide any public support for what must be regarded by the *laïcs* as private schools. Four years ago, in 1959, the Prime Minister of the day (Michel Debré) carried through Parliament a series of measures which now allow private (most of which are Roman Catholic) schools to enter into contractual arrangements with the State for the provision of education with financial support from the State, and provided always that certain conditions are observed. It is impossible to predict how permanent or stable these arrangements will prove to be, and whether they will lead to a progressive fusion of what have often been competitive and hostile systems of schooling.

These are matters on which the FEN, and especially those parts of it most sympathetic to the traditional values of the Left, is deeply opposed to the tendencies of the present government. In 1963 and for the moment, at least, the prevailing commitment among teachers is to an educational system which is national, public, free of cost to the parent, and secular.

Implicit in these practical notions – of Paris as centre, education as a public service, the coupling of equity and uniformity, administrative systems as emanations of a central democratic power – is a deep and complex doctrine of The University, not as an institution anchored to the soil in one place but as somehow constituting in itself the national system of education (Aulard, 1911). This doctrine is, to be sure, less potent in 1963 than in the past, but it has not yet been formally abandoned. It is visibly expressed in the two related terms, Academy and Rector. In a superficial sense, the Academy corresponds to the British Local Education Authority (LEA), and – although even less satisfactorily – to the American School District. But each of those foreign authorities is locally elected, and at present their responsibilities flow from the locality in which they are rather than from a central government of which they are the agents. In neither country would the notion of an Academy as the local expression of a central University be intelligible. The overarching authority of the unitary University at the same time deprives local universities, even when they exist at the level of formal definition, of any substantial identity or autonomy: nor can they develop strong links to the communities in which they are implanted. It is the same unitary, if currently invisible, University which bestows degrees and diplomas, including of course the baccalauréat itself as the school-leaving examination. Against such a background, it ceases to be surprising that the official nominated by the Minister to be accountable to him in Paris for the educational system within the boundaries of the Academy should be a Rector: a professional university academic, established as a specialist in one of the acknowledged disciplines of higher education and expecting at the end of his uncertain period of office to return to the certainties of his university career.

The messages conveyed by such a doctrine, and by the arrangements which throughout France depend upon it, are unambiguous. An educational system to be fair must be national and unitary, just as to be efficient it must be centralized. Paris is the centre to which all is related: if a university exists anywhere it exists there, with the venerable Sorbonne as its symbol. Yet even in the Latin Quarter itself the titles cut into the stone walls of the Sorbonne hesitate between "The University of Paris", "The Universities of Paris", and "The Academy and Universities of Paris". The most prestigious forms of national higher education, concentrated of course in Paris and in the grandes écoles, are found not in the facs but in institutions specializing in engineering, or administration, or commerce, or preparation for the academic profession. Students win places in these establishments as well as money to attend them after a ferocious competition. This competitive entry examination, or concours, is attempted after an extended education within the lycée for two years beyond the level of the first university degree (the bac): the lycée is itself an important part of higher education. Such messages reinforce a curricular preoccupation, in French secondary schools above all, with the intellectual matter of education, the academic imperative, the established disciplines. Latin and mathematics persist as the ideal disciplines, and therefore the most noble school subjects. In France, and only in France, is philosophy taught as a major subject in the final year of preparation for the bac and regarded as of almost mystical importance in the perpetuation of a high French culture.

The progressive articulation of primary and secondary education, epitomized and accelerated in 1963 by the President's decision to impose the collège (the CES) by decree and throughout France has blurred the traditionally rigid distinction between these two sectors of education. It is true that a closer association of the two sectors has already led to the recruitment of former secondary school teachers as trainers of future primary school teachers: but this is a recent and in many ways anomalous development. Now, however, there is to be intruded into a dual system a collège (the CES) which is neither a secondary nor a primary school in the long-established sense of those terms: much has yet to be clarified even in the administrative texts, as the new collèges begin to draw both pupils and teachers from both educational worlds. But for the present these do remain separate educational worlds, and it is already clear that a battle to control this new intermediate territory will rumble on for many years to come. Meanwhile, the entrenched and separate habits of mind persist. These habits prevail at the heart of the Ministry itself: efforts to assimilate the administration of primary and secondary schools were made as long ago as the 1930s, when Jean Zay was Minister, but the hermetically sealed divisions persist to this day (Zay, 1945). The primary school is organized on a Departmental basis (in terms of the mechanisms of control and the deployment of teachers, for example), whereas the secondary school functions within the framework of national provision and the division into large Academies. The key Inspectors of secondary schools proclaim their affiliations to the dominant academic subjects. Those in the primary sector have appropriately different titles (IDEN and not IPR), concern themselves with the whole of the basic curriculum and exert authority over a group of schools, none of which is directly supervised by the equivalent of the American Principal, or the British Head Teacher. On the other hand, each of the lycées is directed, albeit within a framework of detailed national policy, by a *Proviseur*, a highly qualified and senior teacher who, although without any formal training in administration, is expected to govern the daily life of an institution that is always complex and often large. Many of these schools have roots in the last century, while some in Paris and the great provincial cities can claim continuities going back four hundred years. Because they must serve older pupils whose homes may be at a considerable distance, the lycées not infrequently make provision for boarders. Even although the demography of the country is now undergoing rapid change, many of the primary schools are of necessity in rural areas and have only one teacher. The primary school provides a basic curriculum for pupils aged six and above and jealously preserves its function as a channel of social promotion for those who have generally been excluded from the bourgeois world of the lycée. In recent years, growing numbers of determined pupils of ability have pressed through the doors of the lycée, but the expectation that all or even most of the older pupils of the primary schools should so advance is not yet institutionalized, nor even generally accepted as desirable. It is the recently proclaimed determination of the President of the Republic to widen the base of recruitment to the lycée that makes 1963 a turning point in the history of educational policy in this country.

Although the primary school has regarded itself as part of a closed world, it has enthusiastically incorporated within its mission the extension of genuine opportunities to those able and willing to advance beyond the legal minimum age for schooling (still fourteen but to be raised by law to sixteen in 1967). For many decades the primary school sector, rather than providing an avenue onwards into the secondary school, has promoted its own specific form of higher primary education. An understanding of this apparently exotic distinction between higher primary on the one hand and secondary on the other is fundamental to any appreciation by a foreigner of the significance of current reforms in France. More advanced schooling within the primary sector has been provided either in separate and carefully nurtured schools, the écoles primaires supérieures, or in special sections attached to regular primary schools, the *cours complémentaires*. The subjects studied in such programmes have been shorter, less traditional and more modern or more vocational than those exalted in the lycée: modern languages, the applied sciences, technical studies, rather than mathematics or the classics. They have certainly not included philosophy, a noble subject reserved for the last year of study for the bac in the lycée. In the 1950s establishments making such provision were rebaptised or regrouped as CEGs. The tentative effort to align them with the work of the earlier years of secondary education proper, in the lycées, has enjoyed only limited success. In principle, the CES will now begin to achieve precisely that alignment.

The Teachers

Each of these distinctive features in today's educational system has helped to shape the principles and the patterns of the education of teachers in France. Preeminent among these features is the dominance of centralist assumptions about how schooling should be provided and supported. These centralist assumptions are articulated in an elaborate Parisian bureaucracy, and a regular and uniform delegation of Ministerial authority to the Rectors in the provinces. Inspectors, teachers and administrators see themselves and are perceived by others as public servants, sustaining a national system within which inequalities must be systematically minimized. As a public system, it enjoys many of the characteristics of a monopoly. That same system, consciously or not, owes much to a characteristically French understanding of the nature of the University, impacting most directly on the élite secondary schools and inhibiting the development outside the capital of varied and distinctive institutions of higher education. Assumptions about the nature of knowledge and of worthwhile learning engrained in the culture of European higher education determine the curriculum of the schools and especially of the lycée. What matters are *les savoirs*, les connaissances, knowledge as interpreted in a scholarly tradition and as incarnated in the professional lives of the Rectors. Such a dogma has its own limitations of plausibility, and has hardened (to a degree unusual even in Europe) the distinction between secondary schools providing a classical humanist education, and a primary school network providing schooling for the people of the Republic and protecting its own distinctive form of education beyond the normal school leaving age. All of these features stand out clearly in 1963, are organically linked and interact upon one another. All of them are now modified by the creation of a new type of institution, neither école nor lycée, with a new style of teacher, neither instituteur nor professeur. All of them have interacted and continue to interact to produce distinctive patterns of teacher recruitment and teacher education.

The most visible and impressive form of teacher education is the école normale. In each of the Departments of France there are two such establishments: one for men and one for women, or rather (as they are still significantly known) one for boys and one for girls. These schools are an undoubted and integral part of the primary sector, managed at national as at local level by the hierarchies of the primary order. They have no connections, even of an informal kind, with higher education as it is expressed in the fac and, until quite recently, held themselves at a proud distance even from secondary education. The primary sector in the past educated all its own leaders, and many such women and men still occupy senior positions in the écoles normales. The Director of each école normale is at the same time an Inspector (an IDEN, of course) who has under her or his supervision a group of schools in the neighbourhood of the training establishment: it is in many of these schools that teaching practice and other practical experience will be provided for the students in training. Many écoles normales have annexed to them a practice school, directly under their own control. The buildings of the école normale itself are the property of the Department, whereas those of the lycée belong directly to the State. For that reason, the local pride of the Department has resulted in impressive and occasionally ostentatious buildings, designed to convey the message that the locality supports and celebrates the patriotic effort of providing an education of quality for all its citizens.

In the eighteen years since the end of the Second World War – which (in ways which are not always obvious) generated a series of major changes in education, and especially in the traditional relationship between primary and secondary education – the entry of students to the école normale has been possible at two stages. At either of these stages entry is by a concours, a competitive examination by which students are arranged in an order of merit and the predetermined number of places is distributed among those standing highest on the lists. These annual competitive examinations are conducted, as the geometry of the French system requires, on a strictly Departmental basis. The recruitment, training, supervision and deployment of the instituteur are tasks which have been delegated by the State to the Department, by the Minister to the Rector, by the Rector to the Inspector in charge of each Department (the Inspecteur d'Académie), and finally by the IA to the IDENs, two of whom direct the pair of écoles normales. There can within this system be no distinction between admission to training and recruitment to the public service as a trainee teacher: recruitment in effect precedes training, as it would in the armed forces (and for similar reasons). The student admitted to training is paid during that training, and may well be offered board and lodging: in the past, indeed, that student would have been required to reside during term in the école normale so that the process of induction as an instituteur might be even more effective and total. At the end of the course of training (nowadays a period of variable length) and success in a non-competitive examination, the newly fledged teacher is appointed to a first post within the Department where training was given. It is the same Departmentally based authorities of the national system who will be responsible for induction, monitoring, evaluation, in-service training and promotion.

Who, then, are these students who purposefully set out to become teachers? Most of them are recruited, as they have been for a century and a half, at the tender age of fifteen. Up to that point, their education has usually been not of course in the lycée, but in the most advanced sectors of primary education itself from which they progress along the royal road of the competitive examination into the école normale. In this respect the students of 1963 do not differ from generations of their predecessors marching along this route. Once over the intimidating hurdle of the competition, they embark on a three year course leading to the bac, which had for so long been the exclusive hallmark of the traditional secondary education. In this respect, of course, they do differ from preceding generations, who would have been admitted only to the advanced examinations of the primary order itself. This requirement and this opportunity to achieve the bac before beginning teacher training proper have been in place only for two decades. The old frontier between primary and secondary is indeed eroded. In particular, all of the teachers responsible for teaching students for the bac itself will have been drawn from the secondary school culture, and in most cases have had some experience of teaching in the lycée. The next chapter will show how sharp a break with long tradition is represented by this simple fact. Nevertheless, these students – recruited at the age of fifteen – will in most other respects relive much of the experience of their predecessors in the 1930s. They will for some four continuous years attend, and in many cases inhabit, an institution which is dedicated exclusively to the preparation of primary school teachers, and is dominated by the traditional ideology which drives that mission. Most of them are recruited within the Department, and expect to serve in that same Department: indeed, they are effectively guaranteed employment in it. They may now, to be sure, be taught in growing numbers by teachers whose background is in secondary education, but they will have no direct experiences in common with their contemporaries in the lycée.

These students, after completing their bac within the école normale, devote a fourth year of study and practice to sharply focused professional training. A great deal of attention is given to the development of the practical pedagogical skills which are held to define the *métier* of the instituteur. Substantial periods of time (the *stages*) will be spent working under supervision in several of the schools annexed or attached to the école normale. At present (1963), this pattern of study and experience – three years to the bac and a year of professional training – represents the norm: it is this route to the status of instituteur which is followed by 90% of the candidates (Charles 1988, pp.232-3). But a growing minority is now recruited after completing a full course of study leading to the bac in the lycée. They must, of course, then succeed in a competitive examination organized on a Departmental basis before being recruited to the école normale for a two year course of professional preparation, similar to that already outlined but also including further work in the subjects which these aspiring teachers will need to teach in the primary school. The frontiers between primary and secondary are therefore neither as clear nor as impassable as they were before the last world war. All future instituteurs now take the archetypical secondary examination, the bac. Most of them in the 1960s still enter the école normale at the age of fifteen, but a minority will first have completed a general education within the lycée. The historic distinctions between primary and secondary are being further eroded, since many of the professeurs teaching within the école normale will themselves have qualified as secondary school teachers, often as agrégés. How else could teaching for the bac be undertaken?

The contrast between the instituteurs who attend and often live in the Departmental training establishment, and the professeurs who migrate from the lycée to teach them for the national university baccalauréat degree is sharpened by an exploration of the kind of education and training received by those same lycée teachers. If traditional primary school teacher training is represented (still in 1963) by the pupil recruited some three years before the bac and spending the next four years in the same institution, linked neither to secondary nor to higher education, the experience of the secondary school teacher is epitomized by the educational biography of the agrégé. No term in educational and social discourse is more resonant of dignity and tradition than this, for the foreigner, somewhat mysterious title. An agrégé is the most esteemed and protected of the various categories of secondary school teacher, favoured in terms of his career and postings, a scholar in his own discipline, dominant in the upper reaches of administration as of teaching, standing with one foot confidently planted in secondary education and one in higher. Consider the 1963 example of a typical (and fictitious) young *professeur*.

Jean-Paul was born in 1935 in the city of Lyon, and is too young to remember the War or the agonies of the city of his birth in the years that followed it. His father was a Professor of History in the Faculty of Letters on the banks of the Rhône, who well understood the importance of choosing for his son the best ways through the public system of education to the pinnacles of Paris. Jean-Paul attended the preparatory department of the Lycée Ampère, where fees were paid by his family, and at the age of eleven secured without any difficulty a place in the most junior class (the sixth) of the Lycée itself. No fees were paid for any of the pupils (nor had been since 1932) but there were additional expenses incurred by attending this successful school. The young Jean-Paul was already well grounded in Latin and Mathematics, and all his contemporaries came from comfortable families, many of them with one or two parents who were themselves teachers. He flourished in the academic environment of his secondary school, where the teaching was rigorous and the style formal. When he was fifteen he began to make choices which determined the nature of the bac in which he then specialised: for him, mathematics were for the rest of his life to be dominant but his course of study was widely based, and in the last year included philosophy. His parents doubted whether the courses of study available at the fac would be sufficiently demanding for him or open to him any of the best careers, and so a transfer was arranged to the classe préparatoire (the "prépa") of the Lycée le Parc. Admission was preceded by a series of tests and oral examinations and the next two years were the most hard-working of his life, so far at least. The Lycée specialized in the preparation of candidates for the competitive examinations, the concours, for entry to one or other of the grandes écoles concentrated in Paris.

Jean-Paul was again successful, and in 1959 secured admission (being placed twenty-seventh on the list) to the Ecole Normale Supérieure (the ENS) in the rue d'Ulm, close to the Pantheon and at the heart of the university quarter of Paris. As a *normalien* he received payment as well as free board and lodging, being now a trainee member of the public service. He was free to attend the lectures given in the various university establishments of the capital, but the core of his work was more systematically developed within the walls of the ENS itself. Teaching was intensive and in small groups. Many of his contemporaries had, at the age of twenty or so, migrated the few hundred metres from the preparatory classes housed in the venerable Parisian lycées, three of them within easy walking distance of the Sorbonne itself. The traditional mission of the ENS (which nobody confused with the more humble écoles normales maintained in each of the Departments) was the preparation of the highest category of teachers for secondary and higher education, the cream of the professeurs. Unsurprisingly, that function – given the success and prestige of the ENS – had already become more general: the current Prime Minister (Georges Pompidou) was himself a student there from 1932 to 1935. During his own three years at the ENS, entry to which is confined to men and which is one of four – two for men and two for women – in or near Paris, Jean-Paul entered a number of university examinations and (just like his father's students in Lyon) secured national diplomas. These presented no difficulty for him, for his driving preoccupation was with preparation for the agrégation.

This ferocious examination was in 1959, as in 1963 it still is, a national and annual competition for a number of places defined in advance by the Ministry in accordance with its own predictions of and provisions for the number of posts in each major subject that will each year fall vacant or be newly created. In mathematics in 1959 there were relatively few but fortunately for him Jean-Paul was ultimately placed in the first twenty on the order of merit. The examinations were supervised by a jury made up of academic specialists and representatives of the General Inspection (in fact, of course, equally "academic" and impregnated with the values of the university). The written papers and, for those who struggled over this first hurdle, the oral examinations were focused upon virtuosity in the discipline of mathematics (in this case), and only to a modest degree on any matters related to teaching capacity or likely effectiveness in a classroom. The successful candidates become agrégés, that is to say (literally) associated with or incorporated in the university. Jean-Paul now joined the highest category of teacher. More than status is involved in this: from the beginning he received a higher salary, taught fewer hours each week, and (perhaps most important of all) was given much more freedom in choosing his first teaching appointment. Nor are these hard-earned advantages ephemeral: throughout his career in the public service, he will be equally favoured – in terms of hours "of service", salary, access to promotion, choice of region and institution. The title of agrégé, which is neither an office nor a degree but a public rank, can be held only by those who are and remain in the public service, unless special dispensations are granted, and cannot be conferred upon or employed by those teaching in private schools, whatever their quality and however close their contractual relationship to the State.

This is the high road to the agrégation, and although it is now travelled only by a minority, it remains the ideal route. Most now follow more varied paths. It is, for example, possible to prepare for the agrégation in many of the facs dispersed throughout France and concentrated in Paris itself. A student following this demanding path first completes the required university degrees, and then prepares intensively for the same examination as the élite students of the four ENSs. In many of the Faculties of the capital as of the provinces special courses of instruction are available for such students who, in some subjects at least, are now regarded as the most promising, and therefore rewarding to teach, of all higher education students. The requirements of the concours are identical, and the competition is for entry to the same list of defined vacancies, discipline by discipline and for the whole of France. Other teachers already in post may also enter the same competition and in many cases will take advantage of any special courses of preparation in the region where they are working: for such reasons there will always be pressure by secondary school teachers to be appointed to a school in a town which also boasts a university Faculty. Failure in one annual competition is not finally decisive, and the battle-weary candidate returns to the contest year after year. In all cases entry to the oral examination is conditional upon prior success in the written tests. So rigorous are these and so honourable is success in them, that candidates who have twice passed the written examination but twice failed the orals are admitted to a separate category of the teaching service. They join the respected ranks of those who have twice been judged worthy of admission (to the oral examination itself): the *biadmissibles*, who enjoy their own slightly attenuated privileges in the system, and their own salary scale.

Before World War Two, the agrégés enjoyed in effect a monopoly of the higher reaches of secondary school teaching. They were the only established body (*corps*) of professeurs, although assisted by other teachers, often without tenure and employed in various auxiliary categories. The school system was seriously and deliberately disrupted by the Vichy regime, which deeply distrusted what it perceived as the secular and republican prejudices of the primary sector. Some of these changes have since been reversed, while others were consolidated during the fifteen year life of the Fourth Republic. As a result, two new categories of teacher now exist, the first unambiguously secondary and the second growing more uncomfortably in the ill-defined territory which at present exists between primary and secondary.

Nobody now questions the desirability and quality of the certifiés who in the thirteen years since 1950 have established themselves alongside, or more precisely a little below, the agrégés. The *Société des Agrégés* was nevertheless suspicious and hostile when it was first proposed that the number of established and tenured secondary school teachers should be increased by the addition of this new group. They believed then, as some still do, that this was a serious threat to the rigorous purity of the French system. The CAPES (*Certificat d'Aptitude au Professorat de l'Enseignement du Second Degré*) in many essential features resembles the agrégation. It is a competitive academic examination, taken one year after the Licence, a degree awarded after success in an examination at the end of three years of study in higher education – the equivalent, that is to say, of the baccalaureate in other countries but never to be confused with the baccalauréat in France itself. The agrégation, on the other hand, requires at least one year of further study and the possession of a Master's degree. By such distinctions are the necessary hierarchies ordered and defined. Not only is the CAPES, like its elder brother, a competitive examination, but the number of places to be filled is again defined each year by the Ministry in Paris after a review of the needs of the system and of the capacity of the State budget to meet these needs. The concours is therefore conducted on a subject by subject basis, while the jury system and the two stage examination (written and oral) is also constructed upon the established model.

There is one important difference between the two categories of senior secondary school teacher. For the agrégé, as more generally for the scholarly student moving forward into a teaching career within higher education itself, no form of professional training has been thought necessary or even desirable. It is the mastery of a subject which guarantees quality and confers high status. Such a teacher is not required to undergo any further formal training, but simply to demonstrate in his or her first appointment that the necessary if ill-defined skills of teaching have indeed been acquired. Given the selectivity of the system of secondary education, together with the pupil motivation and parental support which can therefore be assumed, these doctrines have not so far been seriously challenged. But the tasks of the successful candidate for the CAPES are often different. The certifié will be required to deliver more hours each week of teaching service (as well as receiving a lower salary) and may well be required to teach younger pupils. When this new concours was introduced, it was therefore decided at the same time to require of such teachers than they spend their first year of paid employment, while working of course in a lycée, attached to a new institution called the Regional Pedagogical Centre (the *Centre Pédagogique Régional*, or CPR). The CPR, even if for the agrégé attendance is not required, is an important innovation.

It is directed by an Inspector, an IPR of course nominated by the Rector, who therefore adds to his mixed portfolio of responsibilities the duty of preparing (for all the new certifiés in the district for which he is responsible) a one year programme of professional training which will support their work in schools, and supplement in more practical ways the academic knowledge which they have acquired through the university. This programme is in part subject based, so that all the teachers of mathematics or of English or of philosophy will be summoned together at regular intervals for a lecture or demonstration. An event of this kind might be planned on one day each week. The CPR must also provide an introduction to more general questions related to school organization or educational law or psychology. The Centre has no permanent and full-time staff: those who provide such courses will be, like the Director himself, employed for most of the time on other duties – as Inspectors, specialists teaching in higher education, experienced secondary school teachers. Nor does the Centre have its own lecture rooms and other facilities. Its administrative base may be located in the headquarters of the Rectorate, or in modest premises elsewhere, but most of its teaching will be delivered on the premises of secondary schools or other educational establishments. It has, of course, no links with either of the écoles normales which exist in each Department since these belong to a separate order, indeed to a separate world.

From that separate world are now being drawn teachers who will be of great importance in the new collèges which the President has determined shall be created throughout France for pupils aged between eleven and fifteen. At present, pupils of this age are to be found either in the lycée or in the upper reaches of what has traditionally been defined as primary schooling. These two separate sectors are now to be integrated, although this work may well take the rest of the decade of the 1960s to achieve. Some progress in this direction has, of course, already been made – which is precisely why to-day's Government has been able to take so dramatic a decision. For the past four years, since the reforms associated with the name of the Minister of Education Jean-Marie Berthoin, the upper primary schools or primary classes have been regrouped and reclassified as Colleges of General Education (*Collèges d'Enseignement Général*, or CEG). These are not, of course, to be confused with the new CES. They cover only the early years of schooling above the age of eleven, although (in principle at least) the first two of these years run partly in parallel with the same phase of education in the lycée, so that transfers might be possible in appropriate cases.

Educational change rarely takes place overnight, and most of the teachers in those CEGs which now exist are in fact former instituteurs, trained in the école normale and accustomed to teach a wide range of subjects. For them already, and even more for their successors, different forms of preparation will be needed: this is because they will no longer be teaching pupils below the age of eleven, they will need to specialize in a smaller number of subjects if they are to give appropriate instruction, they will need in the new collèges of 1963 to provide education of a quality comparable to that previously monopolized by the exclusive lycée. For the past four years opportunities for primary school teachers, whether novices or well established in their careers, have therefore been widened by the creation of a third category of teacher, distinct from the general instituteur. These are the PEGCs – the *Professeurs d'Enseignement Général de Collège*, the Professors of General Education in the Collège. They receive special training, as well as education in the two subjects in which they will now be required to specialize, in Centres attached (significantly) to the écoles normales. As the number of PEGCs grows, so will the tensions within the geometry of the long established teacher training system. The PEGCs belong neatly to neither of the classical worlds of primary and secondary. They are indeed called professeurs and not instituteurs. But they specialize in two subjects and not one. They already teach pupils who are of the same age as those who are at present in the lower classes of the lycée but who are now to be regrouped in the new CES. They receive supplementary education and training beyond that given to instituteurs but are still required to teach two school subjects: they are, in French terms, neither polyvalent nor monovalent but bivalent. Their salaries are lower and their hours of service higher than those of the certifié and agrégé, but their salaries are higher and their hours of service lower than those of the instituteur. Their own teachers in the Centre at the école normale may be, by an odd paradox of history, agrégés from the university world, but in their own education and training there is no formal or informal connection to that world. This will be the group to watch carefully as the story of the relationship of teacher training to the university in France unfolds over the coming years.

The simple geometry of the relationship of the university to teacher education now begins to disintegrate. The agrégé and the certifié have been the pure products of the university world, although the latter is required to undergo formal training for the tasks of the teacher under the supervision of Inspectors accountable to the Minister. The instituteur is admitted to the public service at an early age and receives all his training within the framework of that service which, although controlled regionally by the Rector, has no organic links to higher education. The Director of the establishment he attends and through which he is paid is also an Inspector for the Ministry. It has in practice, of course and even before the injection of the new element of the PEGC, never been as simple as that, and lines have often been blurred. Many of the certifiés use much of their time during the year of attachment to the CPR to prepare themselves for the agrégation. Some of those entering the école normale have already secured a university degree. Many of those who are already instituteurs in service attend the local fac in order to prepare themselves for such a degree. The postwar world is not that of the 1930s. Above all, the realities of life and of the budget mean that the demand for teachers in classrooms far outstrips the capacity of a neatly ordered system to deliver the properly qualified teachers divided into the appropriate categories: the schools are now full of auxiliary teachers, substitute teachers, temporary teachers and all the rest – many of them awaiting an opportunity to receive the training which should in principle have preceded even their provisional entry into the public service. Yet, in contrast to the patterns in many other countries, the geometry of the French system of teacher education does remain both precise and distinctive.

An analysis of that system, as it operates in 1963, brings into yet sharper relief those dominant characteristics of the French public system as a whole which have already been identified. It is the Ministry which establishes the institutions and arrangements for the training of teachers (the CPR, the école normale, the national competitions) and which, officially through Parisian texts and less formally through control by Inspectors, determines the nature and content of all forms of teacher education. It is the Ministry which appoints all those responsible for the training of teachers. More even than that, the Ministry determines the number of teaching posts to be created each year, and the areas of specialization, as well as the nature of the competition of entry into teaching. This is necessary if Paris is to ensure that the universal requirement to deliver the same curriculum throughout France is to be honoured by the formation of correctly qualified teachers. The Ministry pays teachers, secondary as well as primary, once they have succeeded in the entry competitions and are admitted to training. Recruitment precedes training, as is only sensible in a great public service, where the notion of the *fonctionnaire* is more potent than that of "the professional".

Strong national policies, once again in teacher training as in all aspects of the service, are effected through a firmly managed network of local control: authority moves downwards and outwards from Paris, and not upwards from local powers jealous of their own autonomies. The Inspectors, organised by Academy and by Department, secure the unity and coherence of the system. The IDEN dominates the primary sector; the IPR manages the vocational sector of secondary teacher training. The distinction between primary and secondary is fundamental, here as everywhere: the former is organized by Department, the latter at the national level. What is true of teacher deployment is equally true of teacher training. The two forms of teacher training are presented in fundamentally different and essentially unrelated institutions. For the secondary school teacher, vocational training is delivered by the system of Inspection, through the CPR. And such training is in 1963 less respected and less structured than the disciplinary subject based knowledge delivered by the university and attested by a national examination (CAPES or agrégation) impregnated with the traditional academic values. Knowledge – *les savoirs* – is to be nurtured and perpetuated, in secondary as in higher education. Binding together such notions is a historic conception of The University, epitomized in the career of the Rector, a university professor holding the highest academic degrees, who directs the whole of the educational system within the territory for which he is accountable. This is the system which has stood the test of time, and survived the rapid changes of the post-war years.

Notes

[1] In these chapters a consistent, if necessarily arbitrary, method has been adopted in rendering French terms in English.

Most readily understood terms (like "examination") are simply translated. Where the meaning is clear but a special sense is implied, a capital letter is used (for example: Prefect, Department, Rector, Academy, Director, Faculty, Licence). In an attempt to avoid an excess of italics, frequently used terms which either cannot be translated (or for which the English equivalent would be misleading) are given in the French form and in normal print: for example, lycée, collège, instituteur, professeur, agrégé, certifié, concours, baccalauréat and bac, école normale, grandes écoles. Where the reference is to particular institutions, capital letters are used: Ecole Normale Supérieure, Lycée Henri IV. Less frequently occurring terms, which cannot be conveniently translated into English, are given in italics: *fonctionnaire, proviseur, les savoirs, stage, métier*.

[2] See Chapter 3 for the background to these events, and Chapters 2 and 3 for most of the information in this chapter.

Oxford Studies in Comparative Education, Vol. 4(1/2), 1994

CHAPTER 2

France: before 1963

Continuities

There are good reasons for choosing 1963 as the year for which to offer a static account of the French system of teacher training, as of the educational system of which it was and is an integral part. 1963 lies midway between the crisis which inaugurated the Fifth Republic in 1958 and the deep fractures of 1968. It was the year when decisive steps were taken to redesign the framework of schooling throughout France, and in so doing to challenge the deeply ingrained separatism of the primary and secondary sectors. President de Gaulle, in whom were embodied many of the national values of patriotism and centralization, was then at the height of his power. Regionalism had not yet begun seriously to affect policy and practice. In short: neither the universities in their modern form, nor the Regions as important units of government, nor the comprehensive secondary school, nor the systematic training of secondary school teachers yet existed. But 1963 can be explained only in terms of the previous history of France, and it is the purpose of this chapter to explore relevant themes in that history. Only when the portrait of 1963 is placed in that perspective will it be possible to interpret the changes which have, in the thirty years since 1963, overtaken education in France.

This chapter draws the year 1963 into perspective, not by rehearsing the story of the evolution to that date of the French system, but rather by isolating three highly specific questions: How did the agrégation come to be so powerful and distinctive an institution, and not only for secondary teachers? What had been, and in 1963 still was, the University, and how did it relate to the lives of teachers? What had been the importance of the école normale, in political and social history as well as in the specific activity of training elementary teachers?

These questions are themselves played out in terms of the succeeding phases in the political history of France. In that eventful narrative the deeper continuities are often as important as the more violent disruptions nearer the surface of public life (Bosher, 1988): the roots of two of the three questions posed in this Chapter are buried in the centuries before the Revolution of

1789. The events of the political calendar on either side of the Revolution are however not simply chronological pegs on which to hang an account of educational change. There is an important link between political events and educational development. The politics of the Ancien Régime were marked by a tension between the ambitions of a centralizing Bourbon monarchy and the stubborn independence manifested by the corporate powers of the Church, the Law and the ancient universities. That tension had important effects upon education. 1789 and the immediately succeeding years of the First Republic were indeed distinguished by a frontal attack upon many established institutions, and not least in the world of education: old universities disappeared, along with and for the same reasons as the professions, the Church, the guilds and the nobility. The Directorate, in the last years of the century, attempted to reestablish as part of a more orderly society some more formal patterns of schooling, albeit with uneven success. It was left for Napoleon I to manufacture an imperial State, with a common and rational system of law, civil administration, and (especially) education: to that end, he designed the Imperial University, established the dominance of the lycée, and consolidated the influence of the grandes écoles. The restoration of the Bourbons in 1815 led inevitably to the restitution to the Catholic Church of much of its historic power, and most notably in primary education. The 1830 Revolution marked the beginning of a period of purposeful, and relatively liberal, educational reform and the extension (although still heavily under the influence of the Catholic Church) of primary education. The return of the Napoleonic family to power in 1848 led, after the brief experiment of the second Republic and in the Second Empire of Napoleon III, to a succession of educational changes, most of them designed to modernize France. This was a period of considerable, and often neglected, development in both secondary and higher education (Anderson 1975). The defeat of France by Prussia in 1870 precipitated the collapse of the regime, and (after a period of deep uncertainty) provoked the sustained reforms of the Third Republic: according to the still prevailing myth, these were the decades of the creation a great system of national education which was free, public and secular. The Third Republic ended with the defeat of France by Germany in 1940: the Vichy regime introduced a surprisingly wide range of changes, some of which survived the Liberation of 1945. The end of the Second World War made possible the inauguration of the Fourth Republic and, during the thirteen years of its constitutional life, a series of relatively modest adjustments to the classical pre-war system was made. The return to power of de Gaulle in 1958 and the firmer style of the Fifth Republic promoted a succession of more fundamental changes, exemplified by the decree of 3 August 1963. Beyond the horizon imposed by the themes of this chapter lie the ideological revolution of 1968, the accelerating changes of educational policy in the 1970s, the accession to power in 1981 of a confident Socialist party determined to give educational change (and not least the reform of teacher education) the highest priority, and the swing back to the parties of the Right and the Centre in the parliamentary elections of 1993. During each of these succeeding stages, shifts in teacher education policy reflected wider educational change and were embedded in the political narrative. They cannot be interpreted in isolation from it. At the same time, the continuities of institutions, values and conflicts persist.

Nowhere is the paradox of the cohabitation of assertive change with underlying continuity better illustrated than in the unbroken history across these years of one Parisian educational establishment, the Lycée Louis-le-Grand (Palmer, 1985). Across all the mutations in power and ideology, this proud institution has preserved its preeminence: the successive changes of name evoke the subtlety and suppleness with which it has adapted itself to the changing circumstances of France and of its capital. Other educational arrangements negotiated, if less visibly and colourfully, similar transitions. The Collège de Clermont, which was founded in 1563 by the Jesuits in the heart of the university quarter, took in 1682 the name of Louis-le-Grand as a prudent compliment to the most powerful of the Bourbon kings. Not only did it survive the expulsion of its Jesuit proprietors from France eighty years later, but in some ways it enhanced its position, adopting after the Revolution the new name of the Collège de l'Egalité in another effort to reflect changing political preferences. In 1795 it briefly became the Institut Central des Boursiers, and in 1799 temporized further by taking the label of the Prytanée Français: titles that, in uncertain times, had the important advantage of being imprecise. In 1803, the very first year in which such a title was on offer, it was rebaptised the Lycée de Paris, and later in the same year preempted a larger place in the new world as the Lycée Impérial. No sooner had the former Emperor been expelled from France than the place once again acquired monarchist respectability as the Collège Royal Louis-le-Grand, a doubly convenient name as the newly restored king was of course himself a Louis, although hardly a great one. The title of lycée, tainted with Bonapartism, had temporarily disappeared. The Revolution of 1848 restored that title to respectability but, in order to avoid what would have been at that time an indiscreet reference to the Bourbons, the establishment took the politically neutral but honoured name of Descartes. The triumph of the Second Empire ensured that the best could now be made of all possible worlds, and from 1851 until the catastrophe of 1870 the resonant if eclectic title of Lycée Impérial Louis-le-Grand was employed. That had to be briskly dropped when the Empire fell, and the formerly serviceable transitional name of Lycée Descartes was resumed: at least the designation as a lycée had by then become sufficiently French and non-partisan to survive revolutions. By 1873 the world seemed safe enough, at least from the attacks of the discredited extremists on the Left, to allow the buildings to be known for the first time simply as the Lycée Louis-le-Grand: a Republican establishment with the title of a Napoleonic institution under the nominal patronage of a Bourbon monarch. And so it has remained – throughout the lives of three Republics and a German occupation.

The successive names of Louis-le-Grand illustrate both the continuing and central importance of this prestigious Parisian establishment, and the interaction between the events of the political calendar (with all that they imply) and the development of education. Moreover, they conveniently link that story to the themes of teacher education and, even more directly, to the agrégation, the first of the three central themes to be developed in this Chapter.

The Agrégation

From the beginning, the Collège de Clermont enjoyed a close if tense relationship with the University of Paris. There was – in the sixteenth century as in later periods – no clear or formal distinction between schooling that would now be labelled "secondary" and higher education as the twentieth century understands it. The three traditionally senior Faculties – Theology, Law, Medicine – stood aloof from the Faculty of Arts, whose business had long been understood to be the teaching of the seven liberal arts (Brockliss, 1987). The teaching of these liberal arts had become the exclusive business of the colleges which, in Paris as elsewhere, operated under a variety of legal arrangements and whose professors constituted the Faculty of Arts. Of the ten major colleges within Paris nine were more or less directly under the control of the University, whereas the tenth – Clermont itself – was in the hands of its entrenched rivals, the Society of Jesus. But it was the Jesuits who had been most successful in developing education at this level, designing new methods of teaching and cultivating great social influence (Compayré, 1885). The expulsion of the Jesuits from France in 1762 therefore left an alarming gap in the supply of schools and, more especially, of competent teachers. Action was taken, not by a clerical University which had long proved incapable of reforming itself, but by the lay powers, as represented in the Parlements: corporations of lawyers enjoying considerable powers and increasingly impatient of the obstructionism which they detected in the University (Chervel, 1993).

The Paris Parlement determined to use the former Jesuit college of Louis-le-Grand as a centre for training a small number of teachers for the colleges of the capital, and to prescribe the competitive conditions for their recruitment. Those who succeeded were given the title, together with modest emoluments, of agrégé: that is, a teacher associated with or incorporated in the Faculty of Arts. The title was already in use within the higher faculties, which is doubtless why it was not deemed necessary to explain it: the novelty lay in its extension, by the authority of the secular power, to members of the Faculty of Arts teaching in the colleges. An agrégé was traditionally a teacher who assisted or substituted for a professor: in that sense, it was at first a modest title, although it was ruled that in future the professors of the Royal Colleges in Paris must be recruited from among those who had already been admitted to the new category. Each year from 1762 until 1791 there was an examination, and aspiring agrégés competed for admission to one of three categories: Letters, Philosophy, Grammar, which corresponded to the levels or classes of schooling rather than to demarcated disciplines in the more modern sense. The oral examinations were well attended by other members of the Faculty. Membership of the jury was confined to those teaching the Arts, and the chair was occupied by the Rector of the University, who was himself required to be a member of that same Faculty. Some sixty candidates, after undergoing written examinations (fortified by a half-bottle of wine) and oral tests, were admitted each year. The exercise remained modest in scale, and confined to Paris where problems were most severe: some comparable action was however taken by Parlements in other parts of the kingdom. Although the examination did not yet attract candidates of the stature of the intellectual giants of the next century, some salient characteristics of the institution were evident before 1789. They included a rigorous academic examination alongside rather than within university structures, a jury, a concern with the independence of a corps of superior teachers, a sense of occasion, a direct connection to a favoured career on the frontiers of secondary and higher education, concentration on Paris and an association with a prestigious establishment. No examinations were held after 1791, and four years later all the colleges were abolished – except, of course, the resilient Louis-le-Grand itself, which again changed its name and waited for better times.

Those times came with Napoleon's Empire, and in the laws which between 1802 and 1808 laid the foundations for much of French education as it still was in 1963. This period of intense reform was initiated with the creation of the General Inspectors and of the state controlled lycées in 1802: these were to constitute the core of the public system, later to be drawn formally into the structure of the Imperial University. Secondary, or higher, education could hereafter be provided only by these State establishments, or by the colleges maintained by the municipalities and other voluntary bodies. The payment of a tax on the teaching of Latin in schools secured at once the exclusiveness of this system and its legal dependence upon the University (in the contemporary sense of that term, to be explored in the next section of this Chapter). The agreement with the Papacy, achieved in the Concordat of 1801, effectively entailed the separation of primary and secondary schooling, as responsibility for the teaching of virtually all younger pupils was then conceded to the clergy. Napoleon took little personal interest in primary education, and the division of responsibility between Church and State deepened the schism between primary and secondary. The schooling system therefore became dual in two mutually reinforcing senses: primary and secondary, clerical and lay.

It was therefore clear that responsibility for recruiting, training and employing all the Professors for the lycées rested with the State. For this reason, and in an effort to secure both continuity and quality, the title of agrégé was revived in 1808, although not (of course) within the context of any local university, whether in Paris or là-bas: all such old regime establishments had been abolished during the excitements of the Revolution. It was now to be recreated as a national title to serve the needs of a national system. The concours, whether local or national, was not however revived, either under the Empire or during the early years of the Bourbon Restoration. Instead, the title and its privileges – financial and other – were conceded to some experienced teachers and conferred automatically upon the graduates of the specialised training establishment that was to become the Ecole Normale Supérieure (ENS), as constituted in the capital in 1808. These favoured students were selected from the whole of France by the General Inspectors for admission to an examination to enter the public service. From that moment the histories of the agrégation and of the ENS, soon to become one of the most prestigious and distinctive of French academic institutions, were intimately linked. Those histories will be clearer if the institution is consistently referred to in these pages as the ENS, although it was not until 1845 that it secured the title by which it is still known. In 1808, the new establishment was housed in the rue St Jacques (in the premises formerly occupied by the Collège de Plessy) with the unassertive name of *internat normal*. It was, albeit in an imprecise sense, a successor to the very different but ephemeral Ecole Normale, which had itself been called into existence in 1794 as an emergency measure intended to produce at speed trainers of teachers for key posts in the newly created Departments.

The short period after 1808, when the ENS enjoyed a near-monopolistic control over the agrégation and produced only a small trickle of future teachers for the lycées of the capital, was abruptly concluded in 1821. In that year, the competitive examination was reintroduced, and the ENS abolished: it closed its doors, but not for long, in the following year. The two institutions, the examination and the preparatory establishment, were then seen as alternative rather than complementary while the reactionary government – for politics are never distant from the history of teacher education – was suspicious of the ENS. The agrégation itself was at the same time strengthened: only those who were successful in its examinations could be appointed as professeurs in a lycée. The concours itself became a regular annual event, and in 1963 was still the only path to agrégation: the examination, during that long period of its monopoly, was held in every year except 1852 and 1870. The ENS was restored in 1826, this time with the title of *école préparatoire* and appropriately in premises at Louis-le-Grand, where the long story of the agrégation had begun sixty years before. The examination was open only to those already teaching or (which technically amounted to the same thing) already students at the ENS: not until 1881 was access to it widened beyond those who had already been admitted to the public education service. In 1830, the training establishment resumed the 1794 title of Ecole Normale, to which the final dignity of being Supérieure was added fifteen years later, when it became necessary to distinguish it from other establishments being proposed for the provinces.

Until this point, the examination had not been national and was conducted (allegedly with uneven standards) in the Academies. But from 1830 the examinations were held in Paris only: standards were to be defended, and centralization was once again strengthened under pressure from the Government of the day. The capital and its grande école had triumphed. The three-year course of the ENS and the growing number of subjects that could be presented for the agrégation accurately reflected developments in secondary education: in 1840, for example, science was divided into two sections. The oral examinations became a metropolitan event, comparable with the opera as a dramatic occasion attracting public notice. The determination of the most able candidates to remain in, or at least return to, Paris further reinforced the intellectual power of the capital. By the middle of the century, some five hundred agrégés were in active service, with a status indubitably higher than that of mere graduates of the Faculties. Moreover, what had been designed as a stage preparatory to the professorship had in practice become the principal means of direct entry to that status. Many of the teachers in the provinces were understandably resentful, especially as Paris was associated with the exaltation of intellectual gymnastics and the neglect of teaching skills and experience (Chervel 1993, p.108). In 1847, one year before the revolution that was to threaten it with major changes in its mission, the ENS moved to the premises in the rue d'Ulm which it still occupies. The end of the July Monarchy stimulated a reaction and the Minister Fortoul suppressed all the competitions in 1852. For a while, a determined effort was made to dampen the intellectually critical enthusiasms of the agrégés and to make both the examination and the ENS courses more practical and pedagogical in emphasis and therefore more conformist in orientation: all candidates were required to be at least twenty-five years old and to have had five years of teaching experience, reduced to two in the special case of the élite of the ENS. But other pressures soon prevailed, and the essentials of the traditional order were restored.

Some concessions were however made in response to demands for widening the entry: from 1856, the written but not the oral examinations could be held outside Paris. The number of subjects available was increased steadily as the staffing needs of the lycées themselves changed. The efforts, and especially those of Fortoul's successor Duruy, to weaken the grip of the traditional classical curriculum were less successful. A new branch of secondary education ("special") was founded, with its own agrégation and even its own ENS at Cluny in Burgundy. The importance of linking a competitive national examination with a training institution of high quality had become part of the conventional wisdom. Cluny survived only until 1893, partly because of the difficulty of breaking the monopoly of the classical style of French secondary education. Its distance from the centres of power in Paris doubtless contributed to its difficulties. A separate competition for the general agrégation was established for women, and in 1881 an ENS for them opened at Sèvres. In these same years, new institutions of a high quality were provided for the primary sector, but their story and that of their effective fusion with the dominant ENSs of the rue d'Ulm and of Sèvres belong to a later part of this Chapter. So does the evolution of the University and of its Faculties, which from the late 1870s also began to prepare candidates for the concours. Until that time, an experienced teacher or a young student, whether in the provinces or Paris itself, received no formal assistance in preparing for the examination: unless, of course, he (or, after 1881, she) was fortunate enough to be admitted to an ENS. So important was the concours that the monopoly of the two powerful establishments in Paris could not be indefinitely protected. Their preeminence, on the other hand, was now secure. The introduction in 1877 and 1880 of bursaries for students preparing for the agrégation in the Faculties throughout France attracted a flood of new and able candidates: these younger postulants, whether from the Faculties or from the ENS, were innocent of teaching experience and came to dominate the examination.

Competition intensified as unsuccessful candidates returned year after year: already by 1865, 74% of the candidates had faced the ordeal at least once before (Chervel 1993, p.126). The academic and theoretical emphasis of the examination became yet more uncompromising: even simple practical exercises in correcting the work of school pupils had all disappeared by 1885, and teaching practice was peripheral to the central purposes of the academic exercise. By 1885 a general set of regulations could be drafted for an agrégation now in more or less its final form. Nothing fundamental would change until the years after 1963, and even under the Fifth Republic the central principles of the institution proved surprisingly durable. Although numbers grew throughout the nineteenth century, there was no massive expansion: a steady figure of thirty a year in 1830 had become one hundred by 1900. Between 1900 and 1971 that number was multiplied by twenty. By the 1880s, the agrégés were in a majority as teachers in the (secondary) classes of the lycée, although there were wide regional variations. Even in 1936 a figure of 97% in Paris contrasted starkly with an average of only 54% in the provinces. A President of France, himself a pupil of the ENS and an agrégé, reported that in the lycée which he attended as a pupil there was not even one agrégé. Much of the teaching was in the hands of graduates who had earned a Licence after some three years of study in a Faculty, and who had received no formal training for the tasks of the teacher. By the late nineteenth century, the agrégation had come to mark two boundaries: one between the professeurs of the State lycées and those of the municipal colleges, and the other between those teachers in the lycée who enjoyed tenure, and those who did not. The qualification also became an increasingly important condition of promotion, for example to the ranks of Proviseur or *Inspecteur d'Académie*.

At the same time, the value of the title (for it was not of course in any strict sense a degree) became generalised: even if the Ministry recognised the successful candidate simply as *Agrégé des Lycées*, convention allowed the more noble ascription of *Agrégé de l'Université*. Many who had succeeded in the competition, and especially if they were former pupils of the ENS, earned recognition in a range of careers: the proportion moving into occupations outside education altogether – in literature, journalism, politics – rose from 10% in 1870 to 29% in 1900 (Karady 1976). Even more significant, of course, were the growing numbers choosing to make their mark in higher education and in research: the frontiers between secondary and higher education remained vague and permeable. There is a sense in which, in the phrase of André Chervel, a competition for entry (into teaching in the lycée) became a competition for exit (Chervel 1993, p.189). Such powerful tendencies helped to ensure that the examination remained severely academic, and was infected by no taint of pedagogical or professional values. Efforts to change this focus – notably those made by Lavisse in 1899, before he himself became a few years later Director of the ENS at the time when it was first attached to the Sorbonne – were consistently frustrated (Isambert-Jamati 1990). The agrégation served purposes other than preparation for teaching, and in any case even for the lycée teacher practical experience in the classroom before being employed was deemed unnecessary while courses in educational theory were disdained as both useless and irrelevant.

The solitary competitive examination, with restricted possibilities for success imposed by the Ministry's own quotas, could not of itself supply all the teachers for the nation's secondary schools, nor even for the lycées. Although many more or less competent teachers, without enjoying tenure, filled the inevitable gaps in the classrooms of the secondary schools, there was little official or parental confidence in the standards of the Faculties (especially those outside Paris). The government had nevertheless ruled that a new category of secondary school teacher should be created – the *Professeur Chargé de Cours Licencié* (that is, a teacher who had earned a Licence by studying at a Faculty), who could become titulaire (tenured) after twenty years of satisfactory service. The *Société des Agrégés* was founded in 1905 in order to keep a watchful eye on this potentially damaging dilution of standards. The more youthful ENSs at St Cloud and Fontenay-aux-Roses (which will be further discussed in the last section of this chapter) diversified their primary role by preparing the best among their students for the agrégation (Luc & Barbé 1992). The seductions of the market were irresistible and by 1941, one hundred and fifty-eight of the graduates of St. Cloud were already agrégés. Between 1942 and 1953 two-thirds of each generation were successful in the examination. The ambitions of these students, as of those of their contemporaries dispersed throughout the Faculties constituted no threat to the integrity of the agrégation: on the contrary, the standards of a national and competitive examination were strengthened by such stimulating rivalries. But the *Société des Agrégés* did for many years successfully resist all efforts to introduce a second State examination alongside, or more precisely below, that which had now been established for over one hundred and fifty years, and to which the high quality of French secondary education was widely attributed. So dangerous an innovation had to await the unusual circumstances of the

Vichy regime. The hatred of Pétain and his colleagues for all that was represented in French life by the primary school tradition and by the pernicious école normale (never to be confused with the ENS) stimulated the régime to weaken the primary school by decapitating it, and converting the upper primary schools into collèges. These colleges would be secondary and not primary schools (a distinction to be further explored in the later pages devoted to the école normale) and would require appropriately educated and trained teachers. Obviously, these would not be agrégés, and a new qualification had to be invented for them: the *Certificat d'Aptitude à l'Enseignement dans les Collèges*, (CAEC). The monopoly of the agrégation had been breached, and yet the result proved to be a further strengthening of its old power.

Teachers armed with the CAEC were qualified to teach two subjects at the newly defined lower secondary level, and were therefore by definition less specialized (and for that reason less scholarly) than the agrégés. Although the upper primary schools (the EPSs) were restored to their pristine republican virtues after the Liberation, the need for such teachers – more specialized than the regular primary instituteur but less learned than the secondary professeur – persisted. Indeed, the upper primary schools were after a decent post-Vichy interval once more in 1959 dignified as collèges. Meanwhile, in the academic secondary school the shortage of teachers of attested quality persisted. That gap was filled in 1952 by the transformation of the transitional CAEC into the CAPES – the *Certificat d'Aptitude au Professorat de l'Enseignement du Second Degré* – which rapidly established itself as a second order agrégation. It differed significantly from the CAEC by requiring a traditional specialization in only one academic subject. In the following year the regional pedagogical centres (the CPRs which, as has been shown, were in 1963 an important part of the teacher training scene) were established throughout France, initially in order to provide practical training for students from the Faculties who had succeeded in the competition for the CAPES, the procedures of which mirrored in principle and in detail those of its elder cousin. Moreover, it soon became standard practice for many of the newly named certifiés during the year of attachment to the CPR to devote their energies to preparing for the agrégation itself (Leselbaum 1987). Moreover, the CAPES could be awarded as a consolation prize to those who had narrowly failed to achieve the agrégation. The new competition and the new category of tenured professeur were neatly assimilated to the established order. Nor did that established order fail to adapt itself internally to the changing conditions of the mid-twentieth century: as the rigid grip of the classical model on the secondary school curriculum weakened, so the number of subjects available in the great annual concours was widened. In 1962, Management was admitted to the canon, and other new fields of study followed in rapid succession. The agrégation had triumphed again, and was still commanding the heights of the educational system in 1963, as indeed for long after that. A national, State directed, centrally organized and assertively academic examination continued to dominate the French system of teacher preparation, now diversified by the acceptance of novel subjects and buttressed by a new but entirely compatible concours. An academic enterprise to be sure, and yet not controlled (as might have been supposed) by the universities. What, in the French experience, explains this apparent anomaly?

The University

The Imperial University, which (like many things in France) changed its name almost as often as its function, was created by Napoleon in 1806. It was to be "a body with exclusive responsibility for public education in the whole of the Empire...." By the law of 1908 it was ruled that

> no establishment may be formed outside the University without the authorization of its head. No-one may teach without being a member of the University and a graduate of its faculties. There shall be as many Academies as there are Courts of Appeal. Five orders of faculty are created: theology, law, medicine, sciences, letters (Verger 1986, p.269).

The head upon whom the Emperor conferred authority was given the impressively solemn title of Grand Master. In each Academy of the University he delegated authority to a Rector. This was a University in no way comparable with those which existed in France until their abolition on 15 September 1793, or with those which currently existed in other European countries. It was a State body, a corporation of teachers established by law and enjoying a monopoly not only in higher learning but also in secondary education. Indeed, secondary education in the modern sense constituted its core, in the shape of the lycées and the General Inspectors already established in 1802. The Napoleonic innovation was to bring those schools, together with their teachers and supervisors, within a unified structure. Bodies other than the State were permitted to provide education at the higher levels, but only with the hierarchical approval of the University. Although the laws formally applied to education at all levels, in practice the University concerned itself only with schooling beyond the elementary level (Aulard 1911).

When the ancient universities along with the colleges were abolished during the Revolution, some institutions of advanced teaching nevertheless survived. There was in France a long tradition of founding, outside the ossified structure of the universities, special institutions for carefully defined purposes: for example, the Collège de France (1530), the Jardin des Plantes (1626), the Observatoire (1672), the Ecole des Ponts et Chaussées (1747) and the Ecole des Mines (1783). Some of these were preserved or reconstituted during the Revolutionary years, and in 1794 both the Ecole des Travaux Publics (which shortly became the Polytechnique, and eventually the most famous of the grandes écoles) and the Ecole Normale (Supérieure) were created. All these represented attempts by the Directory to meet specific public needs, but without any serious effort at articulation or integration.

Essays in providing some form of secondary education, to precede specific training in the Ecoles, were even more haphazard. Although some one hundred Central Schools were opened in Paris and the Departments, they offered only fragmented courses of instruction in particular subjects: the secondary curriculum had disintegrated. It was for this reason that Napoleon created the lycées as the basis of a truly national education, and then brought them within the legal framework of "the University".

The special institutions, or grandes écoles as they came to be known, provided a form of professional education (at this time principally for engineers and teachers) alongside the higher faculties of the University itself: law, medicine and (although never on a significant scale) theology. In effect, therefore, there was no distinct form of general "undergraduate" higher education other than that provided in the lycée and the college. The Faculties of Letters and of Science existed primarily in order to furnish the juries which would award the degrees of the University: the baccalauréat at the end of studies of a lycée type, and (but in much smaller numbers) the Licence and the doctorate. Little or no formal instruction at these higher levels was provided in the Faculties of Letters and Science, which were to be formally constituted alongside the principal lycée of each Academy, with the senior administrators of that school as members. It was normal for a Professor of the Faculty to teach in a lycée, and of course to receive a salary for doing so. The only source of income for a Faculty as such was derived from the examination fees which the law required it to levy. Throughout, and even beyond, the long history of the University, these Napoleonic principles determined much educational behaviour in France, and explain the special (if not unique) relationship of that University to the education of teachers. The "academic" Faculties (Letters and Science) were weak, and provided little instruction outside the lycée, to which they were formally attached. The University, as originally constituted, was a corporation of teachers with a monopoly protected by law. The boundaries between secondary and higher education were vague and shifting, in the professorial career as in administrative definitions. The academic Faculties shared neither values, resources, interests nor buildings with the professional Faculties of Law and Medicine (themselves equally isolated from one another). The University was the employer rather than the educator of teachers, or future teachers. It was, under another name and through the powers delegated to the Rectors, the public authority responsible for secondary education. The best, indeed for many decades the only, form of teacher preparation was delivered outside the Faculties and the University, in the ENS. The agrégation was not a University degree or diploma.

At first it seemed that this grand display of imperial architecture would not survive the fall of its creator in 1815. In the first flush of the Bourbon restoration, the unitary University was dismembered and replaced by seventeen smaller universities. But after the Hundred Days and the second departure of Napoleon into exile, the University was reborn, albeit without its name and suffering from reduced powers and dignity. The Grand Master disappeared (but not for long) and a Commission formally replaced the University, reporting directly to the Minister of the Interior. The Commission was soon renamed the *Conseil Royal de l'Instruction Publique*. In 1821, the University recovered both its name and its Grand Master, while three years later the Ministry of Public Instruction emerged. The Church, deeply resentful of a monopoly (the essentials of which had now been restored) was temporarily pacified by the appointment of a bishop as Grand Master and Minister and by the purging from the University of some of its more offensive liberals, as well as (of course) by the closing of the ENS. But the University was there to stay, and profited from the more liberal spirit prevailing after 1827, and especially from the Revolution of 1830. It was entering upon its golden age.

The great men of the University – *les grands universitaires* – were now near the springs of power. The long dominance of Victor Cousin in philosophy was inaugurated, while Guizot occupied a central position in a succession of governments. He was especially energetic in developing primary education (for which see the last part of this chapter) and in securing in the education of younger pupils a larger influence for the State at the expense of the Church. Both he and Cousin favoured a restoration of the corporatist power of the University, rather than an extension of the central political and administrative authority. They did not prevail: the enlarging administrative powers of the twin Ministry/University were in the 1840s brought together in the rue de Grenelle, where they remain, although the University in its traditional form preserved a monopoly in the granting of degrees and maintained a solid legal position. But control over educational administration, the management of careers in the education service, and the deployment of finances were all kept tightly in the hands of the Minister and his officials. Those powers were to some extent held in check by the General Inspectors, who were more permanent than politicians and came increasingly to represent the interests of the University, of which they had been from the beginning a key part.

The popular disorders and rhetorical extremism of the Revolution of 1848 drove the middle classes into a working alliance with the Church, in which cautious politicians like Thiers recognized a strong bulwark for the maintenance of their power and respectability. This new coalition enabled the passing of the Falloux law of 1850, which severely restricted the monopoly of the University (although not in the granting of degrees) by extending to the Church the right to establish its own secondary schools. The Grand Master and the old Council of the University disappeared, and although much of the former terminology survived (including of course that of the Academy and the Rector) what had once been a corporation defending its privileges now in effect became a public service, comparable to many others furnished by the State. The enemies of the Napoleonic corporate University secured an impressive but impermanent victory by increasing the number of Academies to coincide with the civil Departments in France: this limited the range of their authority and made them more amenable to the influence of the bishops. The former and larger Academies were however restored in 1854, and the critics of clericalism recovered their nerve. Under the guidance of the effective (and *universitaire*) Minister Victor Duruy (1863-69) more power was devolved upon the restored Rectors and the administrative map of French education acquired the shape it still enjoyed in 1963 (Rohr 1967, Horvath-Peterson 1984).

In these final years of the Second Empire, the University recovered, if not the direct power it had once exercised, then at least an enhanced measure of influence: the Minister was careful to consult its distinguished leaders on a variety of themes, several missions were despatched to Germany to examine the worrying phenomenon of the uninterrupted advance in scholarship and research within the universities of that country, so different in character from their French counterparts in the Faculties and the professional grandes écoles. More influence was acquired by educational reform groups often led by Protestants, Jewish thinkers, Freemasons and Positivists: the *Ligue de l'Enseignement* was founded in 1866. A model for the development of a university institution dedicated to research was furnished in 1868 by Duruy's creation, although with meagre resources, of the *Ecole Pratique des Hautes Etudes*. For their part, the Catholics pressed forward from their victory in secondary education in the 1850 law, to demand a corresponding freedom in higher education. The defenders of the University as a secular and public institution were not content to sit by and wait for the Catholics to repeat the success they had, since 1850, enjoyed in dramatically enlarging their share of secondary schooling. They now redoubled their efforts to reform THE University from within.

The shattering defeat of France by Germany in 1870 and the abrupt ending of the second Bonapartist empire mobilized enthusiastic support for those determined efforts at reform: many attributed the German victory (as was again the case in 1940) to the weakness of the French educational system and the strength of the universities across the Rhine. In the 1870s the influential *Société de l'Enseignement Supérieur* was founded, and the Review which it published contained in the years before 1890 no less than thirty articles on Germany, nine on England and only five on the United States. The German example had a hypnotic effect. A principal motive of the emulation and the reform was the urgent need to produce for France élites of high quality: trained in the rigours of positivist science, secular in spirit, republican in loyalties. The private sector continued to offer lively competition to the monopoly of the University: Sciences-Po, (*L'Ecole des Sciences Politiques*) was founded in the very first years of the Third Republic. In 1875 the Catholics were successful in extracting the concession that any three free Faculties (not being, that is, part of the State system) could now combine to form a free university, although control of degrees was still in the hands of the legally entrenched University of France. Even when that right to the university title was surrendered in 1880, the reality of the competition and of an alternative to the public University persisted. In 1881, with financial and other support from the municipality of Paris, the powerful *Ecole des Hautes Etudes Commerciales* (HEC) was launched.

The competition of the grandes écoles, new and old, and the magnetism of the German example encouraged in the last decades of the nineteenth century a strengthening of the professional Faculties of the University, and specifically of law and medicine. The curriculum in law was widened to include political economy, as well as international and constitutional law. The Licence in law in effect prepared for entry to a number of careers, both public and private. Medicine acquired a firmer clinical basis in the hospitals, and was given a fresh character and rigour by the scientific revolution springing in particular from the work in Paris of Pasteur. This fundamental change in the nature of medical education in turn enlivened the Faculty of Sciences, and not least because future doctors were now required to undertake preliminary work in the basic sciences in that Faculty before entering upon the clinical phase of their preparation. But the two "academic" Faculties, and especially the Faculty of Letters, remained weak and fragmented. Science was relatively advantaged (as the medical example itself suggests) by the opening up of a widening range of careers, beyond the traditional one of teaching. The teaching of applied science acquired a significantly higher priority and promoted the growth of new institutes in the provinces, while many agrégés in science (but not in letters) moved directly into careers in higher education, without passing through the lycée. In any case, the continued predominance of the classics in the secondary school curriculum produced an imbalance in the employment opportunities in teaching for the graduates in the two academic Faculties: across the half-century after 1876, only 32% of those appointments, carefully measured out each year by the providing State, were attributed to the scientific disciplines (Verger 1986, p.349). The share of Paris in the science undergraduate market did decline under the Third Republic: between the two world wars it steadied at about one-third of the total for the whole of France.

The situation in the Faculty of Letters differed in significant respects. Although career opportunities remained restricted, there was indeed, in contrast to the elegant ease of the earlier part of the century, a new urgency in the development of research and serious scholarship. The *Ecole Pratique* earned its international reputation as a centre for research in the humanities and the social sciences. Vidal de la Blanche in geography, Durkheim in sociology, Buisson in pedagogy, Ribot in psychology, Lanson in the history of literature, Langlois, Lavisse and Seignobos in history: such names were associated with schools of thought and the foundation of academic dynasties. The preparation of the thesis for the *Doctorat d'Etat* was elevated to a task of Teutonic scale and seriousness. The building of the New Sorbonne symbolised the vaulting ambitions of both the academic Faculties. Paris itself of course remained very much the centre of intellectual and cultural life, partly because of the concentration there of resources and therefore of

51

scholars: even after 1918, it kept the lion's share of half the national total of enrolments in the humanities.

For both the Faculties, but especially for Letters and not least in the provinces, it was however the preparation of teachers (but not their professional training) that proved to be the engine which drove the whole enterprise: this is one of the reasons why, in contrast with Britain or the United States, the historical question of the relationships between the universities and secondary school teachers is of such fundamental importance. Opinion about the appropriate education of such teachers continued to be dominated by the prestige of the agrégation and the ENS, which began to change their functions as higher education expanded. The ENS became the preponderant institution in providing the academic talent to staff the lecture rooms and laboratories of the reviving university world: in the 1890s, no less than 76% of the posts at the Sorbonne (that is, in the Paris academic Faculties) were in the hands of normaliens, graduates of the ENS (Verger 1986, p.362). These standards and these ambitions set the tone for all else in the education of teachers for the secondary schools and for higher education, between which no clear distinction should yet be made. A teacher was above all else an academic. This perception was important for the Faculties, since it was to them that the government of the Republic looked to produce the many necessary teachers of attested quality for an enlarging secondary school system. This was moreover a sharply political issue, since the elevation of standards and therefore of middle-class confidence in the State lycées was a necessary condition of meeting the challenge posed by the growing number and size of Catholic schools.

It was now the task of the Faculties to produce the *licenciés* who would replace the *bacheliers* in the colleges and the lower classes of the lycée, and to polish the agrégés who would then replace the licenciés in the upper classes of the lycée, as well as in the still higher classes for older students preparing for the competitions controlling entry to the grandes écoles. It was for this reason that bursaries were provided in the Faculties throughout France for students preparing either for the University degrees or for the competitive State examinations. The provision from the late 1870s of such bursaries became and remained a major charge upon the budget of the State. It brought to the Faculties in Paris and the provinces new students and locked those Faculties into the tasks of providing an academic education of a traditional kind for future teachers. It enabled them to develop, by teaching for the agrégation, work of a demanding and postgraduate character and, by increasing the number of serious and full-time students for the Licence, provided a steady financial base for their academic work. It further entailed that the Faculties of Letters remained for the most part bodies preoccupied with the supervision of the arrangements for the award in the lycées of the baccalauréat, and with the teaching within the Faculty of future teachers. Neither for the future lycée teacher, nor for his less well qualified colleague in the college, was any form of serious professional or pedagogical training proposed.

The University existed, and Faculties were growing in importance. But did universities exist? The reformers of the Third Republic were determined that they should, and that the power of Paris should be balanced by that of six or seven great universities in the provinces: only in this way could the dangers of excessive centralization be avoided, and excellence widely cultivated in the German manner. Such was at all events the ambition of Louis Liard, who was for eighteen years (1884–1902) Director of Higher Education at the Ministry. His career epitomises that of a *grand universitaire* under the Republic. He was educated first in Falaise and then at the Lycée Charlemagne in Paris, from which in 1866 he secured entry to the ENS in the rue d'Ulm, becoming an agrégé in philosophy three years later. He taught in lycées for five years, before taking his doctorate and joining the Faculty of Letters in Bordeaux. After spending four years as Rector of Caen, he began his long reign at the Ministry as Ministers came and went. That concluded, he was Vice Rector of Paris until his death in 1917 (Nique and Lelièvre 1990a, p. 245). At the Ministry, he worked closely with the reformers active in the Ligue, and struggled tirelessly to create a national system of universities and to ensure that the State budget should support them adequately. Although politicians and bureaucrats continued to dominate the University (in its administrative form), he did succeed in strengthening the *Conseil Supérieur de l'Instruction Publique*, and was careful to consult his reforming friends in the world of higher education. Greater autonomy was conceded to the Faculties in determining their own programmes of study and methods of teaching. For twenty years, hampered by the sustained opposition of local interests to any plan which might seem to favour one region against another, he struggled to create a new generation of regional universities, and to end the isolation from one another of the Faculties. In 1885 the Faculties had conferred upon them the status of a civil personality, which meant among other things that they could receive gifts and operate with a measure of independence within the framework of the law. In cities where Faculties coexisted, without previously cohabiting, they could now constitute a General Council with opportunities to form a loose federation and to provide certain common services. In 1889, Liard fought to confer legal status upon the largest and most effective of the general Councils, but the Senate – always attentively jealous to local interests – insisted that what was granted to some should be extended to all. As a result, even those General Councils which embraced only the two academic Faculties were allowed the same formal position as the great provincial centres. In effect, this created the framework (although not yet the title) of a university in each of the fifteen Academies then established in France. The title itself was conferred upon each of the fifteen in 1896, and they were then allowed to award their own diplomas alongside those sanctioned by the State. The university map was tidied up in 1922, when Algiers was added, but no further changes were made until the convulsions of the 1960s (Verger 1986, p.333).

French universities therefore kept their distinctive characteristics well into the present century. The term "University" carried, and in some ways still does, many of the overtones of its Napoleonic origins. The University continued to be a corporation of teachers with their roots in the lycée and kept a tight grip upon the conferring of all degrees, including the baccalauréat. It continued to claim, if no longer a monopoly, then at least a predominance in secondary as in higher education and was jealous of opposition from the Church or from private bodies. Its General Inspectors remained integral to the University establishment and promoted its interests and values, while its Rectors directed all educational services within the territories for which they were responsible. It was weakened by the flourishing outside the structure of its constituent Faculties of the grandes écoles, some of which fell under the jurisdiction of other ministries, while others lay outside the frontiers of the State. During the nineteenth century the University, although never clearly or completely, merged with the Ministry in the rue de Grenelle, as the Grand Master faded into an administrative mist. Yet even in the 1980s, a Minister could adopt the tone and even the robes of that anachronistic office. The higher professional faculties achieved a greater measure of visibility and power under the Third Republic, although they continued to operate in isolation from one another and from the academic Faculties. Some of their undoubted success was shared with the Faculties of Science, although many of the latter remained ill organized and scattered. The Faculty of Letters was, and especially outside Paris, debilitated by its entanglement in the business of supervising a large, and for the most part external, system of examinations and by a preoccupation (imposed by circumstances) with the education of future secondary school teachers. Traditionally, the most successful even of those teachers had been educated outside the Faculties themselves in the ENS, and were dignified by the conferment upon them of a jealously guarded title that was not a University degree. The prosperity and status of the academic Faculties were however greatly enhanced by the introduction of bursaries and by the responsibilities which they acquired at the same time in preparing able candidates for the agrégation, as (later) for the CAPES. Paris remained dominant at the heart of a centralized system. The larger provincial centres of excellence – Lyon, Lille, Bordeaux, Montpellier, Toulouse, Nancy, Marseille – did acquire impressive new buildings, as did Paris itself. But the effort to create a network of major and relatively autonomous universities was only partly successful. Not until the 1960s finally shattered the structures and assumptions of the monolithic national University would it be possible to redefine the relationships between "the university" and the education of teachers. And until that time, it would not seem practicable even to the most imaginative of reformers to raise in this context the question of the relationship to the University of the primary school teachers. They belonged to an altogether different world: that of the école normale.

The Ecole Normale

In 1963 the most obtrusive institution devoted to the education of teachers was the école normale (the EN). Other establishments were, in different ways, engaged in this enterprise, but they were not so impressively visible and their missions were more varied. The Faculties and the University had an essential part to play in the preparation of students for the agrégation and the CAPES, but these were essentially examinations in the subject matter of a discipline, dispersed across the range of academic departments within higher education. Practical training for secondary school teachers was delivered through the CPRs, but these were dispersed institutions without any strong institutional life of their own (Leselbaum, 1987). The ENSs of the capital had been founded in order to prepare teachers for the schools, but by the early 1960s had been drawn away from that original commitment and were now concerned more with research and preparing the cream of the professoriate for higher education. But in each administrative Department of the Fifth Republic there stood two écoles normales, one for men and one for women, preoccupied exclusively with the preparation of teachers for the primary schools. As such, they were the inheritors throughout France of a self-confident and distinctive tradition. They would, while undergoing significant changes, preserve for another three decades their institutional identity. The golden age in their history lasted from the 1880s until 1940, but their origins lie earlier in the nineteenth century, and especially in the work of Guizot in the 1830s. At every point in that history, and even more dramatically than was the case for the University or the agrégation, their development reflects the changing politics of successive regimes in France.

The Revolution of 1789 released a flood of speculative proposals for the educational future of France, and destroyed the traditional structures of the universities and the colleges, as well as the uneven pattern of primary schooling dominated by the Church. Theorists like Condorcet argued that all that was required of those who would teach younger pupils was the mastery of a subject: special training was unnecessary, and the future primary school teachers would therefore be produced within the new Central Schools. In the shorter term, emergency measures were however required to fill the alarming gaps in the provision of such teachers, and in 1794 a model was to hand in the shape of the recent and successful arrangements to produce with great rapidity men competent in the manufacture of cannons and gunpowder, trained in Paris and then despatched to all the corners of France to scatter their new-found knowledge and skills. A decree in that same year first made use of the term école normale in an official text: one was to be created in Paris (the somewhat shaky ancestor of the present ENS) with the mission of distributing the necessary knowledge to candidates selected by the civil authorities throughout France. The best scholars in each subject would in a four month course convey their wisdom to this elite, the members of which would thereafter return to their native Departments and in turn train the urgently needed teachers for the primary schools. The only course which this first Ecole Normale of Paris ever delivered opened under the direction of Lakanal early in 1794 in the Museum of National History, with well over a thousand chilled students in attendance. The principles were simple, rational and uniform. "The art of teaching is the same in the Alps as in Paris" (Nique 1991, p.28). This bold experiment was not successful.

After the end of the Terror a good deal of control over primary education was recovered by the clergy, while the State paid more attention to the effort to develop the Central Schools, which would themselves (it was hoped) in time produce a better supply of teachers. Napoleon, as has already been argued, had little interest in the lower levels of schooling: only in the most formal sense did his University include the primary school teachers. Although the 1808 Law did allow, without requiring, the organization in the lycées and colleges of special classes for such teachers, only in Strasbourg (where German influence was naturally strong) did the Prefect in fact decide to make such provision. Students in that city could, at any point between the ages of eighteen and thirty, be admitted to a course which lasted four (soon to become three) years. The first école normale in France was therefore effectively founded in 1811, and survived continuously until 1991.

The early nineteenth century was marked by a fashionable interest in the new monitorial schools invented in Britain: these were schools where one teacher could, with some help from older pupils who had received a basic training as assistants, take responsibility for very large classes. Several model schools of this type were opened with strong (but temporary) support from the government. They were seen as a useful check upon the power of the Church, and especially of the Brothers of the Christian Schools. The political reaction of the 1820s produced a reversal of this mild policy and elevated to the revived office of Grand Master of the University Bishop Frayssinous, who closed the ENS and withdrew government support of the monitorial schools. Responsibilities for education and for ecclesiastical affairs were merged in one Ministry. In the last years before the overthrow of the Bourbons in 1830 policy began to shift, and the new Minister went out of his way to praise the example of Strasbourg and call for its emulation: in 1828-29, eleven new écoles normales were opened, including those at Orleans and Rouen (Nique 1991).

The crisis of July 1830 marked the beginning of the Orleanist regime, whose policies were marked by a new emphasis upon the importance of public education and (within a few years) an accompanying revival in the fortunes of teacher training. This was preceded by a quickening of local initiatives, especially the opening in 1831 with strong government endorsement of an école normale to serve the needs of the Academy of Paris. The detailed regulation by government of the new establishment prefigured many of the features of the next generation of teacher training establishments. The school was deliberately opened not in Paris (where the influence of hot-blooded revolutionaries might corrupt impressionable trainee teachers) but in the countryside at Versailles, where more solid rustic virtues of an unambitious kind might be cultivated. Students were to be at least eighteen years old on admission, which was determined by a competitive concours for the number of places made available each year. Those who succeeded were supported by bursaries during a year of residence as boarders. The programme of studies was carefully limited to the material which the future instituteurs would themselves later be required to impart to their own pupils. Teaching practice was to be completed in special classes annexed to the school, the Director of which was nominated by the Minister. The classical features of the école normale were therefore now all in place: a concern with social order and the preservation of traditional values, especially those of the countryside; admission by a competitive examination to a course of study that was supported by public funding and required students to be boarders; an unambitious curriculum that would not give students ideas above their station; an emphasis on practical experience in classes controlled by the school itself; prescription by the government of the day, which would also appoint the Director; strong roots (unlike the lycée) in the local community.

In the following year François Guizot became Minister of Public Instruction and generalized these principles: the law of 1833, which carries his name, required each Department to maintain an école normale, or at least to contribute to the costs of such provision in the same region. A deliberate appeal was made to the precedent of the ENS, recently reopened in the premises of Louis-le-Grand:

> Primary écoles normales are indispensable. Secondary education has emerged from its own ruins, being founded in France on the day when Napoleon simplified and organized a great idea of the Revolution and created the central Ecole Normale of Paris. This simple and fruitful idea must now be applied to primary education. We therefore propose to establish a primary école normale for each Department. [1]

Continuity was claimed by Guizot the conservative, and symmetry asserted by Guizot the Frenchman. It was the business of the Department to fund and provide the institution, which was nevertheless to remain firmly under the control of the Minister in Paris. No regime was prepared to sacrifice this principle. The famous letter which the Minister sent to all the primary teachers of France reemphasised the principles already clarified in creating the school at Versailles. Above all, the école normale was to be a means of controlling public opinion, fighting disorder, and maintaining the status quo in society. The number of institutions grew within three years from forty-seven in 1832 to seventy-six: only eight Departments were without one. The restrictive control of the ambitions of the establishments became tighter as the government moved to the right, in response to growing middle-class concerns about public order. Attacks on demi-savants became sharper: teachers must not be educated "above their duties" (Nique 1991, p.93). The programme of studies was for that reason more precisely and narrowly defined, and some fifty Directors were dismissed from their posts: in 1845 it was ruled that in future these powerful agents were to be recruited not from secondary education (where they might have acquired inappropriate ideas) but from the supposedly more docile ranks of the primary school teachers themselves.

The agitations of 1848 and the fall of the regime introduced a (very) short period when the teacher training establishments were lauded by the new tenants of power for their part in bringing about revolution and the end of the monarchy. It was proposed that the number of écoles normales be increased to the full quota of eighty-six. The Rectors were required to instruct the teachers to do all that they could to encourage the population to vote well in the new elections and one influential teacher proclaimed:

> I have no doubt, dear brothers, that you will be among those who greet with enthusiasm the new revolution. You have been too disdained and oppressed by the old government not to rejoice in its fall, and you are too intelligent and enlightened to fail to understand the immense advantages for France that will flow from the establishment of the republican regime (Gontard 1976, p.65).

Such unambiguously partisan language, confirming the worst fears of the apprehensive conservatives, would soon be repented. The summer of 1848 was tumultuous and the so-called Party of Order preyed upon the anxieties of all those who had anything to lose if all order collapsed. Louis Napoleon Bonaparte, the nephew of the Emperor who had laid the foundations for the educational system, became President in December 1848, and new legislation was rapidly prepared: freedom to provide secondary schools was, of course, conceded to the Church and the monopoly of the University broken. Adolphe Thiers, who had been hostile to the interests of the clergy, now became one of the most vocal political critics of the instituteurs. Throughout the long series of complicated parliamentary negotiations leading to the Falloux law he battled to eliminate the pernicious école normale from the life of France. Teacher training should take the form simply of periods of supervised teaching practice in carefully selected schools. Thiers admitted:

> under the regime which has collapsed, I feared certain influences of the clergy; today, I regard religion and its ministers as the allies, perhaps even the saviours, of a threatened social order... The village curé is to be our one support against the demagogic and communist teachers who are to be sent forth to every village.

Or, more concisely, "I prefer the teacher who is the bell-ringer to one who is a mathematician". No priorities could be more explicit: the instituteur exists to serve social and political rather than abstractly educational purposes. In a curious sense, all shades of political opinion remained sympathetic to this key principle of the école normale (Nique 1991, p.110).

Napoleon Bonaparte, ever a skilful tactician, wished to keep a certain distance from the clerical party and therefore resisted the pressures for abolition. He and others were also well aware of the practical problems that would be created if the training establishments, which produced about one half of the 1700 new teachers required each year in France, were simply shut down. Formally, the choice between a school-based system of stages and dependence upon the existing école normale was left to each Department, while the Minister himself could also abolish an establishment if he chose. Although this left these institutions in a dangerously exposed position, the government in the event preferred a policy of control (with all its advantages to them as the party in power) to one of extinction. Only eight were closed. Evidence of a determination to control and restrict was however clear as early as 1851, when the competitive examination was replaced by an enquiry into the moral (and therefore political) character of applicants for training. The age of admission was raised from sixteen to eighteen, the curriculum was further restricted, insistence on boarding strengthened, while daily prayer and Mass on Sunday became an integral and obligatory part of the routine. Since even the Rector might show some independence of spirit, the Prefects were given the duty of choosing and expelling students.

The disintegration of Louis Napoleon's uncertain alliance with the Catholic party propelled his government in a slightly more liberal direction. In the early 1860s, six écoles normales were reopened and, in an eloquent gesture, two new establishments were opened in Chambéry and Nice when these territories were annexed to the Empire. They plainly had their uses to any established power. During the Ministry of Victor Duruy, who did much to prepare for the more spectacular reforms of Ferry and the Third Republic, the Prefects were reminded that they must prefer as candidates for posts in primary schools those teachers who had attended the EN. In 1866 the concours was restored. Not only geography and geometry but even so dangerous a subject as history were added to the list of what might be taught, while the age of admission was lowered to seventeen. The fears of corruption, so obvious in the early 1850s, had apparently evaporated. Although eighty ENs for men existed when Louis Napoleon fell from power, no systematic provision was yet made for women. They had to be content with only eleven training establishments of any kind, and of these eight were controlled by the Church.

With the dramatic end of the Second Empire in 1871, the lines of battle between Church and State, as between monarchists of all kinds and republicans, were clearly drawn. They ran right through the world of the école normale and particularly affected the education of women. The feeble provision of teacher training opportunities for women reflected only too clearly the imbalance within primary education as a whole. Although at the beginning of the Third Republic there were 2.350.000 girls attending primary school, compared with 2.5000.000 boys, only 1.100.000 of those girls were in lay schools, compared with 2.000.000 boys. Consequently, there were nearly twice as many male lay teachers as female (Nique 1991, p. 136). Jules Ferry, who was the most prominent of the educational reformers of the 1880s, made explicit as early as 1870 the ideological reasons for according a high priority to the education of girls and the training of women teachers. The Church understood well enough, he argued, the importance of capturing and exploiting the influence of women over their children , and indeed their husbands. "Democracy must choose or it will perish. Citizens, the choice must be made! The woman must belong either to the Church, or to knowledge (*la science*)." [2]

These were the accents of a disciple of Positivism and of a fervent republican (Legrand, 1961). These were the principles to be systematically applied after the cautiously conservative decade of the 1870s. The Catholics correctly saw the effort to establish lay teacher training for women as the critically important first stage of a larger and more sinister plan to make the whole of primary education free, public, secular, republican – and, by implication, anticlerical. They presented the battle as being fought for the very soul of France. For Ferry and the republicans the issue was of central importance: education needed to be mobilized to support – and indeed to create – a new Republic, the very existence of which was menaced by the sympathies of the Church for the royalist and imperialist causes.

The teachers must therefore be equipped to become the apostles of that Republic, and they – but first of all the women – must for that reason be given a sound and appropriate preparation. A legal obligation was placed upon each Department to provide an école normale for women as well as one for men (or, more exactly, for girls as for boys). And yet, once again, the responsibility for ordering the purposes and programme of the EN rested with the State – with the "Teaching State" (*l'Etat enseignant*) as Ferry significantly called it. "I assert that the education of girls, like any other education, is the property (*le bien*) of the State..." [3]

It was the business of that State to produce teachers who would in turn produce good citizens. Once again, the image of downward diffusion – already clear in the Ecole Normale of 1795 – is dominant. Once again, the imperative of political and social control is as assertive as it was for Guizot or in the Second Empire, even if the purpose now is to produce not good Christians but good Republicans. Changes were for this reason imposed by the Minister in Paris on the structure and contents of the curriculum of the training establishments. Given that the induction of docility, in teachers as in pupils, was no longer the main purpose of the enterprise, the definitions of desirable knowledge must be correspondingly widened. French literature and even foreign languages were now admitted to the canon. The teaching of religion was prohibited and the office of chaplain abolished in 1883. The EN became less monastic in style, without losing altogether the flavour of the seminary.

Jules Ferry and those who worked with him believed that all citizens had a right of access to a sound education, and that the survival of the Republic depended upon the equal right of all citizens to benefit from such an education. This did not, however, mean that they for one moment envisaged a classless society. Their vision was of a new social contract between classes, between employers and workers, with the dignity of the latter secured by free access to a general culture and by a conscious acceptance of a defined place in society. It was therefore essential that primary education should be of good quality and held in high regard, while at the same time representing a different Order from that of secondary education, the lycée, and the University. The category and title of *Professeur d'Ecole Normale* was created to endorse this newly bestowed dignity of the primary Order: these Professors, and not their noble University cousins teaching in the lycée, were to convey to "the People" the general culture of France. But the people and the bourgeoisie were to remain distinct. The parallel hierarchies of the two Orders were completed with the creation of two new and specifically primary ENSs: at Fontenay-les-Roses for women in 1880, and at St. Cloud for men in the following year. The function of these great national establishments was to educate and train the Directors and Professors for the écoles normales themselves, as well as for the higher reaches of the primary schools (Luc and Barbé 1982). The geometry was now complete: the best of the pupils of the primary schools went forward to the EN, from which the best pupils were selected for the primary ENSs at St. Cloud and Fontenay, from which the graduates returned as leaders in the primary sector. That sector now had its own self-sufficient hierarchies and selective mechanisms and values: the values of the Republic and of an instructed and loyal People. At the head of the new ENSs Ferry – working closely with the Director of Primary Schooling, Ferdinand Buisson, and Octave Gréard, the Sub-Rector of Paris – installed two of the most influential and scholarly of the General Inspectors. Emile Jacoulet reigned at St. Cloud and Félix Pécaut at Fontenay. Ferry was a Positivist and a Freemason and Buisson a liberal Protestant. The hortatory speeches of Pécaut to the students of Fontenay remain the classic statements of the values and principles to be inculcated in all the écoles normales of the Republic (Pécaut 1904).

The tensions between Catholics and those who preferred the secular power of the Republic were raised to a critical pitch by the Dreyfus case and by the feverish propaganda which accompanied it. They led to the formal separation of Church and State in 1905 and absorbed much of the political energy of succeeding governments. A logistic argument, based on the growing shortage of candidates willing to be recruited at an early age into a system dedicated exclusively to the training of teachers, was exploited by the Right, which argued for the suppression of the EN as a hotbed of radicalism and republicanism. The critics wanted to create a training institution which would recruit its students only after they had completed their general education, and which would provide only a short course of focused practical training. Although such proposals were successfully resisted, the logic of the system of the 1880s was weakened by new regulations made in 1905. The three year course of study (which had hitherto integrated professional and general studies) was now to be sharply separated into two phases: two years of general education (albeit within the EN), leading to the Higher Diploma (the *brevet supérieur*) and then one year of practical and pedagogical training. The concept of a distinct kind of general education, suitable only for those who were themselves going to teach in the primary sector and integrating general and vocational education, became more vulnerable. Why should general as distinct from vocational education be delivered in a specialized institution, dominated by the ideology of a primary sector and the orthodoxies of Fontenay and St. Cloud? The logical connection between the strength and survival of the EN and the dual worlds of primary and secondary Orders was explicitly, and prophetically, acknowledged:

> The day will come when the primary school and the lycée will be one. Many signs prove that we are moving towards an organization which will merge the programmes of the primary and the upper primary school with those of the first cycle of the lycées, so that secondary education becomes the natural continuation of primary. At that time it will perhaps be possible and desirable for future instituteurs to follow the courses of the lycée, while the école normale preserves, within such a system, its proper role as a professional school. But this ideal is still in the distance. [4]

Indeed it was: such a development was accomplished only by the intervention of de Gaulle in 1963, the year which marks the terminus of this chapter.

The devastating loss of life in the war of 1914-1918 aggravated the problems of recruiting teachers, and an emergency measure of 1919 allowed recruitment into a short period of training after a general education had been satisfactorily completed. Although this was potentially a serious compromising of the integrity of the EN tradition, within a year the école normale appeared to recover its original purity. The reforms of 1905 were reversed, perhaps because they did indeed challenge the distinct and wholly separate character of the EN: the closely integrated three year course was restored, with teaching practice introduced into the first year and a general education extended across all three. Although that principle would not again be violated until the fall of France in 1940, criticism of the institution once again surfaced: this time, it came from the Left and was grounded in a rejection of the dual system of primary/secondary schooling which was powerfully linked to a particular view of social structure. The Companions of the New University campaigned for the *école unique*, the junior comprehensive school (to employ a later term), and for a common education for all pupils up to the age of fourteen. As for teacher training, the Left argued for a concours after the baccalauréat or the higher qualifications of the primary sector. Jean Zay, as Minister of Education in the government of the popular front, recalled in his memoirs that "the 1937 plan aimed...to improve the training of primary teachers by giving them the advantages of secondary studies, and by mixing them on the benches of the lycée with the other students of the University ..." (Zay 1987, pp. 226-7).

But nothing was achieved before the fall of France, and (ironically) it was Marshal Pétain who – for reasons fundamentally opposed to those of Jean Zay – killed the EN of Ferry and Guizot. This was part of his vision of a reborn France, dedicated to the values of work, family, and country. It was directly derived from his diagnosis of the causes of defeat, foremost among which he placed the betrayal of the soul of France by teachers who were socialists, pacifists and corrupters of youth (Halls 1976, Giolitto 1991). All the écoles normales were closed on 1 October 1940, and their training functions assumed by one institute of professional training in each Academy. Trainee teachers were required first to complete their studies for the baccalauréat in the lycée, after which they were to move through a one year course, to include teaching practice as well as experience in centres for physical education and for agricultural or vocational training.

Although these changes were promptly cancelled in 1945, the baccalauréat remained the standard by which the general education of future primary school teachers was to be assessed. This represented a fundamental and permanent change. The major report on the future of education produced in 1947 went further in its recommendations, arguing that primary school teachers should first have completed some studies within the University itself [5]. Students were however still to be selected for teacher training at about the age of fifteen and were, for some years, still admitted after success in the competitive examination to one of the restored écoles normales. But for the first three years of their residence there, they concentrated exclusively on studies of exactly the same kind as those being pursued by their contemporaries in the lycée. There was no attempt to restore or defend either the distinctness of a primary school culture (in a broad educational sense) or an integrated course of general and professional education. Professional training had to be concentrated in a separate period after the bac. Moreover, some students who had already completed a bac elsewhere could now be admitted directly to the EN and a course of exclusively professional training. The distinctness of the EN became even more blurred as a growing number of Professors in them were agrégés, recruited either from the traditional secondary schools or directly upon graduating from an ENS or a Faculty. The primary ENSs at Fontenay and St. Cloud had similarly over the years been carried away from their original functions, and so become indistinguishable (except in historic reputation) from the establishments of the rue d'Ulm and of Sèvres. There was no longer any rational justification for the recruitment of primary school teachers in a manner which had already been vigorously attacked in the 1930s: the EN had perhaps been reprieved only by the bitter hostility to it of Pétain, and by the later rejection of anything that could be associated with the Vichy regime. Yet the reprieve was surprisingly prolonged, and this was the system still essentially in place in 1963, still boldly if romantically defended in the name of a noble republican ideal of popular education, still buttressed by the vested interests of the EN Professors and their allies in other teacher unions. It could not, however, survive for very much longer (Laprévote 1984; Charles 1988).

Notes

[1] *L'Instituteur*, nos. 1-2, January – February 1833.

[2] Robiquet (1893-8) *Discours et Opinions de Jules Ferry*. Paris: Colin, p.303.

[3] *Journal Officiel*, 2 August 1879.

[4] *Revue Pédagogique*, no.2, 15 February 1906, p.139.

[5] The 1947 document is reprinted in *Le Plan Langevin-Wallon de réforme de l'enseignement. Compte rendu du colloque organisé par le groupe français d'éducation nouvelle et la Société française de Pédagogie.* Paris: 1964.

Oxford Studies in Comparative Education, Vol. 4(1/2), 1994

CHAPTER 3

France: since 1963

The Crisis of 1968

The long histories of the agrégé, the University and the école normale hold rich clues to identifying the principles underlying the preparation of teachers in France in the 1960s. But, more fundamentally, they serve to illuminate many of the key assumptions underpinning the structures of education in France. The agrégé (at the end as at the beginning of the twentieth century) epitomises the French concern with national academic standards, maintained otherwise than through the institutions of higher education themselves. The University and its Rectors in 1963 express the Napoleonic devotion to order and discipline, sustained by constant pressure from Paris. The 1963 école normale still embodies a patriotic, republican and popular tradition of schooling, rooted in each of the Departments into which the French State organizes itself, and complementary to yet distant from the noble traditions of the University. The three, taken together, were historically integrated in a socially and politically determined pattern of educational provision in which the lycée served the needs of a powerful bourgeoisie, the primary order with its own hierarchies and centres of excellence formed the foundation of a parallel system, the grandes écoles stood outside and above the loose network of university Faculties, and the university Rector applied within his assigned territory policies determined by his Minister in Paris.

The Presidential decision of August 1963 and the dramatic events of May 1968 profoundly affected not only schools and universities but also the lives and education of the teachers in them. The details of that Presidential decision are themselves illuminating, when interpreted against the background of the last chapter. The influence of the agrégé seems pervasive, and the powers of a centralised state unlimited. Christian Fouchet became Minister of Education in December 1962 and on 16 February 1963 his director general, Jean Capelle, was summoned for a conversation with the President. Jean Capelle had attended the Ecole Normale Supérieure in the rue d'Ulm and became an agrégé in mathematics before teaching first in a lycée and then in a Faculty. He had been Rector of Nancy before joining the

Ministry in 1959. Jacques Narbonne, who remained active in these discussions, was technical adviser to the President and (it is tempting to add "of course") also an agrégé. Moreover, The Prime Minister himself, Georges Pompidou, was both an agrégé and an exact contemporary in the rue d'Ulm of Capelle. As the President accompanied the former Rector to the door, he observed: "I understand your difficulties. Take heart. The decision will be taken here" (Prost 1992, p. 115). Here: that is to say, not in the Matignon, the headquarters of the Prime Minister, and not in the rue de Grenelle.

The next important meeting at the Elysée was on 4 April. The President remarked: "I believe, Mr Prime Minister, that generalising the first cycle colleges will best deal with the problem of orientation and provide the best conditions for a genuine equality of opportunity. You do agree?" Monsieur Pompidou replied, without enthusiasm and without making any comment, that he did. In August the formal decisions were taken, with consequences that have already been described. The CES now became an important, and within a decade a dominant, part of the educational landscape. The CEG did nevertheless survive for some years, providing only limited opportunities for those advancing into it from the primary schools, whereas the CES was now able to offer a full range of courses preparing for the lycée itself. Pompidou, as an agrégé in classics, was anxious to preserve such protective distinctions for as long as possible. The simplicity of the two-category pattern of teacher careers (the instituteur and the professeur), which had already been eroded by the reforms of 1959, was now to be finally destroyed. Alongside the traditional teachers of the primary and secondary orders there now stood an expanding and ill-defined group: the PEGCs, already teaching in the CEGs and about to join the agrégés and the certifiés in the newly designated CES. Special centres had already been set up to train them in the ENs, although they would have to wait until 1969 for formal recognition by the Ministry as a distinct corps.

General de Gaulle continued to be much preoccupied with orientation. For him, the so-called democratisation of access was quite simply a necessary prerequisite of the more efficient recruitment of an able élite from a wider basis than that offered by the old system. It was, however, equally important to avoid any dilution of quality, and (in his view) only authoritarian guidance and direction (for which "orientation" became a transparent euphemism) could reduce the perils of Americanising the system. In particular, the baccalauréat and the Faculty must be protected: they were indeed, in his view, already in serious trouble (Prost 1992, p. 116). Pompidou, however, was – as a good universitaire of the traditional school – opposed to any such violation of the sacred principle of open access to higher education for all bacheliers. The President did not succeed in finding any effective method of restricting access to the traditionally esteemed courses and programmes within the CES. Within a few years, the General would have to find another line to defend, and his determination to do so contributed in no small measure to the crisis of 1968. The wave of demographic change had already flooded through the primary schools and, enlarged by a remorselessly increasing demand for a longer secondary schooling, was now threatening to engulf secondary schools and higher education alike. This is the background to the crisis of 1968, and to the changes in both university and école normale to which it led.

The years immediately after World War II generated in many countries a "baby boom", but in few was the change so dramatic as in France. The Government took a series of measures to encourage larger families: the 1930s had seen a falling birth rate, accompanied by a national anxiety about the decline of France. In 1938, the birth rate (live births per thousand inhabitants) was only 14.6 but rose to 21.3 in 1947 (Michaud & Kimmel 1990, p. 316). As these pressures pushed into the higher age ranges, so the system began to buckle. The population of the *cours complémentaires*, the primary sector's version of the lower secondary school, doubled between 1946 and 1956, and yet again before 1961 (Albertini 1992, p. 136). The Berthoin law of 1959 decreed that the minimum school leaving age would be raised from fourteen to sixteen and the secondary school population grew within ten years from just over three to nearly four and a half million. The upward pressure from these secondary schools was in its turn irresistible: in the mid-1960s an average of one CES each day was built, while within the lycée the number of baccalaureates awarded increased by a factor of 3.6 between 1956 and 1967. In 1965, the examination was radically reshaped to allow for more options, and to incorporate technological studies (Prost 1992, p. 143. Albertini 1990, pp. 136-7). The efforts of the General to hold back from the Faculties the flood of students (many of them, in his view, inadequate) were as determined as they were unsuccessful. In 1966 ONISEP (the national agency concerned with improving the quality of guidance and the effectiveness of orientation) was created. Selection, whether by parent or by system, was to be at the end of the first cycle of secondary education and not – as the General and others had originally hoped – at the beginning. This critical shift marked the end of Pompidou's efforts to maintain the CEG alongside the CES: hereafter, the CES would become the common lower secondary school for the whole population and new kinds of teachers would be needed. De Gaulle could now only hope to hold back the flood by "orientation" autocratically imposed at a later stage. Final decisions, he argued, must be taken neither by the student nor by the family, but by the competent authorities: in November 1967 he pronounced that "There can be no compromise on this point since the national interest is involved. The State must accept its responsibilities" (Prost 1992, p. 110). Such haughty and principled attitudes exacerbated the crisis of 1968. The number of students within higher education more than doubled, only to double again in the twenty years that followed. However severe the logistic problems in making provision for younger pupils in lower secondary schools, it was in the fac and the lycée, that the results of this expansion were most dramatic and colourful. Given the rigidities of central control and the absence of local autonomy and flexibility, it is not surprising that the facs failed to adapt themselves to the multiple pressures of the 1950s and 1960s. Some modest changes were made in the historic order: a degree (the Licence) in psychology was introduced in 1949 and one in sociology ten years later (Passeron 1986, p. 370). The most visible problems in higher education were those of overcrowding: lecture halls were packed, university teachers had even less time than in the past for attending to the needs of individual students, residential conditions were poor and library facilities worse. All these problems were at their most acute in the capital. The first year of higher education (the so-called *année propédeutique*) was loosely organized and many students dropped out in disillusionment. The most able and determined students continued to stay on in the best lycées and to fight for a place in the safe havens of the grandes écoles. For those who had to content themselves with the fac, there were (especially in the Faculty of Letters) few career opportunities apart from secondary school teaching, with which the Faculties had of course from the beginning been intimately associated. Even for those wishing to become such teachers, the traditional courses of study – even when supplemented by a year's attachment to a CPR – were an inadequate preparation for work in the new CES or the rapidly changing lycée.

In any case, the traditions of the Professoriate were ill-adapted to meeting the challenges of mass higher education. It was the duty of the Professor to expose to docile and attentive students the high culture by which he had himself been impregnated, and never to compromise the purity of that noble task by adapting his style of delivery to a changing student population. Still more unthinkable would be a serious redefinition of the content of such courses. The so-called *cours magistral* was at its best a high art form, but one that made a number of assumptions which could no longer be justified: in any case, even the best lecture fails if it is rendered inaudible by the unsuitability of the building or the press of students. Moreover, much of the teaching of the growing numbers of students was in the hands of Assistants: many of these younger teachers were resentful of professorial privilege and became eager leaders of the protests which increasingly disrupted the 1960s. In such an atmosphere, even the efforts of the Government to introduce overdue reforms were greeted with suspicion and demonstrations: education moved to the centre of the turbulent politics of the Parisian streets. Fouchet, still Minister in 1966, sought with the active encouragement of the Elysée to address the problems of overcrowding and of vocational irrelevance by introducing the IUT (*Institut Universitaire de Technologie*), an institute of technology attached to the university system but standing outside the crumbling structure of the nineteenth century Faculty. These innovations, which later came to enjoy a great success, were resented on the grounds that they provided only a two year course and – worse – required selection before admission.

In the same series of reforms, the Minister replaced the inadequate introductory year by a two-year course, leading to a Diploma either in Letters or in Science. Unfortunately, the content of these courses and the methods of examination were specified in great detail by the Ministry which irritated the Professors by imposing new and complicated tasks upon them, and the students by subjecting them to a process which was perceived as being oppressive and selective. Similarly, the Minister's efforts to respond to the different needs of students in higher education by adapting some courses to the needs of future teachers (the *licence d'enseignement*), while reserving others for those contemplating more advanced studies, were rejected by an increasingly radicalised student body as both divisive and directive. The growing isolation of research itself from the mainstream of university life contributed to the prevailing sense of feebleness and drift. Serious scholarly work was for the most part undertaken by full-time researchers within the CNRS (the national research body), just as serious preparation for some careers of high prestige was concentrated in the powerful grandes écoles. The higher Faculties of Law and Medicine stood apart from the "academic" Faculties which were left only with growing numbers of increasingly resentful students.

The 1968 troubles in France, and especially of course in Paris, were part of a wider international pattern of discontent and inter-generational conflict. In France they were given a particularly sharp edge by the tensions generated between on the one hand a government which was technocratic, and on occasions authoritarian, working within a system of education that was tightly controlled at the national level, and on the other hand a student body that had particular reasons for its disaffection. The temperature of the conflict was raised by a concentration of student population and problems in Paris itself, a long tradition of activism on the streets, a cautious and conservative university tradition (which forbade, for example, the sharing of halls of residence by men and women), and by the ending of the French colonial empire. The last stages of the Algerian conflict provided a focus for student and other radical protest, which readily transferred itself to engagement in the bitter disputes surrounding the war in Vietnam, a country of great historical and emotional importance to France. The crisis broke in the new and anarchic campus at Nanterre in May 1968, and quickly spread to Paris. Nanterre was closed on 2 May and the Sorbonne itself on 3 May. The movement broadened to include trade unions and other groups and generated a major crisis for the Fifth Republic itself. Paris and other major university centres became the scene of energetic and often chaotic debates. When the Prime Minister returned from a journey to Afghanistan he resolved to adopt a policy of reconciliation, accepting that the old system of university governance, with many of the values which it embodied, had in effect collapsed. Alain Peyrefitte resigned as Minister of Education, and his temporary successor was in turn replaced by Edgar Faure after the parliamentary elections of 23 and 30 June, called by the President as an appeal to the people to assist him in bringing to an end *la chienlit* (the havoc) which the students had caused. The elections produced a massive reaffirmation of confidence in the rule of General de Gaulle, who appointed Couve de Murville as Prime Minister in place of a resentful Pompidou. The President had formed his last government.

Edgar Faure, a wily and successful politician who had twice been Prime Minister in the 1950s, undertook the most fundamental reshaping of the French system of higher education that had ever been attempted. His reforms, developed at remarkable speed, created universities for the first time and still provide the foundations for higher education in France. "Our country had never known universities, only Faculties of a classical type existing in narrow compartments" (Faure 1971, p. 170). His methods were bold. All existing institutional arrangements were suspended, and university teachers and students alike invited and empowered to regroup themselves in new and more appropriate patterns of organisation. Faculty members with similar interests, or prejudices, could form themselves into new Units (UERs – *Unités d'Enseignement et de Recherche*) and these could in turn negotiate themselves into groups and alliances, on the basis of which by government decree the new universities would be formed. The problem of French higher education was solved by being dissolved: for once the State stepped back (but not for long). The key principles, as articulated by the General, were those of autonomy, pluridisciplinarity and participation. Experimental universities were not only allowed but encouraged: Vincennes, for example, would admit students who had no bac and had not followed the conventional paths through schooling, and would as a matter of policy be open to the outside world. (Unsurprisingly, and partly as a a result of falling under Communist influence, it was to become a target of public controversy and polemic during the less enthusiastic decade that followed). All depended upon local initiative and enthusiasm, and in particular on a high level of participation by students in the elections of 1969, which were required to establish the governance of the new units upon a permanent and acceptable footing (Prost 1992, p. 136). By early 1969 no fewer than 639 UERs had been constituted, and in May the first list of universities was issued: thirteen "new" universities were created in and around Paris alone (Minot 1983, p. 13).

A new suppleness was injected into the planning and conduct of courses: programmes organised in year-long blocks were replaced by shorter and more flexible components (the so-called UVs, or *Unités de Valeur*), which owed much to the transatlantic example of "credits" and credit hours. Yet the central authority of the State remained in important ways unimpaired. It was generally accepted that all diplomas and degrees should be given on the basis of national rather than local approval and control. Nor was it supposed that the sources of funding for higher education would be found elsewhere than in the coffers of the State. Nor were serious questions raised about the necessity of continuing to regard university teachers as part of a national force, available in principle to be deployed in the best interests of the system. This principle was applied even more clearly to the management of the teaching resources of the secondary sector: that is, to the recruitment, training, funding and disposition of teachers for the lycée and the CES. The secondary schools were themselves directly affected by the aftermath of 1968, and indeed the lycées played a considerable part in the events of that year. Lycée and university students, and again especially in Paris, cherished a strong sense of solidarity, again reflecting the impossibility in France at this time of maintaining any precise distinction between secondary and higher education. The gap between students and teacher, and even more perhaps between older and younger teacher, was as keenly felt in the lycée as in the fac.

Discontent within the expanding lycées and an activist spirit were reflected in the formation during 1967 of action committees: the CALs (*Comités d'Action Lycéenne*), which mobilised support for strikes and occupations in the following year (Winock 1987, p. 139). Many professeurs joined in debates on the reform of the curriculum, calling into question the very foundations of formal learning as expressed in school systems and curricula. Knowledge was to be invented rather than transmitted, and the relationship between teacher and taught must be denounced as inherently oppressive (Prost 1992, p. 411). There was a natural alliance between youthful revolutionary theorists and those students, without strong ideological commitments yet profoundly dissatisfied with their studies, who longed simply for an education somehow different from that experienced by their parents: "*transformer le lycée de Papa*" became the embracing slogan (Winock 1987, p. 139). But, after the effervescence of the summer months, the changes were less dramatic and less permanent in the world of the secondary school than in the realm of the university. Patterns of governance and control were modified, for example by introducing parents into the deliberative bodies within the school, and by pursuing (not always successfully) a greater transparency in the affairs of the institution. Some ancient fortresses were indeed stormed, and Latin was no longer to be taught to younger pupils: one of the most effective methods of distinguishing between pupils of different aptitudes or social backgrounds was thereby weakened (Prost 1992, p. 149).

The traditions of the academic secondary school were of course threatened by the growth in student numbers and to some extent by the incorporation of a new and less respectful type of student. But the teachers were themselves changing. Retirements and expansion had produced a remarkable change in the age pattern of teachers: in 1966, 51% of the professeurs were under thirty-one years of age, compared with only 17% ten years earlier (Albertini 1992, p. 140). The strong tide of teacher recruitment continued across 1968 until 1975, five-sixths of the teaching force in the latter year having been recruited since the beginning of the 1960s (Passeron 1986, p. 411). This growth was reflected in the rising number of admissions to the élite body of the agrégés: the annual number of such posts offered advanced from three hundred in the early fifties to two thousand by the end of the sixties (Albertini 1992, p. 140). The heady radicalism of 1968 led even to the questioning of the appropriateness of the agrégation, as a symbol of conservatism and (literally) Bourbon tradition: aggressive committees were mobilised, and prevented (but for one year only) the holding of the concours.

One permanent if modest result of this turbulence was the fracture of the absolute monopoly of the concours: in future it would be possible to gain access to this high status on the basis of seniority, achievement and repute with the endorsement of an official recommendation (Chervel 1993, p. 256). In the same year (as has already been noted) the lower status PEGC achieved recognition as belonging to a corps, distinct from and superior to that of the primary teachers: one paradoxical result of the dislocation of the traditional system was the strengthening and complicating of hierarchies among teachers. For the moment, the system of secondary teacher training was left largely in place: certainly nothing was done to strengthen the CPR, or to give new weight to professional training for teachers facing new populations of students, or to modify the predominantly academic approach in the preparation of the lycée teachers. In many ways, the training given in the special centres for the PEGC, which were created in 1960 and based in the ENs – and which now recruited a growing number of candidates already holding qualifications from higher education – was more appropriate for the new teaching styles and content needed in the lower secondary school.

The universities, like the Faculties which were their immediate ancestors, preserved a safe distance from the professional training of teachers. Although in 1967, on the eve of the troubles, the Government had in a number of university centres created Departments of Educational Sciences, those same departments eschewed links with the CPRs and were regarded as interlopers by the traditional academic departments. They concentrated instead, by preference or necessity, on the conduct of research and on delivering services to student populations other than those made up of intending teachers (Albertini 1992, p. 156). They will reappear in this story of the relationship between the university and teacher training. Much more striking was the series of structural changes brought about by the crisis of 1968 in the écoles normales. These were in the circumstances of the day vulnerable institutions, still isolated from other establishments of post-school education. They had never recovered a distinctive sense of purpose since their abolition by the Vichy regime and their reconstitution after the Liberation (Nique 1991, Laprévote 1984, Zay 1988). Since the second world war their younger students had not been prepared for the qualifications of the primary order in which they had once been deeply rooted, but for the very different baccalauréat and by teachers who were themselves agrégés and certifiés. Moreover, a growing number of their students had already been prepared for the bac elsewhere and arrived in these departmental institutions with very little sense of *l'esprit normalien*. The time that could be devoted to professional training for primary teaching was consequently limited, generally to part of one year. This was moreover not always a task for which the professeurs of the EN were best prepared: in many cases the only member of staff who came from the primary tradition and had some experience of teaching younger pupils was the Director. The demand for teachers during the fifties and sixties was such that, in most years, the EN could provide only about one-half of those required for immediate service in the primary schools: the rest had to be recruited from whatever sources were available, and although most of them did later receive some formal training, the tough monopolistic grip of the EN was now weakened. Moreover, as with the passing of the demographic wave the demand for primary teachers eventually declined, the ENs began to develop a new and important role. They came to be of central importance within the framework of government policy in delivering courses of in-service training to teachers already in service. Such teachers were indeed given the right to such training, of course on full pay, amounting to the equivalent of one full year across a full career of service to the State.

These changes interacted to produce a dissolution of the old tradition: the professors in the EN now came in overwhelming numbers from the secondary sector, just as the (originally) primary Ecoles Normales Supérieures created in the 1880s were by now indistinguishable in function from their cousins in the rue d'Ulm and Sèvres. A growing number of students in the EN arrived already furnished with a bac, and even those students recruited at the younger age studied for that characteristically "secondary" examination. The content of their formal studies differed in no way from those being undertaken by their contemporaries in the lycée. Some of the best qualified of the EN students chose to become teachers of older pupils in the new Colleges (the CESs established in 1963) rather than to work in the primary sector itself. Increasing attention within the EN was given to the needs of older teachers already in service, either to provide them with the formal training they lacked or to raise the levels of their competence. A familiar world was dissolving. Many of the ENs nevertheless struggled to preserve the older characteristics of a seminarial tradition. Discipline was strict, and increasingly resented by older students – not least because great importance was attached to the segregation of the sexes and to the maintenance of compulsory residence within the institution (the internat). One student arriving at an école normale in Paris in the autumn of 1956 recalls:

There I found a seminary, a lay seminary...Reveille was at 6.30. At ten minutes to seven, you had to be in the study hall, which left you with twenty minutes to make your bed, sprinkle water on your face and air your little cubicle. From 6.50 until 7.30: forty minutes of study. 7.30, breakfast and at 8.20, back to the dormitory, to make your bed and sweep your cubicle, and then the cleaning of the whole school: every one had his own job... From 8.30, classes until noon. At noon, a meal until 12.30.... Classes again at 1.30. From 4.30 until 5.10, forty minutes of freedom when dry bread was distributed. The study hall until 7.00. Supper from 7.00 until 8.00, and free time to go to the library until 8.15. From 8.15 until 9.30, study and then to the dormitories with lights-out at 10.30....All this marked our training, and our view of the métier of teaching. For four years during our formative years, we were subjected to so rigorous a regime, that we inevitably carried forward that rigour into our own classes. We could behave in no other way, for that is all we had known (Charles 1988, p. 41).

If this was still the pattern of life in the école normale in 1956 it is unsurprising that 1968 was greeted with enthusiasm and disorder in many of these places, which were now about to be driven even further from their anchorage in the noble mission they had inherited from Guizot and Ferry. Vocal dissatisfaction with the EN was not of course new in 1968: the institution had been attacked from the Left in the 1930s and from the Right under Vichy. The critics of the sixties in their turn saw no good reason why, at a time of insatiable demand for teachers, the EN should be devoting valuable resources to teaching students before the bac. Between 1960 and 1962 there was a flurry of media interest in this apparently anachronistic institution; sober newspaper articles asked such questions as "Should the écoles normales be burnt down?" (Nique 1991, p. 186). The EN professors, marshalled of course within their union (the SPEN), valiantly defended themselves against criticisms of ruling "a provincial parish" (ibid., p. 188). It was inconceivable that much could survive of the old EN after the dislocation of 1968. The preferences of Edgar Faure himself were clear: "My instinct would be to turn the EN into an institute of teacher training in which the teaching would be given in association with the university" (Nique 1991, p. 188). The changes that in fact emerged in the immediate aftermath of 1968 may have been more modest but, in their longer term implications, nevertheless marked the end of the life of these resilient institutions.

In 1969 the Government decreed that the post-baccalauréat training course be extended to two years. The declaration that the work of the EN should now be linked with that of the newly constituted universities remained (for the moment) no more than a pious aspiration: the universities had other more urgent worries, while the ENs never after 1968 recovered their stability. Within them, no further efforts were made to impose on students the discipline of residence: the *internat* survived in some places but in a relaxed form, and only for obviously practical reasons. The seminary was dead. The effects of such a change were reinforced by the rule that teaching should no longer be provided within the institution for classes below the level of the baccalauréat. Some students would for a few years still be recruited at the younger age, but responsibility for their general education must now be committed to a lycée. The required changes were completed before the end of 1973: within what was still left of the EN, only a diminishing rôle was temporarily preserved for the agrégé and the certifié, the successors of those recruited to teach academic subjects when the post-Liberation government reversed the radical policies of Vichy. Some relaxation of content and style was attempted within the primary school for which the instituteur was being prepared: a little time was to be freed for activities that were not determined by decree (Prost 1992, p. 148).

The rule of the General did not for long outlast the events of 1968. In the following year, he attempted another trial of strength with the professional politicians by once more and for the last time making a direct appeal by referendum for the direct support of the citizens of France. He chose to make two questions – affecting the powers of the Senate and the pace of regionalization – issues of principle and therefore of confidence. On 28 April 1969 the vote went against his proposals, and he resigned at midnight on the same day: he died at his home in Colombey-les-Deux-Eglises on 9 November 1970. The presidencies of Pompidou who lived only until 1974 and of his successor, Valéry Giscard d'Estaing, saw an acceleration of the changes in the educational system that had been stimulated by the General. The world of teacher training in 1970 reflected the uncertainty of the transitions in which that system was now enmeshed, and especially by the growth of the CES coupled with profound changes in the culture of the lycée. The PEGC had just been established as a corps, albeit with a life that was to prove vulnerable and short, and a distinct and appropriate form of training did indeed exist for these teachers. But they sat uneasily alongside the instituteurs, from whose ranks they had originally been drawn, and the agrégés and certifiés who jealously preserved the university affiliations represented by their high academic qualifications. The two great secondary concours preserved much of their established form and character. Professional preparation, taken with a measure of seriousness only in the case of the academically less illustrious secondary teacher, survived in the CPR, directed by members of the powerful Inspectorate and distanced from the new universities as much as they had been from the old Faculties. But it was in the école normale that the uncomfortable mismatch between a traditional system of teacher training and a changing pattern of demography and educational policy was most painfully obvious. The EN was beyond all doubt no longer what it had been, and yet at the end of the 1960s continued to recruit the majority of its students through a competitive examination for which they entered at the age of fifteen. It still at that time provided within itself a general secondary education for many of those students. But these younger students were diminishing in number, and the discipline of residence had been swept away in 1968. The EN had lost its roots in the old primary order – the order which had been capped by its own ENS – and while most of its professors were academically well-qualified, they lacked direct experience of teaching in the primary school. In which direction would and could the école normale now move? In particular, when and how would substantial connections to the world of higher education be made? These now became the dominant questions in the history of the relationship between the reshaped university and the increasingly fragmented world of teacher training.

Holding the Line: the Right and the seventies

The impetus of growth in higher education continued across the seventies and into the eighties, although not at the headlong pace of the sixties. Demand remained high, as did the commitment of the State to remaining internationally competitive by recruiting from a widening pool of talent. The oil crisis of 1973 and the succeeding economic problems applied only a partial check to development, as higher education now also served the supplementary purpose of reducing or at least camouflaging unemployment. The number of students, which had been a mere 311.300 in 1960 rose from 854.000 in 1970 to 1.176.900 in 1980. The fifty-six universities accorded a legal personality in 1970 (as *établissements publics à caractère scientifique et culturel*) had grown to seventy by the end of the decade. Yet Paris, with its thirteen universities, maintained and even enhanced its relative power within the system, advancing from a share of 33.7% to one of 34.7% of the national total of students between 1961 and 1975 (Passeron 1986, p. 387). Some at least of the rigidities of the Fouchet reforms of 1966, which had already been eased by the introduction of UVs (credits) and more flexible courses, were further relaxed in 1973 by the introduction of a general diploma of university studies – the DEUG – awarded at the end of the first two-year cycle of higher education. In principle, some alignment with the programmes in the EN , for which Edgar Faure had called, should now be possible. The universities did meanwhile acquire a more substantial life and autonomy of their own, individually and locally as well as collectively and nationally: powerful consultative bodies, including a Council of University Presidents (the CPU) were established in these years (Minot 1983).

Those who had hoped that the growth of the system under the Fifth Republic and the major shocks of 1968 would together lead to a major democratisation of higher education, or even a mutation in its relationship to established social patterns, were however doomed to disappointment. As early as 1964, the influential work *Les Héritiers* had raised doubts about the truth of the cheerful proposition that increasing numbers in education would inevitably lead to a greater equality of access (Bourdieu & Passeron 1964). Paradoxically, an increase in educational provision led to a redistribution of national tax income which favoured those already privileged: the workers who composed 41% of the population contributed 21% to the total yield of taxation but made up only 12% of the student population. The corresponding figures for the professional classes were 17%, 30% and 40%. In any case, the parts of the system did not and would not grow with any kind of symmetry, so that the power of such institutions as the ENS - now much more loosely connected to the education of secondary school teachers – was being reinforced by the growth of mass education in the Faculties. Over the thirty years between between 1950 and 1980, the number of bacs multiplied five times, whereas the number of candidates preparing for the grandes écoles (in the *classes préparatoires*, the *khâgnes* and the *taupes*) only doubled (Passeron 1986, p. 398). A detailed examination of the data for the Academy of Orleans led the scholar Antoine Prost to a compatible conclusion: such "democratisation" as had indeed taken place occurred in the years before and not after 1960. The history of the ENS at St.Cloud reflected similar trends as it moved remorselessly away from its origins in the popular primary sector: in the 1960s and in terms of recruitment, it became a thoroughly bourgeois institution. (Prost 1986, Albertini 1992, p. 141, Luc & Barbé 1992).

Access to the more noble tracks of higher education, for the protection of which the General had striven, was in part achieved by a Gaullist government: for the first time a numerus clausus was established, in medicine in 1971, and the long cherished suspicions of the students seemed in part justified by events. In that same year the ENS in the rue d'Ulm, which had enjoyed only an uneasy peace since the disruptions of the summer of 1968, was closed (Passeron 1986, p. 390). The published reactions of its Director survive as an eloquent testimony to the width of the gap in understanding and sympathy within that haven of excellence for the preparation of teachers for the university, in the Napoleonic sense of that term. The students of the classical scholar, Robert Flacelière, were in his view preparing for another night like August 4 1789 (when feudalism had been at a stroke abolished), during which they would "renounce everything which set them apart from the student mass". With a fully developed sense of history, the students chose to celebrate the centenary of the Commune of 1871: on the night of 20 March, both the library and the war memorial were attacked. Flacelière had already sent his resignation to the *"Ministre de l'Education Nationale, grand-maître de l'Université"*. Here indeed was a man unwilling to acknowledge change. He was further disillusioned by the silence of the Elysée, especially as an agrégé ruled there (Flacelière 1971, pp. 43,45).

Such events were reminiscent of the 1960s rather than characteristic of the 1970s, although Vincennes did continue to live up to its reputation for ideology and unorthodox innovation: by the end of the decade, a very determined Minister for The Universities (Alice Saunier-Seité) felt strong enough to uproot the dangerous place and move it to another and less salubrious part of the capital. But behind the posturing and confrontations of the politicians, the basic restructuring of secondary schooling continued, making daily more obsolete the divisions of teachers and teacher education in terms of the categories of a now vanishing system. René Haby, as Minister of Education and a former close colleague of Jean Capelle (as well as being an agrégé and originially an EN-trained instituteur) made the CES the universal vehicle for lower secondary education: the *Collège d'Enseignement Général*, heir to the traditions of the EPS and the *cours complémentaires*, now finally disappeared. France, in the lower secondary sector but not in the lycée, now had a common or comprehensive school. At or before the end of the period of compulsory schooling, choices still had to be made – on the basis of an increasingly contested orientation – between the well-established general lycée, and its less esteemed alternatives in technical or vocational education.

Little of significance changed in the education and training of the teachers for the upper secondary school, most of whom competed in the appropriate concours and began their teaching careers with the professional support of a CPR. The economic and demographic decline of the later seventies led to a sharp reduction in recruitment: partly no doubt for that reason in 1978 the Government abolished the highly prized IPES, which had provided subsidised opportunities for students for the DEUG and the Licence to become secondary teachers. Recruitment for the CAPES declined sharply, and especially in the years 1979-81, the last years of rule by the parties of the Right and Centre. In 1980, for the agrégation in mathematics and letters even the number of candidates from the four Ecoles Normales Supérieures was itself greater than the number of new posts available! Problems, and not least for teachers ill-prepared for work with less academic pupils, were exacerbated by over-selection for the posts available coupled (or so it was alleged) with the under-selection of the students. Many of the most academically qualified teachers found themselves, as a result of the practices of *mutation*, assigned to a CES, which was frequently in a difficult or unfamiliar area (Hamon & Rotman 1984).

Within the primary sector, the decade of the seventies was to be one of deepening uncertainty. Although the EN formally survived, scarcely a year passed without some new attempt to modify its programmes, clarify its mission or redefine its relationship to higher education. Its character was speedily modified after 1968 by a continuing shift away from "early" recruitment towards a pattern of student admission after the bac – or even later, as a growing number of students began to arrive from the expanding universities already armed with a DEUG. In 1970, three quarters of the normaliens had been recruited three years before the bac. Between 1974 and 1976, the proportion of those who had travelled that route dropped to one fifth (Charles 1988, pp. 232-3). Since most secondary pupils now attended a CES as a matter of course, why should they enter for an examination which at the age of fifteen committed them to a career in primary teaching, when they could freely transfer to a lycée without making any such commitment and defer any decision until they had completed their bac? There was moreover a strengthening demand for places in the EN from candidates wishing to become PEGCs, so that even those students who had been accepted at the earlier age for training as instituteurs were diverted in growing numbers to complete their secondary studies in a nearby lycée: there now seemed little reason to preserve two ages of admission, one before and one after the bac. In the late sixties at the EN at Auteuil all the younger pre-bac students had been taught for the bac within the EN itself and by the professors assigned to that place. Between 1965 and 1969 that was the case for no more than half of them, and between 1969 and 1973 for none at all. That is to say, in the case at least of one typical EN, the involvement of the institution with younger and more malleable students had by the early 1970s been broken. The école normale abolished itself before it was abolished. As opportunities within the educational system opened up, so students within the EN were increasingly drawn into careers other than that of the instituteur. Not only was the opportunity to become a PEGC attractive to many, but the IPES continued until 1978 to draw many of the more able students into the universities. Of the boys and young men admitted to the Paris EN between 1960 and 1973, whereas 79% of those who prepared their bac within the école normale itself finally became primary school teachers, that percentage was a mere 49.2% for those who took the more seductive route through the lycée (Charles 1988, p. 55). These shifts, taken with the parallel movement away from early recruitment, changed the historically distinctive social character of admissions to the EN: that legendary "popular" institution was no longer the necessary and principal escalator of social promotion for the children of the working classes.

Any foreigner reviewing these developments is correctly impressed by the quality, power and durability of the traditions underlying teacher education in France. Ministry control of numbers and admission standards, coupled with the jealous concern of university specialists for the integrity of their disciplines as taught in secondary schools, guaranteed the value and reputation of the venerable agrégation and of its younger brother the CAPES. At this level, the comprehensive character of secondary schooling could not and did not entail – as it did in some other countries – any reduction in the emphasis on academic rigour, as epitomised in the baccalauréat. Less emphasis, and indeed almost none within the university itself, was placed upon professional preparation for teachers. This was the responsibility of the CPR (*Centre Pédagogique Régional*), a somewhat shadowy institution which was not well placed to address the tough problems of adapting high quality academic teaching to the needs of all pupils and students in schools. At the end of the 1960s, the prevailing assumption still was that the higher the level of academic expertise in the teacher, the more modest the need for any form of "training".

The very different traditions of the école normale proved for many years equally resilient and impressive. The EN had its origins in a social and cultural world distant from that of the University, the lycée, and the bourgeoisie. In its golden age, the EN had embraced and disseminated the ideals of the Republic: proud of its lay virtues, providing a steady supply of teachers for the primary Order (including those for the EPS, the upper primary school), and drawing many of its leaders from its own metropolitan versions of the Ecole Normale Supérieure. It recruited its students in their early adolescence and grounded them thoroughly in the basic subjects and the essential teaching skills. Its strength was the key to its survival through many externally generated changes. Compare its position in 1970 with that in 1930. Vichy had attacked its dangerous distinctiveness by depriving it both of younger pupils and of its esteemed qualification, the *brevet supérieur*. Although the younger pupils did indeed return after 1945 (but never again to enjoy their previous monopoly), the rule of the bac was never again challenged. From the different world of the University, first the agrégé and then the professeur certifié therefore descended to impart the high culture of the baccalauréat to the normaliens. The prestigious ENSs of the capital, founded to provide the leadership for the école normale and the upper primary school, shifted from their original mission to become in principle indistinguishable from the rue d'Ulm. They too prepared for careers in higher education, research, public service – and for the agrégation.

Although each Department continued to recruit primary teachers at the age of fifteen as well as eighteen, the balance shifted upwards: more candidates presented themselves at the higher age, while a growing number of those selected at the age of fifteen were redirected to a lycée to complete their secondary education before joining the EN for their professional training. The events of 1968 and the regulations of 1969 ensured that the EN would never again be a lay seminary, grounded in its own distinctive ideology, and that (before long) all teaching within it of students of secondary school age would cease. The soul of the old école normale had withered, but the body lived on. It was of course never short of work: one of the reasons for the displacing of the younger *normaliens* was the pressure generated by the need to train growing numbers of PEGCs, teachers for the lower secondary school. The dilemmas presented to the classical French system by these new teachers – neither primary nor secondary in the typology of the Third Republic – finally broke the older system and led (but not rapidly) to the reforms of the 1990s. Like so much else, therefore, structural reform in the education of teachers can be traced back to the August 1963 decision of President de Gaulle.

Although it took nearly thirty years for the transition to be accomplished, the introduction of the universal CES in 1963 injected into the geometry of the teaching profession in France an insupportable anomaly. Logic and history distinguished between the professeur and the instituteur, in terms of the Orders of education to which they respectively belonged. The professeur in the lycée is protected in his central rôle by the perpetuation of the baccalauréat and the power of a university conception of culture and the curriculum. For the professeur in the CES, where he will encounter pupils of all abilities and aspirations, the position is now much more ambiguous. He will, to take the simplest example, need to teach more than one subject. Similarly, the central rôle of the instituteur in the école primaire is protected by the official ideology promulgated by Jules Ferry or Félix Pécaut and rooted in the école normale. But the former instituteur who is now teaching in a CES, or the new PEGC teaching in that place and prepared in one of the training centres located in an école normale, can be less precisely located. He or she will, to take the simplest illustration, teach two subjects and therefore be neither a specialist nor a generalist. And it is precisely in the college, the CES, that the lives and experiences and needs of these different categories of teacher intersect. All this suggests, as of course it did to many contemporaries, that the map of teacher training needed to be redrawn in order to reflect these emerging realities. Boundary lines which were clear in theory were in practice becoming blurred, especially as a growing number of entrants to the école normale arrived already equipped with a DEUG from a university. Why did the task of assimilation take so long?

Much of the answer to that question lies in the very strength of the arrangements which have been described: such strength can easily become rigidity. It was no easy matter, given the depth of loyalty on which they could draw, to sweep away either the école normale or the agrégation; yet they could no longer easily coexist. The persisting centralization of educational governance – plainly another distinctive strength of the system and a formal guarantee of equity – made it hard to adapt, to experiment, to allow flexible and evolutionary adjustments. Wholesale change was further inhibited by the importance at that time (although since much diminished) of the unions, whose centralised authority mirrored that of the apparatus of the State in the rue de Grenelle. Dominant in the world of these unions was the FEN, the Fédération de l'Education Nationale, a powerful yet loose coalition of often conflicting interests (Aubert & Others 1985). The FEN had chosen in 1947 the path of autonomy when disputes about communism broke the trade union movement in France into two competing confederations: the CGT and FO (Clark 1967). But about the FEN, which survived it its original form until the schisms of 1993, there was never anything monolithic or simple. It had in the 1970s nearly fifty affiliates, covering the whole territory of the national education system and each enjoying considerable autonomy. They also appeared to enjoy quarrelling with one another in public and private. The largest of these groupings was the SNI (the *Syndicat National des Instituteurs*) significantly renamed and enlarged as the SNI-PEGC: the instituteurs were staking a claim to the growing territory of the CES. Many of the college professeurs, notably those who were agrégés or certifiés, belonged however to the SNES (the *Syndicat National des Enseignements du Second Degré*) which, within the FEN, dominated the world of the lycée. By the end of the 1970s the SNI-PEGC commanded 260000 members (including some 80000 PEGC) while its rival the SNES mustered some 70000 (Hamon & Rotman 1984, p. 232). Relationships were yet further complicated by the fact that the SNI-PEGC was generally socialist in its tone and sympathies, whereas since 1967 the leadership of the SNES had been predominantly Communist. Such differences always mattered, and were to be even more influential when a Socialist government came to power.

Even the sprawling FEN, strongly represented on the joint committees which since World War II had managed much of the educational system and especially the postings of teachers, did not provide a union affiliation for all teachers. The SGEN (*Syndicat Général de l'Education Nationale*) represented different policies and tendencies, and was affiliated to the CFDT – a broad confederation which had itself broken away from the mainstream in 1919 and renamed itself (dropping the title of "Christian") in 1964. The SGEN traditionally espoused a mild form of socialism, stressing progressive values and the importance of self-government (Singer 1993). It enjoyed considerable influence on educational opinion in the 1970s, and even more after the Socialist victory of 1981. These groupings, and especially the FEN, derived considerable wealth and power from an involvement in a wide range of services for teachers: finance, housing, health, welfare, retail sales, insurance. The tangle of cross currents was and is often baffling, and not least in discussions of teacher education policy. The SNI-PEGC was well disposed towards the école normale (whose professeurs and directors were themselves grouped in syndicates affiliated to the FEN) and suspicious of the élitism and privileges – not to say the politics – of the SNES. It was in direct competition with its fraternal organisation for membership in the colleges. Its members sought equality with their secondary cousins, and that of course implied access to university qualifications and courses. At the same time, they did not greatly respect the forms of training provided in the CPRs. The SNES on the other hand was sceptical of the pedagogy (*pédagogie* is in French often an emotive term redolent with the ideology of primary schooling) of the école normale, contemptuous of efforts to export primary methods and thinking into secondary preserves (*la primarisation*), suspicious of extending the university association, and wary of weakening the value of the qualifications of their own members. The SGEN apparently took a more open and liberal line, arguing consistently in favour of a more flexible and less bureaucratic mode of education. Since all teachers were civil servants, whose scales of pay and conditions of service had to be integrated within an elaborate set of rules, issues such as the type of qualification and length of course enjoyed an importance that was more than symbolic. Professeurs who qualified to become teachers at the level of "bac plus four", that is after four years of university education beyond the bac, could not accept that instituteurs should be promoted to a comparable level. Powerfully entrenched traditions, the centralisation of policy making, the national uniformity of rewards and recognition within a confident public service, the strength of a union movement which was nevertheless riven with conflict: such factors inhibited and delayed the acceptance of changes which could in any case be demanded more easily than they could be defined.

The line could no longer be confidently held, but neither could a new policy yet be articulated. As the seventies advanced policies emerged in rapid succession: between 1979 and 1985 no fewer than thirty-eight texts were issued (Zay 1988, p. 218). Policies were reversed and reversed again, within a context of instability well diagnosed by Crozier: society, he argued, cannot be changed "by decree" (Crozier 1976). In 1973, as has been noted, a significant and irreversible step was taken in the abolition of the concours for entry to the EN before the bac. The two year course (a simple bac+2) was for the moment maintained, but lengthened to three years by a decision taken in 1976 under sustained pressure from the SNI-PEGC. The universities were somehow to be involved in this readjustment, and in 1979 the short-lived and ill-fated special Diploma for primary school teachers was introduced. The three year course was to be taught cooperatively by the professors of the EN and of a university, and lead to the DEUG *premier degré*. It was to be valid only as a qualification for primary school teachers and carried no general right to proceed to a Licence or other higher general qualification. Attempts at cooperation between the two very different, and often mutually suspicious, institutions foundered and further adjustments were made in 1981 in an attempt to make the Diploma more like a mainstream university award (Bourdoncle & Zay 1989). In the same year François Mitterrand was elected as President of France, on the basis of a programme giving high priority to wide ranging reforms in education. By the end of the decade teacher education and its relationship to the university were to be transformed, although not without hesitations, interruptions and controversy.

Pressures for Change: the Left and the eighties

The Presidential election of 1981 was the first in the Fifth Republic to be held at the regularly prescribed time: de Gaulle had departed abruptly after a plebiscite had rejected his policies, and Pompidou died in office. The candidates were on this occasion well prepared, programmes had been clarified, and alliances as well as enmities confirmed. François Mitterrand, with the support of the Communists, won 51.76% of the votes in the second round (Becker 1988, p. 166). Education figured prominently among his declared targets for reform and no less than 34% of the elected members of the National Assembly were teachers, and of those 58.7% were Socialists (Hamon and Rotman 1984, p. 259). The unions had been hard at work. Mitterrand had promised to promote "a great public education service" that would be nationalised, free and lay (Albertini 1992, p. 148). The mood of the early days was euphoric and confidently left wing: the French appeared yet again to have proved their exceptionality in swimming against the Anglo-Saxon tide that had carried Margaret Thatcher to victory in 1979 and Ronald Reagan in 1980. Alain Savary, with impeccable credentials provided by his engagement in the Resistance and his devotion to liberal causes, became Minister of Education and gathered like-minded supporters around him in the rue de Grenelle (Savary 1985). A French minister had the legitimate means to ensure that throughout France his policies were attended to: within two years twenty-one of the twenty-seven Rectors had been replaced by candidates supportive of those new policies.

Central power was employed in order to reduce central power and in an effort to encourage stronger local and professional participation. The supervisory and directive authority of the General Inspectors was moderated, and in future they were to be recruited by special commissions instead of being internally coopted to a body of *universitaires*. In the same spirit, the Government committed itself to a massive programme of decentralization and of devolution from the capital of administrative authority (the so-called *déconcentration*). Prefects lost some of their glittering prestige, while Regional and Departmental Councils were given real powers. These major changes were accomplished in 1983 (Perié 1982, Deyon 1992). The Regions, which in spite of encouragement from de Gaulle had so far enjoyed only a phantom existence, acquired responsibility for the building and maintenance costs of the lycées, while the Departments were given matching duties towards the collèges, and the communes preserved their relationships with the primary schools. The rules of geometry, even in the context of these radical changes, were preserved. Equally important, however, was the consolidation of central power: not only would the curriculum of course continue to be matter of passionate concern at the national level, but the Ministry would still keep a tight control over the recruitment, training, payment and deployment of teachers. It was not conceivable that teachers would cease to be civil servants. Teacher training would therefore keep its high place on the national agenda.

Alain Savary, although unaware of just how little time he would have in which to act, knew that he needed to move quickly and appointed a series of special commissions to attack key areas of policy: within two years Antoine Prost (the historian and SGEN activist) had reported on the lycées, Louis Legrand (for long the Director of the National Institute of Pedagogical Research) on the colleges, and André de Peretti on the training of all the personnel employed by the *Education Nationale*, including notably the teachers (Legrand 1982, Peretti 1982, Prost 1983B). Critics detected in these three documents a unifying ideology and a determined conspiracy to undermine the classical doctrines of Jules Ferry and the Third Republic. The emphasis, they alleged, was being shifted from teaching to learning, from academic content to pedagogy, from scholarship to interdisciplinarity, from the teacher as instructor to the teacher as guide and friend. Such changes were profoundly unwelcome to many, already made nervous by the rapid expansion of secondary education, the creation of the CES, the opening up of the lycée and the explosion of the bac. For this reason the crisis of 1984, although undoubtedly provoked by Government attempts to define a new relationship to the State for the private (and mostly Catholic) schools, reflected an opposition that was deeper and wider than the religious interest alone. It was a protest against "liberal" educational policies, and massive demonstrations in July led to the resignation not only of the Minister of Education, Alain Savary, but even of the Prime Minister himself. Both had become an insupportable embarrassment to Mitterrand whose aggressively socialist policies had already been softened by an economic crisis (Lelièvre 1990, p. 207, Prost 1987, p. 231).

These themes were to be resumed in amplified form when, in the late 1980s, the principles of the Peretti report were applied to the reform and incorporation within higher education of teacher training. The publication in the year when Savary left office of an influential if vehement book illustrates the nature and force of the objections that were soon to be mounted to such a reform. The arguments which it powerfully deployed were to be widely echoed and proved to be of particular importance when the Right returned to power in April 1993. (Milner 1984, Romilly 1984, Finkielkraut 1987, Association 1991). Jean-Claude Milner had no doubts about what had happened or who was to blame. The attack on the Catholic schools was but one expression of the determination of "the Corporation" to establish its complete monopoly of all education. The Corporation he characterised as the teachers and their union leaders organized in a series of groups which not only brought pressure to bear upon policies but were also heavily implicated with the Ministry in administering the details of a monolithic system. The SNI-PEGC were especially culpable since they represented an assault on the intellectual foundations of French education. Their *frères ennemis* within the FEN, the SNES, were of course the valiant defenders of tradition and the agrégation: their Communism rendered them perhaps even more conservative when confronted with their rivals outside the FEN, the SGEN-CFDT. The SGEN represented those who had delighted in the effervescence of 1968 and, which made it worse, who were in a special sense "Christian ": vaguely progressive, hostile to traditional institutions which they saw as oppressive, as suspicious of the traditional scholar and his grip upon cultural capital as of the economic capitalist himself. They champion pedagogy precisely because it substitutes form for content. This is as equivalent to substituting education for instruction (or rather *éducation* for *instruction*). The business of the teacher should rather be to transmit knowledge, *transmettre les savoirs*. Milner was predictably hostile to the Peretti report, which argued for the merging of all forms of teacher training in new University Institutes at Regional and Departmental level and for the assimilation of pre-service and in-service training. Although an increasingly cautious and bruised Government took no immediate action, decisive intervention could not be indefinitely delayed: it came in 1989. Meanwhile, the logistical problems became more acute, as the rising tide of student numbers reached the lycées in the early 1980s. At the secondary level in 1985 the pattern of massive recruitments was resumed: thousands were harvested through the CAPES, as they had been in the early 1970s (Albertini 1992, p. 161). Within the next few years internal versions of the agrégation and the CAPES were introduced, to enable teachers already in service (many of them PEGCs) to secure a higher status: the tightly controlled university system for entry was thereby weakened and the boundaries between instituteurs and professeurs weakened while, even more significantly, the emphasis in these new national competitions was shifted from academic knowledge towards professional skills. New values were now infecting the admired purity of academic criteria. A direct assault on the problem of bringing order to the system was inhibited by the political fluctuations of the decade: the disappearance of Alain Savary marked the end of innovatory reforms. His successor was Jean-Paul Chevènement, who proclaimed his loyalty to the values of Jules Ferry and "the School of the Republic". "The Christians" lost their influence. The electoral victories of the Right in the quinquennial parliamentary elections of 1986 introduced the Fifth Republic to the experience of cohabitation, with a Socialist in the Elysée, Jacques Chirac in the Matignon, and René Monory in the rue de Grenelle. But only for two years: in 1988 Mitterrand's second Presidential victory allowed him to call special elections which brought the pragmatic Michel Rocard (an ally if hardly a friend of the President) to power as Prime Minister and Lionel Jospin to the Ministry of Education.

Chevènement committed himself to a bold policy of expansion, but along traditional lines: 80% of the relevant age groups were to be brought to the level of the bac (the figure had been 33% when the Socialists gained power and was to be 60.6% when they lost it). Yet traditional standards were to be maintained, even if a greater diversity flowed from the creation of a new vocational baccalauréat and lycée (Croissandeau 1993, p. 44). Between 1985 and 1990 one new lycée was completed each week. So rapid a pace of expansion raised urgent questions of teacher supply: but it also sharpened the question of the appropriateness to the needs of the late twentieth century of the deeply entrenched patterns of recruitment and training. The termination by the Chirac Government of recruitment into the category of PEGC was rapidly confirmed by Lionel Jospin: neither the SNI nor the SNES could be comfortable with this hybrid form of teacher, but were now more directly committed to supporting some more general reforms (Alexandre 1991). The expansion in secondary teacher training, the introduction of internal competitions for promotion within existing categories, the abolition of recruitment for the PEGC: all were designed to tackle immediate problems, yet all served to expose the growing anomalies within the existing system.

The problems for the primary sector were even more pressing: for the first time since the Liberation, the écoles normales in 1986 failed to recruit their assigned quota of students (Charles 1988, p. 1). The competition from the secondary sector and the attractions of higher education no doubt contributed to the shortages: already in 1982 a supplementary concours at the level of the DEUG had been introduced and four years later entry at the level of the bac was finally abandoned, as were the uncertain efforts somehow to integrate the école normale with work at undergraduate level within the university context. Meanwhile the shifting status of the écoles normales was formally acknowledged when in 1984 they were redefined administratively as belonging to the higher education sector: no longer were they in any residual sense the official crown of primary schooling, and they passed into different hands in the corridors of the rue de Grenelle. The 1986 reform was the work of Jean-Paul Chevènement, whose preferences were often closer to those of his Gaullist successor than to those of his Socialist predecessor. The intention of this reform was plainly utilitarian. Now that the general cultural level of the entrant to primary teacher training was (it must be hoped) guaranteed by the holding of a DEUG, the business of producing the new teacher should be focused on the needs of pupils in schools. The first year of primary training is to be about subject matter, and the second about practical competence. The CPR is extolled as a model of the kind of practical device which should be extended to the primary sector: it is praised, in spite of such well attested disadvantages as a lack of a sense of identity or continuity in staffing (Leselbaum 1987). René Monory could happily endorse these principles when he became Minister. A former director of his cabinet wrote to a senior civil servant:

Why not adopt in the écoles normales the practices of secondary education, the engineering schools, the schools of administration, as also of the IUTs and indeed of professions of all kinds? Make use of people in the business, in this case experienced instituteurs, to train these student teachers for the whole of the year....Imitate what happens in secondary education (CPR) and in all vocational training: put the apprentice under the guidance of an older person and in the real world, that is to say in a classroom (Zay 1988, p. 95).

Nothing could be clearer than that as an assertion of the primacy of a practical approach to teacher training, and nothing further from the emphasis in the Peretti report on the importance of the university connection. The Government's early responses to that report had indeed been cautious: new arrangements were to be made, but only for the in-service training of teachers, and even then only through a "Mission" in each Academy (the MAFPEN) and not through an Establishment (in the juridical sense of the term). The more challenging principles of the earlier report reappeared in policy only after the Socialist victory of 1988, and in July of the following year the outline of the new reforms was set by Lionel Jospin. The urgency of training large cohorts of new teachers was now overwhelming: 30000 would be needed each year until the end of the century. Jospin confronted two problems: the écoles normales survived, but without any clear mission since they had become establishments to serve the needs of university graduates seeking a career in primary teaching; the responsibility for training new teachers for rapidly changing secondary schools was divided between university departments and the CPRs, while the PEGC had been abolished. The unions could not be allowed to squabble for ever, and it might be simpler to dissolve both problems in one new solution (Nique 1991 p. 192). The Peretti principles were significantly modified and incorporated in a report prepared for the Minister by a committee under the leadership of Daniel Bancel, Rector of the Academy of Rouen (Bancel 1989). In each Academy and under the general supervision of the Rector there was now to be created one IUFM *Institut Universitaire de Formation des Maîtres*. By 1994 there were twenty-nine Academies (including those overseas) and therefore twenty-nine IUFMs. Three were established as pilot schemes in 1990 and the rest followed a year later. The IUFM was to be not part of a university but a free-standing "Public Establishment of an Administrative Character". The Director of each is to be nominated by the Minister and accountable both to him and to various local bodies. All the écoles normales were abolished, together with the CPRs. Their buildings were to be used by the IUFMs, but the Departments were in 1990 given the opportunity of continuing to own them if they wished: the fact that two-thirds of them chose so to do indicates the strength of local pride in these popular establishments of the Republic. The IUFM in each Academy operated in, on average, ten scattered sites. The former teachers in the EN were either redeployed (a fate which some preferred) or absorbed into the establishment of the new

Institute: more than 90% of the trainers and teachers in the new Institutes came from the EN. But twenty-five of the new Directors came from the university world, while the remaining three were Inspectors.

All those training to become teachers in the public system must in future do so through an IUFM, although not necessarily the one implanted within their own Academy. Whether seeking to enter primary or secondary teaching, all must posses a university Licence, obtained after at least three years of higher education. The separate and often conflicting worlds of teacher training are now unified within one structure, at least on paper: the qualifications at entry are the same, and – with many a nostalgic twinge – primary school teachers trained under the new dispensation are now to become professeurs and not instituteurs, albeit *professeurs d'école*. The programme of study and activity has three principal elements: knowledge of and about the discipline or disciplines to be taught, the management of learning (pedagogics and didactics), and familiarity with the educational system. Enrolment for the first year of the IUFM course is not obligatory: the concours for admission as a teacher-in-training is held at the end of that first year and by law no-one can be formally excluded from entering an examination giving access to a career in the public service. The nature and timing of that concours proved to be deeply contentious. The original proposals of the Peretti plan had required that the competition for entry should take place before the beginning of the two year course, and would assess academic progress to date and aptitude for teaching: in that sense it would be like the old EN concours. But the SNES and the pressure groups associated with it could not accept this relative "lowering" of the standard for admission to secondary teacher training, from the level of bac+4 to that of bac+3. Bancel therefore recommended that the competition should be at the end of the first year, and that attendance for that first year should not be compulsory: this inevitably had the effect (and especially since candidates not in the IUFM must in equity be allowed to enter for it) of making the process of selection essentially academic, at least for secondary teachers, with an unequivocal emphasis on subject-matter knowledge. The CAPES was thereby preserved, in something very close to its traditional form. Enemies of the new changes were nevertheless incensed by the requirement that the examination for selection should for the first time include some tests of professional competence and aptitude: the compromise was an uneasy one, and continued to be a subject of lively debate and political resolution. Predictably, there was opposition to the dangerously new notion that future primary and secondary teachers should undertake some study and exercises in common and, in spite of the modest weight of that requirement, the cry of *primarisation* was raised. Many for the same reason opposed as absurd the whole idea of assimilating the agrégé, the PEGC and the instituteur.

The EN and the CPR had been merged in the same Institute, all teachers were to have the same title of professeurs, paid on the same salary scale, trained after obtaining the Licence in the same Institute, entering at the same time for separate but parallel competitions at the end of the first year. At the same time, the CAPES was in all its essentials preserved as an essentially disciplinary examination, while the agrégation and the five (Lyon had recently been added to the list) écoles normales supérieures remained unscathed. Teaching for the agrégation remained an integral university responsibility, although the successful candidate would now be required to undertake a further year of preparation in the IUFM. But for the CAPES and its associated qualifications, the 1991 arrangements did represent a significant departure. Whatever the daily realities, the resources for this work were now assigned by the Ministry to the IUFM and not to the university subject department (such as history or mathematics). The Director of the IUFM was charged with negotiating with a university or universities a contract (a *convention*) which involved a complex exchange of funding and services. This control by the IUFM was especially important at a time when extra staffing resources were made available for the new enterprise: in 1991 alone, for example, three hundred extra posts. Many of these, as well as existing positions, now carried responsibilities divided between the IUFM and the subject matter department of a university. These arrangements became especially complex in the many large cities where there was more than one university. The IUFM is indeed an institution of higher education with a university character, but it is not an integral part of any one university institution and neither is it a university in the juridical sense. The very title of the new Institute reveals the specificity of the French case, and the extent to which problems as well as opportunities are generated by the particular circumstances of France, and indeed the uniqueness of the French language. The term *institut* may not present difficulties for an English speaking observer. But *universitaire* cannot be translated as there is simply no English adjective derived from the word university. Something is either a university or it is not: it cannot be universitarian or universityish. *Formation* cannot be adequately translated as training, while *maîtres* defies exegesis.

Such ambiguities, and the unresolved tensions they concealed, did not prevent the confident launching of the IUFMs: in 1991 they enrolled 60.000 students. But the critics were not silenced, and the success of the parties of the Right and the Centre in the regional elections of 1992 foreshadowed the shattering defeat of the Socialists in the parliamentary elections of April 1993. The shifting winds of politics encouraged those who hoped that the radical surgery of 1991, achieving the incorporation of a unified form of teacher training within the university context, would soon be reversed.

An Uncertain Outcome?

A meeting of critics of the new dispensation held at the Sorbonne in April 1991 gives a good sense of both the substance and the tone of their objections: indeed, the very title of this influential minority group reads like a manifesto – The Association for the Quality of Teaching and of the Concours for Recruitment. For these defenders of high standards traditionally defined the IUFM is a plot to strengthen the unions and weaken the university, and the abolition of the IPES which had drawn able students into the true university was a criminal mistake; the IUFM is a ghetto on the periphery of knowledge. Teaching and the curriculum should not be adapted to the character of particular regions or groups: the principle of equality requires national uniformity. "I am one of those", observed a Professor of Latin from Grenoble III, "who believe that you can only teach well what you know well." The widely repeated, if highly dubious, rumour that at the IUFM in Grenoble primary and secondary students were taught together how to make pancake batter (*pâte à crêpes*) is repeated yet again. An American plot is detected: "IUFM, MacDonald, Disneyland, all represent the same battle" (Association 1991, pp. 6, 51, 32, 18, 17).

During 1992 the General Inspectors and the Senate published reports that were critical of the haste with which the reform had been pressed through, as of several other aspects of the changes. The Senate commission, for example, objected that the IUFM had made the problems of recruitment even worse: the requirement that all applicants should have a Licence cut by one half the number of primary candidates between 1990 and 1992 (although it should be noted that there were still 19,395 candidates for 4900 posts). Worse: many even of these candidates were qualified only in psychology or the social sciences, and only 0.2% of them in mathematics. In the secondary sector the number of postulants for the CAPES fell by 5.2% over the same period of transition. In this case, the number succeeding was smaller than the number of new posts available.

There was no clear policy for the IUFMs , which had to work with no less than seven directorates in the rue de Grenelle. They had fallen prey to "the obscure language of the psychopedagogues". Theory and practice had not been integrated: the university continued to provide the scientific knowledge (by teaching the disciplines), while trainers from the EN or the Inspectorate got on with the training in the second year of the course. The placing of the entry concours at the end of the first year was an anomaly in the public service and sharpened this problem: it should take place before entry to the IUFM while the criteria at the end of the two years of training should be toughened and refer to progress in subject-matter knowledge as well as in professional skills. The IUFMs were shadowy bodies: some of the nine relating only to one university should be fully integrated with it, as the 1984 law had anticipated, but on an experimental basis. The quality of the Institutes should be enhanced by building bridges to the ENSs. Research was by international standards weak in France and attention should be paid to the fifteen University Departments of Educational Sciences which already existed, and to their two hundred and fifty professors. The Senate report was not uniformly hostile to the IUFM and at several points argued for a strengthening and closer association with the university, noting that the universitarisation of teacher education appeared to be a world-wide phenomenon (Senate 1992).

Nevertheless, hard things were said and bold promises made in the period leading up to the legislative elections in the Spring of 1993: the Gaullist party (the RPR) was vehement in its denunciation of the sins of the IUFM. The Socialists were overwhelmingly defeated (although Mitterrand was of course secure in his tenure of the Elysée until 1995) and Edouard Balladur became Prime Minister. The Government was supported by a coalition of the parties of the Centre and the Right, notably the RPR itself and the UDF, the party of Giscard d'Estaing. The responsibilities for Education were divided in a way that could prove to be especially harmful to hybrid institutions like the IUFM: Higher Education and Research were assigned to François Fillon (RPR) and National Education itself to François Bayrou. The latter was an agrégé and former professeur who had written about the recent errors of French education (Bayrou 1990). But he was less fierce in his critique of the IUFM than his colleague, and more aware of the problems of recruitment and management that would engulf him if he supported extreme demands for their abolition: a position taken by the end of 1993 only by the Society of Agrégés. The determination to modify the IUFM settlement was in no way softened by an apparent success in attracting many more applicants for 1993 than for 1992: the general increase was of the order of 50%, with a quintupling of primary applications in the Academy of Montpellier (*Le Monde*, 24 June 1993). Some of this increase could be attributed to the making of multiple applications, and even more to the current restriction on opportunities for employment generally.

The unions were weaker than they had ever been, and in any case not well placed to resist any attack on the gains they were believed to have made in propelling the ideas of the IUFM throughout the 1980s. The mighty FEN, already affected by the decline in the power of unions nationally and indeed internationally, had finally shattered. Its membership dwindled rapidly from a peak of 550.000 at the end of the 1970s. The divisiveness of its multiple factions became insupportable, and there was growing disillusionment with the achievements of a decade of Socialist government. In 1992 the SNI was recast within the FEN as the SE, the *Syndicat d'Enseignants*, while the FEN was reshaped in an effort to isolate the minority which had long controlled the SNES. These tactics misfired: the SNES left the FEN in the Autumn, and in April 1993 the new FSU (*Fédération Syndicale Unitaire*) was created, with fourteen constituent unions, including the SNESUP (higher education) as well as the troublesome SNES itself. At that time, the FSU enjoyed an estimated membership of between 130.000 and 150.00 and the FEN of between 160.000 and 180.000 (*Le Monde*, 21 April 1993).

François Fillon decided to force the pace, and succeeded in irritating his ministerial colleague by inviting André Kaspi, Professor of American History (of all things) at the Sorbonne, to prepare a report on the IUFM: this unfriendly document was completed late in June 1993 and on 1 July the Minister made a speech before the National Assembly which echoed its language and approved its conclusions (Kaspi 1993). The IUFMs were in the hands of mediocrities and illuminati – presumably a coded reference to their ideological commitments and enthusiastic lack of rationality. They had created a heavy administrative machine which then developed ambitions to become an alternative university (*université bis*), already employing four to five hundred professorial persons (the *enseignants-chercheurs* of the authentic university). They had no business to be meddling in the world of research, of which they were no part. The competition for entry to teaching, the concours, should be purified of its professional elements and restored as an academic exercise of high quality. Primary school teachers had no need of a Licence in order to teach young children. The Minister for Higher Education had no patience with the "useless and deceptive" doctrine of a unified teaching force, the *corps unique*, and obstinately referred to the instituteurs under their old title (*Libération*, 1 July; *Le Monde*, 3 July). The FSU (including the SNES) was appropriately horrified, while the SE-FEN and the SGEN-CFDT were no better pleased (*Le Monde*, 8 July).

Nor was François Bayrou himself enchanted: the future of the IUFMs greatly concerned his Ministry, and the concours was his responsibility, as was the allocation of bursaries to support teachers in training (a matter on which M. Fillon had also pronounced). There followed a public wrangle between the two Ministers and their cabinets, terminated only by arbitration in his own office by the Prime Minister. Much of the substance of the Kaspi report did find its way into statements of government policy. Some primary candidates were to be admitted at a future date into the IUFM on the basis of a DEUG (bac+2 again), but would work towards a Licence at the end of their first year and before admission to the concours. There should now be more differentiation between primary and secondary training. The test of professional competence (the by now notorious *épreuve professionelle*) of the first year of the IUFM was to be replaced by an oral examination based upon a dossier. More significant in the longer term were the rulings that all *enseignants-chercheurs* (including those already appointed) should hold their tenured appointments not in the IUFM but in a university associated with it and be chosen by normal university criteria and procedures, that as far as possible appointments to a IUFM should be neither full time nor permanent, and that the financial credits assigned to fund teaching for the CAPES should go directly to the university departments, not to the IUFM. Research, except of a limited and applied nature, was off the agenda.

The IUFM had survived, but with its aspirations held in check and its roots in the university world loosened and its status vulnerable. It may now be consigned indefinitely to that uncertainly classified world which is part of higher education, but only partly so. The Ministers, having reestablished cooperation between the domains of higher education and of the schools, might have moved on to further clarifications of an uncertain future. But, once again and as in 1984, the issue which many thought extinct was resurrected and startled the politicians: the relationship between the Republic and the Catholic schools (Lequiller 1992). Balladur had been anxious to amend the Falloux law in order to enable more state support to be given to those schools, but his efforts provoked a storm reminiscent of July 1984 – although this time it was the partisans of Jules Ferry who took to the streets. The massive manifestation in Paris on 15 January 1994 frightened the Government away from any further provocative acts: the rival teacher unions competed with one another to proclaim their loyalty to Republican principles (*Le Monde*, 26 January).

François Bayrou confined himself to promoting a large number – one hundred and fifty-five in all – of relatively anodyne propositions for the reformation of education (*Le Monde de l'Education*, June 1994). From 1995 some future primary school teachers – still ennobled with the title of professeur – might indeed be admitted to the IUFM at the level of the DEUG, and the universities would develop a special polyvalent Licence better adapted to their needs, and to those of the pupils they would teach. And at Proposition 147 (of 155) it is conceded that the flexibility of arrangements surrounding the introduction of the IUFM without firm central planning had perhaps been an error: for the future more national definition might well be needed. Centralism was still dominant in the debates on educational policy, thirty years after de Gaulle had stimulated a movement of power away from Paris. The instituteur and the professeur still lived in different worlds and their professional training was again being kept apart from the university, thirty years after de Gaulle had intervened from the Elysée to soften the hitherto absolute distinction between lycée and école primaire.

By that same year of 1963, in the United States any sharp distinction between teachers in elementary and those in high schools had long been forgotten, while professional training for all teachers was already a well established if not universally admired part of the life of the university. How would all this appear to a French observer?

CHAPTER 4

The United States: 1963

Towards 1963

My memories of 1963 are inextricably linked with the USA. I had just married a twenty-year old school teacher, fresh from her école normale in Orleans. I was a postgraduate student in English at the Sorbonne in Paris, preparing for that tough national competitive examination for teachers, the agrégation , which, if you were lucky enough to be among the ten per cent of successful candidates, ranked you among the elite of the profession. I thought (wrongly) that the odds were against me, that I would never pass, but still the quality of teaching at the University was so high that this alone was a source of considerable excitement and an encouragement not to give up. France in those days was making a splendid economic recovery under de Gaulle – even though, as I ruefully experienced, the housing problem was still to be taken care of – and on the whole one could look to the future with reasonable optimism.

America seemed to be light years away. What few scholarships there were to spend a year or two in an American University were not for people like me, with humble working class parents. Visiting the States, or so I thought then, was a form of class privilege. And yet America was a dream. We had a passion for its music and the movies. I had seen the huge cars, with only one person inside, pass the diminutive French vehicles with four or five people crammed together and squeezed for space: those had been the pre-de Gaulle days when American soldiers were still present, in Orleans or Fontainebleau. But above all, America loomed large in my imagination through its literature. Hemingway was our hero. We would spend hours in the cafés of the Latin Quarter discussing his merits, or demerits, for he had his own enemies too. We found Nabokov and Lolita perplexing, not quite knowing whether we should like it or not, and Faulkner enthralling, though we were not quite sure if we understood everything. Walt Whitman had scope and tempo. Steinbeck stood up for the oppressed and the poor, and was for us a political giant. Stephen Crane was in a world of his own, with all the mysteries of his metaphors and deeper and still deeper levels of meaning. And we loved Hawthorne too, and Thoreau, Dos Passos, Mark Twain and Stephen Benèt...

America was far away. America was a land of literary fantasy. But America was also throbbing with life; it was beckoning to the young; it symbolised the long-expected post-war revival. America had Kennedy for President. The youths of my generation were never wholly able, however desperately some may have tried, to identify with de Gaulle. He was not even a father figure: he could have been our grandfather. Kennedy we saw as an elder brother. Thirteen days after my twenty-third birthday in November, I heard the crushing, devastating news. I remember all the circumstances with vivid accuracy. After a day spent at the Sorbonne, I had taken the train from Paris to Montargis where my home was. My wife had come to meet me at the station. She looked terribly upset. She broke the news to me. We both felt betrayed, bereaved and dispossessed by that abominable assassination.

America was to us a paradox on at least two accounts. The Left, as the 1968 revolts were soon to prove, exercised a powerful influence over us, including the Communist Party which in those days still enlisted the support of one French voter in four. Yet, to most students, Khrushchev was a caricature while Kennedy had charisma. Many believed in Castro, but it was J.F.K. we loved. There was an immense economic and cultural distance between France, so much impoverished by the War and still predominantly rural a decade earlier, and the United States which generated so much wealth and looked like a model, even though in public no words were harsh enough to condemn capitalism. And yet John Kennedy seemed to have abolished the political distance: he had bridged the yawning gap between us and the other side of the Atlantic ocean. We are much wiser now. Having grown older and learned a thing or two, we know that our enthusiasm for the man had been exaggerated and that he deserved condemnation as well as commendation. But this cannot alter the facts of the time: it was good to feel America was our ally.

The cultural distance could be measured in all sorts of ways. My own experience as an aspiring teacher in France may help to illustrate the huge differences between the two countries in 1963. I had been going through a harsh, unrelenting process of selection from the age of eleven. That I was studying at the Sorbonne was to me a miracle. And statistically, I was an aberration, like a handful of my lower class contemporaries. Over the Atlantic, at the same period, there would have been some hurdles, of course, but access to secondary and then higher education would have been much easier. The high school had for a long time been regarded as an extension of the elementary school. Not so in France where mass education was still synonymous with primary schooling. Lycées creamed off their students and were a preserve for the social elite. Selection, in public establishments, was no longer achieved by the charging of fees. But you still had to pass an examination, essentially based on French and arithmetic, before being allowed access to secondary schooling at the age of eleven. Only a very small minority ever went to lycées.

For most of the children, education came to an end at fourteen, when they went into the world of work. I had been lucky to have been spotted by my primary schoolmaster who had put me up for the exam. Through yet another stroke of luck, I had come out top of the list and, as a special favour, I had been allowed into the classics track: doing Latin in those days carried a lot of prestige ; mathematics was for the less gifted, the coarser kind. At sixteen, after five years of secondary schooling, my parents encouraged me to take the competitive examination that would let me into the école normale: they were quite poor, and the advantage of being offered free board and lodging if I passed was to them an opportunity that I ought not to miss. What is more, I would leave the école normale four years later, at twenty, with all the professional qualifications and the salary of a primary school teacher. That would be a symbol of social promotion, if ever there was one. Everyone before in the family had either been a peasant or a worker. I would climb the social ladder, no longer work with my hands, and become a civil servant since all teachers are State employees. My fate was thus sealed: I would be an instituteur. I took and passed the competitive examination and went to Orleans, which is sixty miles south of Paris, as a boarder. Oddly enough, I felt both triumphant and depressed.

What I was yet to learn was the reality of two worlds which, instead of being complementary, saw one another as rivals, if not enemies. The primary sector, proud of its historical achievements as the promoter of mass, popular education, was prone to look upon the world of the lycées and universities as essentially bourgeois and elitist. Primary schools had a mission towards the nation. Lycées and universities, in comparison, were seen as citadels of privilege. So the two worlds preferred to ignore one another. The primary school, with its teachers, inspectors, administrators, existed on its own planet. To a certain extent, this remained true until the early 1990s. And I was sharply reminded of this implacable truth when I was eighteen: because money had been placed on my head by the powers-that-be to train me as a primary school teacher, I was publicly called a traitor when I apprised them of the news that, having passed yet another competitive examination (the IPES) at the Sorbonne, I had now been chosen to be trained as a lycée teacher. I had crossed the enemy lines and betrayed my side. I was given to understand that this was a shameful thing to do.

Even to me, with my very limited experience, entirely contained within the educational culture of my own country, this seemed odd and not quite acceptable. But little did I know in those days that such attitudes would have appeared utterly nonsensical if viewed from the other side of the Atlantic. For it is indeed in these years that, at least until the mid-sixties when sweeping reforms were introduced in France and mass education was gradually extended to the secondary sector, the histories of our educational systems offer the sharpest contrasts. Our views of what education, its organisation, objectives and profession should be like were simply poles apart. During the past generation, some major differences have vanished, though by no means all. Thirty years ago, we might have lived on different planets.

It would be easy, of course, to overstretch the point. There were some common features, the main one being that, since our national histories converged towards the end of the eighteenth century and we felt equally fired by a Republican zeal, there has persisted, however intermittently, an egalitarian streak within our conception of education. The French and the Americans have similarly thought in terms of educating the citizen. They have associated education and freedom, education and democracy. Differences should not obscure this basic historical fact. But we have certainly not acted in unison on this: our chequered histories have not allowed this to be, nor has our sense of space – a tightly packed nation on the one hand, the whole chunk of a continent on the other.

In 1963, the contrasts were indeed striking. American teachers had long been described as K12 teachers. Whether they were dealing with six-year-olds or eighteen-year-olds, they saw themselves as one undifferentiated professional group. K12 implied that the whole process of educating a child was continuous; the code also indicates that any barriers that might have existed before had been pulled down. The elementary school leads naturally towards the high school, which is a step ahead, but in the same direction. This was and still is taken for granted, so much so that commenting on it may well seem superfluous. But it is not so on the other side of the Atlantic. Many European countries, and some even to this very day, have long drawn a line between the primary and the secondary sectors, the mass of the people and the learned minority. As the story of my own experience revealed, instituteurs and professeurs were still in separate worlds: not only were the latter considered to be more than a notch above the former, but they did not receive the same salaries, their teaching loads were different, they did not join the same unions and they went through very contrasted forms of training. This was so true that it was not until 1991 that the two species of teachers were given the same name (professeur) and trained in the same Institutes of Education (though rarely in the same classes and sometimes not even in the same buildings).

If comparison is best achieved through contrast, this K12 issue, especially when seen in the light of 1963, is particularly relevant. American educational egalitarianism on the one hand, persistent French elitism on the other, offered two clearly distinctive approaches and strategies. The conceptions of the role of the State in France and of the Federal Government in Northern America were even more dissimilar. In one case, centralisation was the key and the Ministry of Education in Paris was all-powerful; in the other, the role of the local community was paramount, and the Federal power in Washington played a minor part. The antithesis is perhaps a little less obvious today, but it was emphatic thirty years ago. Teacher education itself illustrates this. In France, écoles normales for the training of young primary teachers formed a national network. Strict rationality prevailed: they were impressive, expensive stone buildings, often with elegant slate roofs, erected in each Department. There were normal schools for the girls and normal schools for the boys: in Orleans or Versailles for example, as in many other regions, they had been built at the opposite ends of the town so that the twain should meet as seldom as possible. Seen from this consistently rational perspective, the 1,150 American institutions involved in the big business of teacher education could appear as the haphazard products of unplanned proliferation (even after allowance had been made for the sheer differences in the size of the two national territories). The overall pattern might equally be seen as rather messy and chaotic. In France the hand which pulled all the strings was there for all to see. What invisible hand was at play in the United States? And what was the fate of these tens of thousands of trained teachers? Could it really be that they had to play by the rules of the market? That they effectively had to seek employment, send applications, go for interviews? In the best of circumstances, was it really possible to pick and choose one's school? France followed a totally different logic. The State took charge of the trainee elementary teacher, providing free board and lodging, free tuition and training, while insisting that the young pupil teacher should upon entry (at the age of sixteen, that is to say) sign a pledge to serve the State for a minimum of ten years. This contractual obligation worked both ways: the State was pledged to provide you with employment, obviously not in a school not of your own choosing, since that appointment, strictly within the Department, depended upon the decision of the local Inspector. It is hard to think of two more distinct systems.

The contrast did not stop here, however, and the list of dissimilarities could be extended ad nauseam. Let us simply concentrate on one other major difference: the role of higher education in the sphere of teacher training. It is a theme lying at the heart of this study. Comparing 1963 and the early 1990s may prove particularly useful. 1963: in the United States the whole of teacher education was already firmly embedded in the system of higher education. Normal Schools were a thing of the past: by the 1940s they had disappeared as such and been turned into colleges. They were about to go through the process of becoming full-fledged universities. 1963 in France: primary school teacher training is still kept totally apart from higher education. Between the two sectors, there stands a high, solid wall. Secondary school teachers take their degrees in universities, and upon completion of their studies, receive some professional training (the higher their academic achievement, the shorter their period of practice teaching) outside the boundaries of higher education. The lecturers and professors who have taught them hardly ever know (unless they have started their careers as high school teachers themselves) what goes on during that period of training. And to tell the plain truth, they do not very much care. They have performed their academic duty. The rest is the teacher trainers' responsibility. Early 1990s: higher education in the States has retained its virtual monopoly over teacher education, although there had been threats of closures of some institutions in the late 1970s and early 1980s, and there has been talk, in some cases, of transferring teacher training away from the campuses and into the schools proper. France today has its network of regional IUFMs most of which were set up in 1991. Teacher education, the government said, should be the business of higher education. A peaceful revolution is under way. Old academic traditions and corporate hostilities die hard, but the reform seems to be taking effect.

The system of teacher education in France by 1963 was ossified. But there is little doubt that, in the eyes of contemporaries, it looked healthy enough. Pressures for reform were not strong. In the same year, in the United States, an appreciably more flexible system, already under the aegis of higher education, was under very heavy fire. By a coincidence which fits well with the focus on 1963 of much of this volume, in these very months there appeared two books analysing the problems of teacher education and its relationship to higher education on the other side of the Atlantic. A discussion of them will provide the substance of the third section of this chapter, after the history of that relationship has been reconstructed.

Normal Schools and Universities

The salient feature of American teacher education in 1963, especially when compared with the French or British systems, was that the evolution towards total higher education hegemony was already complete. In this sense, 1963 was in the United States the end of a journey which had started roughly half a century before, whereas in both France and Great Britain the same movement was yet to affect the training of primary school teachers. This institutional characteristic (teacher preparation wholly embedded in higher education) remained unaltered from 1963 to the present day. The system therefore suffered no great structural upheaval during those decades: there was no attempt to go back to institutions which were monotechnic, that is solely dedicated to teacher training; nor was there any shift of professional preparation away from college or university towards schools. Thus the main features of teacher education remain basically the same. Preparing to be a teacher still consists in taking courses, in most cases at undergraduate level, in a school, college or department of education (SCDE) set in a higher education institution offering dozens of other subjects and preparing for a multitude of other professions.

Unsurprisingly perhaps, one of the main issues for discussion nowadays is whether such a higher education monopoly of teacher preparation is a good thing or not. The point will have to be dwelt on at some length in the next chapter. What must be noted at this stage are primarily the circumstances and nature of this evolution, which France and Great Britain were to emulate two or three decades later. Seen from a 1963 perspective, and without being unduly deterministic, this evolution seemed irresistible.

The provision of teacher education in 1963 in the United States was very much diversified and located in a context much closer to a market than to a managed system. Teacher education in America was provided in 1,150 institutions, varying immensely in size, output and prestige, and vying with one another for clientele. At a national level, the Federal government's involvement was minimal. The constitutional division of powers placed the entire responsibility for teacher education training in the fifty States, which alone provided the norms for teacher certification. No national rules, regulations or standards were applied. Admittedly, there was a great deal of homogeneity across the nation, as States were applying implicitly accepted norms, but no single conductor ruled over the huge orchestra. In the main, States refrained from being unduly intrusive in their control over certification, and the overall result was that, for good or ill, most of what was going on in the world of teacher education was effectively in the hands of the teaching profession, and especially of educators. One striking illustration of this had been the setting up, in 1954, of the National Council for the Accreditation of Teacher Education (NCATE), operating as the name shows at the national level for the accreditation of programmes, and selecting most of its members from among the educational establishment. The National Education Association (NEA) was thus made a major participant and has continued ever since to play a key role. Locally, school districts, albeit the foundation of the whole American system of education, were concerned hardly at all with the training of the teachers whom they hired, apart from cooperating in the provision of teaching practice and placement of students.

This general picture of a system largely controlled by professional educators operating within the context of higher education, although reduced as it is here to its simplest and barest forms, continues to provide an adequate representation of the current situation in the mid-1990s. As will appear, every single detail of the picture hides layers of difficult issues beneath the apparently smooth surface, and there was already in 1963 much wringing of hands about the wisdom of the prevailing arrangement. Seen from outside, however, the brighter spots far outnumbered the darker ones: surely, the institutional context of higher education could only raise the status of teacher preparation, and the absence of excessively bureaucratic control must guarantee a fair measure of professional autonomy. In other words, America in this field as in so many others was clearly leading the way. Whatever dissatisfaction might be expressed internally was not likely to detract from the two apparently natural goals: teacher education placed near the apex of the system, at a point of vantage, and the teaching profession playing a key role in the preparation of its own members.

The historical move of teacher preparation towards and into higher education in the United States is, especially for a French observer, a compelling object of study. At the beginning, identical labels are to be found in both nations: elementary teachers were likewise trained in "normal schools". But whereas the French écoles normales survived until 1991, the American normal schools enjoyed a much more brief existence – hardly even a century – and had all disappeared by 1940. Why should there have been such a difference in the pace of development? American historians of education have located in the 1830s the origins of a normal school "movement" (Altenbaugh & Underwood 1990, pp. 136-186). This movement developed in unison with the growth of the common or elementary school (Urban 1990, pp. 59-71). The first one was established in 1823 as a private institution in Concord, Vermont, while the first public normal school was created by Horace Mann in 1839 in Lexington, Massachussets. The normal school was opened for women elementary teachers hoping to be employed in the earliest common schools, whose three main characteristics were to offer free tuition, require universal attendance and depend on local tax support. By the end of the nineteenth century, private and public normal schools had grown side by side in roughly equal numbers, to a total of about three hundred. In the early twentieth century, the public sector began to overtake the private sector of normal schools, which experienced a marked decline and by the 1920s had virtually disappeared. This was in any case the time at which transformation on a much larger scale was about to take place.

In large measure because the system had grown locally, there was no single form of provision for elementary teacher preparation, and normal schools never prepared the majority of teachers. In fact, by 1900 no more than a quarter of all new teachers were trained in them. The notion that the education of children should be exclusively entrusted to the care of young ladies and occasionally young men who had enjoyed proper forms of professional training was still in its infancy, as indeed was the insistence on state licensing or certification. But normal schools, conceived as an adequate institutional response to the problem of training teachers, naturally grew in number throughout the States. The movement spread from New England towards the Midwest and the West. It was slower to take root in the South.

The normal school movement, developing alongside and in tune with the expansion of common schools, rested too much on local initiative ever to become a tidy, well-orchestrated affair. The reasons for this unevenness are bound up with the history of the United States in the nineteenth century, when strong dissimilarities opposed the East, where in the 1830s the din of the battles fought during the American Revolution had died down and settlement was ancient, to the West with its ever receding frontier and the dynamics of territorial expansion. The line of fracture which split the nation in the middle between North and South, and with them divergent economies and cultures, also accounted for very diverse approaches to education. No wonder that the normal school movement occurred at different periods in different parts of the United States, and that there never was any unitary conception of the role and function of normal schools.

A rough map could be drawn along the following lines. New England acted as a pioneer and started the movement. The system which the state of Massachusetts adopted was borrowed from Europe and more especially from

Prussia: between 1839 and 1854, four state normal schools were set up in rural areas in Massachusetts. Two were for women only and two were mixed. The original intention of the state and of the founders was to focus the activity of these normal schools on the training of elementary school teachers, and nothing else. In other words, they were conceived as single-purpose institutions. Young ladies outnumbered their male counterparts. Since from the beginning the underlying philosophy of the new institutions was to emphasize character first and knowledge second, the prospective teachers taught and trained in the normal schools were expected to be well-behaved and able to stand as moral examples. That they should be fountains of science or fine scholars obviously mattered less.

In the Midwest, to which the normal school movement spread from Massachusetts, there was greater diversity: the concept of the normal school sometimes followed the original model and sometimes differed markedly from it. In Michigan, the state normal school which opened in 1853 was conceived along the same lines as in New England and was therefore exclusively geared towards the training of common school teachers. Kansas followed suit in 1865. But the state of Illinois adopted another solution and its first normal school was in fact a multi-purpose institution offering vocational training and traditional academic courses to the local youth alongside teacher education for elementary school teachers. The state of Wisconsin emulated none of these models. It was content with providing such teacher training, until the end of the Civil War, in high schools as well as in private colleges and academies. Only after 1865 did it plump for specialised institutions.

Normal schools were much slower to come into existence in the Southern states. The movement did not occur until the 1870s well after the Civil War, and it was oriented along the lines of racial divisions. Normal schools for the Whites were kept remote from the few provided for the Blacks: separate development in this area as in the whole field of education had become the norm before the end of the century.

The historical evidence on the evolution of normal schools which has been brought to light by J. Herbst reveals an interesting phenomenon, probably unique to the United States at the time (Herbst 1989, pp. 213-36). His observation is that even those normal schools which had been set up as single-purpose establishments solely dedicated to the training of young ladies as elementary school teachers soon became impatient with what was deemed to be a narrow definition of their role. Before the end of the nineteenth century, most of them had therefore taken on a wider range of activities, offering as high schools did vocational and academic courses to a larger number of students than before. Many had at the same time launched into the training of secondary school teachers. That normal schools should have been turned into community or "people's" colleges at such an early period and diversified their role to such a degree offers a striking contrast to the institutional stability which, by comparison, was in those years the hallmark of teacher training in France or Great Britain.

At least two main reasons can be found to explain this early metamorphosis. In order to account for what he analyses as the normal schools' "persistent tendency to move away from what had been the initial and never quite fulfilled demand to prepare teachers for rural classrooms", Jurgen Herbst has argued that the model introduced into America had been conceived in European class-bound societies where educated élites were trying to adapt a bourgeois system to their views of democracy. In nations where country and city were opposed, and where the middle classes were not inclined to mix with the populace, it was perfectly logical to keep elementary and secondary schools in separate worlds and therefore also to offer distinct forms of training to common school teachers on the one hand, and secondary school teachers on the other. Such a conception of things soon proved to be ill-adapted to the United States, where the notions of caste or class never prevailed to the same degree, and where on the contrary flexibility and mobility ruled. Even elementary school teachers were not willing to be confined to rigid structures and lifetime occupations. They saw normal schools as opportunities for social mobility, and teaching in elementary schools as a preparation for something else: teaching at a higher level, moving into a different profession, or, as far as women were concerned, matrimony. In Kansas, where the Massachusetts model had been adopted in 1865, the normal schools soon followed what can be regarded as a general trend: they "deserted the field of classroom teaching for the education of specialized and high school teachers, administrators and educational leaders "(Herbst 1989, p. 229). By 1900 most normal schools had already begun to raise their sights towards more diverse and allegedly nobler activities. Their original role had often been taken up by county or city training schools or high schools.

A second reason helps to explain the institutional instability which characterized normal schools as they developed into "people's colleges". The new roles which they were asked to fulfil must be seen as an effect of a massive development which began to take place at the turn of the century, namely the growth of the high school as an extension of the elementary school. The two sectors were complementary and easy passage between them became the norm: there was no reason, therefore, why walls or partitions should as in Europe be erected to separate or isolate them from each other. Naturally enough, normal schools were carried along by this powerful current and tended to perform the role of high schools and/or take on the responsibility of training the teachers and administrators employed in the new high schools.

The beginning of this dramatic development can be traced to the 1880s. In 1890, roughly 200,000 students attended 2,500 high schools. From then on, enrolments in secondary schools were doubled every decade until the 1930s when a decline in the birthrate slowed down the process: in 1900, there were 520,000 high school students; in 1912, the figure had grown to 1,105,000; in 1920, it reached 2,200,000, representing 28 per cent of the 14-17 age group. The following decade, when the high school really began to offer mass education, saw a similar pattern confirm itself; once again, the number of high school students doubled over the period and reached 4,400,000, or 47 per cent of the same 14-17 age group. Despite the relative drop in school rolls in the 1930s, the high school population in America had jumped to 6,500,000 by 1940, an increase of 3,250 per cent over fifty years. It was not yet secondary education for all, but access to the high school had been made much more democratic than anywhere on the old Continent (Cremin 1964).

This remarkable expansion of the secondary school sector produced a sea-change in the educational world. Normal schools became more and more involved in this process, at the expense of their initial role as training places for common school teachers. In the 1920s, when the current was at its strongest, most of these normal schools went through yet another transformation, casting their old slough and shedding their very names in the process. This was when they became known as Teachers' Colleges, and courses were extended from two to four years. As the transition from one type of institution to the other depended on decisions made by individual states, it took some time before it became a national characteristic. Figures for the 1920s show, however, that the process was rather swift: at the beginning of the decade, there were 137 state normal schools as against 30 teachers' colleges; ten years later, the proportion had been reversed, with only 46 normal schools left and as many as 146 teachers' colleges in existence. Another illustration of this change in status and activity can be found in the number of MA degrees in education awarded over the same period: while only two were registered in 1900, the figure had grown to 125 by 1930 and to 146 three years later.

Doubts have nevertheless been expressed about whether this evolution can be regarded as a story of unqualified success. It may indeed have been a good thing for normal schools to keep abreast of the times and follow the upward progression of the educational system. But some have deplored that they should have been left free, or sometimes required, to perform functions other than those for which they had been specifically established. This evolution may be interpreted as "a deliberate neglect by the states of the overwhelmingly female ranks of teachers", whose would be professional status suffered in the process (Herbst 1989, p. 233). This may indeed go some way towards explaining the comparatively low status at all times accorded to elementary school teaching. Had normal schools remained the professional citadels of this educational sector, it could be argued that higher status might have been achieved.

After the setting up of the normal schools and their subsequent transformation into teachers' colleges, the third stage of their evolution towards the 1960s strengthened the connection between teacher training and higher education, but also precipitated the transformation of teachers' colleges into wider, more diversified, multi purpose state colleges or state universities. Teacher education, in this process, ceased to be the central function of the new institutions, and became one of several or many competing activities. Teachers' colleges, in short, became places where students could train not only as teachers, but also as lawyers, or businessmen or architects. The new colleges or universities began to offer liberal arts or other degrees. In the early 1960s, this evolution from normal schools through teachers' colleges to multi-purpose colleges or universities was virtually complete: the world of teacher education had been thoroughly transformed by a series of what some authors have called institutional "displacements".

Posing the question whether this series of institutional changes has been wholly beneficial to the practical job of training teachers is likely to spark off animated debate among educators and historians of education in the United States. And this is indeed one of the key issues which this collective study wishes to tackle. Responses in the institutions which I have visited have been extremely varied, ranging from total indifference to visible and audible concern about the fast-declining status of teacher training now that other degrees for other professions are being awarded. Not a few prominent educators and experts in the history of teacher education in the USA agree that the process of integrating such training into higher education has had some regrettable effects. To put matters simply, there is undeniably a consensus that higher education, whatever its disadvantages, is the only appropriate place where teachers should be prepared: it is the vital prerequisite if teaching is to be elevated to the status of a profession. But controversy revolves around the question whether teacher training has gained in quality or not. John Goodlad, one of the keener observers of the scene, recently concluded that in the multi-purpose institutions, where it is no longer the central activity, "teacher education was not so much pushed aside as overshadowed" (Goodlad 1990, p.21). Clifford & Guthrie have expressed a general judgement which broadly concurs with this. They have argued that with the disappearance of normal schools and teachers' colleges, two professional assets have sadly been lost: one is the idea of the autonomous professional school devoted solely to the "exalted preparation" of teachers; another is a dominating concern with "practical pedagogy" (Clifford & Guthrie 1988, p. 61). There was already in 1963 ample evidence of uneasiness about these issues. In the early 1990s, the terms of the debate had not changed to any remarkable degree, and there was still plenty of talk among professional educators and deans of leading schools of education about ways and means to secure better understanding and closer cooperation between SCDEs and the world of academe.

The matter is made all the more complex since, when teachers' colleges underwent their thorough transformation from single to multi-purpose institutions, teacher education was by no means a newcomer or a sudden intruder in higher education. Schools and departments of education had long been in existence within universities. The first "permanent" professorship in education was established in the state University of Iowa in 1873. The chair was in "didactics", a word which is no longer in frequent use among American educators, who prefer to speak about "pedagogy". As didactics focuses on the art of teaching a given academic subject while pedagogy centres on the teacher–student relationship, this linguistic shift mirrored the typically American evolution in this century from a subject-centred approach to a student-centred one. Five years later, in 1878, the same University of Iowa set up a College of Normal Instruction. In 1879, the University of Michigan at Ann Arbor shunned both the explicit reference to didactics and to the "normal" tradition and, in a rather grandiloquent style, created a Department in "the Science and Art of Teaching". It was followed in 1881 by the University of Wisconsin which created a Department of Pedagogy and then by Columbia University which opened its still illustrious Teachers' College in 1887 (Cremin, Shannon & Townsend 1954). By the turn of the century, nearly 250 universities had set up their own Chairs or Departments of Education. A whole new territory reserved for the training and the study of teachers had been carved out within the sphere of higher education.

Historians do not agree about the usefulness and the quality of the university departments and schools of education which began to proliferate as the nineteenth century was drawing to a close. It is often pointed out that while they undeniably enhanced the status of public school teaching by conferring degrees on practitioners, they themselves had to struggle for status among other academic departments in their own universities. Another common observation is that while the new units offered advanced courses at a higher education level, they were prone to involve themselves in a great deal of useless research. Uncertainty is also sometimes expressed about the quality of the professors of education who were appointed to staff these new schools and departments. Theodore Sizer and Arthur Powell have observed that positions in schools of education were often filled, in the early part of this century, by people who had acquired experience as teachers or administrators (or both) but lacked academic scholarship and felt out of their depth when confronted with theory or genuine research (Spring 1990, p. 254). One of the worthwhile contributions of the early schools of education was the introduction of a scientific study of education, which acquired its modern form, characterised by the collecting of statistical data, the elaboration of standardized tests, the working out of procedures for measuring intelligence and the quantification of education results. The leading schools of education also played a key role in training professors and top administrators of very high standing. These alumni in their turn helped develop national networks, disseminate new ideas, place efficient people in positions of power, and eventually produce major changes in educational theory and practice. In a country where such change in education rarely proceeds from a national centre the function performed by these professionals at a regional or national level was of crucial importance.

Neither should the ability shown by these top institutions to adapt to changing circumstances and to attract high quality faculty be underestimated. The list of the most famous schools of education which was drawn up in the

1930s included many of those which were still rated as being top of the league fifty years later: Columbia (Teachers' College), Harvard, Stanford, Berkeley, Chicago, Michigan, Ohio State and Minnesota. Yale was on the list of the 1930s, but it subsequently closed its school of education. Although UCLA and the universities of Illinois and Wisconsin should now with others be added to the league table, on the whole it has not been modified to a substantial degree. But a critical issue is whether the role assumed by schools of education set in their university environment had been totally beneficial or not for teacher education as a whole. It is clear that since normal schools were deserting their original field (the training of elementary school teachers) and taking on the training of high school teachers and administrators, they were set on a collision course with the university schools of education on whose territory they were encroaching. Wayne J.Urban considers that this led in the end to a regrettable confusion of roles. His conclusion is that the normal school eventually "developed into a pale imitation of the university, doing what the university does, namely research, less well than the university and not wishing to do well what it historically did, prepare teachers" (Urban 1990, p. 66). This somewhat abrupt judgment reflects the recurrent tensions between the academic tendency towards research and the practical requirement to prepare teachers for their classroom tasks.

The emphasis laid in major schools of education on teacher preparation proper, or on education as a wider concept and object of study, has shifted periodically. Concentration on, and interest in, what was going on in the classroom has been seen to wax and wane in cycles: it is difficult to achieve the right sort of balance between academic research, for instance in child psychology or the sociology and history of education, and applied pedagogy, concerned with teaching methods and strategies. Environment and context are here a strong determinant and most leading schools of education have been located in universities encouraging their students to go on for their PhDs, and offering a stimulating academic environment. This has acted as an incentive for such schools of education to produce scholars and researchers, elite professors and administrators.

It is often argued that the leading institutions in the long run acted as magnets and pulled the whole system upwards. Or, to adopt the metaphor of Clifford & Guthrie, the university department, school, or college of education became like suns or beacons toward which other training centres gravitated. "It was the preferred means", they add, "to dignify education as a career for the better-educated and ambitious, to develop competent practitioners, and to build and codify a base of technical knowledge to guide practice and free professionals from outside interference " (Clifford & Guthrie 1988, p. 63). This last point is especially significant: the move of the whole system of teacher training upwards into higher education, where a tradition had already been built up, was a means of strengthening professional autonomy. Here was an enclave into which laymen could not easily trespass. Autonomy, however, equally implied accountability. That implication has ensured that whenever doubts and fears are raised about the quality of schooling, teacher educators are easily and readily taken to task. This was certainly the case in 1963.

1963: Two books

1963 does not assume in the United States the same significance as in France or Britain. Of course the year is remembered because of the traumatic impact, at home and abroad, of the assassination of J. F. Kennedy. But major political change cannot be traced back to this particular year. In the field of education, nothing strikingly innovative occurred. America seems more immune, in any case, to abrupt swings or turn-abouts in educational policies than France or Britain, where oscillations of the pendulum between the right and the left are often followed by swift initiatives for radical change. Much of this is of course due to the minimal role which the Federal government has by tradition been content to play where schools and universities are concerned. When no strong Ministerial or Presidential hand – think of Anthony Crosland as Education Secretary in Britain in 1964 or of President de Gaulle in France at the same period – is visibly reshaping the educational landscape, the system is to a much greater degree left to evolve through its own momentum.

This should not be taken to mean, however, that the Federal government by 1963 had remained totally unconcerned by the issue of education or still less that it was to remain passive in the following years. In fact, one momentous decision had been taken some twenty years before with the passage of the G.I.Bill, offering grants to war veterans going into higher education. Almost overnight, with one million such veterans enrolling, the college population had doubled. Between 1944 and 1951, more than two million grants had been distributed. Financially, the boost to colleges and universities had been considerable. Socially, the grants had done a great deal to promote the idea of greater equality of opportunity in higher education.

Another federal initiative was the passing in 1958 of the National Defense Education Act. Issues of defence and education are seldom discussed together. They are even more rarely the object of decisions meant to affect them both at the same time and in unison. In this particular instance, the Federal government deemed that unless standards in education were raised, American superiority in the world would be in jeopardy. The Act therefore stipulated that federal money should be massively invested in the teaching of subjects whose mastery was deemed to be an essential asset for national defence policy: they were mathematics, science and foreign languages.

The G. I. Bill as well as the 1958 Act were waves that rocked the educational boat. But they sent only gentle ripples into the relatively quiescent waters of teacher preparation. The same can be said of the historical decision to desegregate schools, following the 1954 Supreme Court's ruling in the case of Brown vs Board of Education of Topeka. In the wake of this and other powerful incentives from the Federal government, the world of education, in the southern and then the northern States, was irrevocably transformed.

Desegregation was achieved, and racial mixing in schools promoted by means of bussing, but the institutional characteristics and the essential nature of teacher preparation were not to any substantial degree affected.

Turning points in the 1960s might more legitimately be placed a few years later, in 1965-66. This was the time when President Johnson, who had succeeded J. F. Kennedy, was waging his War on Poverty. One battle in which he asked Congress to join him was on the school front. Two Elementary and Secondary Education Acts (ESEAs) were passed, through which federal aid could be released specifically to help disadvantaged families. Funds were allocated to schools on the basis of the number of poor children attending them rather than in an undifferentiated form as before. Like the two previous examples, this political initiative illustrates the subtle interplay of forces operating in the world of American education and it can be seen as an historic shift in the constitutional balance of powers; as an unprecedented form of Federal incursion into the world of schools, it marks an important departure from tradition. But on the other hand, it did not, nor was it ever meant to, seriously impinge on the traditional training of teachers.

And yet, despite all this, teacher education in 1963 was at least in one sense very much on the public if not political agenda. If one special reason must be given for singling out this particular year for attention to this matter in America, it is this: teacher training suddenly became the focus of close attention, and a target for a great deal of adverse criticism. 1963 was an *annus horribilis* for teacher educators. It was the year of the publication of the two major books which have already been mentioned: Conant's *Education of American Teachers* and Koerner's *Miseducation of Teachers*. Such a coincidence is rare, and was not in fact to be repeated until 1986, when similar anxiety about the standards of schooling and the quality of teacher training led the Carnegie Forum and the Holmes Group to report and issue their recommendations within weeks of one another.

What was the main issue at stake in 1963? It was not mass education, for this had become a reality and was now the object of a nationwide consensus. Mass education had expanded not simply in the elementary sector, but was already (unlike in the UK) in the process of being achieved in higher education. It was generally accepted that economic success and international prestige rested on a wide diffusion of knowledge and distribution of educational opportunities for the greatest number. The principle of the universal secondary school had been fulfilled in America in the first half of the century. As for higher education, the percentage of eighteen to twenty one year olds attending colleges and universities in 1960-61 reached 37%, a figure which, incidentally, was still a target which Europe was setting for itself in the early 1990s.

The debate over whether higher forms of schooling should be reserved for an elite or based on equity was no longer felt to be relevant. There were other deep anxieties, however, which were voiced far and wide. Issues of race and urban poverty were one source of such national concern. The scientific and strategic advance obtained by the USSR, still then a "superpower", after the successful launching in 1957 of Sputnik, the first satellite ever put into orbit, was another. Race, deprivation and disadvantage were topics around which debate continued to rage throughout the 1960s and 1970s. Anxiety over an alleged inferiority of the United States compared to the Soviet Union led, in the words of Diane Ravitch, to a "bitter orgy of pedagogical soul-searching" (Ravitch 1983, ch. 7). In a sense, the two issues collided and called for contradictory reforms. Concern about the lower standards in American education, exemplified by the inability of American scientists to do as well as their Soviet rivals, could only be relieved by making the pursuit of excellence and genuine scholarship a national priority (Gardner 1961). Inversely, the glaring economic and social inequalities linked with race and urban poverty made it an urgent necessity to provide for the needs of the disadvantaged, among whom the Blacks were in a majority. The solution, if there were any, lay in fighting inequality. If this objective was accepted, the pursuit of excellence could only come second. It was extremely difficult if not impossible to fight on both fronts simultaneously. The Federal government did not flinch, however, and made two attempts at dealing with these burning issues. It helped to beef up the school curriculum in mathematics and science; but the major thrust of President Johnson's policy was his War on Poverty.

Dissatisfaction with standards in American schools lingered on. Although the launching of the Sputnik gave it a dramatic emphasis, there had been rumblings for some years. In 1953, A. Bestor had published *Educational Wastelands : the retreat from learning in our public schools*. The book had had a considerable impact and was still regarded forty years later as a major contribution to the diagnosis of what had gone wrong with American schools. Six years later J. B. Conant, a figure of great prestige and influence in American life who had been President of Harvard for twenty years and then Ambassador in Germany, published his study on *The American High School Today*. This is a volume of particular importance to this study, since it was followed in the year 1963 by his discussion of teacher education. In the earlier work, he concluded that there was nothing basically wrong with the structure and direction of education in the United States. When compared with European systems, it even appeared more advanced and progressive. He did however argue that more encouragement should be given to students to learn more science, mathematics and modern languages, and that there should be more academic stretching of the better, brighter minds. Teaching all the children from all the homes in high schools was a principle of equity with which Conant whole-heartedly agreed. But his message was that quality ought not to suffer in the process.

From our comparative perspective, bearing as it does here on the late fifties and early sixties, there is one remark made by Conant which is particularly thought-provoking. A foreign observer looking at the American education scene, he felt, would find it almost incomprehensible. Was this a polite way of saying that schooling in the United States was following an erratic path verging on the absurd, in the cool, unbiased judgement of an outsider? Not in the least. Conant was convinced that America had made such great strides in the world of education that others had been out-distanced, and would be unlikely even to understand what was going on. For them, America had moved into strange, inhospitable territory. Not so, said Conant: America was on the right track.

When he thought of the "foreign" world, it was Europe that Conant had in mind. What he saw there was excessive waste of talent, due to the early selection of pre-university students. To make matters even worse, such creaming off was all too often class-based. By comparison, colleges and universities in the United States appeared much more diverse and open. The same was even more true of the American public high school, with its truly comprehensive intake, and the social role which had been assigned to it: namely to accommodate all the youth of a community. "The American high school", he wrote with undisguised pride, "is an American development of this century. It has no equivalent, so far as I am aware, in any European country" (Conant 1959, p.96). There was indeed much evidence in the educational histories of both France and Britain to justify this conclusion.

The key notion in America in 1963 was therefore that the purpose of the high school was to offer education to all the youth of the community. But, Conant asked, is it right that local communities and their school boards should remain the linchpin of the whole educational structure? Is it a reasonable arrangement to have tens of thousands of tax-supported schools managed through these boards? Can it be called a system, or is it not in fact chaos? Raising the question of the essentially local nature of education in the United States was, again from a comparative point of view, a stimulating enterprise. The issue is perhaps too swiftly brushed aside by Conant who adopts a pragmatic rather than a systemic view: yes, he says in effect, our system looks very untidy and chaotic when seen from outside, but it has one great advantage, namely that it works. And most people like it.

Conant was convinced that the social goals and the basic structure of American education were not to be modified as they expressed a form of national consensus. This conviction provided the rosy background against which the gloomier features of high schools could stand out in adequate relief. What then had gone wrong? Conant put it in a nutshell: "The academically talented student, as a rule, is not sufficiently challenged" (Conant 1959, p. 40). Able boys, he said, will do maths and science, but they will neglect foreign languages, English or social studies. Able girls will readily concentrate on the latter, but be less keen to study mathematics. They, too, will neglect foreign languages. And science will not be their forte either. The social mores perceptible in the affluent suburbs were also a disquieting reality of life. There boys and girls born into well-educated families and with promising futures were found to have dramatically limited ambitions: meeting the minimum requirements for college entrance was the height of their aspirations. Few were prepared to put in the necessary fifteen or twenty hours of homework every week. "It is an uneven contest when the choice between easy and tough programs is left to students with convertibles, plenty of money, and community approval for spending most of their evenings in social activities" (Conant 1959, p. 45). American schools, with society turning a blind eye, were found to be guilty of wasting the nation's social, and potentially academic, elite. For Conant it was not the overall framework and management of education which was deficient, but what was being done, or rather not done, within it. He insisted on tougher programmes and stronger incentives to undertake scholarly work. The pursuit of some form of excellence was in his opinion totally compatible with the democratic ideal of equity.

It was not entirely correct to assume that all European observers found the American system of schooling incomprehensible. Roughly at the same time as Conant was conducting his survey at home, Anthony Crosland, later to become Secretary of State for Education when the Labour Party regained office in 1964, and one of the chief artisans of comprehensive schooling in Britain, was reflecting upon the meaning of the American experience of the high school. He was one of those percipient foreign observers who showed that incomprehension of things American was not a universal failing. He remarked that a great deal of emphasis in American schools was put on co-operation and adaptability; in no schools in the world, he added with some audacity, would you find less insistence on rivalry and competition. He went on to state:

> This may be observed both in the curricula, with classes in "life-adjustment", "group living" and "social integration", and in the studied effort to teach pupils how to "get along" with their fellows .... Promotion by talent or competitive examination has almost everywhere given way to "social promotion" by age-groups, lest the brilliant child be encouraged to be too ambitious, and the stupid child depressed by open proof of his inferiority" (Crosland 1956, p. 158).

It is not clear whether the future promoter of the comprehensive school movement in Britain wholly approved of this emphasis on socialisation at the expense of individual ambition. He simply observed that the "marked tendency to suppress idiosyncrasies" and the "close behavioural conformity" which he he had discerned in the States were in striking contrast with the usual picture of American society as dominated by "ruthless, masterful ambition", and a "reckless, self-regarding individualism". The Socialist in Crosland had little patience with the ugly face of capitalism. But, between the teaching of social skills and the fostering of conformity on the one hand, and encouragement to competition and individual scholastic success on the other, where was his own preference? Or could there be a middle way between the two? Was one condemned to sacrifice one goal while pursuing the other? Or was conciliation of the two possible? One thing is certain, however: Crosland, like Conant, stressed the lack of academic ambition only to deplore it. In this sense, they both passed the same judgement.

It is obvious that what is taught in schools, as well as the pedagogical spirit infused in it, cannot be dissociated from the general philosophy of the training of teachers. It was only natural, therefore, that Conant should go on to engage in a close study of how this preparation was conceived. Educators, to choose as broad a term as possible, together with their shared assumptions of what schooling should be like, might be the faulty parts in the machine, if neither structure nor financial management were a problem. This was the background to his *Education of American Teachers*, published in 1963. The early sixties were a period when the ring of the university monopoly had already been closed for about ten years (Judge 1991, pp. 37-55). Completion of the long process did not mean, however, that pure harmony had been achieved within this ring nor that peace prevailed. The warlike metaphors used by Conant in his description of relationships on the campuses clearly point to a clash between two sides: the camp of the professors of science and the humanities pitted against the camp of the professors of education. The former proved to be in the main dismissive of the latter. Studies in education, they often claimed, were anti-intellectual. Many undergraduates shared similar feelings, and looked down on education courses as "Mickey Mouse courses". The area of teacher education also appeared in academic departments as unduly sheltered by "high protective tariff walls": as state requirements made it necessary to gain certification before getting into teaching, SCDEs could not be bypassed, and prospective teachers had become their hostages. Professors of education, naturally enough, were prompt to disclaim such charges and to assert their exclusive professional competence in their own field. Such mistrust and conflicts seem to occur whenever and wherever teacher education finds itself in close contact with higher education.

Within the world of teacher education, layers of personnel and faculty shared the function of guarding the gates to the profession: as we have seen, they had over the years acquired a large measure of autonomy, and it was possible in the 1960s to see them as making up a whole "educational establishment". They were organised administrators, State Education Department staff, classroom teachers, professors of education, parent–teacher associations' executive personnel, school board associations, all having formal or informal ties with the influential NEA. Within such a mixed group, representing different levels of authority and responsibility, tensions and frictions were perhaps inevitable. But the cement that held it together was the common task of determining the conditions of certification. In a manner uncharacteristic of a scholar steeped in traditional academic culture, Conant refused to lay the blame for what was wrong with teacher training at the door of this educational establishment. Faults could be found, but on the whole, in most of the states, the group had responded to public concern about education. As in the case of the school system as a whole, he expressed little concern regarding the institutional set-up, or the professional group which operated within it. Academic professors were wrong to believe that education professors were a dangerous species. Teacher training, under the control and guidance of the educational establishment, was in relatively safe hands. It was the gap between prescription and practice, the letter of the regulations and their actual implementation, which created a problem. It was the case of right conceptions gone awry. Conant was not a revolutionary. But when it came to the concrete details of the contents of education courses, he could prove to be an iconoclast. What tolerance and indulgence he had so far manifested in his book suddenly gave way to an extremely severe judgement on the quality of teacher training: "The layman cannot know, without special inquiry, that pupils are taught by a teacher specifically prepared and certified to teach on that grade level or in that subject" (Conant 1963, p. 56). Why and how had the system, though not basically flawed, been distorted to the point of leaving so much room for doubts on the real professional expertise of American teachers? Why such alleged discrepancy between the training that was offered and the classroom responsibilities actually assumed by these teachers?

Conant singled out three basic flaws: modes of course accreditation, ignorance of certification requirements, and the selection together with the preparation of prospective teachers.

In the case of accreditation, the role of NCATE, set up less than ten years before, was severely criticised. It was seen as a private, voluntary group which exercised too much power in the field. Besides, its membership was not well balanced. Greater diversification was sorely needed: the NEA had been given most of the seats on the Council, while there was serious under-representation of the academic subjects as well as of the lay public. NCATE was in a sense too parochial, too restricted to a small section of the professional world, and too impervious to outside, lay influence. It seems that Conant had not wished to antagonise the educational establishment and had preferred to approach it with gentle delicacy. But his impatience with NCATE was nonetheless an overt criticism of the misuse of excessive professional autonomy, the danger being that the group's self-interest might in the end prevail over public welfare. Or in other words, that all those who gravitated around teacher education ran the permanent risk of cutting themselves off from other groups which should have been their natural partners and were just as seriously interested in the quality of education and teacher preparation.

The wisdom of the day was that certification requirements had represented a welcome improvement in this field. Genuine professions need fixed rules setting approved standards for entry. But it was common knowledge that, in times of teacher shortages, these requirements were all too easily circumvented, so that incompetent and inexperienced teachers were hired and allowed to practice in classrooms. Unless tougher measures were taken, teaching would be regarded as less than a profession, and its social status would remain notably inferior to that enjoyed by lawyers or doctors: it was a poor reflection on training institutions if hiring authorities could without demur offer similar appointments to people who had been prepared by them and those who had not. This was riding roughshod over the notion of professional competence. Teacher educators were not to be allowed, however, to get off scot-free.

The selection and preparation of student teachers were the responsibility of SCDEs: here was a field ripe for improvement. Raising the status of teacher education began at the very door of the SCDEs. Not enough attention was being paid to the academic levels of intellectual ability of the new entrants. Higher minimum standards before entry into teacher training should be imposed. The desirable levels of attainment, especially in terms of standardised test scores, had been known to bob up and down periodically and among the training institutions themselves. Conant's requirements were ambitious: his suggestion was that only the upper third of a graduating high school class should be allowed to come into teacher education. In addition to this, he stressed the need for entrants to have accomplished a specified length of study in three basic disciplines: English, mathematics and foreign languages.

The preparation of future teachers was certainly the most sensitive area of analysis and it is here that criticisms proved to be the most devastating. Methods courses, designed to instil and develop teaching skills, were found to be utterly inadequate or pointless: in a word, "terrible". Foundations courses were just as summarily dismissed, consisting as they did in "patching together scraps of history, philosophy, political theory, sociology and pedagogical ideology", and being more often than not taught by professors "frequently not well trained in any one of the parent disciplines" (Conant 1963, ch. 7). For that reason, the philosophy, history and sociology of education should be taught by "real" philosophers, historians and sociologists, approved by their respective subject departments. In the meantime, it would be wise simply to eliminate those methods or foundations courses which gave education departments a bad name.

Finally, practice teaching was also seen as a weak spot. While this is a key element in the professional training of a teacher, its supervision and assessment were notably inadequate, being all too often left in the hands of junior faculty and teaching assistants. This prompted Conant to put forward one of his most interesting and controversial recommendations: the creation in SCDEs of a new category of "clinical professors", a term obviously borrowed from medical schools. The special area of responsibility for clinical professors was essentially to be the supervision and assessment of teaching practice. Because genuine professional expertise in the classroom was needed, they would have to be excellent school teachers, hired and promoted as full-fledged professors, and required from time to time to return to their teaching activities in an elementary or secondary school. Unlike other professors, they need not hold a PhD degree, nor do research and publish papers as there was a risk here that they might cut themselves off from their work in schools. Once their quality as superb teachers of children and skilled trainers of college students had been officially recognised by their peers, they were entitled to receive the same salary as any other professor in the institution.

It is not difficult to see how this bold proposal challenged both the in-built hierarchies prevailing in the academic profession and the status within a university context of research (which ceased to be in this special case a necessary condition of appointment). These are potent enough reasons to explain why in none of our three countries have excellent classroom teachers been elevated overnight to the status and salary level of academic professors. Supervision of teaching practice and professional advice to teacher trainees, of however high a quality, have never been seen as of equal value with research activities and production of knowledge. There are of course notable exceptions on both sides of the Atlantic, but scholars and practitioners are seldom seen to be working in close association. And yet the fundamental concern behind Conant's recommendation cannot be ignored. The issue of the close connection between what effectively goes on in schools and the type of courses offered at college level is an essential factor in the quality of teacher education. The art of surgery is taught to would-be surgeons by professional, clinical practitioners, not by doctors remote or removed from the operating table. It is not certain that this simple, commonsense rule is so easily applied in teacher education.

Conant's book remains an excellent guide to the state of teacher education in America in 1963. The tone was never polemical; the author reflected many of the basic, common attitudes prevailing not only among the profession but in the nation at large. There was little dissatisfaction with the historical development of the education system: it had been built up by and for the communities, was in the main supported by them, and had been opened up to progressively larger sections of the population. In a word, it symbolized the ideal of American democracy. The trouble was that schools had been allowed to place less emphasis on academic pursuits, and the nation was therefore slipping behind its powerful rival, the USSR, in science and technology, the determinants of economic and strategic superiority. The solution lay in toughening up the curriculum and setting the academic youth to earnest scholarly work. In order to achieve this recovery and recapture a truly enterprising spirit, schools needed a reinvigorated teacher force. The appeal therefore was to SCDEs to review their strategies, in terms of levels of student intake, recruitment of competent faculty, quality of courses. Hiring authorities were also requested to take on well-trained teaching staff. But once again the institutional set-up was not seriously called in question.

The second critique of teacher education to appear in 1963 was Koerner's *Miseducation of Teachers*. Where Conant was careful not to hurt his colleagues' feelings, Koerner spoke with deliberate bluntness. The mild, wise censor is replaced by an angry, bitter protestor. Though Koerner's book is often quoted in American studies of teacher education, little attention has been paid to the fact that the preface had been written by a former official, Sterling M. McMurrin, who had been US Commissioner of Education. His introductory words set the tone for the whole book: they are harsh, polemical and uncompromising. He, like so many other critics, regrets the prevailing anti-intellectual attitude which has for over half a century characterised schooling in America, and laments the low esteem in which the teaching profession is commonly held; he goes further to openly deplore what he calls the "doctrinaire egalitarianism" pervading the whole system of education. As we shall see, Conant and Koerner shared many common views, and their prescriptions for the improvement of teacher training often coincided to a remarkable degree. But it has seldom been noticed that on the issue of egalitarianism in schools they fundamentally disagreed. Conant would never have accepted a preface containing such strictures on the high school system.

Even if the emphasis laid in 1963 on high schools as places meant to accommodate all the youth of the community did reflect the widely accepted wisdom, minority views like McMurrin's cannot be overlooked. They demonstrate that consensus was not absolute. Conant and Koerner viewed the world of teacher education in radically different ways, the former taking a fairly benign view of the educational establishment whereas the latter had a much more jaundiced vision of the same reality. Teacher education had in his view become by 1963 excessively big business: 1,150 institutions, 20,000 full-time faculty members, 143,000 BA degrees awarded yearly (one third of all degrees in the States), an inordinate number of MA degrees (half the total), from 1,500 to 2,000 PhDs each year. To a European, these figures in the early sixties, even after allowing for differences in scope and size between nations, were astronomical. Although himself an American, Koerner felt they had grown out of proportion. The optimistic view was that teacher education had reached maturity, and proved itself to be an attractive area of higher education study. Koerner did not agree and asserted that it "had grown too large, too fast on too slippery a foundation" (Koerner 1963, p.23).

Excess in growth and quantity was parallelled by depression in quality. Teacher preparation showed multiple signs of intellectual impoverishment. Like Conant, Koerner had a poor opinion of education courses, either in their methods or foundations aspects. "Coursework in education", he wrote, "deserves its ill-repute. It is most often puerile, repetitious, dull and ambiguous". He was just as scathing about teacher educators. "The inferior intellectual quality of the education faculty", he went on to comment, "is the fundamental limitation in the field" (Koerner 1963, pp. 17,18). Distrusting teacher educators as deeply as he did, he was bound to be dismissive of NCATE, which he saw as an "academic cartel", virtually in the hands of the NEA, wielding coercive and abusive power. It was examining what went into training programmes, but showed no concern for what was coming out: the process through which the product was manufactured seemed to matter a great deal more than the quality of the finished product itself.

Occasionally, Koerner tempers his general dissatisfaction with more than a tinge of humour, so that his book becomes at times a source of great fun. The list which he draws of PhD and EdD subjects verges on the burlesque while another extremely derisive and amusing passage in the book concerns the professional jargon, renamed "educanto". Koerner undoubtedly pours too much scorn on the profession of teacher educators and on the work carried out in SCDEs for his strictures to be wholly accepted by the reader. Hostile prejudice seeps through all the pages of the book. This is why, by comparison, Conant's analysis seems today to carry more weight and to be more convincing: a much more charitable mind was at work, with a sense of fairness and a grasp which Koerner lacked of the more delicate issues. Yet the latter's contribution cannot simply be regarded as the work of some bizarre, bilious and disgruntled academic. By tradition and conviction, historians have consistently taken him seriously. His views in 1963 had much in common with Conant's.

Conant and Koerner agreed on the selection of entrants into teacher training and the nature of their preparation. Both insist that admissions levels should be raised. Both think that education courses take up too much of the time of the students, who would be better advised to undergo a proper liberal training, with greater emphasis on academic disciplines. Prospective secondary school teachers, in particular, should be required to possess a much more adequate grasp of their subject. Methods courses are condemned by both. The modes of assessment applied in teacher training were ripe for revision. Koerner perhaps had more to say on this and found the national teacher examinations currently in use in the main ill-conceived and ill-devised. Like others after him, he called for stricter methods for assessing the competence of student teachers. His preference was for formal, written, essay-type examinations as in the case of medicine or law. "Teaching is perhaps the only field that claims professional status", he wrote, "without having professional qualifying examinations of any kind at any level" (Koerner 1963, p. 258).

Undergraduate majors in education should be eliminated. Koerner and Conant were in this area in total agreement: they wanted less pedagogy, fewer educational course requirements, and more depth in the study of an academic discipline. For Koerner "depth in the teaching field is always to be preferred to a broadened general education". Unlike the more mild-tempered Conant, Koerner in the end snapped: "a weak faculty operates a weak program that attracts weak students" (Koerner 1963, pp. 273, 242).

The testimonies left to us by Conant and Koerner provide a disquieting image of teacher education in the United States in 1963. But hindsight, enriched perhaps by observation from outside which adds another form of distance, may help us today to take a more sober, and less sombre, perspective. Teacher education could be judged so harshly by two outstanding academics only because it had moved into the area of higher education. Had it remained at a further remove from the world of the universities where intellectual demands are strongest, it might simply have been ignored and left to its own devices on its solitary island. No doubt it would have been less exposed to the tempestuous protests blowing from the skies of academia In a sense, teacher education in 1963 was being made to suffer for the progress it had been making for several decades. Now that it had acquired higher status, produced a growing volume of research, and set itself more ambitious goals, it was natural that it should come under the stern, cold gaze of scholars.

Nowhere is there the slightest suggestion that teacher training should be as in the past offered in specialised, isolated institutions. On the contrary: the first recommendation made by Koerner insists that the remaining teachers' colleges should either be shut down or converted into general purpose institutions. By proposing the creation of chairs for "clinical professors", Conant, on the other hand, made it clear that he wished to see closer co-operation and still further integration, and did not envisage separation or divorce. Finally, both insisted on a radical revamping of curricula, with more stringent demands on academic training for student teachers: in this sense, they expressed a wish for more links with the liberal arts, not less.

The topics raised thirty years ago are still on the agenda: admissions levels, balance of academic and education courses, in depth versus in breadth programmes, requirements for licensure and certification, the proper status of research in education. They provide the natural background to a permanent debate.

CHAPTER 5

The United States: since 1963

The landscape of teacher education in the United States would, in the 1990s, appear much more familiar to anyone that had surveyed it in the 1960s than would be the case in France or Britain. The reason for this difference is quite simple: thirty years ago in America, an institutional process had just been completed. The other two countries, by comparison, were still only half way there since the preparation of prospective primary school teachers was kept at a certain remove from higher education. It is not surprising that the period is much more eventful on the European side of the Atlantic.

A description of preservice teacher education in a document issued by the American Department of Education in the late 1980s will easily prove the point (USDE 1990). The whole of teacher training is described as being at the higher education level, and provided in public as well as private universities which have departments, schools or colleges of education. SCDEs are also to be found in those institutions which during the past few decades have developed from state normal (teachers) schools into state colleges. Candidates for teacher education programmes must normally have completed one or two years of college undergraduate study. They are then accepted into teacher education programmes on the basis of their college academic records and interviews. The minimum requirement for teaching on the elementary and secondary level in any of the fifty states is the bachelor's degree. All these features and requirements were already in place in 1963. The document refers directly to the familiar practice for hiring teachers which had so angered Koerner: an increasing number of states are trying to meet the growing demand for competent teachers by offering "alternative certification methods". All too often these alternative methods offer training on the cheap when recruitment of teachers is a matter of urgency.

Programme descriptions may vary in detail, but not in essence: most teacher training occurs in 4-year programmes. In most elementary teacher programmes, the core professional studies curriculum consists of an average of 45% theory and 55% methods. This pattern is reversed in secondary programmes, which average 56% theory and 44% methods. Although the "ideal" proportion of theory and methods in professional studies has been a subject for debate, most agree that theory and methods should be, and frequently are, fully integrated in all education courses. The official requirements for teaching practice are, similarly, couched in terms which provide a minimal definition: all states require, the document says, that future teachers have full-time student-teaching experience in a public school classroom, under the supervision of an experienced teacher approved by the college or university teacher education programme in which the students are enrolled. Finally, licensure or certification are defined as being the responsibility of each state: the certification of teachers in certain subjects or at certain levels is regulated by an agency in each state which issues a certificate licensing to teach once its requirements are fulfilled.

Such then are the basic facts, and they suggest that preservice teacher education in America had reached a remarkable state of equilibrium. The metaphor should not be misconstrued, however. It does not necessarily mean that all was well, since any state of equilibrium represents a balance of opposing forces, pulls and tensions of equal magnitude: equilibrium is the result of a permanent struggle and implies conflict. Reading the literature written on teacher education since 1963 amply confirms this. The national mood, and especially since 1983, has tended to be one of gloom and criticism.

Disquietude and anxiety about the quality of public education and teacher preparation in that order became vocal during the Reagan administration. The key year was 1983. It saw a sudden outpouring of reports and writings expressing dissatisfaction, if not dismay, over the low standards of American schools. This soon bred a sense that the educational world was in a state of deep crisis: so many doctors around the patient's bed, all attempting to diagnose the illness and to prescribe the cures, were a visible token – for they could hardly all be wrong – that disease had effectively struck. As in 1963, some dire warnings were issued by outstanding academics speaking in their own name. Diane Ravitch's remarkable *Troubled Crusade*, which explores the cycles of educational reform since World War Two, is an example of this type of critical study (Ravitch 1983). But most contributions in 1983 were collaborative, collective efforts. They assumed the shape of analytical and prescriptive reports and all pointed, in their very titles, to the urgent need of improving standards in schools to meet the challenge of the next two decades before the twenty-first century. Before paying special attention to the message which they collectively conveyed and attempting to decipher its meaning, we must however look more closely, below the surface, at the fundamental and sometimes hidden features of American teacher education, at least as they are perceived by an outsider.

Three basic characteristics may be identified. First, despite all the common traits which have just been underlined, it is impossible to describe the whole area of teacher education as a fully integrated, articulated system. It will be argued that it is in fact a non-system. Second, the institutional diversity and heterogeneity go hand in hand with a widely shared feeling of uncertainty. Unlike medicine, law or many other key professions, teaching and teacher education present a blurred image. This is due mainly to the fact that most of the criteria that serve as emblems of a genuine profession, with a strong academic grounding, are only partially satisfied. Hence much of the uneasiness and uncertainty. Third, an attempt to understand what in America has come to be accepted as the underlying purpose of schooling and teacher training will suggest that, faced with the choice between the academic insistence on scholarship and the social function of schooling, or between the subject-centred and the student-centred types of approach, American teachers and teacher educators have consistently preferred the second option. To put it more bluntly, they have put the heart over the head.

A Non-System?

That the notion of "system" cannot be applied to teacher education (or indeed to higher education as a whole), becomes self-evident when the simplest definition of the word is considered: a whole composed of parts in orderly arrangement according to some scheme or plan. A visitor to SCDEs is often struck by a sense of purpose or dedication, but it is hard to find either order, scheme or plan at the regional, let alone at the national level. This is a particularly striking feature for a European, and especially perhaps a Frenchman, who has been accustomed to see a managed rather than a market system operating, with the central government more or less firmly in control and playing, to a varying degree, an interventionist role. In Europe, the training of teachers destined to serve in the nation's schools is as a rule the responsibility of the State, that is to say of the Government: it is increasingly the case in Britain, for example, and it remains the key feature of the French system. Not so in America where the Federal government does not interfere in the least with teacher education: it does not decide where it is to be provided and has nothing to say about methods, content, certification or licensure. The Federal intervention in the world of education to desegregate schools, promote civil rights, help ethnic minorities and fight President Johnson's war on poverty set off a series of bold political initiatives, but was not followed by any action aimed at reforming teacher training; no national guidelines were ever issued to steer it towards the new goals which had been set for the schools. The States and the SCDEs were left free to decide whether new courses and revised programmes should be elaborated to cope with the sweeping reforms introduced in the education system.

Complexity is the reality that strikes a foreigner exploring the territory of teacher education. The acronym SCDE does not refer to units of roughly similar size and function but conceals great institutional diversity: American teachers can be trained in very small departments with just a handful of educators as well as in huge places which turn them out in their hundreds. Between the tiny workshops on the one hand and the massive factories on the other, almost every variety of teacher training institution can be found among the 1,300 in existence. They differ from their remote English and French cousins on every possible dimension. Many of them are private. Whether private or public, they may be very large or tiny. Whatever their legal status they may be entirely undergraduate institutions, or have strong graduate schools. Little or nothing is revealed by their names: a university with the prefix "State" might be essentially a local institution of modest ambitions or a prestigious international establishment with all the glamour of one of the great private universities. Even the distinction between public and private is slippery, since many public universities enjoy large incomes from private sources while the most famous private institutions draw much of their funding from such public sources as the federal government itself or research bodies. The point is that there is no simple categorisation: even the sub-categories are elusive, and this fact explains much of the resilience and vigour of the system. In this market culture nothing is fixed, and everything may go up or down without any attempt at central direction being made.

A logical corollary of this institutional diversity, over which no hand visible or invisible exercises any real control, is the professional autonomy of those committed to making the whole thing work. This autonomy enjoyed by teacher educators and SCDEs is gained partly by default: on campus, it is not disputed – although it may be occasionally deplored – by academic departments which often prefer to ignore them. The total lack of Federal involvement (but not concern) in the preparation of teachers means that teacher educators are bound by no over-arching national constraints, rules and guidelines. Administrative or bureaucratic control of the kind which Ministries of Education exercise in other countries does not obtain in America. At the other end of the spectrum local communities and their school boards, are hardly involved at all. This professional autonomy is guaranteed and protected by the voluntary nature of whatever submission there may be to national modes of assessment. SCDEs are surely well advised, as a general yet not absolute rule, to seek NCATE accreditation, but they cannot be compelled by any authority to do so. Each individual State can of course impose its own regulations for the accreditation of courses and licensure of teachers. As we shall see, there have been well-known cases of strong State involvement when preparation of teachers was deemed to be inadequate, and the balance between academic and education courses unduly tilted in favour of the latter. But however significant this may undoubtedly be, and whatever unease or wrath it may have caused in SCDEs, such strong State intervention has not become a nation-wide phenomenon. It is also hard to say whether it will remain a permanent feature. The professional autonomy of SCDEs in the United States therefore appears to be far less circumscribed than in Britain today or in France at all times. This is not to say that all is comfortable: less control or direction from above means more responsibility, and especially more efforts to survive in the market place. SCDEs need to attract students and money. They also need to appear to be doing their job properly or to serve a truly useful function: closure on a University President's decision is never too remote a possibility.

Teacher education in America appears at first sight to be made up of an odd assortment of parts of all shapes and sizes very loosely articulated. Such heterogeneity can be blamed or praised: the nature of the judgement very much depends, in the end, on the cultural values of those who pass it. When strong homogeneous national systems are implicitly taken as the norm, the American scene looks pretty messy. When, on the other hand, the extreme variety of human experience and local circumstances is taken into account and given pride of place, it is more legitimate to see such apparent chaos as the reflection of a reality which, by its very nature, is always complex, diverse and polymorphic. The American culture, moulded as it has been by the liberal economic creed of laissez-faire, is apt to find the second version more congenial. While there are undoubtedly good reasons for this placid acceptance of heterogeneity in preference to a form of artificial order that might be imposed from above, attempts have been made to alleviate some of the worst effects of the non-system. First, efforts have been made to provide some kind of national backbone to teacher education. Second, at the State level, politicians and administrators have on occasion interfered with the education professionals' autonomy and issued stricter guidelines for teacher training. Third, the relatively recent move towards the creation of professional development schools can similarly be interpreted as an attempt to stimulate collaboration between SCDEs, academic departments and the world of schools, or in other words provide smooth articulation between units which until then were not systematically involved in a common enterprise.

At national level, two main types of voluntary initiative can be identified as an attempt to provide some broad safeguards. One is the ongoing work produced by NCATE for the accreditation of teacher training institutions. The other is the decision made, in the wake of the Carnegie report in 1986, to set up a National Board for Professional Teaching Standards. Enhancing the quality of teacher education and raising the standards of competence of teachers are their common goals.

NCATE defines itself as a mechanism for voluntary peer regulation of the professional unit – the school, college, or department primarily responsible for the preparation of teachers and other professional education personnel. One part at least of this role definition, from a contrastive perspective, seems quite obvious: institutions whose role is to prepare teachers and other school staff need to have their work watched over by some outside, superior authority. "Regulation" of a kind there must be. The original characteristic of NCATE, therefore, is not to be found in the substantive, but in the qualifying epithets: voluntary, peer regulation. No institution is forced to submit itself to NCATE's review process of accreditation – less than half of existing teacher training units in fact do so. Those that do not wish to apply fall roughly into two categories: a few, in prestigious research universities, feel superior as they do not need NCATE's stamp of approval as a guarantee of quality; but many others simply know that they would fail the test and would not meet NCATE's requirements, and to the humiliation which this would entail, they prefer abstention. Applying for NCATE's review for accreditation is therefore a purely voluntary exercise.

"Peer" holds another surprise in store for a foreign observer. Unlike in France, where the State has consistently called the tune, and unlike in Great Britain, where recent reforms in education have also now placed teacher training under the firm governance of central power, accreditation in the United States is the responsibility of an autonomous, non-governmental organisation largely made up of members of the profession. In a well-coined statement, NCATE describes its work as "a process by which the profession of education declares its expectations for professional education and applies these expectations to units"(NCATE 1993). A glance at its constituent groups indeed reveals that control of NCATE is in large measure in the hands of the profession: teacher educators through the AACTE (American Association of Colleges for Teacher Education); classroom teachers through the two national professional associations, the NEA (National Education Association), which has been a member since the foundation of NCATE in 1954, and the AFT (American Federation of Teachers), a newcomer which joined only in the late 1980s; professional specialty organisations, representing the disciplinary areas. These three groups – educators, classroom and specialist teachers – outnumber the fourth, made up of State and local policymakers (Council of Chief State School Officers and National School Board Association).

In purely formal terms, NCATE wields little authority. Its role should not be confused with that fulfilled by individual States. Their stamp of approval assumes a very different meaning: all institutions need it in order for their graduates to be licensed to teach. Without it, they would have to go out of business. The significance of NCATE's national accreditation is of another order: it provides peer recognition, as the guarantee of the professional worth of what the teacher training unit actually does. Denial of accreditation does not mean closure. But it is surely a blemish on the character, reputation, and ability to attract students, of the unit concerned, all the more so as some States not only accept and use NCATE recognition but are becoming quite keen to hand over their responsibility for programme accreditation to this national professional body through a system of partnership.

NCATE went through a difficult, troubled period from the late 1970s to the mid-1980s, and the denial rate for accreditation was precisely part of the problem. When it starts bobbing up and down as it did twenty years ago, it may well be the sign that the accreditation body itself is becoming unsure of its own standards: a denial rate of less than 5 percent in the mid-70s shot up to 25 percent in 1978 and plummeted down to 5 percent again in 1979 and similar movements were registered in the early 1980s. Such alternate periods of leniency and stringency were taken to mean that it was the thermometer rather than the patient that presented problems. NCATE, whose influence began to wane in the process, consequently went through a period of self-examination, overhaul and redesign. After some drastic structural changes and especially the adoption of new more rigorous standards focusing on the knowledge base for programmes, NCATE appeared to have recovered in health and influence in the early 1990s. This should be good news for teacher education as a whole.

Another response at national level has stemmed from the Carnegie Forum and its call for the creation of a National Board for Professional Teaching Standards. This Board is responsible both for setting up high standards for what experienced (though not beginning) teachers need to know and be able to do and for certifying teachers who have shown ability to meet those standards. For the first time therefore in the history of teacher preparation in America, there will emerge a group of nationally certified teachers. Can this be interpreted as a first step towards further centralization of teacher training? Is this the beginning of a radically new evolution? On present trends, no. The national certification is intended to be purely voluntary and has been conceived not to replace but complement the system of state certification and licensing of teachers. The status quo is slightly altered, but it is by no means upset. The change has been met with general approval and is likely to enhance the image of the profession.

Moreover, some new ideas are being currently developed from this central notion of a national Board. Clifford and Guthrie have for example suggested that, within its overall framework, new modes of assessment should be introduced (Clifford & Guthrie, 1988). They believe that the current tradition of appraising programmes of teacher education should be phased out and that instead emphasis should be laid on assessing individual candidates wishing to join the teaching profession. The new form of appraisal, as they see it, would be carried out in two stages. The candidate's subject-matter knowledge would be tested and then his or her ability to perform as a teacher would be assessed. This can be done by setting written examinations, or by resorting to oral interviews, case analysis and problem-solving exercises. To a French observer the scheme sounds of course very familiar for it bears a striking resemblance to the system obtaining in France where candidates for the teaching profession, either at the primary or the secondary level, are selected on the basis both of their academic knowledge and a prediction of their professional competence. The importance of the shift which this proposal entails should not be underestimated: the talent of individual candidates, and not simply the description or coherence of courses, would now become the yardstick. It might well be the natural evolution of any upgrading of education studies through insistence on an academic major and a fifth-year programme.

State involvement in teacher education is not a clear-cut affair. There have always been great variations of attitude from State to State. Some, like New York, Florida, California and the Southern States, are more interventionist than others, for example those in New England. This inevitably baffles European visitors, who seek for generalisations. Although no unity or overarching single purpose binds the fifty States, it may be worthwhile to seek to identify some main trends. One can be traced back to the mid-1980s, in the wake of the reports which drew national attention to the

127

weaknesses of schooling and teacher preparation: some States have sought to exercise tighter control over teacher training. Another trend is that States have on the whole insisted on a more secure knowledge base for student teachers. This has meant requiring SCDEs to whittle down their professional courses and toughen up academic training.

One example of this can be found in recent decisions made by the State of Virginia. The story of the sudden imposition by the State of new rules for teacher preparation has been elaborately told by Philip Tate and James Cooper, then Dean of the School of Education at the University of Virginia (Cooper & Tate, 1992). It relates how reform of teacher training was forced upon recalcitrant yet passive teacher educators by the Governor and State officials, displeased with the way public school teachers were being prepared. They had been warned by experts that not enough emphasis was being placed on the instruction of prospective teachers in the basic subjects. The Commonwealth of Virginia therefore issued regulations requiring that all future elementary and not only secondary teachers should major in an arts or science subject, thus eliminating education majors which were thought to be too weak in content. Inspectors and investigators had also been convinced that too many professional courses were a waste of time. This led to the rule that education courses should be assigned a strict limit of eighteen hours per semester. State reformers argued that the time thus gained would be better employed in undertaking additional field practice, preparing for an academic major and acquiring a better background in general studies. The shift of emphasis towards the acquisition of knowledge and away from traditional "methods" and "foundations" is an apt illustration of the type of reform which has so often been advocated in the past thirty years by an army of experts, speaking in their own names, or in a chorus. Texas would, like Virginia, provide another excellent example of the same trend, with the State imposing tougher rules on SCDEs and redressing the balance between academic and professional studies.

Although the American system of education has been built from the ground upwards so that local control and accountability remain its hallmark, school districts and their school boards have not attempted seriously to involve themselves in the preparation of the teachers whom they employ. Although some collaboration with the teacher training institutions does of course exist, it is largely confined to matters relating to field practice for student teachers. During the past decade, a great deal of attention has been focused on the cooperation of the schools themselves and SCDEs. It is now widely argued that the present ad hoc arrangements should give way to much closer and more functional collaboration. The deans of the Holmes Group have been the most vocal in justifying this new form of partnership and in devising ways of implementing it. The Group defined itself in 1990 as "a consortium of nearly one hundred American research universities" which incorporated in 1986 "to enhance the quality of schooling, though research and development and the preparation of career professionals in teaching "

(Holmes Group 1990, p.vii). One of their basic purposes is to create bonds between universities and schools and to secure a genuine partnership among peers and not a top-down type of relationship. Their scheme for professional development schools will mean, if it develops into a movement with real momentum, that SCDEs will draw elementary and secondary schools into a collaborative alliance with themselves, as well as the academic departments in colleges and universities. As terminology is more easily bent into shape than reality, the Holmes Group speak, in *Tomorrow's Schools*, of involving the "university faculty": the term is explicitly meant to include both arts and sciences professors and education school professors, as if their partnership was expected to be, against all odds, a natural development. Although many will find such an anticipation excessively optimistic, the spokespersons for the Group must assume the existence of a united university front.

Once the notion has been accepted that a united university faculty will be at work, what role does the new collaboration imply for the schools themselves? The answer lies in two truly revolutionary developments. One is that, through the setting up of professional development schools, all sides will agree to work together: head teachers, deans, academic and education professors and all the school teachers. This would represent a revolution in the mentalities of the persons concerned. A lot of ice will have to be broken, and many corporate prejudices and jealousies will have to melt. The second development is that, once common energies have been mustered, all should invent a new organizational structure like restructuring current big schools, thought to be the plague of American education, into smaller, more humanly manageable units. Greater involvement of schools in the preparation of teachers will, in the opinion of the Holmes Group, also call for a differentiated hierarchy among the school faculty: senior (or "career professional") teachers will take leadership in instructional planning, curriculum, research, and teaching teachers; the monitoring of students will be provided at the middle level by "professional teachers"; the lower level will be occupied by younger colleagues (simply called "instructors") who will still be working under supervision before they meet the full requirements for professional licensure.

A more sharply differentiated teaching force within the schools, with its generals, lieutenants and infantry, is expected to cure the present evil of a relatively "flat" profession, which discourages ambition only to be fulfilled, as a rule, by quitting teaching and taking on administrative responsibilities. In teaching, moving up nearly always means moving out. Prospects of promotion and enhanced status would certainly help to change attitudes. The creation of an elite category of teachers would have an additional advantage: the Holmes Group wishes to see them involving themselves in research conducted in joint projects with university faculty. Such collaboration would not be totally new in America, where numerous examples can be given of research being carried out by a close partnership between academics and school faculty. The novelty with the Holmes Group's proposal is that this is expected to be a systematic activity in the professional development schools.

It is clear by now that nothing short of a revolution is required for this ambitious collaborative scheme ever to expand. Some serious difficulties have been identified which the Holmes Group has preferred to gloss over. Others, on the contrary, have remained very much present in the minds of the deans, who have suggested ways of addressing the problems which they raise. The issue of research is central in the proposed sustained involvement of university faculty in work dealing with schools. Academic tradition sets little store by action-research. Unless this is broken, it will prove difficult to draw university professors into partnership in joint research projects as they are more than likely to feel that their chances of promotion, visibility and improved salary will be blighted. The Holmes Group's response to this does not offer immediate comfort. It is in fact a plea for academics and presidents to change the existing rules, roles, relationships and reward systems within colleges and universities. This is an interesting element in our examination of the issue of teacher preparation set in a university context: improvement in the former cannot be achieved without deep cultural changes in the latter, with the full-hearted consent of academics. Will teacher education, it may be asked at this stage, ever be taken seriously enough to be used as a lever for cultural change of such magnitude in universities?

The second difficulty identified by the Holmes Group seems, on the other hand, much easier to tackle. This is mainly because it is solely the responsibility of teacher educators and school faculty and concerns supervision of teaching practice. This is a time-consuming, unexciting task with few rewards. By long tradition, SCDEs have relied extensively on graduate students and non-tenured staff to do such work. In the new scheme, such ad hoc arrangements will be phased out. Teaching practice will become part and parcel of the new collaborative approach, involving closer contacts between student teachers, SCDE and school faculty.

It is impossible to say whether the deans of the Holmes Group will, within the profession itself and on the campuses, be able to exert sufficient leverage to set their revolution in motion. They were late in 1994 still in the process of identifying the scope and extent of the changes required. Reform of teacher training and redirection of schooling should be accompanied, they were beginning to claim, by a root-and-branch transformation of schools of education. How long will all this take, and what is the force that will impel such thorough change? Meanwhile some effects of the influence of the Group can be detected in the move, in a number of SCDEs, towards the setting up of five-year programmes and the elimination of education majors so that teacher preparation ceases to be a merely undergraduate activity and becomes a more serious enterprise. The Holmes Group should not however be appraised simply in terms of its agenda for practical reform. Seen from outside, it appears to be addressing an ideological message to the nation: it is fighting on the side of democracy and equity with the firm welding together of the two notions and it summons up vast resources of goodwill and understanding. More fundamentally therefore, the question is also whether the ideological assumptions underpinning the whole enterprise stand any chance of being widely shared and whether there exist reserves of sympathy for education large enough to persuade people and institutions readily to agree to change their traditions, conceptions and attitudes.

More than one hundred institutions have joined the Holmes Group and engaged in reforms along the lines which it advocates. No overriding authority guides them all, nor makes them march in step. Local initiative, manpower, needs, resources and constraints again play into the hands of diversity. Any account of the implementation of Holmes Group-inspired reforms is bound to be a motley accumulation of isolated experiments. Some depth here will be preferable to excessive breadth. This is why I have chosen to report in some detail on personal observations made at the Louisiana State University on the early efforts to restructure teacher preparation according to the new spirit of the day. The context of LSU was obviously unique but more important than details and particulars of implementation are the guiding principles: how, in effect, did they inspire the reforms? All the literature and the talk on the subject are embedded in the semantic fields of "collaboration", "cooperation", "partnership" as well as "involvement", "exchange" and "dialogue". These are the key or buzz words. The recurrence of "together", "with each other", "in teams" is so frequent as to provide the dominant stylistic feature of both the written texts and the oral discussions. The new role assigned to the College of Education at LSU is to work actively with other colleges on campus and with local schools. It must be seen to create incentives for school teachers and university professors to work together. This is the conceptual framework, or basic act of faith.

All faiths need places of worship. The new university and school collaborations likewise call for novel sites: the professional development schools fulfil this function as "school–university partnerships". Interestingly enough, much more is said on the relationships to be built up between the College of Education and the future professional development schools and their faculty than between the College and academic departments. No hasty conclusion should be drawn from this, but it may be conjectured that, by nature and by tradition, any Education College can and should move faster in the world of schools, which is part of its own hunting ground, than within the neighbouring forest of university departments and colleges.

Detailed prescriptions are therefore given of methods and strategies for enlisting the cooperation of school teachers who will need to think, plan and develop curricula. This is no minor problem. A typical secondary teacher will teach six periods in a seven period day with twenty to thirty students in each class. Secondary teachers are given a single preparation period daily. Elementary teachers, on the other hand, assume full-time responsibility for twenty to thirty children every school day. To all this, extra-duty assignments must be added: bus duty, hall monitoring, lunchroom supervision, attendance of student or parent conferences. If support and cooperation from these teachers are to be secured, release time must therefore be found. This means additional resources, in the form of grants and contributions. In brief, the reform calls for further investment and financial support.

The experienced teachers expected to cooperate and to assume new roles in the new sites will make up the distinct category of the "clinical adjunct faculty" (CAJ). Their work should cover three broad areas: curriculum development and evaluation, consultation and planning with teachers in training and LSU faculty, and pursuit of collaborative research, again with LSU faculty and teachers in training. They have other partners with whom continuous dialogue is a prerequisite: the school administrators. Here, the area of consultation is that of the instructional programs to be enhanced for all children. Finally, clinical adjunct faculty are invited, away from school and on the university campus, to involve themselves in the ongoing course work with student teachers. This constitutes an impressive list of expectations and duties. Classroom teaching, expertise in curricular matters, supervision of teacher trainers, involvement in research, constant dialogue with school heads, participation in education programmes provided on the campus: clinical adjunct faculty find themselves with a heavy burden on their shoulders. It is true that genuine co-operation implies all this flurry of activity. The question remains whether teachers with so many talents will easily be ferreted out, and whether enough release time will be offered for them to come forward with good will. The future of professional development schools depends partly upon the availability of such dedicated, elite faculty and on the amount of resources which will be readily allotted for them to function adequately as a new category of teachers.

Finally, implementation of the Holmes Group's proposals means changing the framework of education courses provided on the campus. The shift towards a five-year programme – one of the key suggestions made by the Holmes Group – is central to the restructuring achieved at the LSU College of Education. Slight differences must be noted, however, according to whether students prepare to teach at elementary or secondary level. The elementary education program is described as a five-year integrated program. It combines a Bachelor of Science degree in elementary education (having the equivalent of a major or minor in an academic subject) and a Master's of Education degree with state certification. The secondary program, on the other hand, is a *fifth-year* program. This means that entering students will hold Bachelors' degrees in fields appropriate to their projected teaching specialisms. An additional requirement is that they meet Graduate School admission standards (currently a 3.0 undergraduate GPA and a 1000 on the GRE). In this fifth year, they study their teaching subject at the graduate level. They also experience the problems of teaching in schools in ways which are simultaneously theoretical and practical or field-based. It is also emphasized that fifth-year students shall be taught by graduate and clinical faculty, rather than by graduate assistants: this is again a strong indicator of change.

The LSU College of Education reforms are unique – the College has to follow its own path given its particular environment and human resources.

But they are also broadly characteristic of the current movement, and they provide a worthwhile pointer to the general direction of the changes being introduced in many institutions. The immediate goals are threefold: to make the education of teachers intellectually more solid, to raise the standards for admission and graduation and to build up connections between the College and the schools. It is a pity J.B.Conant could not live long enough to witness these changes: do they not express the essence of his own prescriptions for improving American teacher education?

The complex character of teacher education in America perceived as a non-system may now be better understood. It results in the main from the interplay of a series of opposite forces. Some are plainly centrifugal, responding to local conditions and market demands, and producing a motley collection of institutions, public and private, large and small, efficient and mediocre, ambitious or listless. Others are distinctly centripetal, converging towards some sort of centre – however uncertain its geometrical position may be: these forces are more often than not generated by a national awareness among the profession or among the great, the good and the wealthy (a characteristically American category) that the amorphous bulk of teacher education must be given a new sense of direction and purpose. Under these conditions, movement can only be slow, uneasy and uncertain.

The Uncertain Profession

Teacher education as a non-system is an observable fact: it is there for anyone to see from the outside. The uncomfortable position of teacher preparation inside higher education, on the other hand, is the favourite, almost obsessive topic tackled by all those who write about it, most of the time as insiders. It was Arthur Powell who, in his remarkable study of the Harvard Graduate School of Education published in 1980, coined the phrase, "the uncertain profession": a fitting description which conveys the sense of collective unease often expressed by the profession (Powell 1980). Some critics have voiced their regret that a return to single-purpose institutions, bent on the training of teachers and nothing else, was impossible. But in teacher educators' conferences today all the talk, stressing as it does collaborative efforts, may partly fulfil a different cathartic function. The insistence on the need to involve all sides – liberal arts departments, SCDEs, classroom teachers, administrators – in a process of working and pulling together, for the preparation of teachers as well as the promotion of relevant research, may be seen as a method for dispelling the fears of isolation, easing the sense of discomfort, and building up a feeling of common endeavour. Professional development schools, in this perspective, are not simply an instrumental response to the tasks of teacher training but a project for restoring professional self-confidence.

The uncertain nature of teacher education in America can be observed at different levels, as Judith Lanier and Judith Warren Little have well shown:

the problem begins with the teacher educators themselves, often unsure about their own identity and their own role in a university environment; then come the students of teaching, a massive army by all comparative standards, yet not of the highest calibre and with an uncertain dedication to the profession; finally, and in sharp contrast to the course content for other professions, the curriculum for teaching imposes few demands of really complex skills and knowledge, so that the conclusion can easily be drawn that "anybody can teach" (Lanier & Little 1986).

The teachers of teachers wrestle with a twofold problem of identity. One is a question of allegiance: in many cases, it is their basic discipline, rather than the training of teachers in itself, which commands their loyalty. This is true for teachers of foundations courses, whose primary interest is in the sociology, psychology, history or philosophy of education. To them, the real teacher educators are those who teach the methods courses, but the latter in their turn tend to identify more readily with the school subjects of their expertise. So we are left with a narrow definition of the teacher educator as being exclusively the person that coordinates and supervises student teachers in the schools. The second problem of identity is closely related to the first. Lanier and Little, along with many other observers of the teacher education scene, have commented on the inverse relationship between professional prestige and the intensity of involvement with the formal education of teachers. In plainer terms, studying teachers will always be given more academic weight and accorded more academic respect than simply training them. Hence the strong temptation felt by many professors of education to distance themselves from the realities (or the chores) of teaching prospective and practising teachers: research in the history or sociology of education for instance, or else preparing professionals for other than school teaching roles (school administrators, counsellors, psychologists, media specialists and policy makers) are in this sense viewed as more worthwhile activities than being involved with teacher education programmes. Hence also the wide gap between purely academic pursuits, requiring maximum intellectual flexibility and breadth, and teacher training with its practical bias calling for conformity and limited analysis (Wisniewski & Ducharme 1989).

What of the students themselves? If the success of education as a disciplinary area is to be measured in terms of its power to attract large numbers of students, then it seems that there are few grounds for apprehension. The 1970s saw a high proportion of college graduates in the USA pursuing teaching certificates: this varied between 20 and 25 per cent, making education the most popular subject by all accounts. There was, it is true, a steep decline in the 1980s when not a few SCDEs feared that they might have to close down but even then, education on the campuses was still second, behind only business and management. So in purely quantitative terms, the prospects are not at all gloomy. When concern is expressed, it is about quality: the students of teaching are not always those whom deans and professors of education would like to see registering in their SCDEs.

One problem is linked to the opening up of the labour market and increased competition between the professions for good graduates: teacher education suffered in the process and increasingly failed to attract many able, talented women who, in the past, would not have been lured away into other fields of professional activity, often reserved to the males. The over-representation of women among the prospective teacher population still remained a basic factor, however, in the mid-1980s, since they accounted for over three quarters of this population. But the same is not true of the ethnic minorities, for whom the profession seems to exercise little attraction. The rate of the students from these ethnic minority groups (African Americans, Hispanics, Asians, native Americans) taking up courses in education remains much lower than their actual proportion in the population of the United States. Studies of destinations have shown that, as they were entering higher education in greater numbers, they have moved into academic and professional fields like business, engineering, the health sector, as well as biological, physical and computer sciences and have on the whole proved to be more reluctant to commit themselves to educational careers. The teaching population in the United States is over ninety per cent white (Darling-Hammond 1990, pp. 267-290). There is undeniable cause for concern here as, at the same time, the proportion of ethnic minority pupils in the nation's schools is rapidly rising. The situation undoubtedly calls for a fairer ethnic balance among American teachers. In an open, competitive market where the rules of laissez-faire prevail, such problems of matching supply and demand are however not easily solved. They are bound to dominate the 1990s just as they did the previous decades.

Discussion of the composition of successive cohorts of future teachers is a constant theme in the literature on teacher education in America. The common message is that the best and the brightest do not go into teaching. But Lanier and Little conclude that the statement is not only unfair, but also scientifically wrong: teaching does attract and retain persons with high intellectual ability (Lanier & Little 1986). But the basic problem remains that the proportion of those talented people joining the profession is found to be consistently too low. On the other hand, teaching has always attracted a disproportionate number of students drawn from among the least academically inclined. In the competitive world of higher education, where institutions, schools and disciplinary departments are known to be vying with one another for excellence and custom, league tables fulfil an important function. They consistently showed that teaching in the 1980s was failing to draw its due share of the nation's intellectual talent. In one survey, education majors were found to be very close to the bottom of the pile, being second to last in a list of thirteen college majors ranked in terms of mean SAT (Scholastic Aptitude Test) scores (Darling-Hammond 1990, p. 272). In the early 1980s, the gap between national average SAT scores and the mean for entering education majors was, likewise, found to have widened in the course of the preceding decade. As a result, the image of the profession in the public mind is made to suffer, while the overabundance of persons with low test scores inevitably depresses the levels of content knowledge that can be provided in teacher education. As Lanier and Little concisely observed, the teaching force should come from the average and above, rather than from the average and below, as has historically been the case.

A circular effect can be detected: because the expectations of the abilities of teacher students have never been high, the students' own expectations of teacher education have tended in their turn to be somewhat negative. They have seen it as a disciplinary field which was easy to enter, intellectually weak, and possibly unnecessary. This is where education, as an area of study, suffers the most in comparison with other professions which are known to require a great deal of content knowledge and to impose a heavy pressure of intellectual work. It is not true that anybody can be a doctor or a lawyer. But it is often felt, on the other hand, that anybody can be a teacher. The relatively degraded image of education in the eyes of students is, perhaps not surprisingly, shared to some extent by their parents, who have grown more sceptical over the status and merits of teaching as a career. Practising teachers in the 1980s were showing signs of the same pessimistic mood: one in two consistently declared that he or she would not enter teaching again and would not encourage his or her students to make it their choice of a profession (Darling-Hammond 1990, pp. 273-77).

An interesting contrast with France suggests itself at this point, as it appears that the commitment to teaching as a career on the part of the teacher trainees is heavily influenced by the way the whole system of teacher preparation works. Students who pass the competitive examinations giving access to the profession in France will only exceptionally decide (either then or a few years later) that, on second thoughts, teaching is not for them. Once a teacher, always a teacher. Not so in America: there the system is so much more open and market-led that thousands of students may be taking credits in education in SCDEs "just in case". This is why teachers who have been trained but have never or hardly ever practised can be found in great numbers. The image of teaching as an attractive, worthwhile career is bound to suffer in the process.

Another contrast between the two countries must be highlighted: teachers in France are tenured civil servants with elaborate career patterns; their salaries keep evolving and increasing – without admittedly ever reaching considerable heights – as throughout the whole length of their careers promotion periodically rewards both performance (assessed by local inspectors) and experience (measured in terms of seniority). These are strong enticements for sticking with the profession. While teaching in America provides, in many States, more attractive salaries, similar encouragements to make it a lifelong career are rare. Clifford & Guthrie recently observed that out of every hundred beginning public school teachers, almost fifty had resigned their positions by the sixth or seventh year of teaching. With some amusement they added that, because of the sheer numbers of teachers who had left the profession, together with those who had been trained but had never taught, teaching was only second to the military in having its "expertise" so widely present in the general population (Clifford & Guthrie 1988, p.7). Even with the higher rate of job mobility which can be found in America, there is no other profession where one can so easily walk in and out.

Writers and speakers on the subject often sound depressed and discontented. John Goodlad, for example, can hardly be rivalled as an expert on teacher education, and he has also been a dynamic, inspired dean at the UCLA School of Education. The gap between his high expectations of what his own professional field ought to be and his findings after extensive surveys have prompted him at times to write in dismissive terms: "The history of the teacher education enterprise in representative colleges and universities in the United States", he commented sadly in 1990 , "is not one of our most gratifying and uplifting sagas" (Goodlad 1990, p. 37). Clifford & Guthrie in 1988 likewise expressed bitter and even angry feelings. At UCLA, I remember one leading education professor, mocking at the pretentiousness of comparing Teaching and Medicine, who was heard to expostulate: "Teachers are nurses. Where are the doctors? They are certainly not the teacher educators". It was clear that in his mind neither teaching nor even teacher education carried the same professional prestige or required the same expertise as Medicine, although his colleagues were understandably inclined to believe the opposite.

Reasons for this discomfort or discontent are not so easy to identify. They may not be confined to the United States: teacher preparation is often found by academics the world over to be at odds with university culture. Some even claim that it is always out of place on a university campus. But awareness of this international reality does nothing to alleviate the uneasy feeling: all the literature on teacher education in America harps on the theme that it has consistently been felt to be on the margins rather at the centre. It has always stood on the periphery of things.

The metaphor may sometimes mirror reality. At the University of Virginia, for instance, the school of education, which ranks among the best in the nation, is connected to the main campus by a long bridge. Interpretation of this geographical location depends of course on the symbolic significance of the bridge, seen as a link or conversely as a measure of distance. The common perception is of distance – away from Jefferson's Rotunda and the illustrious Lawn. To make matters even worse, the President expressed the wish, a few years ago, that the school of education be moved still further away to the north on the extreme margins of the campus (though in the immediate vicinity of a prestigious business school), and that its present buildings be used for the extension of the chemistry unit. A battle had to be fought (and was eventually won) by the school to keep teacher education in its present place, within reasonable distance of the Arts and Science departments. Undeniably the story is not simply about geography and sites: it is the status of teacher education itself which is here at stake.

John Goodlad has made an additional point about the blurred image from which teacher preparation may suffer on a campus: even in the minds of students taking education courses, it is often seen as being out of focus. Candidates for secondary school teaching tend to identify with their academic departments rather than with the institution providing their professional formation. Education courses may be there for anyone to pick and choose: quite a few students will simply take two or three, just in case they might come in useful, before they even think of seeking admission to a teacher preparation programme. Goodlad and others have furthermore deplored that the student body in SCDEs rarely experiences such strong group identity as is associated with the "class of 1985" or the "class of 1993", traditionally found among would-be dentists, doctors or lawyers.

Schools of education set in research universities, on the other hand, are in a special, ambiguous position with divided loyalties: their commitments are at the same time to the study of education, the preparation of the future educational leaders (as researchers or administrators) and the practical training of teachers. Confusion about goal priorities inevitably occurs at some time or other in the life of the schools. Because they serve several functions, they become the centre of tensions between theory and practice, detached academic study and pragmatic professional answers to the work which has to be carried out in classrooms. Research work on, say, the development of higher education in colonial America is being conducted even as, a few rooms away down the corridor, student teachers are being advised on the handling of a class of ninth-graders or learning the methods for teaching reading to six-year olds. It is not easy to achieve a harmonious integration of such diverse activities within the School of Education. Another even more serious difficulty relates to the cultural perception of these activities: some are in the end bound to appear as more dignified than others. In a university setting, scholarly research will always come out on top, far above the more mundane preoccupations with classroom control or the teaching of social studies. Visibility and prestige are naturally attached to the former and not to the latter. Likewise, promotion of faculty is based on research output and not on levels of professional craftsmanship in classes. Training teachers will never be as good as studying them: here is probably the gulf that divides teaching from medicine.

This was felt in the 1980s to be a matter of considerable concern. Not that it was anything new. Arthur Powell has shown that closer or looser focus on teacher preparation or academic study has never been a stable policy, and that it has in effect evolved in uneven cycles following sudden shifts of mission, which he also calls "programmatic gyrations" (Powell 1980). There was a sense in the 1980s that most schools of education had been drifting away from concrete concerns with school practice and were now bent on pursuing loftier goals (Judge 1982). The ambition of the Holmes Group was precisely to terminate this cycle and to steer schools of education back to the realities and challenges of effective teacher training, regarded as their essential mission. Proposals are currently being made for a complete restructuring of these schools, with a view to making a thorough U-turn: what was until now deemed to be peripheral (teacher training and issues of learning and teaching in K12 schools) should become the central concern of the schools, and whatever was felt to be central (the preoccupations of researchers doing projects) should be pushed back to the periphery. Moreover, the internal differentiation characteristic of the schools of education is, as emphasized above, perceived as an obstacle to be removed. The solution would appear to lie in a twofold process of integration of faculty into a single element on the one hand, and of all programmes under one umbrella, on the other. Existing departments would have to disappear, if this root-and-branch reform ever occurred. The notion of what constitutes genuine scholarship would also have to be totally reshaped: from being non-productive, it would have to show that it can be effective and improvemen-related. This calls for a dramatic redefinition of the role which scholars can play in a school of education. Tomorrow, if the present spirit is kept up, they will have to spend something like half of their time teaching children and their scholarship, instead of being based on disinterested research, will have to rise out of the service which they accomplish in the classrooms. The system of rewards and promotions must, in this perspective, be totally overhauled so that such commitment to the real world of K12 schools can be taken into account and given comparable status with traditional academic research.

This version of the reform that is required if teacher education is to gain efficiency and peer recognition represents an ideal rather than an agenda for immediate implementation. The weight of human and institutional resistance to change has clearly been underestimated. However idealized the prospects of possible change may be, they do point nevertheless to a need which is stressed time and time again by education professors writing on the future of teacher preparation: SCDEs – and schools of education in particular, at the apex of the structure – must redefine their identity so as to be clearer about what they actually wish to achieve. Otherwise the malaise which has been perceptible for quite a long time now will not go away.

The main thesis of Clifford & Guthrie is that schools of education have not only become marginalised, but alienated by the university culture and the obsessive emphasis put on scholarly research. The visible result is that they have in the end betrayed their professional allegiances. Their book conveys a strong sense of institutional misbehaviour, and it is no accident if their condemnation is expressed in words loaded with religious connotations (Clifford and Guthrie 1988). Sins have been committed which must now be atoned for. Vanity and pride are among these. Schools of education, looking down upon their role of training teachers as undignified, have been tempted to rise above their station, and have imitated disciplinary departments by taking on theoretical research dissociated from the world of the classroom. Proper attention towards practice has declined. Hiring faculty with PhDs earned in academic departments has been deemed more important than recruiting able master teachers with thorough experience of teaching as a craft. Such vanity is exposed in a telling metaphor: virtually from the start, education schools have been like flowers turned toward other suns. "In an effort to gain social prestige, academic acceptance, scholarly recognition, and security of resources", Clifford & Guthrie assert, "they periodically have taken on the coloration of social science departments, research centers, management institutes, and consulting agencies. What passed for cachet and fashion in intellectual and scholarly realms outside of pedagogical circles was often imported by schools of education in hopes of attracting similar attention". Education schools should at worst acquire, or at best regain, a strong sense of identity by casting their lot with their natural constituency. If they wish to be whales, let them be whales (Clifford & Guthrie 1988, p. 365).

The prescriptions given for this necessary reorientation of the basic strategies for teacher education include what can now be recognized as the most frequently advocated reform: the scrapping of undergraduate majors in education. It is still too early to say whether all institutions will follow suit or whether the movement will be limited to those set in research universities with strong disciplinary departments. But this is the most conspicuous manifestation of the prevailing spirit of reform.

Since education schools should be reoriented towards the realities of classroom teaching, and cease to prepare for an academic profession, it is argued that they would be well advised to reject the PhD and prefer instead the EdD as the true professional doctorate. This is perfectly in tune with the current discourse on their real mission. But the problem remains that with the closing down of PhD studies, and given the relatively lower status of EdDs, students of the right calibre may be tempted to follow some other professional route. How much impact this proposal will have is hard to predict, but many deans would certainly feel that to adopt it would be to burn their bridges.

Within the non-system of teacher education, an uncertain profession was speaking in the early 1990s with some renewed determination: the talk was unambiguously about making teacher preparation the focus of a collaborative enterprise on the American campuses as well as enhancing its status through more rigorous entry requirements, higher academic demands placed on the students, and a longer, better-integrated form of professional training. Given the structural characteristics and constraints of teacher education in America, the whole problem seemed to be how systematic the process of reform could become and how far it could be pursued. As it was growing from within and was not directed from above, what degree of resistance was it likely to meet and what compelling force would manage to keep it alive?

Heart versus Head?

It would be most unwise to look at the issue of teacher training simply from the point of view of its structural environment. The point of where and by whom it is provided is crucial; but it cannot be dissociated from other related questions: what will student teachers be expected to teach and how ? As Conant, the Carnegie Report or the Holmes Group, among others, have made abundantly clear, it is pointless to discuss teacher preparation while entertaining only vague notions about the purposes of education: decisions that are made about the contents of the curricula, as well as the nature of the schools which the nation needs, should directly influence the training of future teachers. Conant looked at American schools first, and then he reflected on teacher preparation. The Carnegie Forum did likewise, by exposing deficiencies in schools and saying how they could be remedied through radical changes in the teaching profession. The Holmes Group worked the other way round, by reporting on tomorrow's teachers before writing on to morrow's schools, but showed nonetheless that in their minds the two issues could not be disconnected.

Stressing this point may seem to be laying undue emphasis on what is after all a fairly commonsense observation. Reading the American literature on teacher education, however, suggests otherwise: there is much more about structure than about purpose, more on the university or college environment than about academic goals. A large bulk of it concerns the history and evolution of teacher education. Fewer studies have attempted to answer the question: in what sense does current teacher training in America reflect common assumptions about the goals of schooling? To put it differently, it is easier to understand why normal schools have become teachers' colleges which in their turn have been transformed into multi-purpose colleges or universities than to realize in what manner historical conceptions of the role and nature of schooling have led to the system of teacher education as we see it today. Institutional changes, or "displacements" as they have been called, are of course more easily identifiable. They are there for anyone to see. Questions about the ways in which social and political representations of the goals of schooling have influenced the character of teacher training often remain unanswered.

A sense of the contrasts between national systems may, however, help to shed some light. The United States is distinguished by the unrelenting ambition to connect schooling with a specific conception of democracy. There are of course glaring examples to the contrary: segregation in the past between schools for the whites and schools for the blacks provides ample evidence that this sense of democracy was for a long time tragically flawed. With the desegregation of schools that began in the 1960s and the gradual extension of official policies of positive discrimination it is in the 1990s easier to sustain this argument. The early conception of the "common school" as being free, universal and tax-supported, had a lasting impact on the later evolution of the system. It was also a specifically American approach. Two main characteristics seem to stand out: first, mass education developed earlier than in other countries; second, as America was a land of mass immigration, one of the chief functions of schooling – to a degree unequalled anywhere else in the world – has been to educate and socialise the children of immigrants, often poor and illiterate, into good US citizens. It is through this twofold process that the social function of the school was developed to a larger extent and at an earlier period than in Europe. Mass schooling in the secondary sector became a historical reality at a time when France and England, for example, were still excluding a large majority of their youth from their lycées or grammar schools. Likewise, expansion of higher education occurred when European nations were still operating very closed and selective university systems. Openness, flexibility, opportunity and diversity became American characteristics decades before they were taken seriously and accommodated in Europe.

The successive waves of immigration into the United States also posed a massive challenge to the education system: schools had to turn literally millions of young people from deprived families and alien backgrounds into English-speaking, law-abiding American citizens. Schools were used as power houses for the transformation of American society, or, to change the metaphor, as nurseries for the implantation of strange, far-off shoots into the native soil. There is no other example in the world where so much had been demanded of school systems. The social function of the school is still preeminent today. Many would even argue that it has grown to proportions unknown before, as schools are being used not only to impart knowledge, but to attempt to cure all of society's ills, such as combating crime or learning to live with Aids. With just a tinge of exaggeration, it has been observed that "there is seldom a public crisis for which schooling is not seen as at least a partial solution .... Protecting the environment, preventing teenage pregnancy, promoting racial harmony, encouraging world peace, ending world hunger, discouraging alcoholism and drug abuse are but a few of the campaigns currently assigned to schools" (Clifford & Guthrie 1988, p. 6). Bussing as a practice is a perfect indicator of the commitment to turning schools into places where racial mixing and, it is hoped, racial integration and harmony will prevail. The State of California provides yet another example. The role which its education system has to perform is, in its scope, unique in the world. Nowhere else can be found such a variety of immigrants, mainly from Latin America and Asia, whose sons and daughters, speaking dozens of different languages, and bred in scores of different cultures, have to be accommodated, instructed and educated in the schools: this is a basic human right which applies even to the children of illegal immigrants. The shift to this philosophy of education from the earlier conception that high schools should be mainly open to the scions of the middle-class elites represents a revolution of impressive breadth and depth.

The widening of educational opportunities – an integral part of the American democratic ideal – accounts for the power of innovation which America has manifested. It was there that junior high schools were first developed, and there also that, at a later period, community colleges began to expand and allow democratic access into higher education to the less privileged sections of the population. Reading the message conveyed by the Holmes group in *Tomorrow's Schools* leaves the impression that the belief in schooling as an instrument of democracy is still the inspired creed of a burning faith. The Group's definition of a school is, characteristically enough, that of a "learning community", as opposed to the traditional academic model where culture was "rationed to first-class passengers". They argue that "all citizens need a good education as never before", adding: "No one knows whether new and old dreams of democracy will flourish in our precarious world but we in the Holmes Group are willing to wager on *popular intelligence*" (my emphasis). Democratic culture is undeniably the lofty purpose assigned to education. "The ideals of democracy and teaching for understanding are intertwined", the group proclaims, in a statement that rings like a vibrant and passionate tribute to John Dewey, who was still in the early 1990s a source of enthusiastic inspiration (Holmes Group 1990, p. 25).

A brief analysis of the Group's changing definition of the professional development school, which they have been influential in inventing and developing, provides an apt illustration of this point. By 1986, the PDS was introduced as a concept, and not yet as a reality, and its definition was relatively narrow. As a model, it differed little from the "clinical schools" which were being recommended by other think tanks. The comparison with teaching hospitals, viewed as ideal collaborative sites, was quite explicit. Emphasis was laid on the network of relationships which PDSs would help create between schools and teacher training institutions, as well as between all the professional components: classroom teachers, administrators, university faculty and students engaged in teacher preparation. In other words, it was the structural and instrumental function of professional development schools which seemed to be the main objective: they were to be at the very centre of a whole apparatus whose parts had been so far loosely connected. Four years later, in 1990, PDSs were given by the deans of the Holmes Group a much more expressly ideological role. Unlike the laboratory schools of the past, they were now conceived to respond to student diversity and cultural pluralism (Holmes Group 1990, p. 35). Unlike the clinical schools of more recent conception, they were no longer seen simply as centres of a network – even if this in itself was already a considerable advance – but as places for inspiring and instilling lofty values. They were given the exalted function of helping to promote "teaching for understanding in learning communities for everybody's children": here in a nutshell was expressed the ambition for a progressive, comprehensive, egalitarian conception of schooling.

That this educational philosophy should be expressed in the writings and working papers of those SCDEs which are members of the Holmes Group is interesting but unsurprising. The LSU school of education may here again be taken as an example. Its literature on the advantages of professional development schools, to which it has committed itself, does not really provide a fully argued manifesto in favour of education and democracy. It deals essentially with concrete proposals for reform and eschews the philosophical discussion, so that some deciphering is required. Despite all this, the ideological and political purpose soon becomes apparent to the reader: successful mass education is the avowed goal. "The LSU teacher education faculty", one reads, "is committed to developing teachers who are much more successful in helping every child learn". Or, later on: "teachers and professors will together enhance learning for every boy and girl." This short formula is no mere cliché, but the reassertion of a basic statement of principle which, however misleadingly innocuous it may appear, expresses the most ambitious goal to be set for schools: equality of treatment and attention for all children, in spite of their considerable intellectual, social or ethnic diversity. Schools should not be left to operate in a vacuum: the LSU College of Education pledges that its "new bold program" will help strengthen the relationship between schools and the broader political, social and economic communities within which they reside. The setting up of professional development schools cannot be interpreted as simply an instrumental response to the current deficiencies in teacher training. It carries with it a sharp political and ideological view of the role of education in American democracy.

Teaching "everybody's children" in schools conceived as modelling and promoting democracy itself is an ambition of a very high order. When contrasted, however, with the harsh realities of schooling in poor inner-city areas where truancy, drug-addiction, violence and crime are rampant, such a worthy goal may be found somewhat utopian. America, as perceived from the other side of the Atlantic, is torn between a longing for equity and the search for excellence, the pursuit of collective harmony and the belief in individual success. It is not true that such antithetic goals can never be reconciled. But it is also illusory to claim that they create no tensions. The world of education has traditionally stressed the need for equity. To a great extent, it has been shaped and moulded by this central notion. Hence much of its present configuration, and its uneasy relationship with the harsher world outside, whose values and assumptions often clash with its own. It may be for this reason that so much attention is paid in classrooms to peer groups rather than to the achievements of individuals. There was more than a grain of truth in Anthony Crosland's observation that emphasis on cooperation and adaptability, as well as on social promotion by age groups, meant putting less stress on promotion by talent or competitive examination. If the dominant goal is to be that of turning out good citizens, the production of academically successful scholars will not be accorded high priority. Many critics have observed that this may very well pave the way towards utilitarian and anti-intellectual attitudes. Such objections to what are generally perceived as a dominant trend are not, of course, a recent phenomenon. Indeed, one classical statement was made by Richard Hofstadter in 1963 (a year of central importance in this volume), coinciding therefore with the criticims aimed at teacher education itself by Conant and Koerner (Hofstadter 1963). The notion of preparing children for life and helping them to adjust to society is a worthy ideal. It does little, however, to encourage either academic prowess or even an appetite for the kind of abstract knowledge required in a world where scientific advance remains the key for the competition among the world's leading nations. More recently a powerful if sometimes overheated polemic has developed within the United States emphasising precisely such points (Bloom 1987, Hirsch 1987, Schlesinger 1991, Hughes 1993).

Diane Ravitch has highlighted the paradox: the high idea of schooling in America does not go hand in hand with any lofty representation of intellectuality and of teaching as a profession. Besides turning out people with good brains, the school assumes a host of other social functions. This is a legitimate course for them to take. But the rub is felt, of course, when the schools are assessed on their ability to perform adequately on a competitive basis as in international comparisons or, at home, to maintain good standards of scholastic achievement. Taking a happy, leisurely stroll is a far cry from racing against the clock. Group harmony has an obvious enemy, which is the rat-race. The Carnegie Forum protested that high schools had been turned into cafeterias. The same observation applies when they are labelled as shopping malls better suited to accommodate than to educate the nation's youth.

The goals set for schools, as well as their practical achievements, affect the representation of the role which teachers are expected to assume. In a context where equity and preparation for adult life fundamentally matter more than high standards of scholarship and excellence, the image of the teacher cannot be simply that of a scholar transmitting knowledge. He or she must assume much wider responsibilities, the risk being of course that this conception of the teacher's function should clash with the prevalent view of what defines a genuine professional, as is discussed towards the end of this chapter. The commitment of SCDEs to this particular view of the role and nature of education in America is a characteristic which must strike outsiders. Even more striking, perhaps, is the fact that this commitment is in most cases implicit, that it goes, in a sense, without saying. Most of the literature from SCDEs expresses extremely high, lofty expectations of the contributions which teachers and schools ought to bring to the children and to society. Educators are inclined, through the descriptions of the goals which they assign to themselves and their institutions, to sketch the outlines of an ideal world to the point where the line between what "is" and what "ought to be" is sometimes stylistically blurred.

It would take a totally different book to analyze all the beliefs and assumptions which underlie public schooling in America today and underpin teacher preparation programmes. One idealized view which is implicit in much of the discourse on education is that it is possible for teachers, in classrooms with thirty students or more, to discover the learning strategies of every single child and to adapt his or her teaching to each special case. "Teaching for understanding", as advocated by the Holmes Group (but has anybody, one is tempted to ask, ever made a plea in favour of teaching for misunderstanding?) is based on this assumption. It seems that theories of learning evolved from a preceptor-single pupil model are being applied in bulk to serve as guiding principles to teachers who, in the days of mass education, may have to teach up to one hundred and fifty students every day. This may help to explain why, conversely, so much emphasis is laid in SCDEs on courses for class control and management. For here is the double bind: teachers cannot help being torn between their desire to pay individual attention to the child and their duty to keep the whole class attentive and active. Precisely how they are reconciled is the ultimate skill in the craft or art of teaching. No ready, easy recipes can be devised.

The child- or student-centred philosophy or doctrine, which pervades most of the pedagogical discourse which can be read or heard in SCDEs, also emphasizes, quite naturally, the focusing of teachers' attention not only on individual children's learning modes but also on their needs. Pupils express desires which have to be perceived, understood, and satisfied. Here again, beyond the rhetoric of words, this is from any ordinary (or even extraordinary) teacher's point of view an immense, overwhelming task: while attention to what a child longs to learn may realistically be provided for a very small number of pupils, it requires no less than pedagogical genius with groups of twenty-five, in high schools even more so perhaps than in elementary schools. The issue here is whether a child-centred approach is in practice compatible with mass education. The assumption in America is that it is. Teacher educators have yet to prove, however, either that they have solved the conundrum or that they can train teachers to do the job. The faith in child-centredness, widely shared in the profession, does not feed on the positive, visible effects which it produces in schools for if this was the case, America would feel much happier with them.

Child-centredness fulfils another function: not only is it thought to be indispensable for equity, but it is regarded as the only solid foundation on which to build the qualities required for the good, respectable citizen and the loving adult. Only through a child-centred approach in teaching can one ever hope to reach the goal of creating in the child a sense of self-esteem and self-fulfilment. Schools are not simply there for kids to be smart and to be good, but also to feel good about themselves. Faith in child-centredness assumes an indispensable theoretical and functional role. It is of course an admirable concept but part of the American problem is that it may produce a pedagogical impasse, because it requires skills of the highest order to turn it into a reality in the world of mass schooling. Some members of the more affluent middle classes seem to have learned the lesson and have for some time already turned their backs on the public education sector and preferred to send their sons and daughters to private schools. The stress which is being increasingly laid on subject-knowledge both in schools and SCDEs and on academic achievement is a symptom of the same phenomenon. The mistrust of teacher educators often found among faculty in disciplinary departments may by the same token find its source here: an uncertain form of pedagogy produces poor overall results (when measured from a strictly scholarly point of view) and detracts from a more earnest study of subjects.

Another illustration of the preference given to the quality of the pedagogical relationship over thorough mastery of the subject is provided by the training given for teachers of foreign languages. It is always child's play, on a campus, to find where French as an academic subject, including grammar, literature and civilisation, is being offered: in the French department of the liberal arts or arts and science college. It does not take long either to identify where foreign language teachers of, say, Spanish, French or Russian are being trained, practically always together, in the same groups: you simply have to pay a visit to the local SCDE. In the former place, you learn the language. In the latter, you learn the methods and techniques of foreign language teaching. But where do you acquire the specific knowledge or the didactics of French or Spanish as very distinct languages? There are huge dissimilarities between the two languages. It is not only that words are different, but the phonological systems and linguistic concepts are not the same; the notions of time, past, present or future, as expressed by tense patterns and the moods, conditional, subjunctive or otherwise, do not coincide. These are functional elements of any language which require much analysis and refined skills before they can be taught properly to students: in this sense, the training of teachers of French, Spanish, Russian or German has at some stage to be dissociated. Teacher educators in the field of foreign language teaching are legion. Genuine didacticians of specific foreign languages, on the other hand, are quite thin on the ground and much more likely to be found in the language departments than in the SCDEs. Similarly, supervisors of student teachers of foreign languages often insist that they do not need any special working knowledge of the language being taught and that their role is not to check that the trainee speaks the language with reasonable fluency and correctness. What they wish to assess are the teaching skills: attention to children, quality of tempo, questioning, class management and control. Such practices are an index of the gap or perhaps the gulf between academic and education departments.

The emphasis laid by American teachers and professional experts on student-centredness and on the social function of schooling in preference to a subject-centred approach and the resolute pursuit of academic excellence may be expressed in simpler terms by saying that the heart is made to win over the head. But this old, collective wisdom has of course been questioned at different periods and from diverse quarters. Indeed, a number of critics have asked whether such a belief had not caused the education system to be turned head over heels.

Responses

A series of reports published in the early 1980s – 1983 being in fact the crucial year – issued strikingly similar warnings on the state of the nation's schools and produced a whole spate of proposals for urgent reform.

The Twentieth Century Fund Task Force on Federal Elementary and Secondary Education Policy urged the federal government, in *Making the Grade* (1983) to introduce new policies and support programmes aimed at improving quality of teaching in elementary and secondary schools and better proficiency in English, foreign languages, mathematics and science. The Education Commission of the States, made up of an unusual array of governors, business leaders, educators and legislators, issued *Action for Excellence: a comprehensive plan to improve our nation's schools*, also published in 1983. Still in the same year, the National Science Foundation published *Educating Americans for the 21st Century*, while sixteen top corporate executives and university presidents, gathered in a business–higher education forum, in *America's Competitive Challenge: the need for a national response*, made much the same point that students should acquire firmer foundations in mathematics, science and technology.

The educational establishment, putting together eleven national groups in a "forum of educational organization leaders", responded with their own prescriptions for *Educational Reform*. Interestingly enough, part of the message here was that efforts to raise academic standards must not place in jeopardy the gains in educational equity and civil rights made in the 1960s and 1970s. In other words, although it was emphasized that there was no conflict between equity and excellence, the plea made on behalf of the teaching profession was that the agenda stressing equal opportunities should be preserved, as if the pursuit of excellence, so much harped upon in 1983, might after all very well endanger it.

None of these reports, however, ever made so much impact as *A Nation at Risk* which sounded the first warning in 1983 (National Commission for Excellence in Education 1983). Echoes of it were still reverberating ten years later. Quotations from it have become part and parcel of every introduction to a study of American education. It appeared in the form of a report written by the National Commission on Excellence in Education appointed two years earlier by the US Secretary of Education. The educational foundations were being sapped by a rising tide of mediocrity; such assumed mediocrity itself was branded as an "act of unthinking, unilateral educational disarmament". Or else: "If an unfriendly foreign power had attempted to impose on America the mediocre educational performance that exists today, we might well have viewed it as an act of war." The threatening language was certain to catch the attention of the media. What was the nature of the deadly risk? No less than the loss of the economic superiority of the United States and the weakening of its world hegemony: "Our once unchallenged preeminence in commerce, industry, science and technical innovation is being overtaken by competitors throughout the world."

The tone of the report was terse, and the nation listened. Blunt statements soon turned into familiar punchlines. High schools were derided as cafeterias with appetizers and desserts but no main course, and the all-too-wide variety of student choice of subjects was dubbed the "curricular smorgasbord". Two years later, Arthur Powell, Eleanor Farrar and David Cohen were to use a very similar metaphor when they made the point that high schools had been turned into "shopping malls" (Powell & others 1985). One year after the publication of *The Shopping Mall High School*, another similarly striking and abrasive title appeared in the form of an overall indictment of the school system: *Selling Students Short*. Here again, the inability of schools and teachers to reconcile their democratic and academic ideals was stigmatised: "The system's ability to accommodate the aspirations of virtually all constituencies, from the highly to the lowly motivated and engaged, appears both to demonstrate a healthy functional relationship to the larger society and to mask the overall prevalence of low academic standards" (Sedlak & others 1986, p.179).

On teacher education, *A Nation at Risk* reached conclusions which had a familiar ring about them for anyone who remembered reading Conant or Koerner: the same complaint was made about too many courses in educational methods, and not enough courses in the subjects to be taught. Higher educational standards and greater competence in an academic discipline were again required of future teachers. Gary Sykes aptly expressed the wisdom of the day by insisting on the need for "screens" and "magnets". State requirements, he said, provided the former in an effort to keep the unqualified out of the teaching profession; but they failed to offer the latter, in the sense that they were not sufficiently incentives-oriented and did too little to draw in the talented (Sykes 1983, pp. 95-125).

The second wave of reports followed close upon the heels of these earlier calls for reform. Considering the plethora of troubles that had been diagnosed, one might have expected a flurry of surveys going in all sorts of directions: challenging the overall structure of American education or the tenets of the public high school system whose linchpin was the neighbourhood school accommodating the local youth, changing the arrangements for channelling money into schools or assessing students' academic performance with tougher final exams, for example. The many symptoms seemed to call for a whole variety of prescriptions for cures. This was not what in fact occurred. Instead attention was focused almost exclusively on teacher training. In order to improve standards in schools, you have to turn out better teachers: this was in effect the straightforward message of the mid-1980s. It was sent out from two main quarters: the Holmes Group first; and barely a month later, from the task force of the Carnegie Forum. This was in 1986.

The two teams which had been set to work were quite different in their composition, and yet appeared to share many common assumptions. As they published their findings within a few weeks of one another, they can safely be taken in inverse order. The Carnegie Task Force produced *A Nation Prepared: teachers for the 21st century*. It deserved, and obtained, special attention because it approached its subject from an angle very different from that adopted in the past. Previously, reform of teacher preparation had been envisaged primarily from within and much of the attention was concentrated on content. With the report of the Carnegie Forum, it is the reform of the teaching profession itself which is given priority. The core idea is to make the teaching profession more like other professions such as those of accountants, architects or attorneys. Simple, basic rules apply where these are concerned: entrants into the profession must obtain a national certification, no undergraduate major in the professional field should be offered, Masters' degrees are the norm, and high levels of salary the rule. Identical criteria applied to teachers would turn them into a genuine profession. Tougher requirements would produce expertise and quality, and would make it easier to reward experience – all three elements sadly still missing in the 1980s. Most recommendations naturally follow, then, from this central strategy. The Carnegie Forum pleaded for the creation of a national board for professional teaching standards, a proposal which was effectively implemented a few years later and the NBPTS became a reality in the 1990s. Another idea had also by that time been making some headway: it was the requirement that a bachelor's degree in the arts and sciences should become a prerequisite for the professional study of teaching. The last key component of the Carnegie Forum's "professional practice model" dealt with teacher's salaries and career opportunities: ideally, these should become competitive with the conditions obtaining in other professions.

In order fully to appreciate the scope of these changes concerning the restructuring of the profession, one factor must be borne in mind: it is a paradox which has often been mentioned that experienced teachers in American schools are as a rule hard put to it to exercise the sort of influence that would be commensurate with their expertise. Besides, teaching provides few career prospects. For example, the top scale of the salary schedule was never more than twice as high as entry level, the twenty-year veteran being as a consequence hardly distinguishable from the neophyte (Sykes 1983). Hence the notion that instead of the flat marshes where the teaching force has to tread or wade, there should be a more inspiring environment with hills and peaks. A restructured teaching profession was required. The top level would be made up of a new category, that of the "lead teachers", with the role of providing active leadership in the redesign of the schools and in helping their colleagues to uphold high standards of teaching and learning. This was another way of saying that the task of rescuing the school system rested with the teaching profession. However harsh its criticisms, *A Nation Prepared* still held out the promise that reform could be achieved by the chief agents – from inside rather than from outside or above.

It cannot be sheer coincidence that the Holmes Group, in *Tomorrow's Teachers*, had a little earlier followed a similar path. The Group was formally constituted in Washington in January 1987. Its chief characteristic was that it was essentially an insiders' coalition, made up as it was of education deans in research universities. Like the members of the Carnegie Forum, their conviction was that, for education to respond to the nation's expectations, it was the whole occupation of teaching, and not just teacher preparation, which had to change. No wonder if, with a message of this nature, the two reports have remained linked in the public mind, despite their differences on other points. Both their problematics and methodology had quite a lot in common. Some have objected to the "rhetoric of pleading": for them the report reads like "the Sermon on the Mount", promising a heaven on earth (Cuban 1989, pp. 370-92). Yet behind the fervour of the rhetoric, there lie practical suggestions. Some bear a striking similarity to the Carnegie recommendations. Again, the deans themselves wish to scrap all undergraduate majors in education. This means that students in teacher training will have to complete an academic major and a programme of liberal studies. For the teaching force itself, structural changes from a flat profession (with minimal career prospects) to a hierarchical one (with rising levels of expertise, responsibility and salary) are likewise advocated.

A slight difference from the Carnegie report is that the new career ladder which is envisaged by the Holmes Group looks more elaborate, being three-tiered: the bottom rung is for "instructors" (beginning teachers); the middle one is for "professional teachers" (proven competent at work); the top rung is reached by "career professionals" (demonstrating outstanding achievement), the first cousins of Carnegie's "lead" teachers. Both reports insisted that schools should be restructured and working conditions within them reformed to provide a new professional environment that is compatible with the enhanced status of the profession. A more significant difference, of central importance to the theme of this book, lies just below the surface of the two reports. For Carnegie national standards to be achieved by individual teachers are all-important. For Holmes, the graduate school of education itself stands at the centre of attention. Without it, as in the case of medicine and law, real professional advance will never be achieved.

What the reports of the early 1980s had in common was an insistence on the need to do more English as well as more mathematics and science in schools, produce teachers who were on the whole more knowledgeable, and restructure teaching along the lines of a genuine profession. While groups of experts, education commissions and forums of every description were busy hammering home their common truths, a lone yet distinguished voice could be heard. It was the voice of Patricia Graham, who was until recently Dean of the Harvard School of Education, and whose message, delivered in 1984, struck an original note (Graham 1984). Her contribution had lost none of its relevance in the 1990s because her ambition was to look beneath the surface and observe both the practice and the purpose of schooling in America – the roots in effect of the whole education system. The conclusion which she drew can be reduced to a simple formula: she found that the practice of schooling was all cacophony while the purpose of education in the nation was shrouded in silence. Her general observation can be interpreted as a variation on the theme of form getting the upper hand over substance, or rites having become estranged from the original faith. As a criticism, it was of a more fundamental nature than anything else that was being expressed during the same decade.

The original faith has a name: it is progressivism in education, as it was popularized in the first half of this century. Patricia Graham does not disown it: in fact she declares herself to be a true believer who expresses no nostalgia for whole-class teaching and rote learning. Student-centredness and progressivism she finds essentially sound. And yet she is harshly critical of current pedagogical practice. This is because she feels that the faith has been betrayed through a twofold process of misinterpretation and misuse: not only has it not been properly understood, but to make things worse it has been only partially achieved. This has led to what she sees as a disaster. Focus upon the child, which she considers as necessary but not sufficient, has led to a dramatic outcome: academic study has virtually disappeared from high schools. The academic curriculum is dead. Patricia Graham breaks the current silence on purpose: here also priorities should be set right. In education, she isolates three simple, basic concepts: citizenship, character and wit. Informed and enlightened citizenship, in a democracy, is the ultimate goal. This is not seriously disputed by anyone in America. Wit and character are the two pillars on which this sense of citizenship can be built up. By "wit", she means mental capacity, intellect and reason. By "character", she means moral strength. As a former dean of a prestigious school of education put it to me once in a slightly different form of wording, "kids have to be taught how to be smart and how to be good". Here again, few would disagree with this emphasis on intellectual and ethical qualities to be fostered in the nation's youth. Where Patricia Graham, however, breaks with the consensus is over the order of priority. Her simple lesson is that wit should regain, or acquire, primacy over character.

The very negation of Patricia Graham's approach can be found in a draft paper which was circulated by the Virginia Department of Education in October 1992. The document introduces the concept of the "common core of learning", based not on individual disciplinary areas, but on "dimensions of living", and it provides a framework of essential "outcomes". The list of such outcomes cannot so readily be broken down into elements of "character" on the one hand, and of "wit" on the other. But the sense of priorities which emanates from it leaves no doubt as to what is intended: personal well-being and accomplishment come first, followed by interpersonal relationships. Thinking and problem-solving are number eight and nine down the list of twelve skills to be acquired. They are given as additional fundamental skills, and they come after work and economic well-being, local and global civic participation, as well as environmental stewardship (meaning preserving the natural world).

These have been the typical orthodoxies, deeply entrenched in American education since the publication in 1918 of *The Cardinal Principles of Secondary Education* (Judge 1977, p. 243). But Graham has stuck to her guns. In another paper published five years later, in 1989, she chose to spell out what her emphasis on intellectual rigour and an academic curriculum meant for schools of education (Graham 1989). Like other critics of American high schools, she deplored that attendance and completion of a high school programme rather than achievement had in effect become the goal of schooling. Here again, the world seemed to have been turned upside down. To set things right, achievement had to be declared the primary goal. This requires a revolution in pedagogy: in particular, instruction must be given precedence over many non-academic activities in which schools are known to engage. Responsibility for the revolution in pedagogy lies with the schools of education. Her analysis is that so far schools of education have trained teachers who could do reasonably well with motivated, academic students, but who have dealt poorly with low-scoring students to whom in the main deeply boring remedial activities have been proposed. From an institutional and functional point of view, this in effect means that pedagogy should be shifted again to the centre of schools of education; this is a role which they had been increasingly tempted to evade in the past decades.

Although there has recently been a good deal of talk about deeper concentration on subject knowledge and a reappraisal of academic scholarship, nothing has yet upset the time-honoured order of priority, the preference given to the heart over the head. Confirmation of this overall judgement can easily be found in the current conceptions and descriptions of what makes up a teacher's identity. Very rarely is he or she expected to be a scholar. The most commonly held belief is that a teacher ought to be a "facilitator " as a "guide" and a "coach" and not someone whose chief function is to impart knowledge. NCATE itself endorsed this view of the teacher as a "facilitator of learning" as opposed to "a dispenser of knowledge" (NCATE 1993). In many classes where I have observed young prospective teachers being trained, the most common assumption was also that methods should assist a process of discovery by the children themselves: finding out was what mattered, simply being taught and passive was ruled out. I have seen this pedagogical approach being applied to six-year olds learning to read the words which they had just been guided to use themselves. I have also been made aware of how it could be used for older students: to take but one example, teacher trainees, in a microteaching group, were asked to devise activities, like games and quizzes, aimed at helping adolescents guess and grasp some key concepts. It was evident that the pedagogical skills to be developed in this instance were far more elaborate and required a much higher degree of initiative and inventiveness than the talk and chalk method. As everyone knows, it is one thing to fill up a vase with water, and it is quite another to nurse a rose so that it will properly blossom in the spring. In America, children are to be the flowers, not the vessels. It is easy to conceive that, when this type of pedagogical relationship is preferred, knowledge of the child's processes of learning should count more, in the teacher's training, than scholarship in a subject. I have personally heard educators claim that teachers should be granted the basic right not to know, and to acknowledge it plainly before their students. For to them knowledge is not something to be poured out over others' heads, but material which everybody takes a hand in collecting and assembling. Since the search for knowledge is more important than knowledge itself – just as being active is better than being passive – ignorance should not be regarded as a shame, but in many cases as an asset. In the same sort of logic, teacher trainees are often advised to learn from their own students: such is the flow of information outside the schools in our modern societies that the image of the omniscient teacher is obsolete, and the collaborative concept, implying exchange between students and teachers, is used as the basis for a truly positive pedagogical relationship. In their vision of to morrow's schools, the deans who make up the Holmes Group have expressed views which are to a great degree consonant with these. In July 1988, they concluded that "the deeper generic task of education is teaching students how to make knowledge and meaning to enact culture, not merely acquire it" (Holmes Group 1990, p. 10). The definition of the teacher that follows naturally fits in with this general notion: he or she is not primarily someone who does things, but "gets the kids to do them". "Teaching", it is claimed, "is essentially helping people to get excited in a subject area."

The metaphor of the caring gardener with his roses comes to mind at this stage. But so might one presenting the image of teachers as watchful nurses devoted to the service of their patients and helping them recover their health and regain their strength.

Underlying all this is the American paradox: while the role of the teacher as a kindler of passions for learning in the students' hearts is a very exacting and ambitious one, it is far from certain that such a belief will enhance the image of the profession in the minds either of the general public or of university academics. When teachers become more like gardeners or nurses, they drift away from the status of lawyers or doctors who traditionally stand for the authentic professionals. The uncertain place of academic knowledge in the educational process, as well as the emotional aura surrounding it, make the teacher's activity less and less comparable to Medicine or Law. So it may be claimed that just as higher demands are made on teachers as pedagogues, their social image as professionals is being degraded. Teaching seems condemned to remain, in the words of John Goodlad, the "not-quite profession" (Goodlad 1990, pp. 70-71). Academic professors, who rate scholarship as a priority, and education deans and professors, who promote learning for understanding as a collaborative process, will never be easily reconciled.

It has, although for quite different reasons, proved no easier to establish effective and comfortable connections between teachers and academics in Britain.

CHAPTER 6

England: towards 1963

1963

The major educational events in England in 1963 were for many international observers overshadowed by the John Profumo scandal and subsequent defeat of the Conservative Party.[1] Although the tabloids were filled with warnings of the damage that Profumo's personal relationships had undoubtedly caused British intelligence and security, three important events occurred that symbolized both the culmination of one educational movement, and the invigoration of another. They would have far-reaching implications for the education of teachers, the institutions engaged in such work, and the experiences of their graduates. The release of the Robbins Committee Report on Higher Education, one of the central educational moments of 1963, appeared finally to open access to higher education and to connect the deeply fragmented array of institutions – particularly those dedicated to educating teachers – that aspired to "higher education" status. The Newsom report and the "science and socialism" speech of Harold Wilson, who would become Prime Minister when his Labour Party seized control of the government in 1964, reflected revolutionary thinking about adolescents and launched a new era of policy in secondary education by stimulating the "comprehensive" school movement, which had languished for nearly two decades.[2]

The Robbins Committee, which had explored a number of issues since its formation in 1961, grappled principally with the implications of the onrushing demographic bulge of the "baby boom," and tried to devise ways of ensuring that every "qualified" adolescent would be able to find a place in genuine higher education. This was a formidable challenge in a nation with ancient traditions of educational segmentation and exclusion from "higher education," which was then available to fewer than 225,000 in just a score of self-governing universities which were nevertheless totally dependent upon public funds.

Lord Robbins' Committee, committed to responding to the anticipated acceleration of demand for access to higher education, recommended that the number of openings be doubled to approximately 400,000 within the decade, and increased to 560,000 by 1980. Such an expansion would require both considerable financial investments – to sustain a half-dozen new universities, for example – and a reconfiguration of existing arrangements and patterns for post-secondary schooling.

For our story the Robbins Committee's vision for the professional education of teachers is most significant. On the eve of the Report's release, a small minority of teachers were educated in universities; the vast majority were prepared in "teacher training colleges," all of which were under the control of either the churches or the Local Education Authorities. The Robbins Committee saw the network of more than 150 training colleges as a potentially rich resource for expanding not only the number of teachers that would be needed to educate the baby boom generation, but also to serve the higher education ambitions of the baby boomers themselves.

To capitalize on this untapped potential, the colleges would have to be more closely connected with the universities, which were, at the time, the only institutions with the privilege of bestowing academic degrees. The Committee recommended integrating the colleges and universities, even to the point of channelling grants to the training colleges through their host universities, and having the universities actually administer the colleges. This, many believed, would be the only way to improve the status of the colleges and secure their position in the new configuration of higher education. The teacher training institutions would also need to broaden their missions, to diversify their programmes and courses into other service industries, such as nursing and theology.

Coupled with renaming the training institutions "Colleges of Education," the Robbins Committee recommended that the Bachelor of Education (BEd) be universally available in the colleges. This was proposed in order to elevate the stature of teaching by making it a "graduate" profession, through ensuring that in the future all entrants to the profession would have been awarded degrees. Most teachers, prior to the early 1960s, received their professional education in brief two year certificate courses. The Robbins Committee wanted to eliminate such routes into licensed teaching positions and proposed as an alternative the BEd, validated by the universities.[3] This pleased the staff and students in the colleges, because it promised to elevate the prestige of their work and credentials. Staff in the training colleges had for some time been envious of their counterparts in the universities whose positions in genuine "higher education" institutions were far more privileged and autonomous.

In unprecedented fashion, the government released a companion "White Paper" within twenty-four hours of the publication of the Robbins Report in October. To display that government's determination to respond to the mounting pressure for opening access to higher education, the White Paper accepted most of the Committee's recommendations. It accepted high enrolment targets, the need to broaden the image and enhance the reputation of the Colleges of Education, and the Committee's proposals on the function and value of the BEd degree. It agreed with the need to connect the colleges and the universities, and to expand enrolment in the universities. But it was outright hostile to the proposal to bring the colleges fully under the universities' wing. Both local and central government officials were opposed to relinquishing control over the colleges to the independent universities. The Colleges of Education were left in a state of uneasy suspense between the government authorities and the universities, a situation that made them vulnerable once the heady expansionism of the 1960s receded.

A second event of unappreciated significance that occurred in 1963 was the release of the Newsom Report, which was followed by the first signs of a reconceptualization of the place and meaning of schooling in the lives of those adolescents for whom the traditional academic curriculum of the grammar school, conceived as preparation for higher education, was inappropriate. In part, the British system of educational differentiation was based on assumptions about the prerogatives and privileges of class: educational opportunities were justifiably bestowed on the basis of social origins. During the twentieth century, however, a meritocratic ideal came to influence access to schooling. The power of the "11+" selection, which determined the educational destinies of children on the basis of their performance in academic examinations taken when they were approximately eleven years old, appeared to reward achievement uninfluenced by class background. Because of success in the 11+ examinations, many working-class youth were able to attend the prestigious and selective secondary grammar schools, and often gain entry to Britain's most desirable universities. Children who did not distinguish themselves in the 11+ examinations had until recently been denied access to legitimate forms of secondary schooling. Since the 1940s some effort had been made to provide for such students opportunities to acquire some secondary education, but typically at less academic and less esteemed "modern" schools or the scattered "comprehensive" schools.

The meritocratic 11+ examination and selection system was based largely on the assumption that "intelligence" was a relatively fixed and probably innate quality, seemingly immune to significant improvement through good early educational experiences. This view was pervasive before World War II, and remained influential through the 1950s. Scepticism toward this belief spread beyond radical egalitarians by the 1960s, however, and in 1963 it was challenged even by leaders of the Conservative Party. The Newsom Report, *Half Our Future*, challenged educational and political leaders to take seriously the educational needs and rights of the mass of adolescents, most of whom had been ill-served by the relentlessly academic and university-oriented grammar schools. The Conservative Education Minister, Sir Edward Boyle, argued in the foreword to the Newsom Report that the nation had finally recognized that "intelligence" could be "acquired," and that "all children should have an equal opportunity of acquiring intelligence, and of developing their talents and abilities to the full" (Ministry of Education 1963, p. iv). In another document released almost simultaneously with the Report,

Boyle admitted, quite prematurely it now appears, that "none of us believe in pre-war terms that children can be sharply differentiated into various types or levels of ability" (quoted in Chitty 1989, p. 37).

The Newsom Report called for raising the school-leaving age to 16 (a recommendation that the Treasury delayed until 1972) and for the design of a more effective educational experience for "average" and "below average" students, many of whom were fully educable and would be able to make vital contributions to the nation's economy if they received an education adapted to the real needs of their lives instead of mimicking the university-driven grammar school curricula. The Committee members were cautiously reformist and seem not to have fully embraced Boyle's perspective on the impact of education on ability. There was for example no call to eliminate selection at 11+. Instead the Committee advocated deeper investments in urban, "slum," and working-class schools. They proposed adapting the curricula in such schools to more practical and vocational ends, giving academically-alienated students more choice of courses, including classes that were "broadly related to occupational interests," or personal and social adjustment. Despite its reservations about embracing egalitarianism, the Newsom Report signalled that government attention and investment could be legitimately focused on the non-college bound, that something other than pale imitations of grammar schools might be appropriate for the mass of adolescents, and that targeting funds toward average students would not be viewed as squandering the nation's resources.

The third important educational event of 1963 was the speech made at his Party's Conference by Labour leader Harold Wilson in which he revitalized the socialist commitment to expanding educational access while addressing the technological and industrial paranoia that was sweeping most of the West following the successes of the Soviet space programme during the late 1950s. Not only were England's segmented social and educational systems unjust, he claimed, but they contributed to the nation's failure to compete economically.

> To train the scientists we are going to need will mean a revolution in our attitude to education, not only higher education but at every level. It means that as a nation, we cannot afford to force segregation on our children at the 11+ stage. As Socialists, as democrats, we oppose this system of educational apartheid because we believe in equality of opportunity.

After taking this strong political stance, Wilson appealed to the good sense of conservatives and the business community.

> We simply cannot as a nation afford to neglect the educational development of a single boy or girl. We cannot afford to cut off three-quarters or more of our children from virtually any chance of higher education. The Russians do not, the Germans do not, the

Americans do not, and the Japanese do not, and we cannot afford to either (Bell, Fowler & Little 1973, pp. 192-94).

Wilson's public dedication to expanding educational opportunity clearly appealed to many in his party and built momentum for enlarging options for adolescents to acquire some form of secondary schooling. It also led to massive public investments in opening up higher education by both increasing the size of the universities and creating an entirely new sector in higher education consisting of "polytechnics," multi-service, often technically-oriented post-secondary institutions tailored to the needs of youth who aspired to more skilled technical careers or who were unable to secure entrance to a university, or who could benefit from a "second chance" educational opportunity.

But despite the superficially revolutionary rhetoric of Wilson's speech, it quickly became clear that the new investments would not disrupt prevailing arrangements and relationships. While challenging the nation to care about the destinies of the great mass of children, Wilson also reassured his countrymen that the symbolic and real bastions of exclusivity and distinction, the grammar schools, would be abolished "over my dead body." His enthusiasm for embracing both rhetorical positions – egalitarianism and differentiation – quickly became understood as "the new educational settlement" of the 1960s (Centre for Contemporary Cultural Studies 1981, ch. 4). In the words of one historian, it was an arrangement "which ensured that the spread of comprehensive education would take place within, and as part of, a deeply divided educational system rather than as its replacement" (Lowe 1988, p. 140). Indeed, as the comprehensive secondary schools became more prominent, critics raised the spectre of severe internal differentiation, which was increasingly recognized as the essence of the "American settlement": students might attend the same schools but would invariably receive unequal educations. And this American approach was about to be further challenged for appearing to offer a public facade of egalitarianism while reproducing class distinctions through grouping and tracking practices. At least the tradition of privilege and exclusivity associated with the more honest British arrangement avoided reproducing inequalities of station under the pretence of offering educational opportunity.

Thus the British educational enterprise was prodded in 1963 to reconsider its historical solutions to the new problems facing societies that had attained universal education for their children: How to respond to pressures for democratization and enlarged access, at least to schools that benefited from the public treasury? How to adapt education to students who had been excluded from further schooling? And how to recruit and prepare not just enough teachers, but how to educate teachers who would have the talent and commitment to engage students in learning who were not particularly motivated by the stick of the 11+ selection examinations.

We turn now to reconstruct the evolution of teacher education and its interaction with the development of schooling more generally in order to understand the ways in which the events of 1963 brought to a close one educational era and opened another.

The Rise of the Teacher Apprentice, 1798-1902

Teacher training began in 1798 in Southwark, a slum district of London. That Southwark rather than Oxbridge was the home of teacher training explains many of the problems facing teacher educators today: its lack of credibility as a discipline; a dearth of academic ability among its students; and the ambiguities of a curriculum embracing personal education and professional training. All of these have denied it money, resources and until recently, talent, and can be said to have their roots in its humble birth in Southwark. Unlike theology, medicine or law, it has no historic claim to a university tradition of academic excellence or respectability. It has more in common instead with medieval craft guilds, whose apprenticeship system preceded modern technical education (Hencke 1978, p. 13).

Over the past two hundred years, the education of teachers in England has been shaped by the aspirations and arrangements for elementary, secondary, and higher education. From an American perspective, one of the most striking features of the educational enterprise in Great Britain has been the depth and persistence of its segmentation. For centuries it has been vertically differentiated: the worlds of elementary and secondary schooling and higher education have never been fashioned into a continuous educational ladder for all children. It has also been horizontally separated as well: commoners and the privileged have had very different educational experiences. Together these historic features of formal education in England have left enduring imprints on efforts to recruit, prepare, and induct teachers into the nation's schools.

The first century and a half of formal teacher education were characterized by the rapid construction and equally rapid dismantling of a series of apprenticeship schemes. But during the late eighteenth and early nineteenth centuries few educators experienced even the benefits of a sound apprenticeship training. Whether at the secondary or elementary level, prospective teachers received virtually no professional education. Educational levels generally remained low. Of children of elementary age, only one quarter received any kind of formal education, and even of these the great majority attended school for only short periods of time. Teachers in the "dame," "common day," and "charity" schools of the time were barely more educated than their students. Often such schools were staffed with young child minders and socially-dependent adults who were "aged, decrepit, and dissolute" (Dent 1977, p. 2). It was a case, in one historian's view, of "the one-eyed leading the blind" (Evans 1985, p. 168). Whatever learning they acquired occurred on-the-job, although rarely under the tutelage of a master teacher. At the time of Lord Brougham's 1818 investigation into the education of "The Lower

Orders of Society," the capacity of the voluntary sector (which was of course largely responsible for providing schooling for all but the most privileged) to free England from its reputation as "the worst educated nation in Europe," was severely limited by a shortage of talented teachers and the difficulties of keeping children away from employment in the factories (Evans 1985, p. 24).

A few individuals, however, were able to take advantage of the rare efforts by such bodies as the Society for the Promotion of Christian Knowledge (SPCK) to provide formal training for elementary teachers. Throughout the eighteenth century guidebooks and manuals encouraged SPCK school managers to allow novice teachers to "observe and practise" in the classrooms of talented, experienced teachers so that they could "gain the art of teaching school on the old master's methods" (Dent 1977, p. 2, fn. 5). Toward the end of the century, the Welsh "circulating schools" and a number of institutions established by the Society of Friends in England moved more explicitly to develop formal apprenticeship programmes, although it was customary for the prospective teachers to secure a "training in content rather than method" (quoted in Jones 1938, p. 101).

The tradition of relying on university degrees as evidence of academic qualification and trustworthiness to teach at the secondary level continued almost without challenge throughout the nineteenth century. This was to be a defining feature of the unique condition of secondary teachers: their distinctive preparation set them apart from their elementary counterparts and helped to shape the way in which many university staff thought about teacher education. Secondary teachers may have been better informed and educated, but like instructors of young children, learned to teach only as they engaged in their practice. It was their good fortune that the traditions of learning through memorization and recitation were so ingrained that secondary teachers had little need of sophisticated pedagogical skills.

These arrangements, particularly for preparing and recruiting elementary teachers, impeded the expansion of popular schooling until the early nineteenth century. After 1800, a convergence of religious and social reform initiatives stimulated pressure to invest aggressively in broadening educational opportunities for working-class children. The form taken by that investment affected the shape of teacher education for a half-century. Although the competing systems of "monitorial" education differed slightly, the versions endorsed both by Andrew Bell and Joseph Lancaster were fundamentally similar. The monitorial system, which was established in France and the United States as well as in the United Kingdom, was uniquely suited to providing mass instruction at little cost, for it capitalized on a division of labour that made it possible for a single master to "teach" a class of hundreds of students, a feature that magnified its appeal for societies engaged in extending elementary schooling to the poor.

The mechanism that made this possible was the deployment of a system of "monitors," who were themselves students responsible for handing down lessons from the master, or "superintendent," to groups of ten younger scholars. Larger schools might use several layers of monitors, so that in the most fancifully extreme forms, one master might instruct 1,000 children. The monitors participated in an essentially apprenticeship relationship with the master, receiving instruction in delivering lessons, listening to recitations, evaluating progress, and even making pens and cleaning slates. The system strengthened both the personal (subject matter) and the professional knowledge of these ten to twelve year old apprentices.

Lancaster in particular demanded that his superintendents ensure that the monitors who served under them were "able, as scholars, to understand and perform the lessons they are appointed to teach," but were also "instructed, under the inspection of the superintendents, in the mode of teaching" (Lancaster 1808, p. 8). Lancaster's investment in his preparation scheme led to the creation of the first "training college" in the United Kingdom when he constructed a hostel adjacent to his school on Borough Road of Southwark in south London. Lancaster's monitors therefore received what was perhaps the first "theoretical" teacher education in England even if that particular form of theory was delivered – significantly perhaps for the future – by lecturers who were themselves school practitioners.

Bell, in contrast, found Lancaster's insistence on subjecting prospective monitors to "lectures" on school-keeping to be "burlesque." It was, he argued, "by attending the school, seeing what is going on there, and taking a share in the office of tuition, that teachers are to be formed, and not by lectures and formal instruction" (Southey and Southey 1844, vol. II, p. 127). The dispute between Bell and Lancaster consequently prepared the ground for the successive ebb and flow of tension between academic and school-based professional education for prospective teachers.

In the 1830s the tradition of voluntary sponsorship of education, dominated by religious organizations such as the National Society for Promoting the Education of the Poor in the Principles of the Established Church (Anglican) and the non-conformist British and Foreign School Society, began to erode. The national government had attempted to mediate between these rival sponsors, and to entice them into supporting less sectarian schools. It was not until the Reform Act of 1832 brought to the House of Commons a number of political radicals who were profoundly disturbed by the "grave defects" in England's provision for the "health, housing, employment, and education of the great mass of working people" that Parliament was able seriously to challenge the monopoly of the churches (Dent 1977, p. 10).

Among the new members of Parliament, John Roebuck of Bath most aggressively argued the case for public support of education. In 1833 he launched an education bill which endorsed "the universal and national education of the whole people" and provided for a "Minister of Public Instruction, elected School District Committees, central and local financial aid to supplement parents' pence, compulsory attendance from six to twelve years of age and normal schools for teacher training" modeled on the French approach to educating teachers (Evans 1985, p. 28). The considerable leverage of the religious lobbies, however, doomed such a radical proposal, even in a reformed Parliament. But a modest step toward reform was initiated within a few days of Roebuck's defeat, when Parliament approved an education bill that authorized £20,000 per annum to build elementary schools and passed a Factory Act intended to curtail child labour and to encourage school attendance. This legislation invigorated aspirations for expanding elementary education. Although the funds were initially restricted to supporting the building costs of schools sponsored by the National Society or the British and Foreign School Society, they did set a precedent for meaningful public support of elementary schools.

By the end of the decade, pressure was building both to increase the scale of the grants, and to support institutions that were not under the control of the two religious societies. In 1839 Lord John Russell pressed for the creation of some sort of "Board or Committee" to oversee popular education. Shortly thereafter the Committee of the Privy Council for Education was appointed, to be chaired by the Lord President of the Council. It is important that rather than creating a "department of state for education," or some similar entity, Parliament attempted to escape the religious struggles such an act would provoke by accepting the "Committee." Although it was chaired by the President of the Council, that Committee's work was actually carried out by an appointed "Secretary," a senior civil servant. The first Secretary was James Kay-Shuttleworth, a former principal at a teacher training institution, who conceived of the Committee's work ambitiously and imaginatively. Kay-Suttleworth's agenda for expanding the educational service included lifting the restriction that dedicated funds exclusively to the construction of school buildings for the churches, thereby supporting the use of public funds for the operation of a variety of schools. His enthusiasm for popular education led to a sharp increase in the annual parliamentary grant to elementary schools from £30,000 in 1839 to £800,000 just over two decades later.

The accelerating pace of investment of public funds in largely private schools obliged the Committee to organize a programme of inspection and assessment. After a brief but intense dialogue with the Church of England (the largest recipient of government grants), the Committee compromised by allowing the Church to play a role in selecting the inspectors who would report on its schools. Essentially denominational in its origins, Her Majesty's Inspectorate (HMI), as this force was known, would become one of the most mysterious and influential forces in British education. Because of Kay-Shuttleworth's perspective, HMI pursued a diplomatic rather than "inquisitorial" role. They were responsible not only for inspecting schools but also for advising central government on matters of policy and practice, and for providing encouragement, advice, and assistance to local communities about educational matters.

The expansion of public support for elementary schooling exposed the inadequacies of existing arrangements for recruiting and preparing teachers in

England and Wales. Kay-Shuttleworth responded to the emerging need with two related strategies. First, he took advantage of legislation passed in 1834 to fund the construction of teacher training institutions. After it proved politically impossible to establish public colleges, he drew on the £10,000 annual grant to help construct voluntary training colleges. He even participated personally in the founding of an institution in Battersea, a suburb of London. Battersea, a residential college dedicated to an array of educational experimentation and innovation, helped to define many of the features that would characterize the model approach to preparing teachers to practise in England at least through the remainder of the nineteenth century. Most notably, it established "the residential college" as the "type," the modal form of teacher training institution, even though, of course, Lancaster's Borough Road school and a couple of other institutions had been residential for some time. Kay-Shuttleworth's campaign to help build training colleges (most of which were Anglican, as in the earlier case of elementary school capital investments) led to a flurry of institution building during the 1840s. By 1850 twenty-five of the thirty or so training colleges in England, which served 2500 students annually, were operated by the Church of England, and all but one were residential (Dent 1977, p. 15; Evans 1985, pp. 169-70).

The first generation of training colleges – accused by one recent observer of "imitating universities in everything but academic standards" (Hencke 1978, p. 18) – were quasi-missionary institutions where religious knowledge and commitment were strengthened. Students of the two-year courses were expected to combine a smattering of educational theory with considerable subject-matter study and even more school practice. The facilities were inhospitable, the workloads were intimidating. As one might expect, the colleges had a difficult time enticing students into potential careers as elementary teachers, a line of work that was neither well-regarded nor rewarded at the time. They had an even harder time convincing many of the students to complete the full course; most defected by the end of their first year.

Kay-Shuttleworth turned his attention to this problem in the colleges. After using public funds to promote the establishment of training colleges, he lent even more central government authority, legitimacy, and resources to teacher education by providing maintenance grants to prospective teachers in 1846. He provided public support for a corps of apprentices, "pupil-teachers" he called them, who were thirteen-year-olds with desirable intellectual, social, and moral qualities who aspired to become elementary school teachers. They received on-the-job training at the hands of head teachers in selected grant-supported schools for five years, until they were eighteen. Those who completed the apprenticeship experience successfully and passed their examinations in both academic subjects and teaching became "qualified teachers." It is noteworthy that the pupil-teachers could become qualified teachers without any distinct, separate formal professional education, a situation that would haunt the scheme for decades.

During the early 1850s, the most talented graduates were then offered Queen's scholarships to complete a two-year course at one of the training colleges. This arrangement pleased not only the training colleges, which welcomed the enrolment of former pupil-teachers supported through public scholarships, but also the young aspiring teachers, most of whom used the mechanism to rise a little above their working-class origins.

Troubled economic times in the late 1850s and 1860s led to several changes in educational policy that deeply affected the nature of elementary schooling and the pupil-teacher scheme for preparing instructors, which had quickly become the most popular route into elementary teaching. First, in order to gain better control over spending, Parliament in 1856 established an Education Department, which replaced the Committee, an agency that had been essentially free to spend Parliament's revenues without being under its authority.

Second, a Revised Code was passed in 1862 that regulated the distribution of public funds to grant-maintained schools through a system of "payment by results," an ingenious but ultimately damaging innovation promoted by Robert Lowe. On the one hand, it enforced a form of accountability that made public funding of elementary education palatable to many in Parliament. On the other hand, the scheme has been blamed for the intensification of rote memory skill development as the prevailing learning style, direct drill as the typical pedagogy, and the "three-Rs" as the dominant curricula of the later nineteenth and early twentieth centuries. This approach to public funding led, many scholars have claimed, to a situation where teachers crammed their pupils "in a mindless fashion for the annual examinations so that grants could be maximized." Schools for privileged children, in sharp contrast, made little use of the "payment by results" system, thereby avoiding its "restricting and debilitating effects" (Dunford & Sharp 1990, pp. 6-7).

This form of educational financing had parallel consequences for the pupil-teacher scheme. As with other students in grant-supported schools, it tended to constrict the general and personal education of the pupil-teachers to the "three-Rs," and in this way combined with expectations of extended school practice to limit further the opportunities of prospective elementary teachers to acquire either a liberal or professional education. In contrast, it should be recalled, secondary teachers, although similarly lacking professional training, did benefit from liberal education at both school and university.

The number of participants in the pupil-teacher scheme sharply increased after the passing of the 1870 Education Act. This Act – the so-called Forster Education Act – was introduced during the Liberal reformist ministry led by Gladstone and represents an important milestone in the development of public elementary education in England. Hitherto, public investment had of course flowed entirely to and through the major voluntary organizations providing denominational education. In that sense, the system remained voluntary and private, albeit with growing support from public funds. By the late 1860s serious limitations were painfully obvious: those who were not Episcopalians objected to the virtual monopoly enjoyed in rural areas by the Church of England, whereas the churches lacked the means and perhaps the will to provide even minimal elementary education in the new urban areas that were expanding as a result of rapid industrial development. The government therefore determined that, while respecting the rights of the voluntary bodies to continue to maintain their own systems, it would be necessary to devise some new arrangement which would "fill the gaps" in that existing provision. No orderly and universal system of local government yet existed in England (nor would it until nearly twenty years later) and the solution adopted was therefore that already familiar in the United States. In those areas where existing provision was inadequate, School Boards were to be elected and empowered both to levy local property taxes and to provide elementary schools for the working classes. These became the so-called Board Schools. As a result, there was in succeeding years a dramatic increase in the number of children attending elementary schools, as well as a growing rivalry between the churches and the Boards.

It was, of course, also necessary to provide for a matching increase in the number of trained teachers. Between 1870 and 1880 the number of "certificated teachers" jumped from 12,467 to 31,422, while the number of pupil-teachers preparing to practise more than doubled, from 14,612 to 32,128. Because the demand for elementary teachers was so great, however, the fastest-growing corps of instructors consisted of uncertificated "assistant" teachers, most of whom were former pupil-teachers who had failed to complete their apprenticeship or could not pass their examinations (Dent 1977, p. 26). The reputation of the pupil-teacher scheme evaporated quickly after 1870. What once promised to save the cause of mass education was seen as an impediment to improving quality and standards for teaching and learning. A number of communities attempted to address the problem by gathering pupil-teachers for advanced professional study in Centres and by raising the age of entrance to fourteen or fifteen.

National pessimism about elementary learning and teaching deepened through the mid-1880s, when the Conservative government appointed a Royal Commission chaired by Lord Cross to review the impact of the education acts of the previous generation. Many of the Commission's members were supporters of the voluntary, religious sector, and were therefore critical of much of the recent expansion of public services. But the Commission was sharply divided, since another constituency was determined to curtail the influence of the churches. These deep divisions led ultimately to the release in 1888 of a minority as well as the majority report.

On most educational issues, including the appropriate place of religious instruction, for example, the two groups differed only slightly. But in the analysis of teacher education, and recommendations for its improvement, the majority and minority reports differed profoundly. The majority was moderately supportive of the prevailing pupil-teacher scheme, suggesting only slight modifications in its operation, such as the expansion of the embryonic "Pupil-Teacher Centres." The minority issued a stinging dissent, arguing that the pupil-teachers were individuals who were "badly taught and who taught badly." The pupil-teacher system had become the "weakest part of our educational machinery," they added, and "great changes are needed if it is to be continued" (Cross Commission 1888, p. 101).

There were comparable differences of opinion on the nature and value of the residential denominational training colleges. Testimony before the Cross Commission, particularly from HMI, applauded the contributions of the colleges, especially their residential expectations, which were seen to provide a homelike atmosphere in which to develop good personal and moral habits. More critical voices condemned the colleges as "introverted, unprogressive, obsessed with examinations, and out of touch with the schools" (Dent 1977, p. 29). The colleges responded in their defence that most of these claims were exaggerated, and that the pupil-teacher and payment by results schemes left training colleges little choice but to accept ill-qualified students who had to be drilled in content to pass examinations imposed by external agencies.

After listening to such conflicting testimony, the liberal minority members proposed a radical departure from contemporary arrangements. They favoured the Scottish model of attaching teacher education to the universities which allowed prospective teachers to acquire a decent academic education as well as a thorough professional training. They challenged the residential religious training colleges by endorsing non-denominational day colleges associated with institutions of higher education.

The conservative majority reacted vehemently to this critique of the apprenticeship and residential college approaches to teacher education. In particular they were troubled by the implied benefits of substituting a university degree and associated professional studies for extended school practice. Such students, they declared, "would be unsettled and unfitted, rather than prepared for their work as public elementary teachers" (Cross Commission 1888).

In the event, the minority voice apparently prevailed. In the decade following the Cross Commission Report, the pupil-teacher scheme was roundly condemned and day training colleges were established, most of them affiliated with the great civic universities founded late in the century. An inquiry into the "workings of the Pupil-Teacher system," chaired by the Senior Chief Inspector, expressed its "emphatic" opinion in 1898 that "the too frequent practice of committing the whole of the training and teaching of classes to immature and uneducated young persons is economically wasteful and educationally unsatisfactory, and even dangerous, to the teachers and taught in equal measure" (quoted in Dent 1977, p. 27). But it acknowledged that the nation had become too dependent on the system for it to be abolished at that time. Despite their preference for a "full secondary education" for all prospective elementary teachers, the committee members had to be content with hoping for further reform and improvement in the fledgling Centres.[4]

The idea of the day training colleges (actually training "departments") linked to universities appealed to virtually all institutions of higher education because of the access to public funds that accompanied the new students, just as the residential colleges had been stimulated by the presence of the Queen's Scholars a half-century earlier. The Education Code of 1890, which laid out regulations for the day training colleges, authorized a programme of study consisting of lectures in the history and theory of education, practice teaching sessions in schools where model lessons were presented, and the dreaded "criticism" events, in which prospective teachers had their pedagogical thinking and delivery publicly assessed. The individuals who were responsible for this work were typically called "masters" or "mistresses of method." Records of a number of masters and mistresses of method held by the History of Education Museum, housed at the University of Leeds, offer a vivid glimpse into the substance and expectations that the departments had for prospective teachers. Several of these enterprising individuals capitalized on the expectations surrounding their positions to publish their own manuals of method and the first textbooks in the history and psychology of education (Thomas 1990a, p. 21).

Some of the masters and mistresses adopted a decidedly modern approach to initial teacher education, emphasizing professional judgment and ethics over technique. One lecturer at Liverpool observed, for example, that it was not the business of the "training department to give students a finished technique. . . . It is their business to show that technique depends upon devotion, upon knowledge – of subjects, and of pupils, and the history of both – upon a philosophical conception of the value of subjects in a scheme of general education, upon laborious and loving practice through a lifetime" (quoted in Kelly 1981, p. 233). More closely associated with the university-based training departments than with the residential colleges, this approach to strengthening the conceptual foundations of prospective teachers set the stage for expanding the theoretical component of the course over the next seventy years.

By 1900 the sixteen university programmes served about 1200 students annually, approximately a quarter of the 5,000 students preparing to teach at the elementary level. The students in these university-based courses were of course academically better qualified than their counterparts in the colleges, and therefore more consistently able to pass examinations and secure certificated teacher status. Since the training colleges were not generally viewed as post-secondary institutions, teacher education was now for the first time linked to genuine higher education. This affiliation raised the stature of elementary teaching and, by exposing the academic weaknesses of their students, forced the denominational training colleges to consider their place in the rapidly evolving higher education sector.

Since many of the participants in the new concurrent (simultaneous academic and professional preparation) university-based venture sought degrees, it provided the first real opportunity for prospective secondary teachers to acquire professional education. Until this time, it should be understood, prospective secondary teachers received no professional education since their university degree studies were assumed to constitute an adequate preparation to teach. And the training colleges were not engaged in preparing secondary teachers. But the promise of "fusing the training of all teachers into a harmonious unity," as one historian called it, never materialized (Dent 1977, pp. 33-34). Despite several instances where the denominational and university training college students joined together to enrol in general and professional coursework, the two institutions typically separated, perpetuating the gulf between elementary and secondary teacher education, while even the university-based programmes customarily split into separate elementary and secondary departments. The universities admitted only a small number of students for teacher training – two hundred a year by 1910 – and their programmes in secondary teaching were therefore much smaller than the elementary provision either in the universities themselves or in the colleges (Thomas 1990, p. 29).

The Cross Commission's minority members, therefore, had taken positions that proved to be either prescient or influential. In one way, however, their efforts were frustrated. They had wanted to go beyond even the connection with universities and to encourage the locally elected "School Boards," established through the Education Act of 1870, to develop their own publicly-funded day training colleges. Such an aspiration was not, however, to be satisfied until the passing of the important Education Act of 1902.

By 1900 the prevailing nineteenth-century arrangements for educating children and teachers were crumbling. The religious denominations were each year less able to protect, let alone advance, their historical claims to educate the nation's children and those who would be required to teach them. The cheap, mass monitorial systems of Lancaster and Bell had succumbed to Glasgow's Normal Seminary leader David Stow's model of a single adult teacher responsible for a classroom of students. Elementary schooling was rapidly expanding. The prerogatives of even the top-tier endowed grammar schools and the great "public schools," such as Eton, which drew their students from across the nation rather than locally, were constantly challenged by a Parliament committed to investing public resources in children from all social classes, by 1900 at the secondary level as well as at the elementary level. The Bryce Commission had just cautiously recommended that prospective secondary teachers should secure some professional education beyond their degrees. And the traditions both of apprenticeship teacher education and of residential denominational moral development in the colleges, although still popular, were being subjected to healthy competition from the university-based academic community.

The Triumph of Academic Credentials, 1902-1963

Nineteenth-century assumptions and practices, already modified in the later years of the nineteenth century, were subjected to fundamental change in the years before World War One. The movement to consolidate the emerging approaches of the previous generation found forceful expression in the 1902 Education Act, up to that time the most far-reaching piece of educational legislation in Britain's history. The chief architect of the 1902 Act was Robert Morant, a powerful civil servant who had formed a strong relationship with Prime Minister Arthur Balfour in order to fashion for himself a major role in shaping educational policy. The Conservatives, who had taken power in 1896, had been diverted from educational reform by the Boer War. When the war ended early in 1902, Balfour and Morant took the opportunity to strike an agreement with the Church of England in order to moderate opposition to their proposed reform. Religious divisions among the Anglicans, Nonconformists and secularists delayed the Act's passage for two stormy months, and forced Morant and the Conservatives to accept a number of compromises.

Morant and the Conservatives wanted to undermine the popularly-elected School Boards, which had been established in communities where the voluntary, religious societies were failing to provide all of the elementary schooling that was needed. Like their counterparts in America and elsewhere, conservative school reformers were uncomfortable with the political ambitions of locally-elected boards, especially in the larger urban centres. They preferred an administrative arrangement that could be shaped more directly by "expert" educational opinion, one less vulnerable and accommodating to the alleged abuses of local patronage politics. The Church wanted a decentralized educational authority, at least for all forms of secular schooling; religious leaders feared a strong central department out of the control of the denominations.

Some proponents of administrative reforms pursued in the interests of benevolent efficiency had long argued for placing public elementary education under the control of authorities elected or appointed to provide the full range of local services: roads, public health, sanitation, water supply, planning, as well as schooling itself. That solution had not been available in 1870 when the powerful School Boards were instituted for the simple reason that no orderly and accountable system of local government then existed in England. That deficiency had, however, been remedied in 1888 when Parliament divided the whole of the country into local administrative areas, known as Counties (a historic term in England) and County Boroughs (large urban areas treated for all legal purposes as Counties in their own right). Earnest reformers like Morant could and did now argue that efficiency and coordination would best be achieved by using this new system of local government to bring order into the local administration of education.

It is ironic that a Conservative administration (whose successors many years later were to denounce the growth of local government powers) should have now proceeded in the 1902 Act to extend and consolidate those powers in ways which dominated educational policy making for most of the twentieth century. The Act abolished the School Boards and committed all their powers to the new local government units (Counties, County Boroughs, and for elementary education only some smaller units of defined size). These Counties and County Boroughs became the Local Education Authorities (the LEAs), whose powers grew steadily and (it seemed) irreversibly over the years. Support, if not enthusiasm, for the LEAs by the churches was secured by permitting the funding of voluntary schools with public revenue. All costs of operating – not just constructing – the religious schools were placed in the LEA's hands. The shift to public funding was accompanied by the placement of all non-religious instruction in the voluntary schools under the jurisdiction of the LEAs. This folded denominational schools more deeply into the public system.

In addition to extending their influence over religious schools, the 1902 Act obliged the LEAs to investigate and invest in education "other than elementary." In doing so it solidified the emerging partnership between central and local government authority, and thrust the public sector more ambitiously into the entire array of educational institutions.[5] For example, the Act's expectation led the LEAs to fashion a national system of secondary education by helping to establish their own grammar schools (called "provided") and to fund the endowed grammar schools (called "non-provided"), thereby expanding access to secondary education for working-class youth. The charge led them to explore and shape the entire domain of "further" (adult and technical) education. And notably for our study, the mandate allowed the LEAs to establish local public training colleges to educate teachers.

In the decade following the 1902 Act, LEAs established twenty-two such colleges for training teachers, all of which were non-denominational. Some were residential, like those of the churches, while others enrolled students who lived independently in the community, like many students in the universities. Much experimentation spawned a variety of institutional arrangements during that first decade. In London alone, for example, in 1902 the London County Council – in fact anticipating Morant's proposals a year later – set up a joint teacher training college with London University, with funding from the public authority. The County Council acquired another college in 1904 and a year later, with financial assistance from the Goldsmiths Company, entered into another partnership arrangement with London University. Given the number of LEAs at the time authorized to establish post-secondary programmes (146), the pace of institution-building was relatively slow. Funding arrangements were not generous enough to encourage the LEAs to maintain a large teacher-training institution, and many officials were disturbed by the potential for "poaching:" the recruitment by an LEA that operated no training college of teachers who had been successfully and expensively prepared by a nearby LEA.

The expanding presence of the LEA training colleges and the accelerating aggressiveness of the government in centralizing control of the teacher education system put the religious colleges in a difficult position. Like the university-based day training schemes, the LEA colleges competed with the denominational institutions for prospective qualified teachers. Troubled by the unused capacity of the church colleges – a result of restrictions on the religious orientation and beliefs of students and staff – the central government moved imperiously in 1907 to abolish tests of denominational faith in the colleges. The churches reacted within days, organizing marches of impressive delegations. The Roman Catholics confronted the Prime Minister, telling him that they "could not possibly accept" some of the new Regulations, and would "certainly disregard" them (quoted in Dent 1977, p. 63). It took a year to hammer out a compromise which permitted the denominational colleges to impose a faith test on one-half of their students. Although it partially capitulated on the matter of restricting religious affiliation, the government did seize authority over setting intake numbers and qualifications, and controlling the length and substance of training courses.

Balfour's 1902 Act stimulated central and local governments to confront the teetering pupil-teacher schemes. Increasingly concerned about the pupil-teachers' weak academic education, Morant began to strengthen standards of disciplinary learning with his first set of Regulations, issued in 1903. Over the ensuing decade he several times elevated the academic qualifications for the apprentices, raised to sixteen the age of entry into the system, and curtailed their access to scholarships enabling them to attend training colleges. His efforts were supported by the National Union of Teachers (NUT), an organization that recognized the detrimental influence that the unprepared pupil-teachers were having on aspirations to professionalize teaching and to attract talented students into the occupation.

The pupil-teacher schemes were devastated by the combined public and private assault. Before the first decade of the twentieth century was over, the official journal of the NUT was declaring that "the old-style pupil-teacher will soon be as extinct as the dodo," and Walter Runciman, President of the national Board of Education (which had replaced the Committee of Council in 1888-1889), observed that the pupil-teacher system was "dying out all over the country" (quoted in Dent 1977, pp. 55-56). Although some survivors lingered on for several decades in a few rural communities, the last of the great nineteenth-century apprentice schemes had disappeared by World War I.

In sum, teacher education had been transformed during the early twentieth-century by the establishment of the university-based and LEA-funded training colleges, the gradual secularization and upgrading of the denominational colleges, and the collapse of the pupil-teacher system. Once these initiatives were under way, reformers moved to realign the balance between academic and professional studies for both elementary and secondary teachers.

A strong body of opinion was emerging and arguing that prospective secondary teachers, trained exclusively in academic disciplines at the university, did need some professional education. Traditions of direct didactic instruction in secondary schools, however, largely silenced voices advocating a change in the way teachers were prepared. It would take several decades for sufficient pressure to be generated in order to alter the pattern that was almost universal during the early twentieth century. Elementary teachers trained in the colleges, in contrast, ordinarily began their careers with little more than the equivalent of a secondary education in the disciplines: indeed, their two-year training in the colleges barely brought them even to that standard. The university-based day training colleges in principle provided the opportunity for concurrent study toward a degree and a teacher qualification, all to occur within three years (which was the maximum amount of time students were supported with government grants). This limited amount of time posed considerable demands on all students. The government went so far as to manipulate the examination schedule to prevent even the most ambitious students from substituting academic, disciplinary studies for their professional lessons in methods of instruction and classroom management.

The Board of Education was worried that prospective teachers who were sponsored with government grants would neglect their professional training and concentrate instead on securing a good degree, which would be more valuable in the open market for employment. Students who had been recruited and financed as potential teachers were therefore being tempted into other careers. This problem plagued institutions in all fields committed to investing public resources in individuals intent on turning that investment toward their own private ends.

The government remained reluctant to permit publicly-subsidized prospective teachers to acquire strong disciplinary or degree-level credentials until Morant eventually conceded the importance of allowing teachers to move toward acquiring degrees. Morant had been uneasy about the potential misuse of public investments, and saw no reason to encourage students to misapply their grants. The universities and many practising teachers did not share Morant's scepticism about the place of academic work in the preparation of future teachers. The universities resisted any restrictions on their students' aspirations while the teaching force, particularly elementary teachers, had long fantasized about their occupation's potential improvement in stature if it could be seen as a learned profession, based on an exclusive university degree.

Morant gradually came to acknowledge the value of providing some degree opportunities for teachers and instituted in 1911 the consecutive "three plus one" model of teacher education: a three-year university degree followed by an intensive year-long professional course that was able to preserve its integrity. In order to deter prospective teachers who intended to abscond with a publicly-subsidized degree and abandon the education force, Morant imposed the notorious "Pledge" that obliged recipients of grants to sign a commitment to teach in grant-supported schools for a specified number of years in exchange for tuition and maintenance support (Gordon, Aldrich, & Dean 1991, pp. 251-53).

The universities responded enthusiastically to the consecutive four-year plan. But the colleges typically continued to offer concurrent two-year or three-year Certificate courses, for their students were often not prepared for regular university degree study and wanted to get into the classroom as quickly as possible. In 1914, this system of concurrent and consecutive courses embraced eighty-eight separate institutions in England and Wales: fifty voluntary residential colleges, twenty-two LEA (municipal) colleges, and sixteen university departments. This dual system of professional courses, with each sector associated with institutions differing profoundly in tradition, authority, and influence, deepened the separation between the two worlds of teacher preparation. The universities provided graduate professional education to those with degrees (particularly those bound toward elite secondary schools) while the training colleges prepared non-graduate teachers for the elementary and less selective schools. It was an arrangement that persisted through most of the twentieth century.

Reform in the education of young children after World War I probably exacerbated the separation of teacher training institutions, as progressive influences created a distinctive culture of elementary schooling in England while secondary education in the decades between the world wars remained comparatively traditional in style. The abandonment of the Victorian practice of "payment by results" gradually opened the door for reconceptualizing the education of young children. By the turn of the century the educational community was willing to listen to the voices of child-centred nursery and primary education, to the descendants of Froebel and others on the Continent who challenged teachers to recognize the distinctive ways that young children learned and to adapt instruction to their students' connection to the world. Nursery and infant school leaders Margaret McMillan, Maria Montessori, Susan Isaacs, and later John Dewey contributed to the formation of a uniquely English culture of education for early learners that celebrated individualization, aesthetic and physical development, and an object-orientation for infants and young children. Robert Morant's 1902 Education Act symbolically acknowledged the shift in direction by declaring nursery education to be a vital stage for the investment of public funds. Indeed, the official Handbook for elementary teachers, released in 1905, captured the evolving spirit when it stressed the "importance of developing individual abilities and interests and the building of character and moral training, thereby identifying a much broader purpose for elementary education." The Handbook also bestowed on elementary teachers an unprecedented measure of freedom in the areas of "curricula and method" (quoted in Evans 1985, p. 86). Successive editions of the Handbook reflected the mounting pace of progressive pedagogy.

While intending to overturn the tradition of relentless separation between "elementary and secondary schooling" in Great Britain in favour of a concept of a "continuous educative process" with primary and secondary phases, a series of reports released in the late 1920s and 1930s inadvertently helped to strengthen the emerging culture of primary education. In particular the Hadow Report on The Primary School (1931) sanctioned a definition of education for young children, "not in terms of subjects to be taught and facts to be learned, but in terms of experiences to be undergone and activities to be engaged in" (Evans 1985, p. 87). Prevailing standards of learning "by listening and mechanical exercises" were to be abandoned in favour of "learning by doing through the medium of purposeful practical and expressive activity." Attempting to strike a balance between virtually universal practice and progressive visions, however, the report admitted that some whole-class instruction was "indispensable," and there persisted a continuing need for "drill in reading, writing, and arithmetic" (Board of Education 1931). Smaller class sizes during the 1930s enabled some teachers to accommodate modest progressive practices even in the face of continuing intense pressure from parents who were unwilling to risk their children's success in the high stakes' "eleven-plus" examinations that played an instrumental role in opening access to desirable secondary schools. But it would take at least two generations for the pressure of the eleven-plus examinations to recede sufficiently for nursery and primary teachers to be in a position to act on the emerging vision of education for young children.

The training colleges, however, did capitalize on the emerging identity of progressive primary schooling. The colleges quickly became havens for proponents of child-centred learning based on new models of developmental psychology. The ideology nicely accommodated the relatively non-academic backgrounds of their students, an increasing number of whom were young women anxious to secure appointments that offered close and affective relationships with young children. The new primary culture was able to thrive in the cloistered environments of the residential colleges. In contrast, the new vision of child-centredness failed to take root in the strong graduate-level, secondary, subject orientation of the university departments.

There were some changes in secondary education between the wars, but they had little effect on the university departments. Although the terms "grammar" and "secondary" school were at this time effectively synonymous, the central government, through the LEAs, did take a small step down the path of opening access to non-fee paying students. An effort launched by the 1902 Act made scholarship funds available to deserving adolescents who passed a qualifying examination to attend secondary schools that received state grants. But progress was very slow. In 1914 only two and a half percent of the eligible elementary school pupils won scholarships. Nearly thirty years later, on the eve of World War II, the proportion had quadrupled, but still only ten percent of the children of appropriate age moved on to secondary schools, in spite of the strong commitment of the trade union movement and the Labour party to a Secondary Education for All, as a significantly named publication expressed it in 1922.

The Hadow Report on *The Education of the Adolescent* (1926) aspired to enhance the schooling opportunities available to young adults, once the school-leaving age was raised to fifteen, as it proposed (but which was not achieved until 1945). It successfully defended the concept of a sequential educational ladder of primary and secondary education, and proposed that all students should receive four years of secondary schooling after age eleven, when they would complete their primary schooling. As they were enacted, however, the Hadow proposals seemed to take a step backward for every step forward. For example, the effort to strengthen the secondary education available to all youth was compromised by the retention of a powerful eleven-plus examination and the establishment of "modern schools," for adolescents who could not win places in grammar schools. The modern schools were supposed to provide a distinctive form of non-academic education that led, if not actually to vocational tracks, then to essentially practical and realistic courses. Although the Hadow committee optimistically anticipated a "parity of esteem" between the modern and grammar schools, the Board of Education shrank from acknowledging the new institutions as "secondary" schools at all, and often refused to use the complete label, calling them simply "modern schools."

The event that did engage the universities was the creation of the Joint Examining Boards in 1929. Historically, neither governmental nor other external bodies had any power to define university organization or practice. Rather, the universities held the right to approve of or validate their own programmes or courses. Several entrepreneurial training colleges for teachers had approached local universities and convinced them to validate their two-year courses, which were already receiving a national "Board of Education" qualification or approval. These colleges, including Goldsmiths in London, believed that a university validation certificate would improve the value of their credentials. A committee under Viscount Burnham, established in 1925 to review the education of elementary teachers, thought that this arrangement was superior to relying exclusively on Board of Education assessments, and would elevate the prestige of the entire enterprise. It proposed that universities and teacher training colleges across the nation should establish Joint Examining Boards to validate all of the courses for prospective teachers, not just those in the university departments (Hencke 1978, pp. 24-25). To set standards for courses and hold examinations twelve regional boards were formed with the collaboration of the universities, training colleges, and LEAs. HMI, which had conducted examinations of prospective teachers, curtailed that work in 1928, as the Joint Examining Boards assumed their responsibilities. The university's authority to dictate the terms of teacher education outside as well as inside its own walls became an early, defining characteristic of the preparation of teachers. It persisted powerfully until the 1970s, when new and very different policies were asserted.

Under Churchill's Coalition government during the early 1940s a number of important actions occurred that changed the nation's educational agenda for the next generation. Planning for reconstruction following the war led to two major events: the passage of the Education Act of 1944 and the release of the McNair Committee Report on teachers and teacher education. Called the "Butler Act" in recognition of the contribution of R.A. Butler, President of the Board of Education, the Education Act of 1944 abolished the Board of Education in favour of a Ministry of Education, an agency with somewhat greater control over the LEAs than the old Board had possessed. The LEAs, consolidated into about 150 entities, rationalized their educational ladders into three stages (primary, secondary, and further), finally eliminating the official designation of "elementary" school, as had been envisioned in the Hadow Report of 1926. Fees were abolished in all types of publicly maintained schools.

The movement toward universal, free public secondary education was achieved in principle, but the architecture of the emerging system was controversial. The "tripartite" model of academic grammar, non-academic modern, and technical schools, proposed in the influential Norwood Committee Report of 1943, was put gradually into place. The committee had argued that children could be grouped by "type of mind" into three categories: the academic children, who engaged in "learning for its own sake," would attend grammar schools; those who were interested in "applied science or applied art" would go to the secondary technical schools; and children who were more comfortable with "concrete things than ideas" would be sent to the secondary modern schools (Dunford & Sharp 1990, p. 20). Although the committee assumed that these alternative schools would enjoy equal status, the public failed to accept a "parity of esteem" across the range of institutions. Professional and middle-class families were convinced that their children's futures would be jeopardized if they failed to win a position in a grammar school, where the only "genuine" secondary education – recognized by institutions of higher education – was available. Even the stumbling effort to create high status technical programmes failed to reduce the pressure on the eleven-plus examinations.

A fundamentally different policy of developing comprehensive secondary schools, providing for all abilities and aptitudes, received only intermittent support in the 1940s and 1950s. Many leaders in the Labour government of 1945-1951, in the LEAs, and in the Ministry of Education, had attended grammar schools and were undoubtedly impressed with the quality of education they had received. Even the more radical among them pressed for the expansion of the state-sponsored grammar schools (now that they were accessible to all on the basis of merit) rather than the comprehensive schools as the institutions that would advance the interests of the working class. The policy leadership was suspicious, if not openly hostile, to the untried comprehensive model.

The secondary education establishment was also visibly disturbed by the concept of replacing the separate academic grammar and practical modern schools with some new amalgamated form of common school. Teachers in the grammar schools enjoyed teaching their elite, selected students, and modern school teachers were no more enthusiastic than their grammar colleagues about working with multi-ability classes. Traditions of selectivity and segmentation had benefited the corps of secondary teachers and discouraged them from pursuing the ideal of common, comprehensive schooling. Further, the history of preparation for secondary teachers had neither developed a notion of comprehensivization nor had it encouraged beginning teachers to think about learners and their diversity. Commitments to subject matter knowledge had largely defined the culture of secondary teaching.

Consequently, in the six years of Labour rule, before Churchill's return with a Conservative government in 1951, only thirteen comprehensive secondary schools were established. During the ensuing thirteen years of Conservative rule, the controversy over comprehensive secondary schooling became an increasingly lively issue, with the Labour Party by the mid-1950s leading the campaign against continued selectivity, in part because the Conservatives were candidly "championing the cause of the grammar schools" (Dunford & Sharp 1990, p. 22).

It was against this background of a fragmented system of schooling, with all that it implied for the lives and training of teachers, and on the eve of the passing of the 1944 Act, that the McNair Committee submitted its Report. Its chairman, Arnold McNair was Vice-Chancellor of Liverpool University and its terms of reference had been to investigate the supply, recruitment, and education of teachers. The Committee's charge grew out of concern with the divided and unsystematic "system" for preparing teachers and the commensurate need for a coherent, integrated approach that was based on new connections among the array of institutions responsible for training teachers.

Within the McNair Committee there existed two approaches to bringing order to the "non-system" of teacher education. A vocal minority, in tones that perhaps foreshadowed later attacks on teacher education, remained sceptical of the "academic" perversion that would inevitably accompany closer association with (or domination by) the university community, an association which was favoured by the majority of the Committee. The minority declared that the university's role in teacher education should remain essentially limited to providing subject matter expertise and research. Professional education was to be a "subsidiary function" of the university departments. In addition to imposing an inappropriate and unfortunate "urban outlook," the universities would inevitably promote the worst sort of "academic" fantasies about what good teachers needed to possess. The minority endorsed an array of "human" qualities and values, which, they declared, "have no necessary connection with university standards at all and are apt not to receive due recognition and encouragement in an academic atmosphere but will be adequately safeguarded in the training colleges" (Board of Education 1944, pp. 183-96).

Supportive of the advantages of a genuine higher education base for teacher education, the majority attacked the isolation of the colleges and universities from one another and proposed the Committee's most enduring recommendation: the creation of regional Area Training Organizations (ATOs) that brought all of the teacher training institutions together under a university "School (or Institute) of Education," an agency that assumed responsibility for setting standards, evaluating courses, conducting examinations, bestowing awards, and undertaking advanced courses and research in education. This placed teachers in the university, although not an organic part of it, since apart from their departments of education, universities were not involved in the work of the ATOs. Other university groups cared little about the education of teachers and were typically unwilling to exercise any responsibility for quality control. In many ways, teacher education had been grafted onto a higher education institution that long predated it and which would never fully embrace it. Teacher education was increasingly able to take on the trappings of many features and traditions of higher education (with course work increasingly relying on theory, for example). But the ATO structure continued to offer the government (embodied in the non-aggressive – but symbolically significant – presence of HMI) distinctive access to one piece of the university. The ambiguities of these relationships – among the university, teacher educators, and the ATOs - would for decades haunt the effort to prepare teachers.

This reorganization was also initiated in order to raise the stature of all teacher education, by associating all of it more visibly with the universities. The universities were initially ambivalent about becoming more deeply involved in teacher education, and troubled by the prospect of HMI visits such as those that were common in the colleges. Despite some interest in using the ATO federation concept in order to gain access to the universities' lectures and tutorials, the Ministry backed off from intervening in the affairs of the universities, in part responding to implied threats such as that offered by G.B. Jeffery, Director of the London Institute of Education: "if ever it was my sad lot to tell the University that its work was not an acceptable guarantee of academic quality unless it was supported by the verdict of HMI, the days of co-operation between the University and Ministry would be numbered" (quoted in Gordon, Aldrich & Dean 1991, p. 255). Within a decade, ATOs had been established across the nation.

Because a severe teacher shortage through the 1950s undermined efforts to raise standards of entry to the profession, the McNair Committee made other recommendations which were not easily enacted, including raising the requirement for initial qualification to completion of a three-year course: teaching would wait for another generation to become a "graduate" profession.

But the infamous "Pledge," a humiliating legacy of penurious times stipulating a minimum tour of duty for prospective teachers receiving government grants to support their academic and professional education, was finally abolished as a result of the McNair recommendations.

The unprecedented expansion in primary and secondary enrolments following the war had an enormous impact on teacher education institutions. Although the university departments grew dramatically, the largest share of expansion occurred in the training colleges. LEAs received considerable new funding to establish additional colleges, while the Ministry of Education curtailed the creation of new voluntary institutions. The expansion occurred in two phases, the first during the late 1940s, when fifty five new institutions were founded (a quarter of which survived as permanent colleges). A miscalculation of the national birthrate led the government to back off from investing further in teacher education, until it was recognized in the late 1950s that far more training facilities were needed. Contrary to predictions, the birthrate remained high and students were staying in school longer. Moreover, teachers were abandoning their careers far more rapidly than had been expected: the "wastage" or rate of defection for women teachers stood at seventy percent.

The expansion in teacher education was coordinated by the regional ATOs, allowing for centralized planning to be translated more efficiently than had been the case when institutional relationships had been far looser. The improvement in the prestige of teacher training, presumably associated with closer university relationships, increased the pressure to raise entry qualification standards from two years to three years, an ambition that had been frustrated by the teacher shortage of the 1940s and 1950s. The Ministry of Education finally capitulated to advocates of the McNair proposal, and taking advantage of a presumed surplus of teachers put the three-year minimum course requirement into effect in 1960. Everyone expected enrolment in training programmes to drop sharply with the increase in entry and exit requirements. But the improving stature of teaching and teacher education (helped undoubtedly by the increase in standards) resulted in continued increases in applications for training places.

The Ministry left the implementation of the three-year requirement relatively undefined. The goal was to produce "the mature, well-educated, and highly skilled teachers" envisioned in the 1944 Act (quoted in Dent 1977, p. 135). But the route to such a goal was yet to be determined. The historic controversy over the balance of disciplinary and professional study continued to stimulate debate over the direction of the new courses. HMI and others had become convinced that the new curricular space should be filled with academic course work because it was critical for the "health of the teaching profession ... that three-year training should give a considerable proportion of teachers an academic standing and confidence which will enable them to take their places alongside graduates" (Ministry of Education 1957, pp. 2-3). The university departments seized the opportunity to augment the prospective teachers' academic and disciplinary qualifications. Responding to the ethos in which they found themselves, leaders in the university departments of education gave "disproportionate weight to the study of academic subjects and educational theory," at the expense of "practical" training and subject methods (Evans 1985, p. 181). Course leaders accepted the prevailing practice of sixty days worth of whole-class teaching for prospective teachers, and saw no reason to expand its place in the training regimen.

On the eve of the events of 1963, therefore, a modern system of educational credentials had replaced the medieval craft apprentice model in teacher education. The Robbins Committee had recommended moving the professional education of teachers to academic degree status, although it would take another generation for that standard to become universal. Qualifications for teaching careers had been based fully on "education" rather than on experience since McNair in the 1940s, but moving to bestow "graduate" status on the occupation was a grand symbolic gesture that fulfilled the dreams of virtually everyone associated with the educational enterprise. Not only was the event symbolic for the profession, it was understood to represent an ambitious step forward that would guarantee both the disciplinary and professional qualifications of the teaching force, a combination that would help Britain reclaim its competitive position in the great global economy that had emerged from the 1950s. Growing comfortable and confident in the academic setting, the teacher education community was poised to claim and extend the autonomy and independence customarily associated with university protection.

Notes

[1] As explained in the Introduction, our focus is on England and not more generally on Wales, Scotland, and Northern Ireland. The experience of Wales has been quite closely aligned with that of England, far more so than traditions of schooling and teacher education in Scotland and Northern Ireland. As a result, when we refer to "Britain" we mean almost invariably "England."

[2] Our understanding of the evolution of teacher education, and of schooling more generally, has been most obviously shaped by the following works: Dent (1977); Dunford and Sharp (1990); Evans (1985); Gordon, Aldrich, and Dean (1991); Graves ed. (1990); Hencke (1978); Judge (1984); Judge (1991); Lowe (1988); and Silver (1990). We have minimized citations of these works, and have attempted to acknowledge only direct indebtedness or verbatim quotation.

[3] The concept of "validation" requires some explanation. Traditionally, English universities held exclusive prerogative to validate or approve the degrees of institutions of higher education. Non-university institutions would apply to specific universities to have various degree programmes (or "courses" in the English terminology) validated. The university staff would evaluate the proposal and decide whether or not to validate the degree and agree to examine the requesting institution's students at the end of their studies. As a result of the Robbins' Committee Report, the Council for National Academic Awards (CNAA) was established as an alternative to university validation. Other

institutions of higher education, including the polytechnics and colleges of education, could seek either university or CNAA validation.

[4] It is useful to recall that until relatively late, at least through the 1920s, "higher education" in England meant essentially secondary education. The division between primary and secondary schooling represented far more than differences in the age of pupils. Secondary education was largely a colonization by the university. The traditional expectations for teachers and their education at the primary and secondary levels parallels this division.

[5] Again, the traditions of university independence and autonomy require a slight qualification of this generalization. Even though they received some government funds, the universities were not subject to government scrutiny and detailed oversight until late in the twentieth century.

Oxford Studies in Comparative Education, Vol. 4(1/2), 1994

CHAPTER 7

England: after 1963

The promises inherent in the major educational events of 1963 – notably the release of the Newsom and Robbins Reports and the speech by Labour leader Harold Wilson – were during the next several years not equally fulfilled. For example, those who endorsed Robbins' ambitious commitment to close the gap between the traditionally segmented array of teacher training institutions, were deeply disappointed. There emerged strong opposition to the proposal for placing the colleges of education under the umbrella of the universities – in terms not only of validation, but also of their administration and financing. Despite the appeal of the proposal to the teaching profession and the staff in the training colleges, all of whom were excited about the elevation of their stature that would surely accompany the proposal's adoption, those who had historically controlled the operation of the colleges were hostile to the Robbins' recommendations. The LEAs and the Minister of Education, Sir Edward Boyle, in particular feared losing authority over the colleges to the universities, whose historic independence would inevitably be extended to protect the entire teacher training enterprise, including the increasingly liberated "colleges of education." The government rejected that portion of the proposal in late 1964. As a result, the colleges' aspirations to be fully legitimized within the university community were left unrealized, a fact of life that has led to a condition of perpetual vulnerability and instability.

Other recommendations embedded in the Robbins Report were, however, received more warmly. Most notably, the goal of making teaching an all-graduate profession, with its own professional bachelor's degree, the BEd, exhilarated the teaching force. And by permitting lecturers in the colleges to teach in degree courses, it also did much to soothe the sting of their continuing humiliating subservience to the universities. But the building of a new relationship between the colleges and universities required by the BEd raised diffciult questions about curricular balance, admissions qualifications, personnel strengths, and was inhibited by the refusal of most universities to award honours degrees. Even by the end of the decade, when all twenty-one universities with schools or institutes of education had established BEd degrees, eleven would offer nothing more than "general" or "pass" degrees to graduates of the new programmes.

The colleges, again made uncomfortable by the behaviour of the universities, had little choice but to accept for the remainder of the 1960s their step-child status, with its commensurate loss of autonomy.[1] The choices of both the colleges and the universities were governed by other changes traceable to the Robbins Report and to the ascension of the Labour Party to power in the mid-1960s. Fundamental to the Labour Party policies of 1963 and 1964 was a commitment to expand educational opportunity at all levels. Harold Wilson's government pursued policies in higher education on the one hand and secondary education on the other which many observers found incompatible. In the expanding battlefield of higher education, Tony Crosland, Wilson's Secretary of State for Education and Science (the old Ministry of Education had been replaced with a Department of Education and Science in 1964), assaulted the monopoly of the universities in his 1965 Woolwich speech and launched a sweeping proposal for imposing a "binary line" between the universities and all other institutions of higher education. Alongside the universities there was to be developed, as a matter of deliberate policy, another system of higher education, within which the leaders were to be called polytechnics – rivalling the universities in importance and prestige while differing from them in academic and social purposes. They were, however, to remain firmly under the control of local (and therefore of central) government.

This shift in policy caught many off guard, particularly Lord Robbins himself, who had assumed that expansion in higher education would occur by increasing the scale and scope of the universities, not by sharply dividing them from the other higher education institutions. Indeed, shortly after Crosland's announcement, Robbins observed that "I just can't understand what has happened." The government, while attempting to extend the comprehensive model at the secondary level, "are deepening the existence of lines of division in higher education and actually announcing as a matter of policy, which has never been announced before, that these divisions are to be permanent. They are making the system more hierarchical than ever before" (Robbins 1965, pp. 6-7).

Even Crosland, who announced the new arrangement with unexpected aggression, found it difficult (according to his American wife and biographer) to maintain some level of "intellectual cohesion" in at one and the same time formally segmenting higher education while unifying secondary education (Crosland 1982, p. 159). Some of Crosland's difficulty may be attributed to interference by other cabinet colleagues and to the powerful influence of his senior civil servant, Toby Weaver, in whom some would recognise a Morant of his day. At all events, influential figures in central and local government were suspicious of the autonomous traditions of the historic universities and understandably wished to continue to exert close control over those parts of higher education that had not enjoyed the privileges of the university sector. The binary system that emerged over the next several years therefore consisted of an "autonomous" sector of about two dozen universities awarding their own degrees and a closely controlled "public" sector of scores of colleges and 30 "polytechnics," large, comprehensive, multi-service institutions established by the LEAs, all of whose courses were validated by the Council of National Academic Awards (CNAA). The CNAA was indeed established in 1964 for precisely this purpose. Hitherto, non-university institutions of higher education – colleges of various kinds, and now the newly-titled colleges of education – had been obliged to seek the validation of their degrees from existing universities. Obviously, this requirement kept them in a condition of tutelage. The non-university sector now had its own machinery for controlling and awarding its degrees. Within a brief period of time, therefore, the landscape of higher education was transformed. Although many individuals in the public sector undoubtedly continued to aspire to university ideals and norms, the binary line also encouraged a group of polytechnic and college leaders to head off in their own direction, to fashion new identities, to begin to compete with the universities. In those early years, the university community was not much troubled by the new venture. In part the universities' ease was attributable to their confidence of superiority. And in part it was attributable to the convenient role that the polytechnics played in the entire system, as "filters, allowing the universities to continue to draw in the abler students, to maintain their style of teaching and research, and to claim that they were the centres of excellence in higher education" (Gordon, Aldrich & Dean 1991, p. 241). At the time, the polytechnics were not seen as serious competitors.

These radical changes in the pattern of higher education in England had strong implications for the world of teacher education and training. So, of course, did the equally profound but very different changes in the world of schools, especially of the secondary schools. Wilson had firmly committed his government to developing, or even imposing on reluctant LEAs, a pattern of comprehensive schooling that would inevitably shatter those assumptions about teaching and learning which had for so long prevailed in England. The tide of comprehensive secondary education had ebbed and flowed (mostly ebbed) since the Education Act of 1944; neither the Conservatives nor the Labour Parties had been particularly enthusiastic about dismantling or challenging the grammar schools. Wilson's speech in 1963 symbolized an unprecedented commitment to the comprehensive model, a promise that was only haltingly fulfilled with the victory of the Labour Party in late 1964. The Labour Party's new posture toward universal common secondary schooling was anticipated, ironically, by the Conservative educational leader Sir Edward Boyle (who had endorsed the comparatively liberal Newsom Report) when he made it possible in September 1964, on the eve of Wilson's ascension to power, for the town of Bradford to abolish "selection at 11," the process at the heart of the British segmented model of education.

Upon assuming power, Wilson and his advisors quickly turned to advancing the cause of comprehensive schooling. Within a year of taking office, Crosland released Circular 10/65, on *The Organization of Secondary*

Education, one of the most celebrated statements of educational policy in the twentieth century. The Circular asked the LEAs to submit plans to move toward the goal of comprehensiveness. It offered the two most desirable models: (1) an eleven through eighteen "all-through" arrangement that retained students in a single comprehensive school over the entire course of their secondary education, and (2) a two-tier arrangement that allowed students to transfer from a junior to a senior comprehensive school at age thirteen. Other models that permitted more segmentation were discouraged (Evans 1985, p. 119).

Despite Wilson's vigorous reiteration of comprehensive ideals, the Labour Party's initial actions, including its most public pronouncement, in Circular 10/65, ultimately did not aggressively advance the cause. Indeed, the Circular itself seemed almost to give aid and comfort to individuals interested in avoiding or delaying the move toward comprehensive schooling:

> The Government are aware that the complete elimination of selection and separatism in secondary education will take time to achieve. They do not seek to impose destructive or precipitate change on existing schools; they recognise that the evolution of separate schools into a comprehensive system must be a constructive process requiring careful planning by LEAs in consultation with all those concerned (Department of Education and Science [hereafter DES]1965, p. 16).

As the Circular moved toward implementation, it became apparent that the government held a somewhat ill-defined notion of comprehensiveness, since alternatives to the more unified approaches were eventually accepted. Few financial resources were provided, at least initially. The DES teams responsible for evaluating the LEA proposals had no unique or distinctive conceptualization of universal secondary schooling. In the absence of a vision of appropriate curricula or purpose for the new institutions, they tended to think of the comprehensive schools as "grammar schools for all," and to accept watered-down traditional subject matter as the best course of study for the masses of working-class children who would populate them. Rather than being prepared and poised to enter a "new age" in British education, the movement stumbled out of the passing age, and thereby largely missed a great opportunity to design and implement a meaningful and valuable experience for the nation's adolescents. Many with responsibility for developing the new comprehensive schools, confronted only by the alternative of adopting a discredited life-adjustment approach to the curriculum, preferred the apparent safety of the grammar school culture, with its emphasis upon traditional academic subjects and conventionally sound teaching (Chitty 1989, p. 39).

Outside the DES, local comprehensive school leaders and advocates were convinced that much of the value of the grammar schools resided in their strong, teacher-centred pedagogy and their commitment to tough academic disciplinary standards. They concluded that this value could be extended infinitely. At least they hoped that the value of a grammar school education resided in the experience itself and not simply in its relative exclusivity. School leaders who paid attention to the American experience recognized that providing universal access to an educational certificate or credential that previously had been bestowed on only a privileged, meritocratic, and social elite would inevitably dilute the credential's value. They also undoubtedly realized that in a system devoted in large part to selection and sorting enormous pressure would emerge to re-establish exclusive credentials in some form, particularly as more and more adolescents came to enter and graduate from secondary schools.

Supporters of mass comprehensive education believed that working-class pupils who distinguished themselves in the public examinations would find new avenues of educational and occupational opportunity. And, despite the contemporary experience of developing nations, they hoped that relying on influential examinations would not convert (or pervert) the entire educational experience into one of preparing for the exams. But some educational leaders did become concerned about the impact of examinations on the nature of schooling itself. Indeed, although it was not quite a reinvention of the nineteenth-century "payment by results" initiative, under which schools were financially rewarded for the examination success of their pupils, HMI began to worry that "the work attempted in the classroom was often constrained by exclusive emphasis placed on the examination syllabus, on the topics thought to be favoured by the examiners, and on the acquisition of examination techniques" (DES 1979, p. 217). Despite the concern of some, most comprehensive advocates were convinced that a version of the grammar school experience – combined with examinations – could provide genuine educational value and meaning for all adolescents. Nearly every society that attempted to extend secondary education to the mass of adolescents had followed a similar path. No one had designed a real alternative. Around the world educators were just as hopeful and unimaginative, just as willing to risk the futures of the masses of adolescents, and equally unable to invent or at least imagine an alternative.

So the effort to expand comprehensive schools (albeit based on grammar school traditions) moved forward during the ensuing decade as momentum increased and resistance became more defensive. Opposition to the movement surfaced publicly with a vengeance toward the end of the decade. In a series of controversial "Black Papers," prepared by prominent conservative voices, the political and educational ambitions of the comprehensive schools were attacked. In 1969 and 1970, for example, Black Papers condemned the movement for attempting to use schools "directly as tools to achieve political objectives," including egalitarian social relations. And, supported by some early social science research, the Black Papers ridiculed the quest to secure social unity and implied that comprehensive schools even exacerbated class distinctions.

The liberal reaction to the Black Papers, and the incipient conservative community that they represented, was vicious. "Enemies of reform," the authors of the Black Papers are "scared men and women – scared of the future, scared of change. The principles enunciated in their dismal essays amount to nothing more nor less than a blue-print for a stagnant, unthinking society, perpetuating itself through a rigid hierarchy of educational establishments." The first generation of the "Blackwards" Papers, as they were labelled, were "voices of the past." One of the most prominent critics of the Black Papers admitted that his reaction was too "arrogant and complacent," given the unwarranted optimism of the comprehensive school advocates about the nation's commitment to genuine educational reform (Chitty & Rein 1969).

Since the Labour Party was turned out a year later, in 1970, it would appear that the critic's observation is justified, particularly since the new Conservative government, led by Edward Heath with Margaret Thatcher as Secretary of State for Education and Science, began to fashion what would become known as the "New Right" ideology of the 1980s. The Conservatives reigned only four years, until 1974, but their emerging principles began to attract a new generation of opposition to virtually all forms of twentieth-century liberal thought and policy, particularly the apparent consensus that had emerged around "progressive" and social reformist educational policy.

The direction of the new conservative movement is visible in several of its relatively ineffectual actions of the early 1970s. Heath and Thatcher pledged to withdraw Crosland's Circular 10/65, the symbolic centrepiece of the educational reformers of the 1960s, and to restore the nation's commitment to the grammar schools. In the face of this bold posture, however, the number of comprehensives more than doubled before the Labour Party resumed power in 1974. Clearly the LEAs, by and large, had embraced comprehensive secondary schooling. It magnified their role and authority dramatically, especially with the associated commitment to expand social and health services through schools at the local level. The entire "educational establishment," as it came to be known – consisting of the LEAs, the universities, teacher educators, the HMI, and even the civil servants of the DES – seemed to embrace, and was determined to impose, this "great roller coaster of an idea," which Thatcher found "difficult, if not impossible, to stop" (Thatcher in *The Daily Mail* [13 May 1987]). Some observers remain convinced that Thatcher's "lingering resentment" over her unsuccessful confrontation with the educational establishment over comprehensive schooling as Education Secretary explains her "contempt" for the enterprise that was evident in her policies as Prime Minister a decade later.

Antagonism toward allegedly professional arrogance, another facet of the New Right perspective, emerged in embryonic form in response to debates over the establishment of a "General Teaching Council" following the release of the Weaver Report in 1970. The concept of a General Teaching Council – an organization of teaching professionals largely independent of government authority and with responsibility for oversight and control of their colleagues – had been proposed and discussed for generations. Various teacher unions had aspired to exercise such responsibility, but divisions among teaching organizations had undermined any fledgling movement toward a general council. Any progress was further inhibited by the refusal of the government to make membership mandatory for those seeking recognition as qualified teachers. During the 1960s the momentum toward forming a general council nevertheless accelerated, particularly after teachers in Scotland were able in 1965 to overcome their differences and exploit their political power, manifested in a strike in Glasgow, in order to form the Teaching Council (Scotland), modeled on other professional councils – including the General Medical Council.

South of the Scottish border the DES remained troubled by the attempt to form a national body comprised of teachers who had authority over control of entry to the occupation. Even the Labour government worried that a union-dominated council might move to protect the privileges of its members by manufacturing an artificial shortage by constricting entry into teaching. But as the birth rate, which had peaked in 1964, continued to decline, making it obvious that some contraction in the teaching force was inevitable, resistance to the concept of a teaching council began to recede. In 1969 the teacher associations managed to persuade the DES to establish a working party to examine the possibility of authorizing a teaching council for England and Wales. Chaired by Toby Weaver, the influential senior DES official, the group reported in early 1970. In order to avoid the touchy issue of ungoverned professional control of entry, the Weaver Report recommended that "general self-government" responsibilities be separated from "supply" activities. The first set of issues and tasks would be committed to a Teaching Council dominated by a majority of teachers, while the second would be handled through an Advisory Council on the Supply and Training of Teachers (ACSTT), with no more than one-sixth of its members drawn from the teaching force.

The National Union of Teachers rejected the Weaver Report, largely because of the working party's refusal to allow teachers to control entry into the occupation, and the campaign to create a general council quickly fizzled out. The government was not interested in negotiating on the matter, even though the ACSTT proposal was adopted in an attempt to address the need for a continuing reduction in the number of teachers. In any case, with the Conservative victory a few months later, the terms of the discussion shifted, as the "consumerism" movement was adopted by the New Right. In a climate of intensifying hostility to even the General Medical Council, it was unlikely that voices for creating yet another professional council – with the authority to exploit and neglect clients – would receive a favourable hearing. The NUT's reaction to the relatively liberal Weaver proposals was predictable, the Conservative leaders observed, and symbolized the sort of unhealthy, even offensive, aggressiveness of protected monopolies (Ross 1990, pp. 124-33).

The campaign to establish some form of professionally controlled teaching council failed as a result of schisms in the profession itself, the divisions among teacher educators caused by the different cultures that emerged through the binary line and the CNAA, and the independence and separation of the most prestigious teacher educators from the schools. The failure contributed to the creation of a policy vacuum in the area of teacher supply and education that ultimately proved too tempting for national political leaders – of both parties – to neglect.

Equally important as an issue related to the professionalism of teachers was the perennial question of their education and training. Vocal discontent with weaknesses in the preparation of teachers, especially in the primary field and even after the introduction of the BEd, had been growing for several years. Moreover, all forms of teacher education, inside as well as outside the universities, consecutive and concurrent, primary and secondary alike, were criticised for being too removed from the practicalities of teaching in schools. "Theory," rooted primarily in the social sciences and the humanities, came to dominate discourse in teacher education. Consider, for example, an article on educational studies that appeared in 1966 in the leading journal Education for Teaching, which was shaped primarily by the work of Karl Mannheim and Robert Merton; two other articles focused on the place in teacher education courses of the sociology of education, perhaps the queen of educational theory. K. E. Shaw argued that "sociology of education is poised to join Educational Psychology as a major component in the professional training given to teachers" (1966, p. 61). Students studying this subject ordinarily did no field work; they learned it through an academic instructional model exclusively. Theory, as a consequence, was typically separated from the analysis of practice.

The staffs of teacher education courses had changed in response to the expansion of the teaching force during the 1960s, yet their backgrounds poorly matched the needs of a changing educational system and the context of teacher education. Many individuals who entered primary teacher training came from a background of teaching in secondary schools, and especially the academic sixth form. They would therefore be, above all, subject specialists and there was a sharp disjunction between their knowledge and the needs of young learners. In the meantime, the so-called "mother hens," who were strongly committed to primary teacher training but enjoyed an expertise in neither an academic subject (such as history) nor an educational discipline (such as philosophy) had all but disappeared from the teaching staffs of the colleges. Teacher educators had either fully embraced the academic culture of the university disciplines or were otherwise determined to flee real classroom teaching. Former subject matter specialists might continue to cultivate their empires in local schools where they had established relationships with department heads who could assist both in the training and the hiring of their graduates. The university subject matter specialists were however themselves disinclined to continue to practice in schools, hoping instead to secure and sustain the prerogatives of higher education faculty members. The teacher education community consequently suffered from problems of credibility that were impossible to overcome, given the higher education norms and aspirations within which it now existed.

Thatcher responded quickly to this mounting pressure by convening in December 1970 a Committee of Inquiry, chaired by Lord James of Rusholme, Vice-Chancellor of York University and an open critic of excessively academic teacher education schemes. Working intensively for a year, the James Committee took seriously its charge to review the education of teachers and proposed a radical new architecture for the entire enterprise. The James Report, released in early 1972, proposed a novel approach to teacher education in differentiating the process into three "cycles:" (1) personal education in one or two of the disciplinary subjects, which a student expected to teach, for two or three years to diploma or degree level; (2) pre-service training (one year in a college or department of education) and induction (another year in a school as a salaried but supervised novice teacher) ; and (3) inservice education for practising teachers (in all forms of continued personal and professional education that would last a lifetime, with paid sabbaticals).

This emphatically consecutive model sought to eliminate the inequities and confusion of the BEd by abolishing that form of concurrent training altogether. It sought to transform professional education during Cycle 2 from traditional university and college-based academic theory to school-based pedagogical studies and internship. And the Committee proposed a new two-year qualification, a Diploma in Higher Education (Dip HE), a form of pre-professional study that would be open both to prospective teachers (on their way to Cycle 2 professional experiences) and to others who were interested in advanced training for other occupations.

Thatcher's DES responded to the James' proposals toward the end of the year in a White Paper called *Education: A Framework for Expansion* (December, 1972), a document that embraced virtually the entire educational system but concentrated on higher and teacher education. The government refused to accept a model of strictly consecutive personal and professional studies, agreeing with much conventional opinion that one year of separate professional education was probably too brief, despite the successful experience of the universities with the (approximately) year-long Post-Graduate Certificate in Education (PGCE) courses for secondary teachers. The government was more enthusiastic about investing in the continuing education of teachers and encouraged LEAs to support an array of proposals for practising teachers.

The government ventured far beyond the teacher training proposals of the James Committee, however, and addressed the broader issue of the future of higher education. The nation was engaged in a dialogue about making access wider than it had ever been in the United Kingdom. Accepting the assumptions of Crosland's "binary system," the White Paper explored ways of expanding the public sector of higher education. In particular, the government focused on the colleges of education, suggesting that some of them should diversify, broaden their mission to include training for a variety of human services, in the health and social welfare industries, for example. Some colleges might become more closely affiliated with universities, even to the point of formally merging with a department of education. Some should consider associations with the increasingly robust and ambitious polytechnics. The strongest colleges could anticipate considering such a rich constellation of destinies, all of which would amplify their stature by bringing them squarely into the mainstream of "major institutions of higher education" (quoted in Dent 1977, p. 153).

But not all of the 160 colleges were sufficiently strong or conveniently situated to be afforded such possibilities. Some of these institutions would perhaps be forced to play smaller roles as centres for inservice education, and, unfortunately, some would "need to close" (DES 1972, p. 44).

As the birth rate continued to fall, forcing the government to acknowledge the unfortunate implications for growth in the title of the White Paper *A Framework for Expansion*, discussions and negotiations among all of the players in the higher education community intensified. Initially it looked as though a quarter of the colleges would become "free-standing" multi-service institutions, with a majority merging either with universities, polytechnics, other institutions of higher education, or one another. Perhaps a dozen would have to close entirely. In 1973 the government had to revise its projected intake for teacher education drastically, from 114,000 to about 65,000. The accelerating recession of the mid-1970s aggravated the situation and forced an even deeper contraction as the demand for teachers (or at least the ability to pay for them) declined. Even the Labour government, returned to power in 1974, could not stem the onslaught that colleges faced and reduced the intake figure to a mere 45,000 by 1978. After successive waves of contraction, by the late 1970s many of the colleges had been closed, and nearly all of the rest had been transformed in some fashion; even the survivors resented and were shaken by the process they were forced to endure.

The government's campaign to "tidy up" the voluntary colleges, allegedly conducted under a cloak of secrecy and misinformation, provided new wealth and broader markets for the polytechnics in particular, many of which were condemned or applauded (depending on one's perspective) for plundering the vulnerable colleges of education. During the waves of "mergers and consolidations," the polytechnics took a strategic stance toward the array of "talent" available in the colleges. Some staff were retired or bought out entirely. Others, particularly younger lecturers with sufficient energy to invest in lucrative teacher education, were retained and used to staff courses that turned excellent profits to the polytechnics. Those who possessed the skills and disposition for more traditional forms of academic work were allowed to join existing polytechnic staff in pursuing grants and engaging in research and publication and other high status university activities.

The universities, too, benefited from the savage reduction of college places. This reduction advantaged those universities that were fortunate enough to acquire comfortable and scenic teacher-training campuses and sufficient staff to allow the university staff to specialize more deeply in traditional academic research and graduate education. In fact, some members of the university community believed that the colleges of education should have been even more deeply curtailed. They maintained that the powerful Bishops were able to protect too many troubled church-affiliated colleges that were engaged in preparing teachers who were ill-equipped to educate the growing number of school pupils, many of them from racial minorities, in urban working-class areas who were beginning to enrol in Britain's schools. The often timid young women who received limited disciplinary and theoretical preparation in the colleges, some university observers claimed, were temperamentally unwilling to provide the aggressive professional leadership that the teaching force would need in its inevitable confrontations with government initiatives.

It might be argued that the turmoil surrounding the assault on the colleges during much of the 1970s contributed to a false sense of security in the universities and polytechnics. The comparatively advantageous fate of the autonomous universities and prominent polytechnics masked the emerging critique of higher education in general and of teacher education in particular. Few leaders in higher education had any reason to be genuinely worried or to feel particularly vulnerable. There were in this sector no traditions of intervention and interference. Their confidence seemed justified as their institutions appeared to be riding a crest of legitimacy and influence that had gathered momentum for perhaps two decades.

Within the long-established universities the teacher education community felt protected by the halo of traditional autonomy. Certainly in their eyes the government had targeted the right culprit, the weak and disreputable colleges. Even with overall intakes reduced, had not the university courses been enriched, with their share of the teacher training intake tripling from a tenth to a third during the 1970s? Did not the stunning breadth of approaches to teacher education hosted by the universities and polytechnics reflect health and vigour? Were not course characteristics most closely associated with the university culture – the celebration of academic theory, for example – almost universally emulated? Yet it would appear that virtually everyone, engaged as they were in fighting about the James Report's more visible observations and recommendations, overlooked one of the most salient points: the need to redress the balance between academic and professional preparation by connecting teacher education to school teaching.

The opportunities presented by repeated accusations of irrelevance and impropriety therefore slipped by the teacher education community. In retrospect it appears that university-based teacher educators in particular missed an unprecedented opportunity for openly addressing public concerns about the political content of professional studies. They failed to consider exactly how "theory" might be applied (or left unapplied) by novice teachers, or whether new teachers might be trusted to apply their theory in practice. They appear to have been, by and large, satisfied with their relationships with cooperating schools. But outside the universities, in the schools for example, others thought that the university teacher training leaders too often operated courses for their own convenience rather than to serve the needs of prospective teachers or the interests of practising teachers who were called upon to become teacher educators. School teachers and administrators often felt that they had little choice except to suffer this arrogance on the part of university staff. Higher education's false sense of security about its invulnerability – grounded in traditions of university autonomy – prevented the universities from anticipating the broad populist critique of their enterprise as too academic, too individualized, and too cavalier about its impact on prospective teachers.

As a result, even after a decade of tremors caused by the shifting tectonic plates below the educational enterprise, the world of teacher education had not by the early 1980s recognized the force of the threats that were breaking toward the surface. The universities increasingly set the tone and aspirations for teacher preparation courses in all institutions. Since the 1960s, "theory," particularly the social and behavioral sciences, had come to constitute the heart of educational studies. Authoritative lecturing dominated instruction in most courses. Regardless of the institution, few lecturers worried much about the "professional" application or relevance of this segment of professional knowledge.

The only real challenge to the prestige and influence of "theory" in the most prominent institutions came from subject tutors and specialists. During the 1970s the dominance of theory was more vulnerable to competition from the inside than from external political intervention. The "Subject Barons," as they became known in a number of universities in all regions of England, began to build powerful individual empires, principally through strong networks with their former students who were employed in local schools. The Subject Barons fashioned good relationships with departments in schools, but not really with schools themselves. Such relationships permitted the subject tutors in higher education to press for autonomy and separation within the teacher training courses, and eventually for parity with the academic theorists. Competition between these two powerful groups often led to fragmentation in courses, to a strong ethos of individualism and mutual suspicion, to an inability to build real conceptual and intellectual coherence. Course leaders did what they could to make their courses appear coherent on paper. They presented imagined sequences, curricular spirals, maps of consecutivity. But their colleagues acted in isolation and built their own definitions of the "courses" to which they contributed unrelated parts.

Such an arrangement served many interests. It undoubtedly encouraged staff to leave one another alone, to allow one another to fashion their own personalized visions of a teacher education course. It probably enabled higher education to avoid connecting "theory" to teaching practice. It probably deluded many into thinking that the universities had established relations with schools, when what many really had were some staff members who were on good relations with their former students who were now teachers in schools. It may have allowed teacher educators to assume that they were fully integrated into the higher education community. Vice-Chancellors and other institutional leaders had little incentive to challenge this arrangement since one of its unintended benefits was to produce a recruiting device for new students for the universities. Subject specialists were able to work with their former students in recruiting their current students into the Barons' universities. Moreover, attempting to enforce the coherence that was evident principally in course descriptions rather than in reality would have violated and offended university-wide academic customs. The embryonic split that was developing within teacher education also came to serve the interests of outsiders committed to elevating the stature and presence of subject methods over social science theory in the initial training courses.

Perhaps their undeserved confidence and the war engulfing the colleges distracted members of the teacher education community within the university from detecting the shift in the tectonic plates beneath the entire educational enterprise, the emerging populist critique of education in general and the reformulation of "New Right" ideology. This distraction allowed the education community to squander a timely moment to review the direction of teacher training, especially as it had taken shape in the university setting. Before the New Right ideologues seized control of the discourse and policy environments, educators – including those involved with teacher training – enjoyed all too brief an opportunity to consider and debate the genuine concerns even of liberal reform interests. Ironically, the teacher educators' neglected opportunity occurred during a period called "the Great Debate."

What eventually came to be viewed as a conservative campaign was launched by the Labour leader James Callaghan, who succeeded Wilson as Prime Minister in early 1976. Disturbed by what they saw as the complacency of the DES, Callaghan's advisors, particularly Bernard Donoughue, encouraged the new Prime Minister to play on the popular concerns about learning in school and possible connections with Britain's continuing economic troubles. As would befit a Prime Minister who had not graduated from university, Callaghan interrogated Fred Mulley, Secretary of State for Education and Science, about the Department's posture toward teaching in the basic subjects, the appropriateness and relevance of the secondary curriculum for adolescents, the accuracy of the examination system, and the availability of educational options for sixteen to nineteen year olds.

Mulley, believing himself to be competing with Donoughue for Callaghan's attention on educational matters, required the DES staff to prepare a lengthy analysis and critique of education in the U.K. Presented to the Prime Minister in July 1976, the "Yellow Book," as it became known, expressed reservations about the nature and scale of educational accomplishments since 1944. It reiterated growing public scepticism about curricular coherence, learning standards, and the effectiveness of teachers. Every level of schooling was probed and criticized. Primary education continued to suffer from four decades of progressivism, and especially from the wrong-headed Plowden Report of 1967, which seemed to excuse and even applaud every form of scandalous philosophy and embarrassing practice. The world-renowned primary schools had evolved into a separate culture of permissiveness, excessive child-centredness, and illiteracy.

Secondary schools had followed the American path of abandoning for the vast majority of students standards and expectations of achievement. The curriculum had become inflated and degraded to such an extent that virtually every student could build a private and unique definition of an "education." Adolescents were out of control; afraid of exercising discipline (or too ideologically committed to egalitarianism and the use of schools to further radical social objectives), teachers had capitulated to their students and were desperately adapting their classrooms to the presumed interests of teenagers. As a consequence of these trends, schools were failing to prepare students to function in a robust and competitive economy. In general the Yellow Book challenged the entire educational community. Its implication was that politically aggressive teachers and the individuals and courses that prepared them had failed the families and employers of the nation.

"Outrageous" in its assumptions, targets, and remedies, the confidential Yellow Book – described by the Times as the DES "Black Paper" — was partially leaked to the press in mid-October, 1976. Most sectors of the educational community, including groups historically influential in policy formation, like HMI, recognized the "freshness" of the Labour Party's perspective and the potential for the Callaghan government to overturn traditions of generosity and non-intervention toward schools in allowing them to define their own roles.

Several days after excerpts of the Yellow Book were leaked, Callaghan delivered an address at Ruskin College, Oxford, in which he developed themes rooted in the DES document. Calling for a national debate on educational issues, the Prime Minister expressed personal sentiments in favour of "a basic curriculum with universal standards," a connection between school and productive – especially technical – work, teachers who would communicate more clearly with parents about their goals and methods, and enabling parents to take a more active role in running their community's schools. In doing this, he took the stance of a lay person asking a well-protected and even arrogant profession to be more visibly responsive to its obligations to its clients. Although he explicitly distanced himself from those who defended "standards" as a way of defending "old privileges and inequalities," his speech clearly legitimized a set of attitudes which the conservative leaders of the 1980s would be able to exploit. The speech also represented the break from the traditional emphasis on the quantity of schooling toward a concern with its quality and meaning for individuals and the nation.

The "Great Debate" that followed Callaghan's Ruskin Speech was formally structured in eight regional conferences held in February and March, 1977. Carefully selected individuals, chosen to "represent" an array of interest groups, including teachers, parents, higher education representatives, LEA personnel, employers, and others in addition to DES staff, discussed four central topics: the curriculum, assessment, teacher education, and the relationship of schooling to work life. A "Green Paper," *Education in Schools: A Consultative Document,* summarized the Great Debate in mid-1977, pulling together and reaffirming the central themes of the Yellow Book, the Ruskin speech and the eight conferences, especially the importance of creating mechanisms for ensuring educational accountability.

Despite this background of all this talk about incomprehensible curricula, indefensible performance standards, and accountability, during the 1970s there were few incentives to rethink the dominant forms of teacher education in any of the varied institutions that prepared teachers. Traditions that shaped the cultures and aspirations of higher education staff and students appeared to be serving their interests well. Only a few gloomy prophets foresaw how vulnerable the entire enterprise would prove to be. Even those few prophets of doom would have been startled by the intensity and success of the impending assault on teacher education in England. The next chapter examines the situation as it had become by 1994, and explores the dynamics of change since the late 1970s.

Note

[1] It is worth remembering that the concept of "higher education" emerged rather late in England, in part, undoubtedly, out of a desire to maintain the distinctive role and values of the universities. Historian Harold Silver recently reminded us that the Robbins Report popularized the notion of a broader community of institutions of "higher education." He drew from a University Grants Committee report on the 1960s in observing that the Robbins Report "significantly changed the demarcation lines which had previously existed between universities on the one hand and teacher training colleges and further education colleges on the other." After Robbins, and the related governmental actions, it was no longer possible "to view the universities as a completely detached group in the educational structure of the country" (Silver 1990, pp. 7-8, 14-18).

Oxford Studies in Comparative Education, Vol. 4(1/2), 1994

CHAPTER 8

England: towards 1994

Over the past two decades dramatic changes have taken place in the structure and provision of teacher education in England.[1] These changes were derived directly from the electoral victory of Margaret Thatcher in 1979 and the subsequent ascendance of Kenneth Baker, who ultimately became her Secretary of State for Education in 1986. The scale of these changes can best be captured by a portrayal of the situation as it had become in 1994. When that has been attempted, it will be helpful to retrace the steps of the narrative and explore the dynamics of change since the Great Debate.

1994

By 1994 teacher education in England had developed a kind of uniformity underlying the continuing tradition of great diversity. Institutions of very different history, organization, staff, students, and culture were now engaged in preparing teachers in surprisingly similar ways. In the early 1990s, British teachers could be prepared in colleges of education, universities, polytechnics, and even outside higher education in school-based programmes. Despite variation in the structure of provision there were common features in much of the training. This relative uniformity had been imposed by government prescription, which had (as in many educational policy arenas) become more universal and detailed than at any time in the past. A Post-Graduate Certificate in Education (PGCE) student, for example, could count on having a thirty-six week course of study, and undergraduate students in BEd programmes were guaranteed a minimum exposure to higher education course work in their subject areas. Whether in a postgraduate or undergraduate programme, participants in initial teacher education tended to be exposed to study in subject application, educational studies, and professional studies. Central to their preparation was an understanding of the National Curriculum, now fully introduced in schools, although being constantly modified by government and still quite controversial. Practice in schools now constituted a major demand on their time; in 1993-94, for example, teacher education PGCE students tended to spend most of their course time in school-based work and, in response to the newest government requirements, courses preparing secondary teachers were moving rapidly towards requiring that students spend two-thirds of their time in schools. Educational theory, on the other hand, had all but disappeared from most courses. The tradition of study grounded in the foundations of sociology, history, philosophy, and psychology had been replaced with a prevalent orientation toward teaching as "reflective practice," which faculty described as characterizing most courses (Barrett et al. 1992a, p. 25). And regardless of the site, a future teacher prepared in higher education would be taught by university or college staff who had to satisfy a government requirement that took them back to classroom teaching in schools.

If these characteristics were in 1994 part of the educational experience for the beginning teacher, what had teacher education become for those higher education faculty who identified themselves as teacher educators? The visitor to English teacher education institutions was struck by common features of the experience of teacher educators as they defined teacher education through their daily work, despite the differences in teacher education courses and the structures which housed them. Teacher educators seemed frantically busy in 1993-94, but their activity was often reactive and anticipatory. They seemed to be forever responding or waiting (and waiting to respond to the actions of others).

In the first place, they were busy in schools. They spent time there, often on a daily basis, observing, consulting with, and teaching alongside their teacher education students. Many met frequently with school staff who served as mentors to novice teachers. Some of them returned to teaching, perhaps for the first time in years, as a way of satisfying the government requirement for "recent and relevant" classroom teaching experience. And many were locked in delicate negotiations with school heads about the costs of collaboration, as higher education institutions were now obliged to pay schools for sharing in the work of preparing teachers. As schools continued to develop ways to live with the Local Management of Schools (a scheme introduced in 1988 to devolve funding responsibility and authority), school heads had become keen to translate into cash the increased responsibility they and their staffs were assuming for initial teacher training. In these negotiations, as in much of the work they did, teacher educators were, as one of them put it, "making it up as they go," trying to find what sorts of arrangements would work with little guidance but much pressure from the outside. Veteran teacher educators had spent much time sharing rumours about what the going rate was in various regions for the amount higher education institutions had to pay schools for each student teacher. Teacher educators worked strategically to compete with other nearby teacher training institutions to secure partnership arrangements with local schools. Squeezed from their own central and college administration, they had to develop agreements which were typically less generous than the schools wanted. Given demands for higher education faculty members to spend time in teaching primary or secondary school pupils, one observer noted the irony of teacher education students complaining that they could not find their university tutors because they were off in schools.

But tutors in 1994 did not enjoy the luxury of just working, observing, meeting, or negotiating in schools. Many had spent the 1992-93 year busily preparing for the next round of the government's research selectivity exercises, the results of which would determine much of the funding and prestige of their department. That activity required an "immense" amount of time and effort, and assumed that teacher educators were heavily engaged in research (Universities Council for the Education of Teachers, (hereafter UCET] 1992, p. 10). For faculty in the new universities, which had been polytechnics until the binary line was abolished, this was their first encounter with this type of evaluation and funding decision. It was also the first time that new and old universities, historically on either side of the binary line, would be in direct competition for funds and would be evaluated, at least formally, on the same criteria. Certainly the financial squeeze on higher education and new management styles which provided funding on a performance basis, combined with the resource drain on teacher education programmes imposed by the need to share funds with collaborating schools, gave research a new meaning to members of education faculties. One department in 1993, for example, was faced with the need to generate £95,000 by September; faculty were informed that they should try to develop lucrative research projects.

Finally, faculty seemed busy responding to (and waiting for) external demands. Teacher education programmes were consumed by outside inspections. For example, within one period of nine months Oxford's Department of Educational Studies endured six audits or inspections. Each required separate and extensive preparation as Oxford and its sister education departments responded to an alphabet soup of old and mainly new organizations created to evaluate and hold accountable their work. While meeting with HMI, the Council for the Accreditation of Teacher Education (CATE), the Higher Education Funding Council for England (HEFCE), Quality Assurance assessors and others, teacher educators also spent much time hurrying to respond to the government's Department for Education's Circular 9/92 on secondary teacher training, or waiting anxiously for the release of its companion primary circular, which together were intended to overturn many of the twentieth century arrangements for preparing teachers. These documents were produced by the newly named Department for Education, which had assumed many of the responsibilities of the former DES.[2] At the heart of the nervousness about these newest governmental requirements was a question about the role of higher education institutions in teacher education. By the end of 1993 debate had begun in the House of Lords regarding the creation of a Teacher Training Agency which would remove the management of teacher education from that of the rest of higher education (Hansard 1993, 1994). What had perhaps long been a semi-detached position of teacher education within higher education was now, in many ways, to become more openly detached.

Teacher educators in 1993-94 spoke with only thinly veiled sarcasm about the need for visitors to see teacher education before it disappeared. Coupled with their cynicism and despair was a kind of surprise. They seemed to ask: How could this have happened? In the trenches of their daily practice, where they felt besieged by powerful forces embodied in regulations, audits, and inspections, they spoke of the tremendous acceleration of change that had beset them in recent years, of change that got "faster and faster and faster," leaving them "punch drunk" and hard-pressed to do more than react. From a comfortable distance outside the battle lines the years 1983-1984 stand as a turning point, midway between 1976 and 1994 and a moment when the first round of fundamental conflict began in ways that may have seemed like skirmishes, rather than defining moments. But initially in government reports, then through the creation of CATE, and eventually in a series of government circulars, teacher education would be reshaped in ways that fundamentally transformed it, changing not just the minor details of its operations, but rearranging the structures, communities, and principles which had come to guide it in the twentieth century.

Towards 1994

During the late 1970s and early 1980s, few seemed to recognize the magnitude of the oncoming change. Some however did. In 1983 Stuart Maclure, the seasoned editor of *The Times Educational Supplement*, warned the Universities Council for the Education of Teachers (UCET) that "the actual details of the [government's] new proposals and the precise educational nuances which will be expressed in the criteria for accreditation are much less important than the assertion of control and the declaration of a readiness to exercise responsibility for it." He went on to say that "this is to be responsibility of a different order from the more familiar obsession with numbers and subject balances – this could go to the basic content and shape of courses" (quoted in Whitty, Barton & Pollard 1987, p. 167).

Maclure's comments proved to be an accurate prediction of the far-reaching changes which would come. The key actors in teacher education policy and the discourse of that policy would change dramatically. In 1994, UCET was no longer able to rely on familiar patterns of engagement with those involved in the provision and control of teacher education. Since 1966 UCET had, in various organisational forms, represented the interests of the university schools and departments of education. It had always tried to work as closely as possible with the former colleges of education, as with their successors in the polytechnics and elsewhere. It avoided confrontation, or espousing policies which might divide the interests of teacher education as a whole. "UCET's traditions have hitherto been those associated with the quiet word, the friendly suggestion and the reasoned position paper," argued its historian in 1987, who thought that "it may be necessary to move towards a more public (and therefore exposed) position in the promulgation of views and policies" (UCET 1987b, p. 28). Certainly by 1994 the civility which seems to have defined the relationship between the universities and the government in decisions involving teacher education had been shattered. The idea that UCET represented an elite group of higher education institutions, distinguished by their royal charter, their history of relative autonomy from government interference, and economic privilege was no longer appropriate: the elimination of the binary line had made the term "university" now apply to a much wider category of institutions. Economic and political pressures had entered the university gates with a vengeance. And UCET was no longer able to separate itself from the practices and concerns of polytechnics and colleges. Moreover, as Maclure predicted, the manner and content of the discourse on teacher education had indeed changed. In fact, by 1993-94, the debates about teacher education had gone beyond even the substance of the content and shape of teacher education: government responsibility had moved to outcomes. And finally, during this decade of rapid transformation, the definition of what constituted teacher education and the population of teacher educators would be significantly altered. As a result, ten years after Maclure's remarks, the shift in responsibility was so great as to make some universities question whether it was worth being in the business of educating teachers.

How could changes come so fast with such far-reaching consequences? How could teacher educators by 1994 be both so discouraged and so surprised? What one university-based teacher educator called the Alice in Wonderland quality of life in his enterprise in the 1990s made sense only if changes in teacher education since the late 1970s are placed in the context of equally important changes in precollegiate and higher education. This chapter therefore explores three themes that help explain how teacher education could have arrived at the point at which it was in 1994: centralization, anti-professionalism, and competition for resources in a destabilized environment.

The Story within Teacher Education: centralization of control

The process of centralization and the deepening of government intrusion into teacher education began with the concerns spelled out in *Teaching Quality*, a major White Paper released in 1983, and the remedies supplied by the ensuing creation of CATE, the accrediting body which, through its process of reviewing for the Secretary of State teacher education courses against explicit criteria, came to exercise much influence on teacher education. *Teaching Quality*, another in a long series of white and green papers, was in some ways predictable in focusing on provision and forecasts for numbers of teachers needed and commensurate intake numbers of students to be admitted into teacher education programmes. Its familiar first section, "Schoolteachers:

Demand and Supply," predicted an upsurge in the need for newly prepared primary teachers and a simultaneous decline in the need for secondary teachers until the early 1990s. Its rational and technical concerns for manpower planning focus the paper's discussion of "mismatches," particularly in subject areas like mathematics and science, and its plan for restructuring the provision of teacher education (Department of Education and Science [hereafter DES]1983, p. 8). The White Paper suggested reducing to eighty-five the number of higher education institutions engaged in initial teacher education, increasing the number of primary teacher training places while reducing the number of secondary, and altering the BEd and PGCE balance.

To engage in this sort of decision-making and control was certainly nothing new for the DES, nor a surprising exercise of power for the Secretary of State. What gave the White Paper its landmark status, however, were the later sections of its text, as it moved from technical discussions about intake numbers to concerns about the content of teacher education and mechanisms for assuring rigour and quality in that content.

In its effort to "strengthen initial teacher training, to promote the recruitment to it of academically well qualified people, and to improve the match between training and qualifications and teaching programmes" (p. 18), the government used the White Paper to outline criteria the Secretary of State should consider in approving courses. The Secretary of State would then review all currently approved courses and "withdraw approval from those courses which do not conform to the criteria" (p. 19).

This emphasis on the criteria raised the issues which would, over the decade, take on greater definition (and, in many cases, engender tensions between the government and providers of teacher education). *Teaching Quality* challenged the traditional place of subject studies, not simply by calling attention to mismatches in supply and demand, but by stressing the need for sufficient "subject expertise" for teaching, which it defined as minimally "two full years' course time devoted to subject studies at a level appropriate to higher education" (p. 19). For intending teachers preparing in an undergraduate programme, this had implications for both the structure and content of their studies. For the postgraduate student, this criterion especially affected selection decisions. There was a related concern that teachers be given adequate preparation in subject-specific and age-appropriate teaching methods, and preservice primary teachers should pay "sufficient, and substantial" attention to language and mathematics (p. 19). The third broad criterion obliged teacher education to be "closely linked with practical experience in schools, and involving the active participation of experienced practising teachers" (p. 19).

While these three criteria – higher education preparation in subjects of the school curriculum, specific methods instruction, and a close link to practice – were described as requirements that should be imposed, in subsequent policy developments several other issues addressed by the White

Paper were added to the list. One which in retrospect is particularly significant was the expectation that teacher educators have not only credentials for teaching in higher education but also experience in school teaching. At this earliest stage in the formulation of criteria, the guidelines remained imprecise: "in order to satisfy the third requirement [of close links to practice], a sufficient proportion of each training institution's staff should have enjoyed success as teachers in schools, and their school experience should be recent, substantial and relevant" (p. 20). The expectation, moreover, was that some teacher educators, those responsible for pedagogy, should have "continuing regular contact with classroom teaching." Another identified need, which would later develop into a formal criterion and encourage closer relations with schools, was for improved admissions procedures to reduce wastage and to involve practising teachers in decisions about selecting teacher education students.

The documents which followed with increasing frequency reiterated the central themes of *Teaching Quality*, honed them, or narrowed them into bureaucratic procedures. The notions that teacher education was principally a process of learning the content of the subject or subjects that the teacher would eventually teach, that it was rooted in practice, and that its practitioners needed themselves to be actively engaged in schools and classroom teaching remained a shaping mantra of policies to come. Intellectual contradictions or tensions inherent in combining these expectations were not addressed, nor was there any explicit articulation of an underlying theory of teacher learning or even of good teaching (McClelland 1989, p. 20). Over time, the notion of good teaching would emerge, as would some outlines of good teacher education practice. Yet the images of these conceptualizations, like those implicit in the initial proposals, were made up of fragments of expectation – two years of subject study, one term of recent and relevant experience – with little glue of a model or theory to connect them. This incoherence has been for institutions both a problem and an opportunity they could exploit. Similarly, practical problems of the resources needed to support these goals were not directly discussed.

In the White Paper's appendix, an advisory report from ACSET (the Advisory Committee on the Supply and Education of Teachers) touched on one issue that was to be far more controversial than any detail of criterion or enrolment contraction. It was the same issue identified in Maclure's prophetic remarks to UCET. And it was to be one of the defining aspects of the struggles in teacher education in 1994. It was what ACSET in its advice referred to as "the distribution of responsibilities" (DES 1983, p. 30).

ACSET argued for ways in which the government could use its power to approve courses as a way to improve initial teacher training. Although it recognized the power of the Secretaries of State in this regard, ACSET's report, significantly at least in retrospect, tried to hold the delicate balance between government involvement and higher education autonomy:

within the existing framework of responsibilities there is scope for securing improvement in professional improvement and monitoring of initial teacher training courses while at the same time preserving and encouraging worthwhile diversity, protecting the autonomy of academic validating bodies, and strengthening processes of individual and institutional evaluation and review (DES 1983, p. 31).

In fact, ACSET advised that the Secretary of State's work should focus on "the broad framework and structure of courses leaving detailed content to academic institutions and their validating bodies" (p. 31). It supported the notion of a General Teaching Council as an eventual gatekeeper for both course approval and entry to the profession. But it suggested that in the interim professional committees, somewhat ill-defined agencies created to discharge some of the responsibilities left in suspense when the ATOs were abolished in the 1970s, be re-established to determine criteria and review courses. Their task, as laid out in the ACSET annex, pointed to the crucial mix of higher education and government responsibility in the education of teachers.

The main body of the White Paper, however, uses ACSET's recommendations somewhat selectively, though appearing fully to endorse its advice. Thus, the DES called for the use of professional committees. Yet it steered clear of discussing issues of higher education autonomy and the importance of diversity. This silence would prove to be at the crux of debate and change in teacher education over the next decade.

Teaching Quality, while setting in motion a series of policies which would dramatically transform teacher education, was received at the time by many in teacher education with a "guarded welcome" (UCET 1983, p. 1). UCET members, for example, saw the proposal of a "national transbinary accreditation council to advise the Secretaries of State as they exercise their powers of approval of courses of Initial Teacher Training" as generally positive and thought that this might even lead to the long-discussed General Teaching Council (UCET 1983, p. 2). Many recognized the tremendous diversity which characterized teacher education in 1983 and which, given the unevenness of expectations about subject matter (for example, where time devoted to this in Initial Teacher Training (ITT [3]) courses ranged from thirteen to fifty percent) worried the government and its advisors (Taylor 1990, p. 112). There was at first no challenge to the principle that teacher education should be improved nor to the legal right enjoyed by the Secretary of State to intervene in such matters. What did worry higher educators, however, were the questions of how this power would be exercised, and how mechanisms created for that purpose might add burdens to the resources of higher education institutions and transgress long-established boundaries of institutional autonomy.

The establishing in 1984 of CATE clarified the criticisms of teacher education, revealed the emerging political motivation of the reform, and threatened teacher educators. As CATE took shape and proceeded with its charge, the tone of the teacher education debate was transformed. The annual bulletins of UCET offer a telling example, as expressions of "some surprise" (1984, p. 2) at the creation of its membership soon became concern and confusion that "no one has at present any clear idea of what will happen" (1986, p. 2), and eventually deepened to sharp criticisms of the ideas underlying government policy as "extraordinary," "ill-researched", and "misleading" (1990, pp. 1-2). By 1992 the cautious concern of the early 1980s had hardened into frustrated anger as UCET's annual bulletin reported "overwhelming dislike [and] condemnation" of government teacher education proposals and their process (UCET 1992, p. 2).

It is ironic that the birth of CATE, according at least to the official story, was based on the advice of professional teacher education organizations such as ACSET and UCET (Taylor 1990, p. 113). While CATE may have emerged from consultation with such professional groups, over time it has often been described as ignoring them, transforming their role, and undercutting their power. When CATE was initially formed, its membership included few teacher educators: of the original twenty-three members, only three were from public sector institutions which offered initial teacher preparation and only one was a university teacher educator (Council for the Accreditation of Teacher Education 1990, p. 2; Taylor 1990, p. 116; Macintyre 1991, pp. 9-17). Whatever its professional origins, few would deny that its effect has been gradually to remove the profession from making decisions about its future (Ross 1990, p. 135). By 1993 CATE included among its members Anthony O'Hear, one of the most visible of critics of teacher education who argued that teachers do not need professional education in college or university (*The Times Higher Education Supplement*, December 24, 1993, p. 17).

CATE has been described as a buffer for higher education's teacher education enterprise, or as a wedge, the first wedge, that began to splinter the relationship between the education of teachers and higher education. The chosen simile – buffer or wedge – clearly reflects its author's own position. But regardless of which of these two interpretations one takes, all would agree that CATE provided a new level of government central control of teacher education.

CATE grew out of the critique and recommendations of *Teaching Quality* and the government's Circular 3/84 on *Initial Teacher Training: Approval of Courses* (DES 1984). Recalling the White Paper's proposal for criteria and a review of courses, the 1984 document laid out the "machinery" for this proposal (DES 1984, p. 18). It outlined the charge and composition of an advisory council for accrediting courses and detailed the criteria with regard to links between institutions and schools, "subject studies and subject methods," "educational and professional studies," and student admissions (pp. 23-27). While these criteria heralded a new level of government involvement in shaping teacher education, they are, when compared to criteria that later evolved, relatively general and devoid of quantifiable indicators.

From its inception, CATE struggled to clarify the elusive distinction between accreditation and validation; the two were often confused (Taylor 1990, p. 114; Macintyre 1991, pp. 18-19). Circular 3/84 argued that while "these two functions are clearly interrelated and cannot be carried out in isolation from each other ... they exist for different purposes" (DES 1984, p. 18). CATE's creators argued for the importance of making this distinction. But by the mission and authority given CATE, the distinction was in some ways challenged. Historically government, academic, and semi-governmental organizations (in the UGC or University Grants Committee) shared responsibility for control of programmes of initial teacher education by dividing authority for determining Qualified Teacher Status (QTS), offering validation of courses, and allocating intake numbers (and hence funds). CATE's birth gave renewed salience to QTS and, in a sense, gave the government veto power over the other controlling bodies. If, for example, the Secretary of State withdrew approval of a validated course of teacher training, that course would in effect be eliminated.

This stark assertion of governmental powers which had long been held but never applied startled many in teacher education. And the language of its "machinery," tinged with industrial metaphors, clashed with traditions of professional relations which had characterized the previous sharing of responsibility for teacher education. The Circular called for members of the Council to be appointed "on a personal basis" by the Secretary of State (p. 19); this small body, not designed to be representative, was deliberately drawn from a diverse group of people with, its defenders claimed, some knowledge of teaching and teacher education (Taylor 1990, p. 116). But its composition came as a surprise to most teacher educators (UCET 1984, p. 2). Although the Council's charge was to advise as "experienced professionals" with knowledge of teacher education, the small number of professional teacher educators actually appointed to it suggested that this group was not taken seriously by the government. "The initial misgivings felt by many involved in teacher education about the criteria for accreditation were exacerbated by the fact that they were to be applied by a council with membership ... which seemed light in the knowledge of what was being accredited,'" wrote one CATE member (Macintyre 1991, p. 15). So far from contributing to professional control, CATE's composition "explicitly excluded representatives of relevant professional bodies and effectively disenfranchised teacher educators and teacher associations except in so far as they came into the accreditation process through the local committees" – which, it should be noted, were later disbanded (Edwards 1992b, p. 284).

After the establishment of CATE and the policies that would follow, teacher educators were made increasingly marginal to policy making. In 1987, UCET's historian captured this change when he stated that "today policy tends to be declared first and consultation is only on the details left unconsidered in the declared position. Committees tend to be composed of government nominees rather than representatives nominated by interests. Indeed interests tend to be disparaged as 'the education lobby'" (UCET 1987b, p. 27). With CATE, the government defined the legitimate interests of teacher education and, to some extent, teacher educators. CATE's creation was part of a move towards central control that accelerated throughout the 1980s. CATE proved an effective stepping stone to greater centralization, but the founding of the Teacher Training Agency, scheduled for 1995, made CATE superfluous and it was abolished. In the intervening years, the original themes enunciated in *Teaching Quality* and CATE persisted: the study of subjects taught in school, relevant school experience for teacher educators, strong links to schools. These were the themes woven through the subsequent refinements of policy in such key documents as the Circular 24/89 on the approval of ITT courses and recommissioning of CATE, Circular 9/92 on secondary teacher education, and Circular 14/93 on primary teacher training. With each effort to apply these themes in regulations, government policy became more prescriptive, higher education's presence in teacher education more constrained, and its institutional autonomy narrower.

The evolving language of the criteria reflects the intensified role of government in defining the practice, practitioners, and location of teacher education. What was initially described in five pages in 1984 expanded to six pages of criteria and nine pages of commentary explaining them in 1989. The language shifted to outcomes and performance indicators. The new criteria reflected the parallel drama of centralization occurring in the schools through the creation of the National Curriculum, an unprecedented curriculum policy for both primary and secondary schools which was introduced as a part of the 1988 Education Reform Act. And the terms of the criteria grew more specific. For example, the original broad goal that teacher educators should have recent and relevant school experience became "at least a term every five years"; school experience for teacher education students was translated into more specific requirements, such as a school placement in their first term. CATE's role was to expand from its work in advising on course approval to include as well ongoing monitoring of courses, review of criteria, identifying and disseminating good teacher education practice, and more (DES 1989c, p. 2).

Government control tightened in 1992 when Kenneth Clarke, the new Secretary of State for Education, made a speech at the North of England Conference imparting a new momentum to the reforms. This declaration led to a consultation document and Circular 9/92 on *Secondary Initial Teacher Training*. This set of reforms introduced criteria aimed at teacher competences, at the same time mandating collaboration between higher education institutions and schools in initial teacher training which was unprecedented both in the pace of change and the extent of partnership required. Clearly Clarke and his successor John Patten, who replaced him in the spring of 1992, wanted to move to a model of "school-based" teacher education, with schools in the lead in all phases of the development and running of courses in ways that would, as Clarke enthusiastically put it, "break the hold of the dogmas about teaching method and classroom organization" in departments of education (Clarke 1992). In calling for four-fifths of the initial teacher education course to be based in schools (a proportion that was eventually bargained down to two-thirds), requiring contracts between higher education institutions and schools, directing that money flow from higher education to the schools, and even recommending the kinds of schools which should be sought for partnership status, the government actively defined course content and location, as well as the relationship between institutions. In other words, it seized control of defining the terrain and boundaries of teacher education, as well as changing the landscape that was mapped. Institutions which would not comply, rejected a school's interest in partnership, or which were seen as treating a school "arbitrarily or unreasonably" were threatened with loss of approval (Department for Education [hereafter DFE]1993a, p. 15).

Reinforcing the government's growing authority was its ability to link directly, for the first time, teacher education content and the content of schooling (through the National Curriculum). Circular 9/92 required teacher education institutions to teach their students about that curriculum. Some saw these changes in teacher education as an attempt to establish a national teacher education curriculum, with the central government "setting limits to permissible differences in course structure, content and (in the 1992 version) the outcomes of training" (Edwards 1992a, p. 2). The government's keenness to open teacher education to regular inspection and the dismantling by 1992 of local CATE committees further illustrate the concentration of authority in the hands of central government.

While the story of central control is fairly straightforward, if somewhat breathtaking in its pace and boldness, the impact of such control is rather more complex. Certainly over the course of the 1980s and early 1990s initial teacher education courses became more consistently school-based. They offered fewer distinct occasions for studying social foundations or educational theory; as one teacher educator described his department's change (inspired in part by internal reform but supported and pushed further by the direction of government policy), "You couldn't say 'where's your psychologist?' now." Departments paid more consistent attention to subject studies and subject applications and these topics were taught by staff with more recent experience in schools. Yet institutions and their faculty did not respond uniformly either to the substantive direction of government policy or to the process or mechanisms which supported it.

All institutions were required to comply with the new criteria. Nevertheless, given their diverse prestige, resources, and institutional histories, the universities, polytechnics, and colleges engaged in teacher education varied in their response to this challenge of top-down reform. Some went smoothly through CATE's approval process, others encountered repeated problems. One college which failed after two attempts to secure

CATE approval eventually found it could only satisfy government concern for subject strength by sending students for some instruction at a polytechnic sixty miles away. Faculty complied with these CATE requests despite their misgivings but eventually the college and polytechnic merged. The pressure from CATE was discouraging for the institution and ultimately contributed to its loss of institutional independence. In a contrasting case, a polytechnic, even though it too initially failed to get approval, took a more assertive stance, did not tailor its course description to fit the government's forms, and openly challenged the grounds for some of CATE's claims about their programme (Barton et al. 1992). While both courses encountered difficulties because of CATE, their interactions with CATE differed greatly because of their different experiences in defending themselves and their different histories of exposure to outside scrutiny. Several faculty members with experience working in CNAA-validated institutions explained to us that this history of preparing course rationales for the external peer review that CNAA required prepared them better for the processes associated with the government's move toward centralization. While they may have been no more receptive than university faculty to the increasing direction from the government, they were, they argued, at least more accustomed to considering the coherence of their course as a course, of arguing among themselves about course elements, and of defending their decisions to outsiders.

Within the university sector, on the other hand, the traditional mantle of autonomy and academic freedom made expansion of government control appear disturbingly intrusive. It could be argued that the concepts of autonomy and academic freedom, although carrying important symbolic value, had not for some time in their pure forms characterized British higher education (Warnock 1992). Yet under these terms fragmentation of work undertaken by many in the same university departments of education had been possible. Consider the experience of a university teacher educator in charge of a course who recalled how he had asked to see an outline of the teaching programme of a colleague and was reported to the department chair as violating academic freedom. That such a culture existed within many university departments of education helps to explain why the 1980s and 1990s reforms, with the movement of standards-setting to the hands of government, were so challenging for the universities.

University concern about the intrusion of government was often symbolized in the debates about HMI inspections. The convention that HMI inspected only public sector institutions was abandoned as a result of CATE's requirements. Course approval depended on CATE recommendations, which were to be based on HMI reports. Although softer language (of "invited visits" rather than "inspections") was used to mask the process, this intervention "effectively breached some of that sector's traditional autonomy" (Whitty et al. 1987, p. 165). Relations with HMI remained relatively cordial, but the publication of their reports on each institution visited – a further symbol of the lowering of university walls – posed what UCET in its typically understated tone called "a knotty problem" (UCET 1986, p. 2).

Like their counterparts on the other side of the binary line, universities varied in the level of difficulty they encountered in responding to the new mechanisms of central oversight. Some university departments of education which enjoyed a relatively easy passage through CATE complained when their courses were later officially held up for emulation, on the grounds that their original intentions and principles had been distorted. Based on a conceptualization of internship which predated CATE and having received a positive HMI report, Oxford's PGCE subsequently was used to support Clarke's idea of school-based teacher education. However, as many both in and out of Oxford would note, this facile commendation of Oxford's course showed little appreciation of the pedagogical principles or resources needed to sustain it.

Despite the variation across sectors and institutions in their experience with CATE and successive policy changes, centralization produced common effects in many institutions. The most obvious and immediate side effect was the massive increase in the time higher education institutions had to spend in responding to government requirements. The dean of education at a polytechnic complained that simply preparing for the HMI visit for CATE approval required pulling together extensive documentation: "Now this was a real problem, we almost stopped doing anything else for a matter of several months, not just weeks, preparing the material for the HMI. Everything had to be copied, typed up and we had to abstract. It was a massive job ... All the resources were going into the HMI visit, so that you know everything else got put on one side" (quoted in Barton et al. 1992, p. 48).

As inspections and the number of government-sponsored supervisory agencies increased, universities complained about the "demands for excessive amounts of information" (UCET 1992, p. 7). Inspectors or others would arrive in a department in a group, sometimes as large as ten, and spend as much as a week observing, interviewing students and faculty, looking over course documentation, and debriefing faculty. Life had to go on hold for each of these visits, even though the preparation for them had already been a significant disruption. Certainly just responding to this degree of outside evaluation put tremendous demands on departments. Of course, the substantive changes that the process was to put in place called for even greater resources, especially the requirements for a longer term, more time in schools, and more extensive school teaching experience for teacher educators (to be subsidized by their employers).

The resource problems were exacerbated by a pace of top-down policy changes and modes of control that were "unprecedented" (Whitty et al. 1987, p. 171). This period saw a rise in the number of papers "requiring reactions and comments, often within a very short time" (UCET 1985, p. 1). Consultation documents proposing a radical overhaul of teacher education were released with little response time allowed. The result was to diminish the ability of teacher educators to engage with or shape central education policy. Major changes in secondary teacher education, for example, were announced on January 4 in Clarke's North of England speech. A consultation document was drafted by late January, and by May John Patten had already succeeded Kenneth Clarke and reached his decisions on the reform of secondary teacher preparation. Many of those with whom we spoke thought this typical haste reflected the wish to make consultation only a superficial process. The new policies, announced in the June 25 Circular, were to go into effect immediately during the imminent Autumn term. The very process became contentious, as UCET claimed that the new scheme produced "real problems ... caused by the speed with which it was supposed to be put into effect and the generally disorganized way in which it has been imposed" (UCET 1992, p. 2).

The pace intensified with the primary reforms. Here, in the wake of the radical transformation outlined by the secondary Circular, primary teacher educators waited for months as anticipated dates for announcing the parallel changes for primary teacher education continued to recede. On June 9 1993 a draft circular on primary teacher education reform was circulated for comments, which were required by the end of July. Many cynically noted a pattern of consultation which was not only swift but also deliberately timed to coincide with school holidays or other periods when responses might be inhibited. Teacher educators, dizzied by this pace of change, spent the decade racing to catch the window of opportunity to respond to government edicts and, more exhaustingly, to put into place courses that met government specifications. This process occupied the teacher education community in a way that, as the polytechnic dean cited above suggested, kept his department from doing other things. This pace also placed teacher educators in a reactive stance.

As government consolidated its control of teacher education, the mechanics and pace of change doubtless allowed some institutions to exploit the circumstances. Institutions that were well-connected to insiders aware of what was about to happen, those with confidence based on their previously successful government assessments or their relative prestige could afford to think more creatively or strategically. Teacher educators spoke of being able to capture the language of government goals in support of championing practices perhaps at odds with such goals. Government criteria which stressed subject study, school practice, and teacher competences were re-translated in some programmes to support courses that fostered critical reflection, an approach likely to fall under the Ministers' list of what a teacher educator called the "woolly liberal targets" of government reform (Whitty et al. 1987, pp. 177-78). Consider the example of John Eggleston's textbook, *The Challenge for Teachers* (1992). His is an upbeat encouragement that, in spite or even because of the National Curriculum, teachers have "a major if not a dominant role in determining the curriculum and its outcomes" (p. 18). Eggleston tells teacher education students, in the language of the new sociology of education which was very much a target for the government's centralizing reforms, that "the curriculum is about the distribution of power" (p. 23).

While few courses or their materials seemed openly subversive of government policy, many institutions quickly learned how to deal with central control. Their responses could become "ritualistic," focusing their energies on presentation and "managing the impressions they gave" while still "creatively attempting to retain aspects of practice in which they believed" (Barton et al. 1992, p. 55). Thus, course elements and rationales would be re-written or re-named, 'creative accountancy' would transform the calculation of hours in particular subjects and activities would be redefined to 'count' in respect of important criteria (Barton et al. 1992, p. 55).

The outsider looking at institutions in 1994 is nevertheless struck by the extent to which the norms of government policy became internalized. The terms of the debate increasingly were set by the government – and, within the government, by politicians. Institutions complained initially about CATE, they strategized to find ways to create for themselves a niche in the market of providers that government policies tried to establish, and they devoted hours to elaborating arrangements to cope with "recent and relevant experience" or with the 9/92 Circular's notions of partnership. Yet their considerable investment in strategizing reveals the power that government had come to have over teacher educators in colleges, polytechnics and universities. In part through internalizing the government framework and in part by sheer dint of necessary compliance with bureaucratic structures, teacher education had by 1994 adapted itself to conform to a model dictated and controlled by central government. Of course, variation still occurred across institutions, but the process of centralization had indeed produced fundamental change.

The increasing concentration of decision-making power in teacher education paralleled centralization in other parts of education in ways that had a powerful impact on teacher educators and their practice and further tightened central control of the teacher education enterprise. Within higher education generally, entire institutions, like their schools and departments of education, were subjected with growing frequency and consequence to government review. Thus by 1994 teacher education faculty had to interact with an ever growing number of outside agencies who were responsible for ever increasing amounts of scrutiny, as well as scrutiny about more aspects of institutional life – funding, programme content, links to schools, students, faculty quality, faculty research, and so on. CATE (and for a time its local CATE committees), HMI, OFSTED (the Office for Standards in Education), HEFCE, research selectivity, efficiency audits, and academic audits within the university consumed the time and energy of teacher education faculty, specifically, and higher education staff more generally, and shaped the definition of issues.

The problems of external scrutiny may have placed exceptionally heavy burdens on university-based teacher educators, living as they did in two worlds. University departments of education "are constituent parts of chartered autonomous bodies organised on the principle of each university taking decisions independently according to the collective view of the members of the academic community. University departments, as providers of teacher education, are, however, also part of another system, increasingly centralised, in which characteristically major decisions are handed down from elsewhere" (UCET 1987b, p. 26).

The government's newly articulated concern with accountability in higher education raised such issues in the sharpest form. Although few institutions had ever experienced pure autonomy in terms of "independence from resource constraints," the values of self-governance have "persisted, but on a steep sliding scale according to the status of the institution" (Becher & Kogan 1992, pp. 178-79). The increasing presence of a managerial style in higher education, with funding determined on a performance basis, represented a break from even the narrowed version of autonomy that all but the elite higher education institutions had experienced for decades. This was translated during Thatcher's years as "funding by and for results."

A key emblem of this policy was the research selectivity exercise. First in 1984-85 and then again in 1988-89 and 1992-93, universities had to submit to a research selectivity exercise as an evaluation which would determine differential funding and serve as a method of justifying some of the funding discrepancies between universities and polytechnics (Williams 1992, p. 9). For teacher educators this process of publicly ranking a department on the basis of published research created what one teacher education course director called "tremendous pressure" to do research. Within departments faculty varied in how they were affected. As he explained, in the past no one expected the same people to do both "high class teacher education and research." But if departments of education were to meet new government standards for higher education, now the same people were expected to do both and this put, in his words, "divisive pressure" on faculty. Some clearly resented the increased burdens on their time imposed by government teacher education requirements, such as the lengthened PGCE term or the recent and relevant school experience. They complained bitterly about the way their departments were resolving the tensions between autonomy and control and longed for a chance to pursue their own interests. Others, while generally supportive of the direction of the government's push in teacher education, anxiously tried to find opportunities to publish. In terms of their daily lives, these twin pressures left teacher educators having to carve out research time (as well as topics) from the edges of their days in schools. For department chairs, the pressures put them in an unenviable position – needing to goad more faculty into productive lines of research while explaining to their fellow chairs why their department's research portfolio or their ranking might not be comparable with those of other parts of the university. The challenge was made more difficult as much of teacher education research, developed along the lines of action research, did not look like research done elsewhere. With

215

the elimination of the binary line, the challenge offered special difficulties for many faculty in polytechnics, where research had not been part of their traditional mission.

As with responses to CATE, this new level of higher education accountability was time consuming for teacher educators. "The amount of time and effort (not to mention expense) put into these exercises is immense" (UCET 1992, p. 10). It led to "many anxious hours preparing research profiles and awaiting the ... pronouncements" (UCET 1986, p. 1). It also helped shape definitions of research, of appropriate knowledge, and of higher education itself. This expansion of government control of higher education put higher education on the defensive and made teacher education more vulnerable than before. Few welcomed these new burdens and the heightened level of scrutiny of their work. A telling episode in the story of the strained relations between higher education and the government was the University of Oxford's rebuff of Margaret Thatcher; while Prime Minister, her nomination for an honorary degree was rejected by the academic parliament of the university.

This need to defend their work to government organizations was especially irksome for teacher educators, who were already deeply affected by CATE and government reforms in schools. As UCET explained for university departments of education,

> In tackling the immediate problems thrown up by the Education Reform Act [of 1988], the national curriculum and the large number of Government initiatives, university staff were pushed toward the "development" side of the "Research and Development" equation. Though there was much British research in education of the highest international significance in terms of "pure" research, a not inconsiderable part of the efforts of university teacher trainers was directed at meeting the challenges posed by the major reforms in education in Britain over the last few years (UCET 1989, p. 6).

Teacher education could not avoid being affected by the realignment of relations between government and schools in the 1980s and 1990s. During the decade in which teacher education decision-making was increasingly determined by government and higher education activity was ever more closely monitored by it, schools underwent a process sometimes described as decentralization but which might, in many aspects crucial to teacher education, be better characterized as consolidation of central government control. The tradition which celebrated British teachers as key decision makers in matters of curriculum, pedagogy and assessment was dramatically challenged by the National Curriculum mandated as part of the landmark 1988 Education Reform Act.[4]

The legislating into existence of a National Curriculum in 1988, however complex the subsequent debate and ephemeral some of the decisions, did profoundly redirect educational decision-making, remove much from teachers' control, and relocate fundamental determinants of teaching practice in the hands of central government. The contrast is sharp, and perhaps like many aspects of reform in this era, made sharper by the speed with which change occurred. Teachers who, like the primary teachers studied by Nias (1989), defined their practice with emphasis on the self, individuality, and autonomy, now had their practice defined by two short lived committees, the National Curriculum Council (NCC) and the School Examinations and Assessment Council (SEAC), with members appointed by the Secretary of State. (By 1994, these councils were to be merged, a decision which simply underscores the process of concentration of power at work during this time.) The "secret garden" of the curriculum had, after years of debate, been opened up for others to landscape in ways that frustrated and disillusioned teachers (Bolton 1993, p. 3).

The introduction of this curriculum represents, in a sharp break with the past, the introduction of central control of definitions and organization of knowledge. In moving towards a centralized curriculum, national policy redefined the role of teachers, as well as the skills and knowledge they were believed to require. Furthermore, the fact that the curriculum came neither from teachers nor from the university means that teachers now looked to the government and official curriculum bodies for crucial information about and understandings of the important knowledge on which schooling is based. British teachers were now not only required to meet objectives set centrally by policy bodies, at a prescriptive level new to the history of teaching in that country. They also were encouraged to see that the sources of knowledge in teaching, or the arbiters of that knowledge, were located outside the university. Higher education faculty were involved in the creation and implementation of the National Curriculum, but their authority came not from their location within academe but from their appointment to the NCC body; their opportunity came through lucrative contracts to implement the government's objectives. A central feature of this process of concentration of decision-making power was the exclusion or marginalization of teachers from the process. The national assessment reforms that were associated with the National Curriculum gave added force to this message. With the introduction of published league tables that allowed the public to compare schools in a competitive market environment, teachers and their schools were held accountable for their success or failure in delivering the official curriculum.

School heads, while critical of some aspects of the National Curriculum, nevertheless explained that they used it in job interviews with teacher education graduates. Student teachers were reported as "demoralized" from their time in schools where they saw how low teacher morale was in the wake of the extensive changes demanded of them. And teacher educators were obliged to teach the National Curriculum in their teacher education programme. In short, the National Curriculum appeared everywhere as a reminder of a process of centralization unfamiliar and generally unwelcome within the teacher education community.

By the end of 1993 the effects of a decade of centralization had led to very clear changes in teacher education. Even the limited degree of local control represented by the local CATE committees had been eliminated since, according to the government, it was no longer needed. With the loss of autonomy, teacher educators worried about a rise of "conformity and mediocrity" (Barton et al. 1992, p. 46). A polytechnic faculty member with an interest in special needs had noted that with CATE's requirements, "more innovative degrees won't be possible" and even early on, UCET said that for its members "the overriding concern is that the criteria themselves and CATE's interpretation of them may well lead to a more standardised, more rigid, less innovative system, which would only be to the detriment of teacher training in particular and eventually to education in schools" (UCET 1985, p. 2).

Was teacher education in fact more uniform by 1994? In measurable terms, certainly. As for the feeling in the hallways, classrooms, and staffrooms, it is harder to say. But it does seem clear that a function of the centralization was to focus attention on government policy rather than on an organic or internal critique of teacher education practice. By deflecting teacher education from the obligation to assess itself, the process of central control weakened its institutional capacity for thoughtful change. Moreover, the vision of teacher education inherent in central plans, fragmented though it has been, has been internalized in interesting and important ways. One particularly significant example is in the redefinition of the teacher educator.

Many of those who by 1994 had become initial teacher educators were new to higher education. Those who had taught in and even run courses a decade earlier were, in many institutions, no longer the core of teacher education faculty. Not only was the psychologist of the earlier quotation no longer visible. Neither were many of the sociologists and other "educationalists," as the critics of teacher education disparagingly called those not primarily identified by a subject specialty. The vision of teacher education embodied in the government's reform, combined with the structural requirements for such courses, resulted in a relocation of responsibility. And many mainstream teacher educators, disheartened by the whole atmosphere of reform in education, had resigned their leadership positions, some taking early retirement, others striking out to develop graduate programmes in management and other areas intended to appeal to prospective international students.

It is not clear always whether many of the teacher educators of earlier days had jumped or were pushed off the main deck on the Initial Teacher Training ship. What is clear is that – although many remained – ITT staff now included a large influx of younger teacher educators, arriving fresh from experience as teachers. As one director put it, higher education administrators could not find researchers with sufficient school experience in order to satisfy CATE requirements. One solution has been to hire school people and let them develop research expertise. While ultimately the aim was to produce a teacher educator firmly grounded in both school experience and research, the insertion of government requirements in initial teacher education brought into higher education many whose prior primary professional identity had been forged in schools. In addition, the push from government for partnership with schools and the strengthened role for practitioners in ITT – as mentors, as admissions interviewers, as course co-developers – changed and enlarged the very definition of a teacher educator. Teacher education's culture became more diverse; its cultural core in higher education was weakened.

These changes contributed to tension between teacher education and higher education. The government's requirements, whether related to the amount and placement of subject studies or the links with schools, affected parts of the universities and colleges outside departments of education and hence forced teacher educators to educate their institution's administrators and faculty. At one meeting we observed teacher educators complaining about how CATE and higher education were at odds. Their universities were calling for greater integration between education and the rest of the university, and in one institution this had produced an integrated four year concurrent ITT course that allowed teacher education students to take courses with students in other fields. Yet CATE's insistence that students' school experience should be organized as block practice meant that students were not available for regular higher education courses other than those specifically provided for them.

These tensions – present in hiring faculty, in scheduling students, and other daily features of higher education operation – were important side effects of centralization and represented the redefinition of teacher educators and the content of their practice. A third dramatic side effect was the relocation of teacher education. As a result of the government's aggressive involvement in ITT, by 1994 teacher education had rapidly moved from its traditional home in higher education to a base in schools. In the wake of the 1992 and 1993 Circulars, teacher education courses for both secondary and primary teachers needed to have extensive and close links to schools. The role of higher education in teacher education was of course significantly reduced by the requirement that PGCE students should spend most of their time in schools. Other changes reinforced these effects, moving teacher education away from its base in universities and polytechnics.

Three alternative modes of teacher training exemplified this process: the Articled Teacher Scheme (ATS), the Licensed Teacher Scheme (LTS), and proposals for school-led or school-centred teacher training. In terms of number of students, these alternatives were small. For example, only eight per cent of ITT courses were organized as an ATS in 1990-91 (Barrett et al. 1992a, p. 11). Yet what they suggested in terms of the balance of responsibilities between schools and higher education for ITT and the degree of direct government control was significant.

These schemes varied distinctively in their structures and the inherent assumptions about who should make decisions about the preparation of beginning teachers. The ATS acted as an extended PGCE course. Lasting for two years, an ATS course was jointly administered by higher education institutions, LEAs, and schools. ATS students spent the majority of their time, eighty per cent in fact, in schools (Barrett and Galvin 1993, p. 5). The Licensed Teacher Scheme was an even more fully school-based approach. The training of Licensed Teachers did not require any higher education involvement. Licensed Teachers could be paid as qualified or unqualified teachers; they were therefore, "literally, training 'on the job'" (Barrett & Galvin 1993, p. 5). The third and most recent initiative of school-centered training, which allowed consortia of schools to develop their own initial teacher education programmes, similarly left no mandated role for higher education. But this approach transformed relations across sectors and commercialized that relationship, as schools could contract with local higher education institutions for contributions to the course, leaving the higher education institution simply to offer services for sale.

These alternatives posed a serious challenge to teacher education as it existed and called into question the sincerity of government rhetoric about partnership between higher education and schools on teacher education. "The concept of 'partnership' was now one in which the HEIs [higher education institutions] figured only if the other partners wanted them" (Barrett and Galvin 1993, p. 6). Hence, these reforms, particularly LTS and school-centered training, were perceived by teacher educators as politically and economically, rather than pedagogically, motivated. Teacher educators saw, as one of them put it, these reforms as government moves to "get teacher education out of the clutches" of departments of education; or, in the words of another, to increase teacher supply through doing teacher education "on the cheap." Despite their relatively small size, these schemes – like other reforms of this era – strengthened central control by reducing the mediating role of a traditionally powerful education sector, in this case higher education.

By redefining teacher educators, their practice and location, the process of centralization politicized the discourse of teacher education. Government reforms in schools, higher education, and especially teacher education directed, as we have suggested, teacher educators' efforts and discussions. These were the highly charged years of the second administration of Margaret Thatcher and the government of her successor, John Major, who, some claimed, tried to "out-Thatcher Thatcher," years when various Secretaries of State for Education were closely identified with policies they pursued very personally or designed in consultation exclusively with ideologues. They announced some of these policies with an eye to generating what one government official saw, not disapprovingly, as "creative destability." In such a climate, teacher educators focused their attention on what they saw as the heavily politicized agenda of reform. For many, for example, CATE seemed, as one department chair claimed, an example of "government interest in policing." Centralization was a process that was inherently about political control, not building professionalism. Thus, for many in teacher education, the theme of centralization as a dominant motif in the turbulent decade of change could only be understood in relation to a campaign of anti-professionalism.

Anti-professionalism: resurrecting the teacher apprentice

The reforms promulgated in 1994 were designed to place a new Teacher Training Agency in absolute control of the financing and administration of the whole teacher education enterprise. Teacher educators and teachers could no longer hope to exercise any professional control over training for and entry to "the profession." The campaign for a General Teaching Council was undermined both by government policy and failure of professional groups to agree on details (UCET 1987a, 1990; Ross 1990, p. 124). Growing central control had proved to be a mighty distraction for teacher educators. It had encouraged compliance rather than critical reflection among teacher educators. And it had further divided an already diverse community. By 1994 the dangers were unambiguously clear to all those affected by them, but for much of the previous decade relations within the teacher education community, and between it and the worlds of higher education, had been badly strained.

The government's vision of teacher education and of teaching, which was to exert such divisive power over ITE was, by 1994, fundamentally anti-professional. It rested on a body of critique, including attacks that were sometimes measured but most often fierce. It produced a view of teaching and teacher education that was technicist, denying any meaningful role for educational theory. The result helped to transform the nature of teaching and learning in teacher education courses and shifted their knowledge base – not just their course hours – to schools.

At the time of CATE's creation, teacher education was still being challenged by the problems which had vexed it for decades: finding an appropriate balance between its many curricular demands, especially between disciplinary and professional studies, and between those involved in the process, particularly higher education institutions and schools. In the early and mid-1980s, as HMI visits reported, teacher education in the public sector and universities offered initial teacher education with great variation in the coherence of their course, their content and its balance, their staffing, and their relations to schools. Courses were generally weak in equipping students with enough depth and breadth of knowledge in a subject and its teaching methods to enable them to attend to the diverse needs of students. Professional issues were often introduced in shallow, optional, or disconnected ways. ITT courses generally were faulted for problems in staffing and management. And teacher education courses were seen as not consistently and sufficiently connected to good practice in schools (DES 1988b; DES 1987).

Most undergraduate BEd courses were viewed by HMI as falling "considerably short of providing adequate subject studies, and ... scarcely any had developed aspects of the course which would equip students to orient the study to the needs of primary school children" (DES 1987, p. 25). Postgraduate programmes, given their short length, were too densely packed and in the primary PGCE this problem was exacerbated by the breadth of subjects involved and the nature of the primary teacher's work. Most staff came with secondary, rather than primary, teaching experience and hence were not as well prepared to help intending primary teachers. And the traditions of institutional and faculty autonomy within the university sector led to a tendency towards the balkanization of courses, with individual tutors pursuing topics without knowledge of or coordination with what occurred in the rest of the course. University courses were seen as having developed in a haphazard manner in a culture unlike that of the CNAA-validated institutions, where the prevailing traditions of peer review encouraged whole course development, reflection by faculty, and consequently greater integration of work. In addition, without a common external process or standard, university courses varied widely in key areas, such as the teaching of theory. Some departments in the early 1980's still had specific theory courses, while others had moved with varying success to integrate theoretical questions into consideration of professional and educational issues. With university tutors spending up to one third of their time in research, and decentralized decision-making for staffing in many departments, HMI found "too few full-time tutors are sufficiently involved in ITT" (DES 1988b, p. 5).

These concerns helped to inspire *Teaching Quality*, Circular 3/84, and CATE. They were echoed outside the government in increasingly harsh and loud tones by a small but vociferous group of New Right critics. They rested their case on two arguments. They first criticized beginning teachers for weakness in their knowledge of academic subjects. What is needed, say these critics, is less time on educational theory and more time actually learning a subject. Their view of good teaching is centred on a teacher's "authoritative" command of a subject (O'Hear 1991, p. 33). "Although the good teacher is unique, he shares one characteristic with every capable teacher: a deep knowledge and mastery of his subject. Any plan designed to improve the quality of teachers should concentrate on ensuring that those in the profession have a mastery of their individual subjects" (Lawlor 1990, p. 7). The second argument, separate although related to the first, alleges that teachers do not need teacher preparation in a higher education setting, which only introduces the teacher at best to irrelevant theory, and at worst to dangerous ideas of Marxism, socialism, or "woolly headed" liberalism. One critic claimed that the "threat today" in teacher education could be readily detected in the course details at any institution of teacher preparation: embedded within these courses are "equality-mongering and the hate-cults, in conjunction with the celebration of childhood hegemony" (O'Keefe 1990, p. 85). What teachers need to learn in order to teach, it is claimed, is pedagogy, particularly exposure to and work with experienced practitioners in schools. Theory is depicted as the villain. Redemption lies in disciplinary knowledge and in school practice. Lawlor argues, for example, that "instead of putting mastery of the subject at the heart of the course, as the essential foundation for good teaching, the training courses demean the subject to being little more than a peg on which to hang modish educational theory. Moreover, unlike other professions where mastery of the subject is followed by practice on the job (whereby the individual develops the methods which suit him best), teacher training courses seek to impose the same style on all teachers, for all subjects, for all children" (Lawlor 1990, p. 42). Her proposal therefore is to abolish the departments of education, eliminate the PGCE and BEd courses, and move entirely to on-the-job training.

Finally, a major source of the problem lies with teacher educators themselves, who, goes the story, are cut off from the realities of schools and classrooms. Teacher education was attacked as removed from the needs of schools for the twentieth and twenty-first centuries yet having dangerously taken over control of oversight for teacher education curricula. Recalling and reworking themes from the Great Debate, the New Right critics laid emphasis upon the assumed link between economic and social strength and schools, with an explicit claim for the special role of teachers in supporting that link. The argument was "not only that the education system was failing to deliver the kind of educated population which a modern economy requires, but also that the country's schools, and that above all means its teachers, were no longer fulfilling their role as transmitters of the values and beliefs of the majority in society" (Perry 1989, p. 147). Teacher educators were accused of ignoring the government's criterion for teacher education which required it to focus on Britain's economic and social foundations.

Books with titles such as *Teachers Mistaught* (Lawlor 1990), *Who Teaches the Teachers?* (O'Hear 1988), and *Education and Democracy: Against the Educational Establishment* (O'Hear 1991) directly attacked teacher education with growing force over the 1980s and early 1990s, inspired new government policies, and set terms for a teacher education discourse over which teacher educators had diminishing control. Even although teacher educators and their courses changed radically over the 1980s, in part as a result of CATE and government demands, the attacks grew (Edwards 1990, pp. 185-87). In 1990, for example, Lawlor questioned the DES's assessment that "the effect of changes since the mid-1980s has been for the best" and finds instead that "these apparently sensible ideas have been put into practice in such a way as to turn the original intention on its head" (1990, p. 12). While the reforms were intended to diminish the stress on theory and increase attention to practice, critics saw the revised courses as still dominated by theory: "practical experience has been manipulated so as to provide a vehicle for theory," they argued (Lawlor 1990, pp. 22-23).

But teacher education was not at this time the only target of anti-professional criticism. In the early 1990s John Major, struggling with being Thatcher's heir while needing to distance himself from some of her policies, drifted toward the left wing of his party on economic and trade issues and policies regarding relations with Europe. On the other hand, he seemed willing to "throw" to the right wing many social policies, including education.

Thus it was that government resurrected anti-professional criticisms that had been popular among radical scholars of the late 1960s and 1970s. Now in the 1990s the government's conservative advisors appropriated the critique to justify a more aggressive market orientation for professional activities. The anti-professional critique pressed for an expansion of consumer – and a matching reduction of professional – power, in part through market mechanisms. This anti-professional culture led to assaults on health care, the police, architecture, and teaching and teacher education. Existing structures for professional education were seen as too costly and their content as too theoretical. Architecture was a case in point. Creating "alternate routes" would appeal to prospective practitioners who would find entry opened to more individuals and individuals with fewer academic credentials. Ultimately, it was argued, the public (the clients of architects) and the employers of designers (the direct consumers) would benefit from the de-professionalization of the field because buildings would be simpler and cheaper, more popular and understandable to the public, and less the product of unrestrained architectural egos. These campaigns, while well supported by conservative propagandists, benefited from the timely participation of others; the attack on architecture, for example, intensified with public criticism by the Prince of Wales of recent architectural projects as inappropriate and frivolous; he entered the dialogue as a voice of a public disenchanted with architectural monstrosities.

In education, as in these other areas, the role of the media in feeding these debates is not to be ignored. Conservatives for example exploited the difficulties encountered by the National Curriculum and assessments reforms in order to indict the destructive role of the professional "educational establishment." Benign reforms, designed to serve the interests of the public as consumer, had been (it was claimed) subverted by the professionals. In assessment, for example, media space was devoted to the charges and counter-charges related to the reforms proposed for a series of tests on the national curriculum. A valuable effort to provide important information to help parents make wise choices was, said the conservatives, hijacked by the professional establishment. For the goal of producing simple and market-directed measures had been substituted that of providing gentler diagnoses of the progress and difficulties of pupils.

Teacher education, as our earlier discussion of Lawlor, O'Hear, and their colleagues suggests, was portrayed as a dangerously subversive activity. But even within the government, it was acknowledged that ITT by the 1990s was in fact essentially conservative, and that an old, outdated image was being promoted for political reasons in order to build the impression that radical theory was still dominant. This helps to explain in part the conflicting images of teacher education that emerged from, on the one hand, DFE/HMI reports, which cite on balance great gains in teacher education, and on the other hand government circulars and consultation documents which are based on the assumption that teacher education has corrupted professional practice.

These attacks were, some would claim, misdirected or ill-informed. They seemed to be aimed at a version of teacher education which had dominated in the 1960s and which was associated with undergraduate programmes. Yet by the 1990s the university PGCE had become a dominant mode of teacher education; in 1990-91, there were slightly more students in PGCE programmes (12,235) than undergraduate programmes (11,934) (Barrett et al. 1992a, p. 8). Still, fighting against that version of teacher education which it saw as predominant, the government and its advisors pushed for more radical reform, for an alternative to teacher education as it existed. Critics of teacher education rallied around the growing number of alternative routes to teaching. Conservatives like Caroline Cox, from the influential New Right Hillgate Group, questioned the idea that the "vast majority" of future teachers needed to come from teacher education courses. Such qualifications were "not necessary for good teaching. They are an expensive practice which hinders the state sector and the sooner they are abolished the better" (quoted in Barrett & Galvin 1993, p. 8). These critics, on economic and ideological grounds, argued that teaching is best learned through an apprenticeship model, such as LTS offered.

LTS was an open challenge to teacher education. Baroness Blatch, an Education Minister closely connected to the Prime Minister, in commending the publication of OFSTE's reports on the LTS's and ATS's first two years suggested "The world of education is changing and the world of teacher education will have to change with it" (DFE 1993d, pp. 1-2). That an Education Minister, rather than a civil servant, should be touting the benefits of working outside the "educational establishment" of teacher education is illustrative of the new style of the anti-professional critique.

The attack upon professional power and autonomy was not without its contradictions, perhaps the most basic being the insistence that prospective teachers should learn by "sitting by Nelly" in the popular phrase: that is to say, directly from those same experienced teachers who were themselves held responsible for the reported deterioration of English education. While the LTS, for example, was held up for emulation by government advisors, Licensed Teachers were not necessarily able (nor were they required) to satisfy the government's CATE requirements for subject knowledge. This contradiction suggests that whereas CATE's own subject matter emphasis related mainly to the importance of ensuring that teachers were in a general sense well educated, the government itself was concerned with the very different objective of securing that teachers would be equipped to deliver the officially packaged basic knowledge of the national curriculum. Baroness Blatch, for example, commended the LTS and ATS for offering "'a sharper focus on the teaching and assessment of the National Curriculum" (DFE

1993d, p. 1). Similarly, while alternate routes were advocated in part for their cost effectiveness, researchers claimed the ATS was more expensive than traditional teacher education. That this conclusion could be ignored by the government suggests that the more powerful motive behind the support for alternatives was the desire to challenge the higher education monopoly in teacher education. Teacher educators ruefully recalled that many of the hard won improvements in professional standards and qualifications were now being sacrificed. In response to the LTS proposal, universities noted that this new zeal for employing unqualified, untrained teachers "came only five years after exemption from that training was finally abolished in all but special cases, and only about fifteen years after teaching became an all graduate entry profession" (UCET 1988, p. 4).

LTS clearly represented an apprenticeship model of teacher education. Subsequent proposals similarly challenged the assumption which had evolved about the importance of teaching being an all graduate profession and the special place of higher education knowledge in the education of teachers. One such proposal which typified the efforts of the Secretary of State to contest professional norms was to recruit what was popularly ridiculed as a "Mums' Army." In his proposed draft of the 1993 Primary Circular the Secretary of State proposed to develop one year courses for "parents and other mature students with considerable previous experience of working with young children (such as nursery nurses who have worked for some time in schools)" (DFE 1993a, p. 12). Intended only for those teachers who would teach young children, this suggestion represented a break with recent traditions of professionalism and a throwback to earlier approaches. It discriminated among standards for teachers of different age phases, suggesting that teachers of young children did not need as much academic knowledge as other teachers. Unlike even the LTS, it did not assume that a higher education background was relevant to teaching. The Mums' Army concept was based on a strong anti-professional assumption that mature individuals who had common sense but who had not been contaminated by psychological and other learning or child-centred theory would be best able to "keep their eye on the ball" of the national curriculum agenda and ensure discipline and achievement. Mature people who were trained on the job could be counted on to break the stranglehold of the professional establishment, in particularl the monopoly of university-based teacher education. A way to circumvent higher education was needed, since, as one civil servant explained, it was seen as "slightly subversive" and "still broadly unsympathetic" to government policies such as the National Curriculum. The Mums' Army proposal would have the potential to drive a wedge of differential prestige between different kinds of teaching, as well as between different kinds of teacher education.

The proposal, although short-lived, served as a decoy to distract attention from other contentious reforms proposed by the government. One such proposal, which underscored many of the assumptions supporting the case against professionalism, was for the introduction of a new kind of BEd degree, the preparation for which would last only three years and would cover six subjects (DFE 1993a, p. 11). Once again, subject mastery was directly related to the content of what needed to be taught in primary schools, and not to the general educational or cultural needs of students within higher education. This proposal challenged the tacit assumptions that had been worked out over the years regarding the importance of higher education to teacher education. Patten hoped this approach would "progressively...replace the current 4 year course" for primary teachers and serve as a model for similar changes for secondary teachers (DFE 1993c, p. 5). Shortening the degree reversed reforms hammered out since 1963 and which had given education some academic respectability. Where the previous certificates had been transformed to the B. Ed.s, the new proposals were chipping away at the BEd degree itself. Moreover, by asking that the degree be a six subject one, the proposal denied the dominant notions of both higher education (characterized by depth of study) and primary teaching (seen as interdisciplinary and focused on learning, rather than subject-defined and bounded).

The anti-professional theme of the attacks on teacher education had at its heart a vision of teaching very different from that which had developed in the previous half century. Good teaching at the primary level had come to be child-centred, focused on holistic learning and the child's individual growth and academic, social and personal development (Osborn & Broadfoot 1992). In this orientation, knowledge is something to be constructed, and teachers were accustomed to impressive degrees of autonomy in determining how to support this learning. The definition of good teaching underlying the government's reforms was very different. It was a narrower definition of teacher competence (Cowen 1990, p. 57). It presumed that teaching consists of delivering a set curriculum, one rooted in traditional notions of core knowledge and the core subjects of "reading, writing, and number," as Blatch listed them (DFE 1993d, p. 2). It valued discipline and student achievement as assessed by pupils' knowledge of the curriculum.

While individual growth defined primary school teachers' culture, it was the mix of egalitarian values and professional discretion that shaped secondary teachers' culture in the wake of comprehensivization. This too was challenged by the anti-professional rhetoric and practices of the early 1990s. For both primary and secondary teachers, the redefined practice of teaching was to be "de-politicized", or in other words to pursue the goals of the state curriculum. And teaching was understood as inherently a technical activity focusing on a combination of specialized subject expertise and management skills. Although the teacher was to attend to the social and personal needs of pupils, those needs were narrowly bounded. For example, government documents directed teacher education to help future teachers attend to cultural diversity but never mentioned social class diversity.

This vision of teaching, and therefore of course of the character of the teacher education needed to support it, is fundamentally technicist. Teacher education was to be transformed into teacher training. Kenneth Clarke could therefore describe educational theory as "'barmy'" and advise teachers to ignore it (Smith 1992, p. 387). Although most theory courses had already disappeared, criticism of them was nevertheless more vehement than ever. During the 1980s, the pragmatic response of teacher education to external criticism and to the demands for more student time to be spent in real schools had been to convert social science discipline-based or foundations courses into issues courses, such as educational and professional studies. In our observation of such parts of the teacher education course, we saw a cohort of teacher education students listening to a black community leader talk about racism and later reacting to the presentation in their school-based groups. We saw preservice teachers presenting research studies on issues in the schools to which they were attached, choosing such topics as the implementation of LMS, special needs students, or the transition to secondary school. We watched students simulate conversations with parents about a pupil's needs. These episodes were typical of the issues orientation we found in courses across the spectrum of institutional types and structures, and allowed students to address topics immediately connected to their experience in schools. Theory for these students was reflection on practical problems. Given this, the teacher educator was "no longer the academic specialist but the facilitator and systematizer of student knowledge and learning" (Young 1990, p. 16).

While we saw great variety in the ways in which a discussion of issues provided learning opportunities for students, equally striking was the relative lack of sustained analysis, the limited use of relevant research, and the strongly personal orientation of much of the discourse. The basis for understanding action appeared often to be the student's own experience. By the 1990s discussions of race, class, and gender – topics which in the past had resided in theory or foundations classes – were treated in a class format that did not seem markedly different from that adopted in other elements of the teacher education course. The disparate pieces of a course were apparently integrated by a hands-on approach, were rooted in personal experience, and were closely connected to schools. Given the virulent attacks on "outdated educational ideology" (Clarke 1992) and the pernicious influence of theory, it was surprising for us to walk through teacher education buildings and see hallways decorated with teacher education students' projects, to sit in on an investigations mathematics class and see ITT students sorting rods to look for patterns, to listen to future secondary history teachers decide how geography could or could not be taught with history, and to observe intending primary teachers trying to make decisions about what art supplies they would buy with the budget their school allocated them. The source for their decision making and understanding was their own experience, typically then discussed with and compared to that of their teachers, who themselves drew on their own time in school.

Given this concern – widely appreciated by students – for learning by doing, the place of theory becomes a complex, subtle question many teacher education courses answered articulately in their brochures and faculty statements but only vaguely in their practice. Certainly among many teacher educators there was a sense of despair, of "powerlessness" as the anti-professional pressure had moved theory to an ever more marginal place in the teacher education curriculum (UCET 1992, p. 10). For teacher educators there was "little doubt that these [government] policies represent a deliberate attempt to de-intellectualize the education of teachers and, thus, the teaching profession" (Kelly 1993, p. 134).

This issue, of course, is not simply one of theory and its place, but rather a question of the distinctive role of the university in shaping the understandings and skills of beginning teachers. But the ability of the government and teacher education critics to portray the problem as a problem of theory set the terms within which most of teacher education responded. And in those terms, much as in the earlier efforts to imagine a new kind of secondary education, English educators could turn to no existing models for promising alternatives.

Teacher educators are finding it hard to respond in constructive ways to the anti-professional critique, and in particular the challenge to theory. Certainly, there is much which is positive about an issues orientation. But this approach did not fully imagine or explore alternatives to simple theory/practice dichotomies, nor consider directly how theory might contribute to teacher education. The issues orientation, as enacted, represented a shift "away from discipline-based courses [and] raised the question as to whether there is anything distinctive about university based teacher education" (Young 1990, p. 17). While the reflective practitioner model, some would claim, offers teacher education students theory-informed lenses through which to understand their teaching, it is a subtle model that does not, in the shrill atmosphere of attacks on teacher education or the daily pressure from teacher education students for practical help, easily make a case for why higher education is essential to developing this practice, why academic knowledge is essential to teacher preparation. The anti-professional critique was an attack on teaching, on teacher education, and on its location in higher education. It was an attack teacher educators were not fully able to counter. It was to thrust teacher education increasingly in schools and in a higher education environment destabilized by a new market orientation.

Competition in a Destabilized Environment

Americans reviewing English teacher education in 1994 are inevitably struck by the extent to which its management has been centralized. Challenges to notions of professionalism underlie much of the substantive thrust of central control. Equally potent has been another distinguishing doctrine of the New Right ideology, namely a belief in the positive effects of the market. As one education civil servant explained to us, the government can control teacher education through regulation or by opening it to market forces. By 1994, it had done both. The effect of the market – of competition in what became an increasingly destabilized environment – was a third significant theme which explains how teacher education had by 1994 come to assume a particular and novel character.

The nature of central government policies in teacher education forced the enterprise into a competitive mode that contrasted dramatically with its traditions. Teacher education institutions were thrust as never before into competing for students at a time of contraction in the primary teacher education sector, for links with schools to satisfy CATE requirements and the demands made in recent Circulars for school-based training, and for research contracts and publications to generate much needed revenues and research ratings. But competition within teacher education was not an isolated phenomenon. In fact, education at all levels had entered the competitive market place in the 1980s.

Anti-professional critiques and central government policies propelled teacher education into schools. Teacher educators and their students became in the early 1990s even more connected to schools, or even dependent upon them. But in moving into more intensive and more intimate relationships with schools, teacher education was entering an environment destabilized by the dramatic reforms of the 1980s. Schools were themselves coping with the wide ranging changes precipitated by the 1988 Education Reform Act. As we have already suggested, the National Curriculum had destabilized teaching. Holding it accountable to a national curriculum in ways unfamiliar to British teachers, the Act violated traditions developed over decades. The introduction of the Local Management of Schools (LMS) had produced a countervailing decentralization, as funding, personnel, and management decisions were devolved from local authorities to individual schools. While welcomed by many school heads as a way to bypass the sometimes slow or unwieldy LEA bureaucracy, LMS nevertheless put new pressure on heads and their staffs as they had to make financial decisions and balance large budgets with little or no training or experience. Often motivated to go into education by a love of children, subject matter, or learning, heads and teachers now had to spend sizable amounts of time balancing books. The change was dramatic and sudden. In one not atypical school, for example, the school head described how his responsibility in 1987 for managing £29,000 of discretionary money had by 1992 ballooned into the management of a budget of £2 million.

Schools now had to compete for funds in a newly created educational market. The 1988 Education Reform Act and later the Government's 1992 White Paper *Choice and Diversity* had expanded the rights of parents to choose a school for their children. As a result, with formula funding based on student enrolments, schools (already under-resourced and in need of funds) had to put priorities on making their school competitive in the market for students. The competitive pressure was heightened by the public manner in which schools could be compared. The government's enthusiastic support for the greater accountability of schools produced new ways of publicising the performance of schools and the 1992 Education Act "which, in line with the Citizen's Charter, made provision for the publication of data about performance and school attendance, as well as four-yearly inspection reports" (DFE 1992a, p. 5). The "League Tables," which compared schools on a number of performance indices, directly challenged professionally oriented ways of measuring and displaying school achievement (DFE 1992a, p. 8).

Finally, associated with the reform themes of choice, autonomy and accountability was a concern for increasing efficiency. Schools were described as holding "surplus places" and otherwise being unnecessarily wasteful (DFE 1992a, p. 13). As part of the reforms, teachers were made more accountable to their newly formed governing bodies, and, many would claim, teachers' work was intensified. This was the destabilized environment which teacher education entered: some were forced, some wandered in, and some went enthusiastically.

Even though teacher education and schools shared a long history of interdependence, the central government requirements for teacher education and the pressures on schools intensified this relationship and added new strains to it. With LMS and the National Curriculum, school people found themselves busier than ever, just at the time that teacher education policy expected them to play a more active role in the education of new teachers. Moreover, these reforms took place at a time when devolution of authority had transformed roles within schools. Thus the relationship between teacher education and school became ever more commercial. And with the declining importance of the LEAs, accelerated by the 1988 Act and subsequent legislation, teacher education increasingly came to be seen as a potential supplier of services to practising teachers. The collegial connection between teachers and university- and college-based teacher educators became one more transaction in a series of potential resource inputs and drains. It also put teacher education institutions in competition with one another for the client school.

This drive by teacher education institutions to consolidate relations with schools was initiated by CATE expectations for school involvement in teacher education, but the pressure was dramatically increased with the 1992 Secondary Circular's demand that students spend two thirds of their time actually in schools, for school-based teacher education, and, particularly, for money to follow teacher education students to schools. Time was already a scarce resource. And funding, which was to be offered as support and compensation, was urgently needed. The result was to strain relations, and often deflect conversations away from professional to practical issues. As one university teacher educator explained, the money "ratchets up the relationship to a new form."

Schools were already complaining of being overburdened. At one meeting between local school heads and a university department of education where partnership was being explored, many head teachers spoke eloquently of their support for teacher education and their desire to have higher education involved in teacher training as support for teacher professionalism. But there was frank and outspoken concern about the added load increased school and teacher involvement put on hard-pressed staffs. One head teacher explained that teacher education involvement was "becoming a burden."

Consider the case of Sussex University, often cited as one of the exemplars of university-school partnership in teacher education. There, a twenty-five year tradition of collaboration was significantly affected by government reforms. Certainly the Education Reform Act and the National Curriculum influenced not only the pace of life in schools, but also the way in which teachers perceive themselves and their work. Local financial management of schools has brought about the accountability of schools to their governing bodies. If this has produced more effective use of resources it has also strained many notions of good will, for example the training of teachers as an uncosted additional school activity (Dart & Drake 1993, p. 178).

Even before the push to move most of ITT time to schools, "mentors were already saying that too much was being asked of them, and insufficient time, researching or recognition provided" (Dart & Drake 1993, p. 178). Early in the partnership the university had offered only a small fee to teacher tutors; this stopped in 1983 and was transformed into "a token £50 ... to each school for each trainee to defray incidental expenses." But with the 9/92 changes, "significant resource transfer has been re-introduced" with £750 paid schools for each trainee.

To many schools the sums being offered were, in the words of one head at the meeting we observed with the university department, "Mickey Mouse, appalling." The sheer size of the jump in costs, however, was shocking to teacher education course directors who had before been able to rely on good will or beneficent LEA support. Now they needed to come up with funds from the money they had been allocated. Apart from a single government grant of transition support (given to higher education institutions on a competitive basis), no special support was provided. It was a recurrent theme throughout this decade of reform that while government demanded more of teacher education, it did not provide additional financial support; UCET and other organizations, as well as individual institutions, repeatedly expressed concern at this. Further complicating the process was the refusal of the government to set any kind of price for such school involvement. The rationale was that the market would lead to a fair arrangement, that higher education institutions had autonomy to make decisions, and that this would be best negotiated on a case by case basis to suit local needs.

Given resource-hungry schools and resource-starved teacher education courses, there could only ensue difficult, delicate negotiations among university (or college) and school people, great variance across the country in fees paid for school involvement, and stiff competition among teacher education courses to strike bargains with schools. In the first year of the new arrangement payment to schools seemed to range between £500 and £1000 per ITT student. Teacher educators spent a great deal of time trying to find out what other nearby institutions were offering while still negotiating their own arrangements in time to find sufficient places. (In a community with several teacher education institutions and a finite number of school places, the need to secure arrangements quickly was especially great.) One education professor reported that his colleagues felt that all the money was "disappearing ... so they want to jump in and make a quick deal." In this deal-making environment, schools, given their more extensive recent experience through LMS and the reality of their resource needs, were able to draw hard bargains and act strategically. As providers of essential places for teacher education students, they were able to play different teacher education institutions against one another. Many carefully chose not to. But one head described how he was accepting ITE students from three different courses at three different rates, a fact he chose not to share with the institutions or his staff. His idea was to charge what the market would bear.

This may be an illustration of the pattern Poppleton & Pullin (1992) observed in a:

> trend ... away from the public service ethos in schools, under which professionalism has been seen as disinterested service, to a market-place orientation. This is particularly marked in the case of senior management teams who have, indeed, been at the cutting edge of the reforms introduced by LMS. In this context, a teacher education programme led by the concept of the trainees' "needs" is giving way to a training programme determined by the schools' "needs" in creating and sustaining a market (p. 127).

For schools, the reality of their life since 1988 gave them a bitter appreciation of the process of negotiating a rearranged relationship with higher education. In fact one university teacher educator reported how, when the university department had complained to schools that the local going rate of £900 per trainee would force staff reductions, some heads of schools applauded, enjoying the fact that the university would finally "bleed" when they had been cutting deeply for some time. Schools were not eager to take on fuller responsibility for teacher education, and they almost uniformly wanted higher education to play a clear role in the preparation of teachers. But they responded to the rearranged relations with higher education in ways that heightened the sense of competition within teacher education and, in so doing, strained teacher education's relations not only with schools but also the rest of higher education.

The strain came in large part from the huge costs now represented by ITT for the higher education institution. Whereas in earlier days teacher education may have been seen as a "cash cow," ITT courses now actually depleted institutional resources. Teacher educators used a range of creative ways to try to reduce the financial cost of the commercialized relationship with schools. Departments offered their faculty as inservice providers or suggested that they could collaborate with schools to help them improve their test scores. One administrator at a former polytechnic explained that their offer of free INSET went "down like a lead balloon." Those schools wanted money. In another part of the country, schools did accept a university's offer of £300 worth of consultancy time from each member of the department's faculty, but this had the teacher educators stretched terribly thin, in a kind of indentured servitude to their course. The costs of the higher education-school relationships were very high and came at a time when there was less enthusiasm than ever in higher education for voluntarism, inefficiency, or financial burdens.

Higher education as a whole had its own problems and entered the market place on terms very different from those which applied in the schools. Given the complexity of the higher education system and the differentiation supported by the tradition of a binary line, it is not surprising that the experience of the market was varied. But across the sector, by 1994 higher education institutions were in tense struggles to develop or maintain their market share and therefore needed explanations of why teacher education should become a drain on resources or should be supported by the rest of the institution.

By 1994 universities and colleges, in spite of a long and very different cultural history, had come to be seen and to see themselves as corporate enterprises. The Jarratt report in 1985 pushed universities in this direction by criticising a collegial model of leadership producing "'large and powerful academic departments together with individual academics who sometimes see their academic discipline as more important than the long-term well-being of the university which houses them'" (quoted in Becher and Kogan 1992, p. 181). It advocated instead a corporate model in which the vice-chancellor would act as chief executive, with department heads in what was conceived as a "'middle management' role." Among other things, "it urged the use of performance indicators" and added force to its recommendations by making their implementation a requirement of the University Grants Committee (UGC), then the funding body for the university sector (Becher & Kogan 1992, p. 47). This broad change in style was not limited to institutions then under UGC authority. Increasingly, said one faculty member associated with a former polytechnic, higher education is being asked to be concerned about efficiencies and the bottom line in a corporate world; universities are asked to make efficiency gains, bidding for course costs, students, and teachers.

Such changes in the control of funding of higher education, as well as demands for increased monitoring of and rigour in standards, have gradually drawn closer together the disparate parts of the loosely articulated system called higher education. By the 1990s the whole of higher education had come under a "unitary but market-oriented system" (Williams 1992, p. 1), what Becher and Kogan term a "command model with market forces" (p. 92). Higher education became what one teacher educator called "a portable commodity" to be sold to consumers. In higher education generally and, with great significance, in teacher education – both inservice and preservice – the market became consumer, not supplier, driven. But this shift in control transformed the role of institutions of higher education. Two researchers write that "higher education institutions [are] losing their role as expert providers of INSET and becoming instead learning support agencies" who may have difficulties being self-supporting, as was now expected (Gilroy & Day 1993, p. 148). The combination of LMS in schools and market motivations for higher education caught teacher education in a tight squeeze.

This squeeze led many faculty to see the administrative and financial reforms in higher education as part of a broader process of attack on and transformation of higher education. A range of significant changes took place during the 1980s to bring about this transformation. For example, higher education institutions during this time saw their numbers of students increase while their funding decreased. Moreover, the Education Reform Act of 1988, in addition to its powerful impact on the finance and governance of primary and secondary education, eroded some of the privileged character of parts of higher education by ending the system of faculty tenure and by making higher education institutions derive from sources other than the government "as much of the funding as possible" (Warnock 1992, p. 120). For those universities which had previously enjoyed relatively generous support from the state, this has been a particular jolt. As higher education institutions were forced to become entrepreneurial, research became an important income-generating activity. Different types of institutions were differentially predisposed to take advantage of the market atmosphere, but those most able to exploit market possibilities were often not the institutions able to capitalize on research. As a result, all kinds of institutions were trying to discover new ways of being. Polytechnics faced a new system in which they had to bid for funds. All these factors contributed to a climate of deep uncertainty.

By 1994 there was a pressing need to contend with altogether new situations, and to do so in a climate that seemed to threaten the traditional character, culture, and organizational styles of much of higher education. The ending of the binary line in 1992 contributed much to this destabilizing sense of unfamiliarity, as well as raising the stakes of an already complex competition. As that line had solidified real differences in funding, governance, and mission, very different cultures had emerged. There had been no institutional and relatively little individual mobility across the line. For years, these two worlds of university and polytechnic could in many ways go their separate ways. They were now thrown together into a single funding body (the Higher Education Funding Council for England), utilizing common funding formulas for the old universities and the former polytechnics, now informally rebaptised as "new" universities. This represented a real change for old and new universities alike. The change, as one administrator from a former public sector institution noted, "exposes the old universities to new accountability." At the same time, it forced new universities for the first time to compete for funds based in part on their research activity, a real challenge to institutions which had not hitherto been expected to conduct research. Although the impact of this change naturally varied with type of institution and the unique situation of each institution, all were now subjected to more central oversight and greater competition. All experienced destabilization. In teacher education, competition for intake numbers and for partnership arrangements with schools became crucial. Institutions which in the past could ignore each other now had to take each other seriously.

These broad changes in higher education were felt with particular intensity in teacher education, given the demands placed on it in the wake of the greater centralization and the need to respond to the anti-professional critique. In making this point, Kelly (1993) summarizes the range of changes in higher education which impinge on the ways in which these institutions responded to the changes in teacher education:

> the developments. . .within education are part of a much broader attack on the very concept of a university. . . .Recent years have seen an erosion of academic freedom; the loss of academic tenure; the creation of a competitive, market-place economy; the application of industrial models to university education which go well beyond mere analogy; pressure for the increasing vocationalising of university provision; the creation of funding mechanisms which place emphasis on competition between institutions, in research as well as teaching, rather than co-operation in the interests of genuine quality control and the furtherance of knowledge and understanding; a new structure of political control and intervention which must militate against the furtherance of free, independent challenge and critique in any area. The CATE exercise...has proved to be the thin end of a destructive wedge for universities and for academic freedom. (pp. 137-138)

The changes in higher education, when combined with the transformation of schools, place teacher education in a vulnerable position. The government-mandated reforms (such as CATE) were seen as expensive and teacher educators as expendable. (We observed many institutions that were in the process of sharp reductions in ITE staff in 1993 and 1994; one administrator of a former polytechnic, for example, explained that the education staff in his college would be reduced by one third in just two years.) Nor was it entirely clear how teacher education justified its existence within higher education. Concerns of this kind were expressed in many ways, but teacher education was especially vulnerable on the research front.

The research selectivity exercise has already been discussed in the context of centralization. The HEFCE singled out teacher education, requiring research reviews to be undertaken in order to "justify a claim for excellence" as a basis for the following year's funding. In so doing, it reminded teacher educators of the central role of research while at the same time suggesting that research in teacher education is suspect. Such an approach exacerbated the long-standing problem of research within teacher education; with much of it developed on action research lines, teacher education research did not fit orthodox notions about the generation of new knowledge in higher education. This tension came to a head in 1993-94 as the government proposed to extract education from its general programme for supporting research within higher education. Separated and made subordinate to research within academe, teacher education would become even more vulnerable.

This vulnerability was the result of a combination of factors related to the changes in higher education and schools. Teacher educators, as has already been explained, found themselves compelled to navigate anxiously between intensive school-based activity (in efforts to satisfy their teacher education policy mandates) and research (in attempts to respond to the twin drives towards entrepreneurism and standards in higher education). At the institutional level, with a focus on the bottom line, teacher educators were required to prove their "value" to the rest of their higher education institution by securing high research ratings.

Of course the whole issue of university funding of its programmes is complex and varied, but in general a department of education was now caught in an uncomfortable squeeze between the university central administration and the schools. Universities expected to have some financial stake in their ITE and other programmes. For example, universities had long and widely practised "top-slicing" in which as much as 35-50 percent of state funds allocated to ITE on the basis of intake numbers was held back for use by the institution's central administration. Teacher educators told us of their interest in putting the longstanding concept of top-slicing on the table for renegotiation (to readjust the rate or the formula) as schools claimed a larger share of ITE funds. But one ITE director said, as did many teacher educators, that this sum was negotiable only within narrow limits. As a result, teacher educators not only had to produce certain kinds of work (such as income generating or highly rated research) under increasingly difficult circumstances for their funding, but they were faced within the university with cries about their becoming too costly. This led to multiple pressures to engage in competitive activity – for research grants, for less expensive partnership agreements with schools, for larger student enrolments and the expansion of graduate courses designed to attract fee-paying students.

These pressures encouraged higher education generally and teacher education specifically to redefine their missions and organizational styles. School partnership, difficult enough to develop even when resources are not an issue, epitomized the ways in which teacher education was caught in a market competition in a period of instability. Teacher education was impaled on the horns of a dilemma: developing good teacher education programmes in order to secure government funding was expensive in terms of faculty time, but devoting time to that task absorbed energies which might have been given to efforts to attract other funding from non-government sources. To develop workable partnership arrangements took significant time; in many courses we visited, working committees had been established which had consumed many faculty members' time for a year or more. Then, with the 1992 Circulars and the impact of LMS, financial costs of such collaboration jumped dramatically, as has already been demonstrated.

The result was that many tried to find the least expensive arrangements. For some institutions this meant creating a cohort of expendable faculty – untenured, often younger faculty who could be the sustaining force for ITE and its school-based work, but who could also be cut off from the university without major administrative problems. Closely tied to schools and in many cases unable to locate time for research, they constituted an academic second-class community. A more radical approach was for the higher education institution as a whole to consider jettisoning not just certain faculty, but its entire teacher education activity. By 1993 this had certainly been contemplated in at least two institutions we visited, and rumours about this as a potentially widespread higher education response to the challenge of teacher education were common.

In fact, by 1994 the market pressures had encouraged teacher education to develop certain kinds of courses which would undercut the rationale for its location within higher education. Competing pressures within higher education more generally would make the question of teacher education's relation to higher education a particularly important one within the academy. It was to be a question which would obsess teacher educators – nervous, overworked, and now defensive.

Concluding the Era: surprise

The question of teacher education's proper place in higher education had for some time been a question which teacher educators had been obliged to discuss in financial terms with their deans and vice-chancellors and directors. By 1994, however, the question had moved into a much more public forum, as the House of Lords debated whether in fact a teacher training agency which would wrest teacher education from higher education was the logical next move for English teacher education. Despite eloquent arguments, in the end the vote went against the modern tradition of teacher education being fundamentally a matter for higher education.

By 1994, teacher educators seemed shell-shocked. One of the defining qualities of teacher education in the early 1990s seemed to be this sense of astonishment. How could these changes have taken place so swiftly and with such force? How could a Teacher Training Agency, centrally controlled and separate from the rest of higher education, come to take responsibility for ITE? By 1993, a Teacher Training Alliance had been formed to try to respond to the government's plans. Yet this effort came much too late. Although some individuals had spoken out throughout the 1980s, the community had not united to respond critically early enough. For too long teacher educators had been both preoccupied with their changing tasks and trusting of authority in ways that were bound to harm them. Given their history of politely deferential relations with the government, they were caught off guard by the vehemence of its critiques of their work and the speed with which and extent to which established assumptions and practices had been overthrown. Gentle nudges would not do; softly spoken protests would not be heard. Too slow, some might claim too cowardly, to develop that internal critique which would allow them to take professional knowledge seriously and develop close relations with schools before they became mandatory and commercialized, teacher educators instead were forced by reforms to become deeply engaged in scheming to develop their own niche within a competitive school market. Teacher educators had lulled themselves into "spurious forms of academicism," some claimed (Kelly 1993, p. 132). When this academicism was challenged, they moved to the other extreme, finding ways to market themselves in ways that were so rooted in practice that the distinctiveness of whatever higher education might offer to the schools was obscured (Young 1990). And in the process of this response, teacher educators were so busy competing for their market niche that they did not foresee what was coming, nor the need to form alliances with schools, with the rest of higher education, or even among themselves.

There is no question that by 1994 the aggressive external attacks had surprised most of the English teacher education community. Teacher educators had misjudged the critiques of their work, the strength of their connections to universities and, like almost everyone in higher education, the autonomy and invulnerability of the universities themselves. Although teacher educators worked daily with great thoughtfulness and energy to support the learning of their students, through these miscalculations and their passive political stance, they gave their implicit assent to severing the preparation of teachers from institutions of higher education. It may be that the growing reluctance of schools to play a larger role in preparing teachers – on the grounds that it might threaten the education of children – will help to preserve a role for higher education. In 1994, however, wrenched from its home of a century in higher education yet unwelcomed by those whom the government hoped would adopt it, teacher education in England appears to be on the verge of becoming homeless.

Why was teacher education in England even more friendless than it appeared to be in either the United States or in France?

Notes

[1] We are especially indebted to the following institutions, and to partnership schools associated with them, for enabling us to construct the data on which these chapters are based: Bristol University, Cambridge University, Exeter University, Keele University, Leeds University, Leeds Metropolitan University, the University of London Institute of Education, the University of North London, Oxford

University, Oxford Brookes University, Reading University, Warwick University, the University of the West of England and Westminster College, Oxford.

[2] The DES had been recently transformed, along with moving to what UCET termed "the rather more lush surroundings of Sanctuary Buildings" (UCET 1992, p. 11). Whether in the removal of "science" from the title or the creation of an atrium-filled office, the remaking of the department seemed filled with symbolism.

[3] The nomenclature, initial teacher training (ITT) and initial teacher education (ITE), is a serious political matter in England at this time. Many influential critics of traditional teacher education prefer intentionally to use the term "training" to reflect their political position on the sensitive issue of whether teachers are trained or educated. Others prefer the symbolic use of "education" to represent their position. We are more sympathetic with the preference to use teacher education over teacher training. But we have used both terms and acronyms (ITT and ITE) in our presentation.

[4] Ginsburg, Wallace & Miller (1988) saw this as already being eroded at the time of the "Great Debate" and budget cuts of the 1970s. But even if we acknowledge that there had been inroads made into teachers' professional autonomy before the 1988 Act, there seems to be unanimous opinion that the National Curriculum represented a stark contrast with what had preceded it.

Oxford Studies in Comparative Education, Vol. 4(1/2), 1994

CHAPTER 9

Reflections

HARRY JUDGE

1963 Again: the University

The title of this last chapter has been chosen for its ambiguity: these pages are meant to offer some reflective conclusion to the whole book, but they will also try to capture some sense of the differences in the three national studies, as they are reflected in the alien perceptions of them described in previous chapters. At the end, as at the beginning, the double argument is that contrasts are more illuminating than comparisons, and that an exploration of the frontier between the university and the training of school teachers is itself an integral part of a broader analysis of the relationships among higher education, national conceptions of the university, the authority of the state, the pattern of public schooling, the structure of society, and the role within it assigned to teachers. The contrasts implied in the previous chapters may best be made explicit by returning to the year of departure, 1963, and by placing alongside one another the three national portraits first of the university and then of teacher training. 1963, it may be remembered, was chosen for a reason of procedure rather than of principle: a contrastive account of the present would be meaningless without an appreciation of its long history, but such an account would be unintelligible if written in terms of a narrative starting at a remote beginning at the end of the eighteenth century, and plodding two centuries forward. 1963 is therefore identified, but not in an entirely arbitrary way, as a point where the continuities with the past were still sufficiently strong and obvious, and before the accelerating changes of the last four decades of the century obliterated many familiar landmarks. Think only of the école normale in France or of the University Grants Committee in Britain.

There is significantly, and this a major part of the thrust of the argument in chapter 4, no example for the United States comparable with the 1963 events in France (the decision to impose the comprehensive lower secondary school) and Britain (the publication of the Robbins Report, and the dramatic advance of the Labour Party). This formal deficiency is neither inconvenient for our argument nor (for the United States) some kind of misfortune. On the contrary: it is argued that there can be no decisive or symbolic events in the United States for the fundamental reason that by intention there is no Federal power, and was in 1963 not a great deal of State power either, able to propel the whole country in one direction or another. It was left to an assassin and not a politician to create the one event in 1963 which made of it an uniquely memorable year. The deep changes in American society were of another order, relating to issues of race and equity which could not be resolved by single decisions, not even those of the Supreme Court. The relative weakness of governmental power diminishes the importance of "the event" in the history of American education: the system might at any one time be moving in many different and conflicting directions. And the whole point of the contrast with France and Britain is, of course, that only in some vague ecological sense is it a system in the first place.

There is another equally important reason why 1963 does not in the States represent some kind of a watershed. The French observer reporting in Chapter 4 knew that many of the changes which were to be initiated over the next few years on his side of the Atlantic had, for good or ill, already been achieved in America. The GI Bill had brought to the gates of higher education an ease of access which had been common for several decades in the high school (but which had not yet been won in France or Britain). The balance between the scale of private and public provision in higher education had indeed been tilted towards the latter, but the coexistence of the two sectors was by 1963 an undisputed fact of life. Institutional variety, sometimes to the despair of the Cartesian French spirit, defied any kind of attempt at classification: not only could a university or college be public or private (or even both), it could also be massive or tiny, grounded in research or teaching, local or international, rich or poor, good or bad, new or old. Variety of an equally bewildering richness was to be found in the content of what was taught, and in the patterns into which that content was organised. A strong Land Grant tradition supported the provision of courses that were useful: think only of the place of agriculture in higher education in our three countries. Nor was there, is there, or should there be any sense of national shame in including courses in mortuary science or hairdressing.

An American student in the 1960s could (already) assemble a tailor-made programme of studies in higher education: he or she could move from one university to another near or far, interrupt studies in order to take up work and return later, take four or any number of years to complete the requirements for a degree, earn a living while taking courses at a university. This was an infinitely flexible and indeed welcoming structure, especially at the undergraduate level. Already by 1963 one of the most impressive transatlantic inventions – the professional graduate school – was deeply rooted in the culture and economic life of universities. In medicine, law and business they often represented the proud crown of the most prestigious of the universities. All this relatively unregulated variety entailed that universities were in vigorous competition with one another, for without a continuing flow of students they could not hope to survive. The rules were (and of course are) those of the market, and universities bid against each other for students, for faculty, and for research grants. This was the open yet tough university context within which teacher education in the United States had by 1963 already found its apparently permanent home.

Although the earliest American universities had, of course, much in common with their English antecedents, by 1963 even Harvard or Yale shared few of the characteristics of Oxford or Cambridge. Not all the continuities to be observed within English universities were superficial: beneath the affectionate perpetuation of ceremony and anachronism persisted powerful habits of mind. In 1963 English (and, here again, that term is more appropriate than British) universities were still designed for an elite, even if that favoured minority was now defined in academic or meritocratic rather than social terms. They were still suspicious of most forms of vocationalism, preferring the rhetoric of pure scholarship, disinterested research and liberal education to that of professionalism, utility and profit. The university scrupulously distanced itself from other forms of less noble and less well endowed forms of education beyond school: Polytechnics (in the special sense enjoyed by that term between 1964 and 1991) did not of course yet exist and the traditional university model for the moment enjoyed a monopoly. Education at English universities had since the end of the second world war nevertheless been free: all students sufficiently able to win coveted places were relieved of any financial problems.

Although the universities had been, and in a juridical sense still were, private institutions, they were fully supported by public funds. There was in effect no private sector of higher education, although for some years yet it suited the interests of universities to claim – and occasionally to exercise – freedom from State interference. The distribution of public funds was the responsibility of the much admired University Grants Committee, which took decisions on the global distribution of funds without seeking to exercise close control either of academic policy or (still more plainly) of appointments. Although habits varied, most universities were in effect run by the academics within them, under the general leadership of a Vice-Chancellor who was himself more likely to be by temperament also an academic, rather than an administrative or entrepreneurial manager. The balance between public accountability, represented by the UGC (itself predominantly academic in membership and sympathies) and the treasured autonomy of each university was respectfully maintained. Graduate work was relatively unimportant, while graduate professional schools (with the significant exception of Medicine) were barely visible. The studies of undergraduates were dominated by the single-subject honours degree, although in some universities (especially the newer ones) an emphasis upon interdisciplinary work was being promoted. A university student would therefore expect to pursue for three years, continuously and in one place, an honours degree in a single subject without necessarily making at that stage any decisions about a future career. Some universities were significantly more attached to their regional roots than others, but all saw themselves as national if not international institutions. Inevitably, they varied both in quality and in prestige but, especially when compared with the luxuriance of the transatlantic scene, the gaps and differences between then were relatively narrow. This university world would plainly have great difficulty in adapting itself to the presence, on any large scale, of programmes for the training of teachers – of primary school teachers most obviously, but of all teachers in terms of their professional training rather than their general education to a high level.

Neither American nor English universities had much in common with the University in France. The complexities of the history of that august institution have been sufficiently explored: it is neither quite true nor quite false to assert that universities simply did not exist in France in 1963, but the University certainly did in the minds of those who knew it. Even five years later, the Director of the Ecole Normale Supérieure addressed his letter of resignation to The Grand Master of the University. Even though my French colleague accuses me of writing as though I believed (which I do not) that education in his country was created by two Generals, the importance of Napoleon the civil administrator in establishing the University cannot be gainsaid. His Republican successors shared with him the ambition to create institutions, or preferably an institution with the same kind of integrity as the legal codes, for the whole of France. As a national institution, its singleness was more important than its local manifestations: the national coherence of each of the Faculties (Letters, Sciences, Law, Medicine) was more important than the solidarity in one localised institution of the *universitaires* who, at least for the moment, lived in the same city. Similarly, within each of the Faculties the various disciplines (history, mathematics, languages) collectively preserved the status and value of the particular knowledge (*les savoirs, les connaissances*) committed to their safe keeping.

The nobility of this task reflected a view of culture – the general culture of France which all civilised men and women had a right to share – and of the education by which it was transmitted. Indeed, and for many years to come, the concept of instruction was preferred to that of education simply because the sense of the universality and durability of its content was so strong: instruction implied the formal transmission of an established culture, whereas education was less precise and even less noble. For precisely that reason all qualifications and examinations of any importance needed to be guaranteed by the University and by the University as an emanation of the State. This was at least as true of the baccalauréat as of the licence: these were much too important to be left to local whims or preferences, or to a particularist as distinct from a metropolitan culture. The Faculties were then preoccupied with general culture (*la culture générale*) rather than with vocational utility, the pursuit of which at the lower levels of achievement could safely be left either to vocational schools lying outside the mainstream of University, Faculty, baccalauréat, licence and lycée. They were indeed so relegated until the creation later in the 1960s of the IUT, one of the many success stories of French higher education. The commanding heights of power and prestige in the specialised professional fields could, on the other hand, be quite safely left to the grandes écoles, most of them concentrated in Paris and enjoying a measure of insulation from the mainstream of the University world.

The University in France was not in 1963, never had been, and was not to become isolated from the rest of public education. In a centralised system it could not be, if all the parts were to be rationally related to one another. As early as the middle of the nineteenth century, the Grand Master became the Minister of National Education, and ruled from the rue de Grenelle. His General Inspectors were scholars of University standing. He and they worked through a national hierarchy of inspectors, penetrating all branches of education, but especially the secondary schools. Within each Academy, the Rector (who was required to hold the *Doctorat d'Etat*, yet another of those expressive if untranslatable terms) was a University personage whose responsibilities embraced the whole of public education, even that provided on a generous scale for the very youngest children. Nor was the vertical integration of the system powerful only in terms of administrative arrangements: a good part of the most esteemed segment of higher education, that leading not to the Faculties but directly to the doors of the grandes écoles, was implanted within the walls of the lycée. One section of that higher education, in the Écoles Normales Supérieures, had been created specifically in order to provide teachers of high academic quality for the secondary schools and for those establishments which would in their turn produce teachers for the primary schools. The agrégation itself, although taught in the ENSs and the Faculties, was a State rather than a University examination. It was for the State to determine the number who should achieve it by defining and funding the number of available posts. By 1963 all teachers – in primary, as in secondary and higher education itself – were public or civil servants (*fonctionnaires*), employed by the State to perform essentially civic duties and paid on nationally determined salary scales. In France the training of teachers could not be anything other than a responsibility of the State: the same State which had established the University. The relating of the two presented in France problems and opportunities which simply did not arise in the other two countries of this study.

1963 Again: the Teachers

Those problems seemed least troublesome in the case of the secondary school teacher – the agrégé and the certifié whose academic preparation was a matter of central interest to the University, its Faculties and the Ecoles Normales Supérieures. The agrégation – hence the impassioned defence of its special position in the 1990s – encapsulated the French emphasis upon the supremacy of academic knowledge and skills: what was well understood would, almost of necessity, be well taught. *Savoir* and *savoir faire* were but two sides of the same expertise and the more a teacher knew the less the need any special training as a teacher (and the fewer the hours of teaching each week that would be exacted, presumably upon the rational grounds that quality compensated for any abatement of quantity). For the agrégé the year to be spent in a loose attachment to the *Centre Pédagogique Régional* was never more than a slight and potentially irritating formality. What was important was the time and energy invested in the subject matter department of the University, studying beyond and above the level of the licence, under the guidance of scholars. Similarly for the certifiés the CPR was a marginalised institution, with no assertive identity of its own, and with no specialised expertise (other than experience in the real world) associated with it. For the best among them, this time could be better spent preparing for the agrégation itself and in the University.

Already by 1963 most of the education of the lycée teacher was therefore integrated in the Faculties of the University, where its scholarly emphasis allowed it to sit comfortably. For many university departments, especially in the humanities, the academic preparation of secondary school teachers was the most prized element of their work: the contrast with England and America, then or now, imposes itself. The lycée teacher who also taught in a *classe préparatoire* was moreover in her or his own right a teacher within higher education, whose work was at a level and standard comparable to those of a university teacher in either of the other countries of this study. For such a teacher the institution which stood at the peak of professional as well as academic prestige was the École Normale Supérieure, especially the establishment in the rue d'Ulm, at the heart of the university quarter. The secondary school teacher was the guardian of a tradition of equal access to the commonalities of *la culture générale* and of the universal and undifferentiated quality of the bac, the university degree which was the culmination of every secondary school career. Such perennial traditions were a bulwark against the erosion of intellectual standards in secondary education in France, and perhaps ensured that when comprehensive secondary schooling was introduced it was to be largely confined to the lower age groups. The common high school of the United States, which was often admired at the time in England, never became a model for the Hexagon.

There was of course a price to be paid for this congruence between the education of most teachers for the secondary sector (as it was in 1963) and the internationally recognised values of a university culture. Sustaining this clear congruence was an equally self-conscious differentiation of values and methods between primary and secondary schooling. The price paid (which many then and now would deem reasonable) for the closeness of the work of the Faculties and of the ENS to the daily lives of teachers in the lycée was the distance that was necessarily imposed between the culture of that same national ENS and its more modest departmental cousin, the EN. That distance between two institutions which sounded as similar as they were in fact different was echoed in the tempestuous debates that surrounded any discussion (then and since) of the difference between pedagogy and didactics – a difference without distinction in the other two countries. Didactics was the business of the universities, bearing as it did upon a particular subject matter as recognised by those universities. Pedagogy was the business of the primary school and of those who trained its teachers, and was by definition unspecific and basic. It was for small children who had not yet begun to climb the academic ladder properly so called. To push its claims further was to declare an addiction to *primarisation* and to be an ally of the SNI.

This difference, which was more than one of emphasis or balance, buttressed the significant social as well as educational categorisations which shaped the two Orders. The primary order had been, and for most Frenchmen still was, an alternative to and not a preparation for entry to the secondary order; the one belonged to the people, and the other to the bourgeoisie. At its best and most confident, this was in no sense a deferential or ignoble position for the instituteur and the class to which he belonged. The primary school had a key role to play in the encouragement of the civic virtues and in particular of lay and republican principles: which was of course why the men of Vichy hated it as they did. At its own summit had stood the primary ENSs of St Cloud and Fontenay-aux-Roses, although they had by now succumbed to the charms of social and academic promotion. Nor was primary synonymous with elementary: beyond a basic education the Order had, in classes for older pupils and especially in the upper primary schools (the EPNS), provided rigorous forms of vocational and professional preparation as an alternative to the University bac. By 1963 these extensions of primary education were straddling the increasingly blurred frontier with secondary schooling, but they remained easily distinguishable from the lycée and the principles of their separation were lucid.

At the very heart of this web of practice and belief sat the école normale. Its students, unlike those preparing for careers in secondary schools, were still recruited at an early age. They, like members of the armed forces and other public services but unlike intending secondary teachers, were recruited before they began their academic training to become teachers. They were recruited through a concours, and paid a wage while they were being educated as well as trained. That formation as well as their deployment within the Department when they eventually qualified were under the direct control of Inspectors and not of Faculty members. They were of course now being prepared within the EN for the baccaluréat and taught by agrégés and certifiés steeped in the culture of the University. But the EN remained at a great distance from that University and the tasks of assimilation, even when stimulated by a reshaping of secondary education itself, proved to be of an intimidating difficulty.

Across the Channel in England the difficulties, although real, were surmounted more rapidly: which is perhaps why the victory may prove to have been short-lived. The system there was centralised when compared with that of the States but not by comparison with that of France. Government policies and initiatives, often at that time based upon reports by specially appointed committees or commissions, did exert strong pressures upon practice even if much day to day responsibility for action rested with local and not central government. Much power locally was deployed by the elected county and county borough councils, and their professional officers who (again it must be added, at that time) enjoyed considerable autonomy in their actions and preferences. The English system of the day and the preceding decades had been frequently and aptly described as a national system locally administered. In some matters, and notably in strategic questions related to the training and employment of teachers, the national framework was strong and clear so that arrangements were relatively uniform and shifts of policy were usually well coordinated at the national level.

The pattern of schooling, although based more upon a broad consensus than upon detailed prescription, similarly conformed to national norms and expectations. National policies on teacher education and on secondary schooling were for these and other good reasons harmonious with one another. For the American contributors to this volume what was most striking about policy and practice in both these areas was the degree of what they call segmentation. In a word: the universities had for long been encouraged to take some interest in the training of teachers for secondary schools, while the Teachers Training Colleges concentrated their attention on producing teachers for primary schools and for the secondary modern schools which had inherited much of the old elementary tradition. This is indeed very different from American practice even in 1963, while the prominence of the word "training" in the very title of the colleges for future teachers rendered highly problematical any effective relationships with English universities which still affected a disdain for the useful and the vocational.

It would however be an error to assimilate at this point the French and English experiences. The Training Colleges were not first cousins to the école normale: they were maintained by voluntary as well as public bodies (and in that they differed from English universities as well); they recruited at the age of eighteen or above students who had already in growing numbers completed a full secondary education; they were not under the direct control of the Ministry; their graduates were not legally committed to a career in teaching and had a relatively free choice of where to seek employment. The immediate difficulties in the way of somehow assimilating or federating them with universities were for these and similar reasons technically less daunting than in France. A parallel error would be to equate the involvement of the university itself in the education of secondary teachers in both France and England. It is obvious that in both countries future secondary school teachers, who need not yet have identified themselves as such, did draw from the University their general, liberal education – an education in form and substance (in this regard unlike the United States) indistinguishable from that delivered to other students envisaging quite different careers. But there the similarity abruptly ends. Most students in the humanities Faculties in France did in fact become teachers, since by tradition few other careers were open to them; most such students in England did not. In both countries, education for teachers immediately beyond the level of the first degree (awarded after three years in both countries) was indeed in the hands of the universities. In France, however, these tasks of preparing graduates for teaching were of course in the hands of the subject departments: what was deemed to be important was above all else a deepening of subject matter knowledge. This was the country of *les savoirs*. In England, the university scholars who had busied themselves with teaching their subjects to undergraduates had thereafter no further connection even with those of their own students who went on to become teachers. Many of those could and at that time did directly enter the teaching profession without any further training or qualification. For those who felt the need for further preparation, responsibility passed to a different group of university staff: the specialists (the French would have called many of them didacticians) who professed an expertise in teaching the teaching of particular subjects. Alongside them worked the specialists (sociologists and philosophers as well as many whom the French would have scornfully dismissed as *psychopèdagogues*) whose concern was with contextual rather than disciplinary questions. For the Training College there were few direct and obvious links with the university. For the students aspiring to become secondary school teachers there were indeed strong links: but they were of two kinds, and it might almost be said links to two very different manifestations of the university. One (the intensive study of a subject at undergraduate level), being subject based and focused on acquiring a qualification in an established discipline, the French would have no difficulty in recognising and approving. But in their eyes the second (the professional training element in the PGCE pursued in a Department of Education) would be more suitably located in an organisation like the CPR, and be better kept apart from the true University: otherwise, as one of their Ministers was to protest in the 1990s, the Education Department might be tempted to acquire the inappropriate characteristics of a *université bis*.

The American university on the other hand was nothing if not single and all-embracing, and this openness (which some native critics chose to dismiss as promiscuity) made a profound difference to the place and status within it of the tasks of preparing teachers. Two dominant and related factors encouraged this style of open-ended development. One has already been identified: the absence of any control even of the strategic development of higher education at a national level ensured that universities would develop in spontaneous and often apparently random ways, most often in response to a market. If society needed teachers, the universities could be counted upon to furnish them. "If the world offers you lemons, make lemonade." Any reader of these pages will be equally well aware of the absence, striking when compared with England and startling when compared with France, of any governmental attempt at national level (in 1963) to control the recruitment, training, qualifications, appointment, licensing, deployment, salaries, pensions or conditions of service for teachers in the public schools. The direct employers of those teachers were the thousands of school boards, some of them small and none of them directly engaged in controlling or even influencing the quality of their future employees. Teacher education was fated to become an expanding business.

It would also, as in all societies, reflect the basic characteristics of the teaching force and of the schools in which its members taught. Those schools, in 1963 standing for once in clear contrast to those of both France and England, were common and unified. Just as there had for many years been no open and public distinction between those schools providing an academic education and those content with more practical tasks, so also there was no formal and absolute distinction between primary (elementary) and secondary schools. They all shared a common purpose. Segmentation, whether vertical or horizontal, was a vice in the eyes of Americans, as of the contributors to these chapters. Schools were schools and teachers were teachers, and the French contributor to these pages is rightly impressed by the force of this K-12 concept. As the implications for teacher education of this openness, of the absolute need in American society for the school to be a force for assimilation and integration, of the emphasis upon adjustment rather than instruction and upon happiness rather than knowledge – as all these are unwound, so his perception is revealingly sharpened into a mood of anxious ferocity. Heart is elevated over head, and *les savoirs* are betrayed. A former President of Harvard and a former Dean of the Harvard School of Education are called as witnesses.

The institutional as much as the cultural implications for teachers and their education are at once obvious. Normal Schools no longer exist because they are no longer needed: in 1963 they have already been painlessly, effortlessly almost, absorbed into the generous university tribe. Meanwhile, established universities have shown their entrepreneurial skills (as they could not have done across the Atlantic) in developing degree programmes for administrators, counsellors and psychologists as well as for teachers of all kinds. The flexibility of course structure and of entrance requirements, the absence of national standards governing the award of degrees, the reluctance of public authorities to protect any kind of monopoly in provision: all these encouraged expansion and integration within a flexible system. But training for teachers – so profoundly unlike that for doctors or for lawyers – cannot be a graduate exercise, for that is an expensive business which the salaries and expectations of teachers are unable to fund. Teacher education is not only inside the university, it is also needs to be dispersed throughout it: the Arts and Science colleges make a contribution as well as the SCDEs. Many candidates take courses designed for teachers without even intending to become teachers. Here is indeed an example of the total integration of a large system (or non-system) of teacher education within the university. The very size and diversity of that system will make it vulnerable to the dramatic changes of the decades after 1963. The two European systems will be vulnerable for quite different reasons.

The Dynamics of Change

The contrasts running across the three systems, as viewed within the relatively static framework of the year 1963, are just as striking when applied to the changes running across the next three decades. In the educational history of the United States there can of course be no key dates and no decisive events. But if change is glacial, it is so in its range and depth as well as in its pace. Teacher education necessarily reflects profound changes in society: and above all changes in ethnic balances as well as in the economic strength of the nation in an increasingly competitive world. The strains within the equilibrium analyzed in an earlier chapter remain profound and constant: the pressure of Japanese competition inflamed the 1983 rhetoric of *A Nation at Risk* and deliberately generated a new emphasis on academic performance in teacher education programmes. But the public reactions to the Los Angeles riots of 1992 epitomised a perennial concern with issues of equity and multiculturalism, in teacher education programmes as in everything else. Yet these were symbolic rather than decisive events and while policy did of course shift, it did so as a result of competing and conflicting pressures as well as of the uncoordinated interventions at different levels by governments, agencies, pressure groups, alliances and Foundations.

The SCDEs continued therefore to develop and display those same qualities already inherent in them in 1963. They needed above all else to defend and enlarge their share of the market and to compete with one another, as well as against an increasingly hostile environment. State governors and legislatures became more critical of them and their products (as indeed of higher education as a whole), and of their tendency to neglect the urgent needs of preparing real teachers for real schools. It was never easy for the SCDEs to respond. The acknowledged, if sometimes resented, leaders among them – that is to say, the graduate schools of education in the research universities – were in reality driven in opposite directions by powerful market forces. An emphasis upon the social functions of the school was reflected in a growing perception of the school as an agent for delivering integrated social services. SCDEs were therefore pulled towards redefining their mission in terms that would not necessarily accord the highest priority to the training of teachers. In many of the SCDEs, but again especially those planted in universities which defined their own mission largely in terms of research, the incentives to produce research rather than classroom teachers were sharpened. The impact of much of that research on the improvement of teaching was, as these pages have suggested, far from obvious. Faculty in the SCDEs were rewarded, as the institutional norms of ambitious universities required them to be, for paying more attention to the research imperative than to teaching or service (in the schools or elsewhere). Polemicists contributed to the criticism by associating the alleged progressivism of Schools of Education with what they saw as the mindless faddism of Political Correctness, the shift away from the established canons of western civilisation, and a dangerous addiction to academic softness.

The Schools of Education responded as best they could, for the most part through a series of self-help efforts and shifting coalitions. John Goodlad, whose views on the place of teacher education in the university correctly impressed a French observer as tinged with pessimism, stimulated the evolution of a partnership of universities and schools dedicated to a particular version of reform. NCATE struggled with the problems of raising the standards of accreditation without inflicting irreparable damage on the widely diverse base of teacher education. It formed new partnerships with States in order to rationalise the elaborate machinery of teacher certification and bring to it a measure of national comparability. The Carnegie Corporation funded a major project leading to the creation of a National Board for Professional Teaching Standards: a characteristically American institution which (like comparable boards for other professions) was to be national without being governmental – a distinction that would defeat the French intelligence (for which language itself is a governmental concern) and make difficulties for the British. The Holmes Group mobilised itself to elevate the intellectual seriousness of teacher preparation, to ally it more effectively with the Arts and Sciences, and to articulate it with the world of practice inhabited by teachers. Yet even between the world views of Carnegie and of Holmes there was tension: the former had little or nothing to say about the role of the university in the advanced training of teachers. It was rooted in the belief, grounded as some would argue in the democratic mythology which applauded the fact that Abraham Lincoln did not attend law school, that the knowledge and skills of teachers mattered more than the name of the place where they might have acquired them. The Holmes Group on the other hand emphasised above all the central role of the university in the education of teachers, which is of course why – quite apart from any question of the value or force of its recommendations – it has appeared so often in these chapters. The Holmes Group, determined in pursuing its university version of what an authentic professionalising of teachers would require, protested that doctors cannot secure recognition without attending a properly constituted medical school.

The sceptics remain unconvinced by the argument by analogy, asserting that the knowledge base for teaching is not to be compared with that for medicine, law, or even business. Useable research which demonstrably contributes to the quality of teaching remains weak, and what needs to be learnt about teaching as distinct from the subject matter to be taught can be acquired on the job or by private study: for such critics this does not require (as medicine most obviously does) years of immersion in a university. Where, it is asked (as Conant asked in 1963), is the sound educational research to be compared either in solidity or indispensability with the established conclusions of the research chemist? The champions of the deep involvement of the university in teacher education are themselves trapped by the logic of their own argument: for them the basic reason why research in education has not as yet been as productive as it must now become is that it has been directed at the wrong questions or (in the case of the Holmes Group) conducted elsewhere than in the Professional Development School, the analogue of the teaching hospital.

This case for the university connection rests therefore upon an aspiration that the Schools of Education should in the near future change fundamentally in order to become what they have never been. It has therefore been hard for those who argue for the indispensability (and not just the general desirability) of a university connection to resist the currently powerful movement towards alternative methods of training teachers. These alternative routes into a teaching career are typically offered by school boards or by States. They may draw upon individual Faculty from universities but without requiring any institutional engagement, and make extensive use of experienced teachers as mentors while relying upon some theoretical work being completed in summer schools and elsewhere. Such efforts are often idealistic in intention and effective in recruiting as teachers those, and especially people of colour and others willing to work in the demanding circumstances of the inner city, who would otherwise not become teachers. The willingness of some universities to accept a degree of involvement in such programmes has tacitly conferred upon them some measure of approval. The largest single programme training teachers in the State of Texas in 1993 was wholly outside its large university programmes. None of this means, of course, that teacher education is likely to be disestablished and summarily banished from the university. But it does mean that its place, or more precisely the survival of the School of Education, in the university remains contentious and problematical. The reformers at the beginning of this century had assumed that by its close this would no longer be the case.

In these developments Washington played no part: some might be tempted to wish that London or Paris had cultivated a comparable reticence. But of course they could not. Her Majesty's Government in London intervened decisively on two occasions during the period and in the issues under review in this chapter of reflections – once from the Left of the political spectrum and once from the Right. In 1964 a Labour government required (even if it employed the more emollient language of requesting) all the local government bodies with responsibilities for education to submit plans for ending the selective patterns of secondary schooling (the segmentation described in earlier chapters) and replacing it by a system of comprehensive schooling already familiar to the United States. This was, albeit with significant variations affecting upper secondary education, precisely what a Gaullist government in France had accomplished in the previous year. The publication of the Robbins Report, also of course in 1963, led to the redesignation of Training Colleges as Colleges of Education and, of especial importance to this analysis, the introduction of a new university degree in those colleges – the Bachelor of Education. These changes in secondary and higher education were by intention complementary : new kinds of teachers (no longer to be classified as the more academic and the less academic) would be required and they would need a new style of preparation. In 1964 the Polytechnics were created, and the frontiers both within and around higher education significantly adjusted: it became very much easier for colleges educating teachers to merge with these new institutions, designed to celebrate the values of utility and training while enjoying a status approximating to that of a university (although, until 1992, not the title that went with it).

Meanwhile, the uncertain life of the BEd began. Although a chilly reception was accorded to the Robbins recommendation that the Colleges of Education should be federated – academically, financially, administratively – with the existing university departments of education in new Schools of Education, a new relationship between teacher education and higher education had indeed now been created. Universities acquired a variable measure of responsibility for the quality of the education provided in the Colleges (without of course going so far as to provide it themselves). Education (with a capital "E") became an acceptable subject of study for a university degree, although not (save in rare cases) within the walls of a university itself. Here was indeed a nearly perfect example of teacher education being part of higher education, but only partly part of it. This uneasy experience found some echoes in the very different world of the French école normale, when a special DEUG for instituteurs was (briefly) introduced to it in 1979. The BEd highlighted the conflicts of definition which bedevil the relationship between the education of teachers and the university. For some the BEd provided an opportunity to enrich the culture of the future teacher, for inducting him or her more thoroughly into *les savoirs* as the university perennially understood them. For others however it should be a professional degree, comparable even to degrees in medicine and attesting a knowledge of the disciplines of education (psychology, sociology, philosophy) as well as a mastery of the professional skills needed by a successful teacher in primary or secondary schools.

For teacher education this was a summer as golden as it was brief, during which it was possible to hope that the triumphs of the great Schools of Education (always glittering more seductively from a distance than on their own campuses) could now be replicated in England. The university schools of education flourished as new academic dynasties were established in the sociology or philosophy of education: the expansion of the Colleges of Education produced a strong demand for new staff, many of whom improved their qualifications as educators by taking advanced university degrees in education. The universities were further strengthened in income and influence by playing an important part in the administration and control of the BEd degree. But it was not to last. Before the new arrangements had had time to prove themselves a new reaction set in: a reaction against the progressivism of the Colleges, against the alleged child-centredness of their teaching, against the pursuit of ethereal theory at the expense of hard-headed practicality in the training of teachers. The polemic of James Koerner was available to furnish a transatlantic warning and a persuasive text, written in the very year that Education replaced training in the new titles of the Colleges. It was a commonplace of the argument that what went wrong in England had first gone wrong in the States. The James Report captured and influenced this mood, and the long jeremiad against the orthodoxies of teacher education (real or imagined) began to unroll. The leaders of opinion in the university Schools of Education thought that they could afford to neglect the warnings, even as the contraction of the Colleges in the seventies, as rapid as their breathless expansion in the sixties, destabilised a fragile system. One common criticism was that the basic values of the old elementary school and the academic values of the disappearing grammar school had been sacrificed to the necessity of meeting the needs, including those of a social and personal nature, of all pupils, however faint their academic tastes or talents. Heart was being placed above head. It is ironical that in their well balanced chapter on these developments the American observers in fact detect a fault which is the exact opposite of this: for them the problem was rather that new methods of teaching and new approaches to the curriculum were not introduced into secondary teacher training, and that attitudes (rather like those of the *Société des Agrégés*, they might have concluded) remained inflexibly traditional. The fault they identified so incisively is therefore the mirror image of that dereliction of the academic mission which their French colleague castigated in teacher training in their own country.

This mood was reminiscent of much that was already being proclaimed about teacher education in the States as of much that was later to be asserted in France after the 1990 reforms: indeed the 1993 Senate report on the IUFM made an explicit and approving reference to *A Nation at Risk*. It was reinforced by the campaign for a return to basics in teaching, heralded by the Labour Prime Minister's speech in October 1976 and given a characteristically new vigour by the Thatcherite victories in 1979 and (especially) 1983. The significance of this was of course not lost on the American contributors to this volume, who have documented the success of the Right in introducing a national curriculum (traditionally rejected as a dangerously French notion) and then using CATE to domesticate the whole of a disconcerted teacher education establishment. The alternative routes of recent transatlantic experience were praised and elevated into the one standard doctrine, in order that the despised "education establishment" of a Conservative demonology might be ejected from its power base in the university. The notion of a partnership with schools in the training of teachers (praised in the James Report of 1972, epitomised in France in the historic connections with the world of practice secured by the authority of the Inspectors and the CPR, and idealised by the Holmes Group in the theology of the PDS) was transmuted by government direction into a cumulative weakening of the very basis of teacher education within higher education. The climax came with the legislation of 1994 creating the Teacher Training Agency, and removing all the funds to support the education of teachers from the mainstream of university financing in order to commit them to a government appointed committee for distribution as it as it saw fit – to schools, or groups of schools, or consortia, or indeed to universities if the latter did what was demanded of them and satisfied the requirements of a powerful Secretary of State. It was now hard to say what, if anything, the distinctive contribution made by a university to the training of teachers might in principle be.

Whatever the complexities of the deeper currents, on the surface at least policies towards teacher education appeared in the nineties to be moving in opposite directions in England and in France. These policies did have common origins in related events of the sixties: in England the government's decision to introduce a comprehensive school followed by a reshaping of higher education, and in France the President's determination to introduce a comprehensive school followed five years later by the reform of higher education. In both countries these were government acts. The changes in England did not require the evolution of a new classification of teacher, partly no doubt because there was at that time no formal or legal distinction between the qualification and status of teachers for primary and for secondary schools. But in France the growing salience of the PEGC, significantly defined as a teacher who was neither a monovalent educated by the university nor a polyvalent formed in the école normale, and the marked differences in style between the lycée and the collège did impose the necessity of such an evolution. By 1963 training for the PEGC had already been placed in special centres in the école normale, which for this and many other reasons was slowly losing its clearly defined sense of mission. Integration of any kind within a university was not an accessible option, as it had long been in the United States and was now coming rapidly to be in England. The universities themselves were not (indeed were not intended to be) strong or acquisitive institutions, while the EN was still admitting most of its students at secondary school age and, more surprisingly for a foreign observer, within the developed structures of primary schooling.

That integration was nevertheless slowly achieved, as universities acquired a sense of local identity and the level of age and qualification rose for the new entrants to the EN. The écoles normales were by government decree reclassified as part of higher education in 1984, and by that time efforts had been made – inspired more by government order than by enthusiasm in either of the partners – to establish connections between universities and the training establishments. In particular, a university award (the DEUG for primary school teachers) made a faltering entrance on the scene in 1979, and within a few years all entrants would arrive at the gates of the école normale already armed with a university diploma and strengthened by at least two years of a university education. The gate of entry to the category of PEGC had already been closed (although the category itself lingered on) and it made little sense to maintain two distinct traditions of teacher education, or to require those who already had a university diploma to attend an institution which had been developed as and still showed many of the characteristics of an upper primary school. Given the intricacies of union rivalries and the labyrinths of academic politics, it was however easier to recognise the problem than to provide an acceptable solution to it.

Only after several years in office, interrupted by a brief period of exile, was the government emboldened to adopt a uniquely French solution. Throughout France new Institutes (the IUFM) based upon the existing institutions were to provide two years of training for teachers of all kinds, all of whom were required to have achieved a three-year university qualification. Since these institutes were given a university label (but not the title or juridical status of university) integration might appear to have been achieved, but it has been argued in a previous chapter that appearances – especially when seen from a distance and from outside France – might indeed be deceptive. Even so, there was more than enough in these new arrangements to startle opponents. The return of a right wing government in 1993 immediately called in question the permanence of these new arrangements for associating the education of teachers with the university, even if it proved impossible (or perhaps in the eyes of its critics unnecessary) to abolish the newly minted IUFM. This alien institution could, they knew, be fatally weakened in other less direct ways. It is no coincidence that such things were argued at a time when the French and their government were manifesting great sensitivity about the influence of what they quaintly call "the Anglo-Saxons" and were anxious to preserve the integrity of the French language and culture. The IUFM and Disney were indeed part of the same threat, and Berkeley might be as dangerous as Hollywood. The relationship of teacher education to the university certainly had, in legislative terms, been more clearly defined in France than in the States or in England, and defined in a way which teacher educators as well as teacher unions might be expected to welcome. But even in France the future of that relationship remains problematical.

After 1995

Within the triple perspective of this volume the United States is obviously the country in which the general relationship between the university and teacher education is least threatened. The reasons for this relative security have been illuminated by this comparative study, and refer in particular to the very different manifestations of governmental power in the three countries and to the unmanageable variety of provision in the United States. No one person or institution can do it very much harm. It could further be argued that teacher education in the States is less vulnerable to sharp attack and dislocation precisely because it is so flabby: its very looseness constitutes a defence. There is of course an obvious downside to this second advantage: teacher education may be secure on its university base on one campus but not in another university a few miles away. It may be adequately protected in one of the fifty States and critically vulnerable in its neighbour. Even within one university, it may be smiled upon by one President or Provost and persecuted by their successors. And even within the same School of Education, most of which have a mandate infinitely wider than that of an IUFM or an education department in an English university, internal as much as external factors can have profound effects upon the prestige and resources accorded to teacher education. It may in public opinion and anxiety be accorded a lowly place (as in the sixties) or a high one (as in the eighties). A SCDE may command a Faculty of only four members or one of two hundred. Teacher education may be more or less invisible, which is not to say marginal, within the general education culture of a liberal arts college or set grandly apart in a palace of its own in a large university. Even within universities which look alike its work may be concentrated in the hands of the Faculty of the SCDE, or dispersed over a large number of colleges, many of them (in English language and literature as much as in music) employing their own methods professors. None of these things is true of either France or England.

Moreover, the relative security of the university base for teacher education depends, as has been noted, on the fact that no person or institution can very much affect it. State politics can indeed influence teacher education, but federal politics do so only rarely and lightly. The Presidential election of November 1996 will have no effect on these matters. But at the national, as distinct once again from the federal, level other influences can be important. Many of them have already been identified. During 1995 the American Association of Colleges for Teacher Education (AACTE) will debate whether its currently wide criteria of membership should be narrowed, so that only institutions seeking and securing NCATE recognition will be admitted. This effort will raise in the sharpest form the question of whether those who defend the engagement of the university in teacher education wish to defend all expressions of that partnership, or only those which achieve a certain quality of output. Many centrally placed teacher educators know, but will admit only in private, that many SCDEs should simply be closed down: there are more of them than the market can bear. In 1995 the Holmes Group confronts a parallel question. Each member university is required to recommit iself not only to the principles already established by that Group and discussed in earlier pages, but also to establishing at least one Professional Development School, designed and operated on a basis now to be defined much more clearly than in the past.

This insistence will thrust upon the universities a decision about how serious, and indeed how exclusive, they are prepared to be in enthroning the education of teachers and other educational professionals at the heart of the reformed SCDEs. It will require an equally delicate and complex choice (as in the example of the parallel AACTE/NCATE debate) between admitting to membership only those elite universities which have a serious claim to have developed research of quality and advanced professional work, or opening the gates more widely. If the more exclusive choice is made – as it certainly was in the history of the university medical schools – minorities and the institutions in which they are best represented are certain to be disadvantaged. Either way, a precarious equilibrium will be disturbed. Moreover, if the universities with a strong research capacity choose to set themselves apart from the mainstream (as graduate schools of law and business certainly have) they will find it difficult to be taken seriously in the business of influencing Statewide policy, either for the education of teachers or for any of the other areas with which it is entangled.

In neither England nor France is there any analogue to the Holmes group, AACTE or NCATE. The strong similarities between England and France become clear only when they are jointly contrasted with the United States. In both countries, the relationship of teacher education to the university will be profoundly affected by the cross-currents of national politics. The French Presidential election of 1995 and the parliamentary elections which may follow it will push policies towards either strengthening or weakening the IUFM as defined in 1990, although it is impossible to know how far and at what pace. The abolition of the IUFM may not be on the agenda, but almost everything else about it is. In any case, in 1995 the resources for teaching for the CAPES go back to the universities from which they were diverted only as recently as 1991, more of the former professeurs of the EN will leave the IUFM to retire into the pedagogical mist, the IUFM will lose those full time faculty members whom it had just acquired, future primary school teachers (to whom the fresh title of professeur seems not yet to have adhered) may once again be admitted to training at the level of bac+2, a new licence specifically designed for such teachers is to be introduced with the hope that it will do better than its 1979 DEUG antecedent. It may be that history will be turned back even further, to the first pages of the first chapter of this book, and that a way will be found to reconnect the Ecole Normale Supérieure to the world of the secondary school teacher. If in 1995 the power of the Right is electorally consolidated, a proposal made by the Senate in 1992 may well be revived. One or more of the IUFMs, currently in the university world without being in a university, may be fully integrated "on an experimental basis" within a university: such a move is likely to approximate to absorbtion, or even abolition, rather than to canonization. It certainly does not appear that the point of equilibrium has yet been found in France.

In the last few years of this century politics may have less impact on the training of teachers in England. Although a general election in 1996 or 1997 could introduce a change of mood or even (for the first time since 1979) a change of government, the willingness even of a new government to reverse the major educational changes of the eighties cannot be taken for granted. The world of 1963, as a previous chapter described it in England, has indeed gone for ever. The withering local education authorities do not (at least yet) have many good friends and seem unlikely to recover their former grip on issues of teacher employment and teacher training, the former polytechnics have disappeared for ever into the family of universities, Colleges of Education will not be magically reconstituted, no government seems likely to relinquish the control now exercised from London over the training of teachers, the autonomy which has been conceded by government to primary and secondary schools (and not only to those designated as grant maintained) is unlikely to be clawed back. The Teacher Training Agency in 1995 begins to do its work, under a chairman just retired from the headship of that ancient grammar school over which Lord James himself presided until 1962. The money which previously flowed to the universities and their schools of education through the Higher Education Funding Council for England is now diverted to that agency. The Secretary of State for Education controls the standards, content, financing and location of teacher education. If that activity preserves real links with the university, it will do so by his leave only. Although these deep changes owe most to the continued and aggressive assault by Government upon the teacher training "establishment" (as it was parodied), the American contributors to this volume, reluctantly and gently, place on the shoulders of the university based teacher educators themselves at least some of the blame for this decline from the high days of the sixties.

The links of teacher education with the university in the United States were extensive in 1963 and appear to be strong today: yet in the minds of many critics doubts about their value and permanent strength persist. In England in 1963 the formal links were strong and given powerful institutional and curricular form in the years of expansion that followed: today they are being broken. In France in 1963 there were strong links in the academic preparation of the secondary school teacher, but none beyond that: today University Institutes exist, although their status remains uncertain and their newly acquired powers have already been weakened. A book which has been built entirely on contrasts can no longer avoid the one comparison which matters. Why, in all countries and in all times, is the relationship of teacher education to the university so problematical?

None of the three countries seems able either to ignore or to solve the problem. In the course of the years new subjects – like geography, or modern languages, or English literature, or economics, or sociology – insert themselves (often against a tide of criticism or disdain) into the university canon. The philosophers or the mathematicians may indulge a measure of residual contempt but come to live with their new cousins. New professions or careers – like architecture, dentistry, engineering, journalism, or business – similarly gain a more or less enthusiastic acceptance. They have, for plain reasons, done so more easily in the tolerant market of America, and with greater difficulty in France where professional education has often been delivered in institutions outside and even above the university: but acceptance is achieved. And yet even in the United States, Education still has to struggle for this degree of acceptance, while such an acceptance has often been paid for by sacrificing teacher education itself to other more glamorous or lucrative occupations – administration, curriculum development, or research. Yet however repetitive the rejection, the effort cannot be abandoned. Teacher unions naturally associate the interests of their members with achieving professional status for them and link that to the university connection. Theorists argue that a healthy society needs teachers who are liberally educated and will not accept a utilitarian or functional definition of their role.

Nor can the state – in the general rather than the specifically American sense of that word – stand aside from this issue or evade the tensions it generates. Teachers are needed as means to an end – whether the end is the civic goal of shaping good citizens, encouraging republican values and patriotism, maintaining the amenities of a class system, or the economic goal of enriching the bank of skills which a developed society needs and the basic skills of literacy and numeracy on which that bank must draw. The state – everywhere but more directly in France and England than in America – also exercises patronage if not control over the university and cannot stand aside, as it might in the case of nursing or architecture, to allow the forces in play to determine without interference questions related to the location, costs and character of teacher education. Rising levels of education will incline the state towards integrating (somehow) the education of teachers within the context of the university. The specialised college for teachers appears therefore to be a transitional institution, and sooner or later is tugged or nudges itself towards the university.

But a university is a place very different from a school, primary or secondary, and the greater the intended academic distance between school and university – contrast the cases of France and the United States in the 1950s – the more that difference matters. The title given to the French university teacher (a term with which we have struggled throughout these pages, since Faculty is a serviceable American term for which academic staff is an inaccurate British equivalent) of *enseignant-chercheur* is in this respect revealing. It appeared in official texts for the first time in 1984 and reflects the duality in the roles of teacher and researcher. Nor is that duality stable, as

France and England become steadily more like America and the life of the researcher moves towards being esteemed and rewarded above that of the teacher. It follows that many "teachers" in higher education shift in their attitudes and preferences away from teaching and towards work associated (somewhat grandiloquently) with the enlargement rather than the transmission of knowledge. Yet most of them still do a great deal of teaching, many of them are glad that this should be so, nearly all of them would find unpalatable (even if they sometimes show a generous respect for it) the idea of teaching in a primary or comprehensive secondary school, and none dare concede that teaching is work for which they are ill-prepared. Here lies the cause of much of the hesitation of the university in accepting the training of teachers as part of the central mission of the university. The Faculty members are themselves teachers and yet they are for the most part untrained, or trained only in a way which is by intention narrowly functional.

No such difficulties, of course, surround the education as distinct from the training of those who will or may become teachers. For them a university education of quality is doubly necessary: first, so that they may acquire a mastery of that disciplinary subject matter which is the foundation of teaching at any level, and second because future teachers need a sound liberal education for exactly the same reason as any other potentially influential member of society. Politicians need, even if they do not always have, education to a high level, but that is not to say that they all need degrees in political science, or that the world would be a better place if they were so endowed. This distinction – between the education which a teacher needs and deserves at a university, and the training which is needed by a school teacher but not by a university teacher – is the fault line which runs through the passionate debate about the IUFM in France, the controversy which surrounds the proliferation of alternative routes in the States, and the debate on the relative virtues of the BEd and the PGCE in England. French universities have never found any difficulty in embracing without reserve the agrégation and the CAPES, but are inflamed by any sniff of a plot which might submit secondary education to the process of *primarisation*. This may suggest that just as teachers teach best what they know best, so universities should concentrate on doing what they do best.

What precisely that is will of course vary in definition and in balance from one country to another, and the three countries of this study will continue to be very different places. Their universities and their teachers, like the societies to which they belong, do not look the same to foreigners as to natives, and certainly do not look the same to all foreigners. This, we hope, is why cross-national studies involving a small number of countries may be illuminating. To our French colleague, the United States is a jungle: luxuriant, confusing, noisy, undisciplined, competitive, diverse, unmanaged, individualistic, unsystematic. To our American colleagues, the world of education in England is less like a jungle but perhaps more like a zoo: caged, segmented, tidy, domesticated, deferential, inflexible, generally docile. But by an Englishman, France is admired as a circus: planned, orchestrated, elegant, geometric, traditional, skilful, moving at the behest of an always visible ring master. Perhaps after all it would have been wiser to choose another subject, even to succumb to the hint in the Introduction that a study of national railways (contrasting British Rail as it disappears with SNCF and Amtrak) would have served similar purposes. Even in that case, however, the last sentences of this chapter might well have been exactly the same.

Bibliography

FRANCE

Albertini, P (1992) L'école en France, XIXe-XXe siècles, de la maternelle à l'université. Paris: Hachette.

Alexandre, J-M (1991) Une espèce enseignante en voie de disparition, Le Monde de l'Education, 187, pp. 52-55.

Allègre, C (1993) L'Age des Savoirs: pour une renaissance de l'université. Paris: Gallimard.

Anderson, R (1975) Education in France 1848-1870. Oxford: Oxford University Press.

Ardagh, J. (1988) Modern France. Harmondsworth: Penguin.

Association pour la qualité de l'enseignement (1991) Main Basse sur l'éducation. Paris: Editions Universitaires.

Aubert, V. , & others (1985) La Forteresse Enseignante. Paris: Fayard.

Aulard, F.-A. (1911) Napoléon Ier et le monopole universitaire. Paris: A Colin.

Avanzini, G (1987) Introduction aux sciences de l'éducation. Toulouse: Privat.

Baker, D.N., & Harrigan, P.J. (1980) The making of Frenchmen: current directions in the history of education in France 1679-1979, Historical Reflections, Réflexions Historiques, Special Issue.

Ballion, R (1991) La bonne école. Paris: Hatier.

Bancel, D. (1989) Créér une nouvelle dynamique de la formation des maîtres. Paris: Ministère de l'Education Nationale.

Baudelot, C., & Establet, R (1989) Le niveau monte. Paris: Seuil

Bayrou, François (1990) 1990-2000: La décennie des mal-appris. Paris: Flammarion.

Bédarida, C. (1991) L'école qui décolle. Paris: Seuil.

Berger, I. (1979) Les instituteurs d'une génération à l'autre. Paris: Presses Universitaires de France.

Best, F. (1987) The Work of the French National Institute for Pedagogical Research, Studies in Educational Evaluation, 13, 3, pp. 289-296.

Bierry, M.C., & Fromageau, M. (1992) Le professeur de collège et de lycée. Paris: Nathan.

Blackburn, V., & Moisan, C. (1986) La formation continue des enseignants. Maastricht: Presses Universitaires Européenes.

Bosher, J.F. (1988) The French Revolution. New York: Norton.

Bourdieu, P., & Passeron, J.C. (1964) Les héritiers: les étudiants et la culture. Paris: Editions de Minuit.

Bourdieu, P., & Passeron, J.C. (1970) La reproduction: éléments pour une théorie du système d'enseignement. Paris: Editions de Minuit.

Bourdoncle, R., & Zay, D. (1989) Ecole normale et université dans la formation des enseignants du premier degré: une expérience pour les IUFM. Paris: Institut National de Recherche Pédagogique.

Bourgeois, G. (1989) Le baccalauréat n'aura pas lieu. Paris: Payot.

Briand, J-P. (1992) L'enseignement primaire supérieur et le développement de la scolarisation prolongée sous la Troisième République. Paris: Editions du Centre National de Recherche Scientifique.

Broadfoot, P., & others (1987) Teachers' conceptions of their professional responsibility: some international comparisons, Comparative Education, 23, 3, pp. 287-301.

Broadfoot, P (1985) Towards conformity: educational control and the growth of corporate management in England and France, in Lauglo, J., & McLean, M. The Control of Education, London: Heinemann.

Brockliss, L.W.B. (1987) French Higher Education in the Seventeenth and Eighteenth Centuries. Oxford: Oxford University Press.

Chapoulie, J.-M. (1987) Les professeurs de l'enseignement secondaire: un métier de classe moyenne. Paris: La Maison des Sciences de l'Homme.

Charles, F. (1988) Les instituteurs: un coup au moral. Paris: Ramsay.

Charlot, B. (1987) L'école en mutation. Paris: Payot.

Charlot, B. ed. (1994) L'école et le territoire: nouveaux espaces, nouveaux enjeux. Paris: Armand Colin.

Cherkaoui, M. (1982) Les changements du système éducatif en France, 1950-1980. Paris: Presses Universitaires de France.

Chervel, A. (1993) Histoire de l'agrégation. Paris: Editions Kimé.

Clark, J.M. (1967) Teachers and Politics in France: A Pressure Group Study of the Fédération de l'Education Nationale. Syracuse NY: Syracuse University Press.

Compayré. G. (1885) Histore critique des doctrines de l'éducation en France depuis le XVIe siècle. Paris: Hachette.

Coutel, C. ed. (1992) La République et l'école: une anthologie. Paris: Presses-Pocket.

Croissandeau, J.M. (1993) Les bonnes notes de la France. Paris: Seuil.

Crozier, M. (1970) La société bloquée. Paris: Seuil.

Crozier, M. (1976) On ne change pas la société par décret. Paris: Fayard.

Desbrousses, H. (1982) Instituteurs et professeurs. Paris: Edires.

Deyon, P. (1992) Paris et ses provinces: le défi de la décentralisation 1770-1992. Paris: Armand Colin.

Direction de l'Evaluation et de la Perspective (1992) L'état de l'école. Paris: Ministère de l'Education Nationale et de la Culture.

Dubet, F. (1991) Les lycéens. Paris: Seuil.

Durand-Prinborgne, C. (1991) Le système éducatif. Paris: La Documentation Française.

Durkheim, E (1969) L'évolution pédagogique en France, vol II, De la Renaissance à nos jours. Paris: Presses Universitaires de France.

Faure, E. (1971) Ce Que Je Crois. Paris: Grasset.

Fave-Bonnet, M.-F. (1994) Le métier d'enseignant-chercheur: des missions contradictoires?, Recherche et Formation, 15, pp.11-34.

Finkielkraut, A. (1987) La défaite de la pensée. Paris: Gallimard.

Flacelière, R. (1971) Normale en péril. Paris: Presses Universitaires de France.

Frazer, W.R. (1971) Reform and Restraints in Modern French Education. Boston: Routledge and Kegan Paul.

Gaillard, J.-M. (1987) Tu seras Président, mon fils: anatomie des Grandes Ecoles et mal-formation des élites. Paris: Ramsay.

Gaillard, J.-M. (1989) Jules Ferry. Paris: Faillard.

Gallot, J., & Gallot, A. (1991) Réussir l'école, démocratiser la réussite. Paris: Messidor.

Gauthier, N., & others (1986) Les Instits: enquête sur l'école primaire. Paris: Seuil.

Gaulupeau, Y. (1992) La France à l'école. Paris: Gallimard.

Gaziel, H. (1989) The emergence of the comprehensive middle school in France: educational policy making in a centralised system, Comparative Education, 25, 1, pp.29-40.

Gentzbitzel, M. (1988) Madame le Proviseur. Paris: Seuil.

Gentzbitzel, M. (1991) La cause des élèves. Paris: Seuil.

Gildea, R (1983) Education in Provincial France 1800-1912: a Study of Three Departments. Oxford: Oxford University Press.

Giolitto, P. (1991) Histoire de la jeunesse sous Vichy. Paris: Perrin.

Gontard, M. (1976) Les Ecoles Primaires de la France Bourgeoise. Toulouse: INRP-CRDP de Toulouse.

Guiraud, M., & Longhi, G. (1992) La république lycéenne. Paris: Payot.

Halls, W.D. (1976) Education, Culture and Politics in Modern France. Oxford: Pergamon Press.

Halls, W.D. (1983) Youth in Vichy France. Oxford: Clarendon Press.

Hamon, H., & Rotman, P. (1984) Tant qu'il y aura des profs. Paris: Seuil.

Hanley, D., & others (1984) Contemporary France: Politics and Society since 1945. Boston: Routledge and Kegan Paul.

Hollifield, J.F., & Ross, G. (1991) Searching for the New France. Boston: Routledge and Kegan Paul.

Horvath-Peterson, S. (1984) Victor Duruy and French Education: Liberal Reform in the Second Empire. Baton Rouge: Louisiana State University Press.

Houot, B. (1991) Coeur de Prof. Paris: Calmann-Lévy.

Hunt, P. (1973) French Teachers and their Unions, History of Education Quarterly, 13, 2, pp. 185-190.

Isambert-Jamati, V., & Henriquez, S. (1983) Le rôle de l'université dans la formation des enseignants en France, European Journal of Teacher Education, 6, 3, pp. 271-279.

Isambert-Jamati, V. (1990) Les savoirs scolaires. Paris: Editions Universitaires.

Joxe, P. (1972) Rapport de la commission d'études sur la fonction enseignante dans le second degré. Paris: La Documentation Française.

Juillard, H. (1985) La Melonnière ou l'Ecole Normale de Besançon de 1819 à 1922. Besançon: Centre Régional de Documentation Pédagogique.

Karady, V. (1976) Recherches sur la morphologie du corps universitaire littéraire sous la IIIe République, Le Mouvement Social, July-September, pp. 47-79.

Kaspi, A. (1993) Rapport sur les Instituts Universitaires de Formation des Maîtres: Jeudi 1 Juillet 1993. Paris: Ministère de l'Enseignement Supérieur et de la Recherche.

Lanson, G. (1926) L'Ecole Normale Supérieure. Paris: Hachette.

Laprévote, G. (1984) Splendeurs et misères de la formation des maîtres: les écoles normales primaires en France, 1879-1979. Lyon: Presses Universitaires de Lyon.

Larkin, M. (1988) France since the Popular Front. Oxford: Oxford University Press.

Léger, A. (1983) Enseignants du secondaire. Paris: Presses Universtaires de France.

Legrand, L. (1961) L'influence du positivisme dans l'oeuvre scolaire de Jules Ferry: les origines de la laicité. Paris: M.Rivière

Legrand, L. (1982) Pour un collège démocratique. Paris: La Documentation Française.

Legrand, L. (1993) Quelle politique scolaire?, Le Monde de l'Education, December, 210, pp.25-26.

Lelièvre, C. (1990) Histoire des institutions scolaires (1789-1989). Paris: Nathan.

Lequiller, P. (1992) La guerre scolaire n'aura pas lieu. Paris: Critérion.

Leselbaum, N. (1987) La formation des enseignants du second degré dans les Centres Pédagogiques Régionaux. Paris: Institut National de Recherche Pédagogique.

Lesourne, J. (1988) Education et société: les défis de l'an 2000. Paris: Editions la Découverte.

Lethierry, H. (1993) Feu les Ecoles Normales. Paris: L'Harmattan.

Letterier, L., & le Marchand, J. (1933) Historique de l'Ecole Normale d'Instituteurs de Calvados (1833-1933). Caen: A. Olivier.

Lewis, H.D. (1985) The French Education System. London: Croom Helm.

Lewis, H.D. (1989) Some aspects of education in France relevant to current concerns in the UK, Comparative Education, 25, 3, pp. 369-378.

Luc, J.N., & Barbé, A. (1982) Les Normaliens: histoire de l'école normale supérieure de St. Cloud. Paris: Presses de la Fondation Nationale des Sciences Politiques.

Lutringer, B. (1978, 1979) Cent cinquante ans au service du peuple: l'Ecole Normale des Vosges. Charmes: Feuillard.

Magliulo, B. (1982) Les Grandes Ecoles. Paris: Presses Universitaires de France.

Malefon, R. (1988) Vivante mémoire 1883-1985: l'Ecole Normale d'institutrices de Limoges. Limoges.

Mayeur, F. (1984) Recent Views on the History of Education in France, European History Quarterly, 14, pp.93-102.

Mendras, H., & Cole, A. (1991) Social Change in Modern France: Towards a Cultural Anthropology of the Fifth Republic. Cambridge: Cambridge University Press.

Mialaret, G. (1983) La formation des enseignants. Paris: Presses Universitaires de France.

Michaud, G., & Kimmel, A. (1990) Le Nouveau Guide France. Paris: Hachette.

Milner, J.-C. (1984) De l'Ecole. Paris: Seuil.

Minot, J. (1983) Quinze ans d'histore des institutions universitaires. Paris: Ministère de l'Education Nationale.

Miquel, P. (1994) Les Polytechniciens. Paris: Plon.

Moody, J.N. (1978) Education Since Napoleon. Syracuse NY: Syracuse University Press.

McLean, M. (1983) Education in France: Traditions of Liberty in a Centralised System in Holmes, B. ed. Equality and Freedom in Education: a Comparative Study. London: George Allen and Unwin.

Nemo, P. (1991) Pourquoi ont-ils tué Jules Ferry? Paris: Bernard Grasset.

Nique, C., & Lelièvre, C. (1990a) Histoire biographique de l'enseignement en France. Paris: Retz.

Nique, C. (1990b) L'éducation devient une affaire d'Etat. Paris: Nathan.

Nique, C. (1991) L'impossible gouvernement des esprits: l'histoire politique des écoles normales primaires. Paris: Nathan.

Nique, C., & Lelièvre, C (1993) La République n'éduquera plus: la fin du mythe Ferry. Paris: Plon.

Octor, R. (1990) La législation du système éducatif français. Paris: Armand Colin.

Ozouf, J., & Ozouf, M. (1992) La République des instituteurs. Paris: Seuil.

Pagnol, M. (1988) La gloire de mon père. Paris: Fallois

Palmer, R.R. (1985) The Improvement of Humanity: Education and the French Revolution. Princeton: Princeton University Press.

Parias, L.-H. (1981) Histoire générale de l'enseignement et de l'éducation en France (4 vols). Paris: Nouvelle Librairie de la France.

Passeron, J.-C. (1986) 1950-1980: l'Université mise à la question: changement de décor ou changement de cap? in Verger, J. ed. Histoire des Universités en France, pp.367-395. Toulouse: Privat.

Pécaut, F. (1904) L'éducation publique et la vie nationale (2nd edn.). Paris: Hachette.

Pelpel, P. (1986) Se former pour enseigner. Paris: Bordas.

Peretti, A. de (1982) Rapport au Ministère de l'Education Nationale de la Commission de la Formation des Personnels de l'Education Nationale. Paris: La Documentation Française.

Peretti, A. de (1993) Controverses en éducation. Paris: Hachette.

Perié, R. (1982) L'Education Nationale à l'heure de la décentralisation. Paris: La Documentation Française.

Peyrefitte, A. (1977) Rue d'Ulm, chroniques de la vie normalienne. Paris: Flammarion.

Pillard, G.-E. (1990) Louis Fontanet 1757-1821, Prince de l'esprit. Paris: Hérauld.

Plaisance, E. (1984) L'école maternelle en France depuis la fin de la deuxième guerre mondiale. Lille: Presses Universitaires de Lille.

Plenel, E. (1985) L'Etat et l'école en France, la république inachevée. Paris: Payot.

Poitou, C. (1987) Centenaire de l'Ecole Normale d'institutrices d'Orléans. Orléans.

Ponteil, F. (1966) Histoire de l'enseignement en France: les grandes étapes 1789-1964. Paris: Sirey.

Prost, A. (1968) L'enseignement en France 1800-1969. Paris: Armand Colin.

Prost, A. (1983A) L'école et la famille dans une société en mutation 1930-1980, (Volume IV of Parias, L.-H. 1968). Paris: Nouvelle Librairie de la France.

Prost. A. (1983B) Les lycées et leurs études au seuil du XXIe siècle. Paris: Ministère de l'Education Nationale.

Prost, A. (1985) L'éloge des pédagogues. Paris: Seuil.

Prost, A. (1986) L'enseignement s'est-il démocratisé? Paris: Presses Universitaires de France.

Prost, A. (1987) The Educational Maelstrom, in Ross, G., & others ed. The Mitterrand Experiment, pp. 229-236. Oxford: Oxford University Press.

Prost A. (1992) Education, société et politiques: une histoire de l'enseignement en France de 1945 à nos jours. Paris: Seuil.

Raynaud, P., & Thibaud, P (1990) La fin de l'école républicaine. Paris: Calmann-Lévy.

Reboul-Scherer, F (1989) La vie quotidienne des premiers instituteurs 1883-1882. Paris: Hachette.

Rohr, J. (1967) Victor Duruy, ministre de Napoléon III. Paris: Librairie Générale de Droit et de Jurisprudence.

Romilly, J. de (1984) L'enseignement en détresse. Paris: Julliard.

Rosanvallon, P. (1990) L'Etat en France de 1789 à nos jours. Paris: Seuil.

Ross, G. ed. (1987) The Mitterrand Experiment. Oxford: Oxford University Press.

Saint-Etienne, C. (1992) L'exception française. Paris: Colin.

Sarrault, M. (1984) Les carrières de l'enseignement. Paris: Génération.

Savary, A. (1985) En toute liberté. Paris: Hachette.

Schwarz, L. (1984) Pour sauver l'Université. Paris: Seuil.

Sénat (1993) Rapport d'Information fait au nom de la commission des Affaires culturelles. Annexe au procès-verbal de la séance du 27 octobre 1993. Paris.

Shinn, T. (1980) Savoir scientifique et pouvoir social: l'Ecole Polytechnique. Paris: Presses de la Fondation Nationale des Sciences Politiques.

Singer, M. (1993) L'école de la république: le SGEN des origines à nos jours. Paris: Cerf.

Sirinelli, J.-F. (1988) Génération intellectuelle: khâgneux et normaliens dans l'entre-deux-guerres. Paris: Fayard.

Smith, R.J. (1982) The Ecole Normale Supérieure and the Third Republic. Albany NY: State University of New York Press.

Snyders, G. (1965) La pédagogie en France aux XVIIe et XVIIIe siècles. Paris: Presses Universitaires de France.

Talbott, J.E. (1969) The Politics of Educational Reform in France, 1918-1940. Princeton: Princeton University Press.

Thuillier, G., & Guiral, P. (1982) La vie quotidienne des professeurs de 1870 à 1940. Paris: Hachette.

Toulemonde, B. (1988) Petite histoire d'un grand ministère: l'Education Nationale. Paris: Albin Michel.

Vallet, O. (1991) L'Ecole: l'Ecole Nationale d'Administration. Paris: Albin Michel.

Verger, J. ed. (1986) Histoire des universités en France. Toulouse: Privat.

Villin, M., & Lesage, P. (1987) La galerie des maîtres d'école et des instituteurs, 1820-1945. Paris: Plon.

Vincent, G. (1967) Les professeurs du second degré. Paris: Armand Colin.

Vincent, G. (1980) L'école primaire en France. Lyon: Presses Universitaires de Lyon.

Weiler, H.N. (1988) The Politics of Reform and Nonreform in French Education, Comparative Education Review, 32, 3, pp. 251-265.

Weisz, G. (1983) The Emergence of Modern Universities in France 1863-1914. Princeton: Princeton University Press.

Winock, M. (1987) Chronique des années soixante. Paris: Seuil.

Wright, G. (1987) France in Modern Times (4th.edn.). New York, Norton.

Wright, V. (1989) The Government and Politics of France (3rd. edn.). London: Routledge and Kegan Paul.

Zay, D. (1988) La formation des instituteurs. Paris: Editions Universitaires.

Zay, J. (1945) Souvenirs et solitude. Paris: Julliard.

Zeldin, T. (1983) The French. London: Collins.

UNITED STATES

Altbach, P.G. & Berdahl, R.O. (1988) Higher Education in American Society. Buffalo: Prometheus Books

Altenbaugh, R. J., & Underwood, K. (1990) The Evolution of Normal Schools, in Goodlad, J. I., Soder, R., & Sirotnik, K. A. eds. Places Where Teachers are Taught. San Francisco: Jossey-Bass.

Anderson, J. D. (1988) The Education of Blacks in the South, 1860-1935. Chapel Hill: University of North Carolina Press.

Best, J.H. (1988) The Revolution of Markets and Management: towards a history of American higher education since 1944, History of Education Quarterly, 28, 2, pp. 177-89.

Bledstein. B.J. (1976) The Culture of Professionalism. New York: Norton.

Bloom, A. (1987) The Closing of the American Mind: How Higher Education has Failed Democracy and Impoverished the Souls of Today's Students. New York: Simon and Schuster.

Borrowman, M.L. (1976) Teacher Education in America: a documentary history. New York: Teachers College Press.

Bowles, S., & Gintis, H. (1976) Schooling in Capitalist America. New York: Basic Books.

Calambos, E.L. (1986) Improving Teacher Education. San Francisco: Jossey Bass.

Carnegie Task Force on Teaching as a Profession (1986) A Nation Prepared: Teachers for the Twenty-first Century. New York: Carnegie Forum on Education and the Economy.

Clark, D. L., & Marker, G. (1975) The Institutionalization of Teacher Education, in Ryan, K. ed. Teacher Education. 74th yearbook of the National Society for the Study of Education, part 2. Chicago: University of Chicago Press.

Clifford, G. J., & Guthrie, J. W. (1988) Ed School: A Brief for Professional Education. Chicago: University of Chicago Press.

Conant, J. B. (1959) The American High School Today. New York: McGraw-Hill.

Conant, J. B. (1963) The Education of American Teachers. New York: McGraw-Hill.

Conant, J. B. (1970) My Several Lives: Memoirs of a Social Inventor. New York: Harper & Row.

Cooper, J. M., & Tate, P. M. (1992) Restructuring Teacher Education: Policy, Narratives, Stories, and Cases. Albany: State University of New York Press.

Cremin, L. A., Shannon, D. A., & Townsend, M. E. (1954) A History of Teachers College, Columbia University. New York: Teachers College Press.

Cremin, L.A. (1964) The Transformation of the School. New York: Vintage Books.

Cremin, L. A. (1978) The Education of the Educating Professions. Chicago: University of Chicago Press.

Cremin, L.A. (1970) American Education: The Colonial Experience 1607-1783. New York: Harper and Row.

Cremin, L.A. (1980) American Education: the National Experience 1783-1876. New York: Harper and Row.

Cremin, L.A. (1988) American Education: the Metropolitan Experience. New York: Harper and Row.

Cuban, L. (1984) How Teachers Taught: Constancy and Change in American Classrooms, 1890-1980. New York: Longman.

Darling-Hammond, L. ed. (1994) Professional Development Schools: Schools for a Developing Profession. New York: Teachers College Press.

Damerell, R. (1985) Education's Smoking Gun: How Teachers Colleges have Destroyed Education in America. New York: Freundlich Books.

Ducharme, E.R. (1993) The Lives of Teacher Educators. New York: Teachers College Press.

Elsbree, W. S. (1939) The American Teacher: Evolution of a Profession in a Democracy. New York: American Book Company.

Feistritzer, E.C. (1983) The Condition of Teaching: A State by State Analysis. New York: The Carnegie Corporation.

Feistritzer, E. C. (1984) The Making of a Teacher: A Report on Teacher Education and Certification. Washington, D.C.: National Center for Educational Information.

Flexner, A. (1910) Medical Education in the United States and Canada. New York: Carnegie Foundation for the Advancement of Teaching.

Flexner, A. (1930) Universities: American, English, German. New York: Oxford University Press.

Fuller, W. E. (1982) The Old Country School: The Story of Rural Education in the Middle West. Chicago: University of Chicago Press.

Geiger, R.L. (1986) To Advance Knowledge: The Growth of American Research Universities 1900-1940. New York: Oxford University Press.

Ginsburg, M.B. (1988) Contradictions in Teacher Education and Society. London: Falmer Press.

Goodlad, J. I. (1984) A Place Called School: Prospects for the Future. New York: McGraw-Hill.

Goodlad, J. I. (1990) Teachers for our Nation's Schools. San Francisco: Jossey-Bass.

Goodlad, J. I., Soder, R., & Sirotnik, K. A. eds. (1990) Places Where Teachers are Taught. San Francisco: Jossey-Bass.

Graham, P.G. (1967) Progressive Education: From Arcady to Academe. New York: Teachers College Press.

Graham, P. A. (1984) Schools: Cacophony about Practice, Silence about Purpose, Daedalus, Winter, pp. 29-57.

Graham, P. A. (1989) Revolution in Pedagogy, in Preparing Schools for the 1990s: An Essay Collection. New York: Metropolitan Life.

Gumbert, E. B. ed. (1990) Fit To Teach: Teacher Education in International Perspective. Atlanta: Georgia State University Press.

Herbst, J. (1989) And Sadly Teach: Teacher Education and Professionalization in American Culture. Madison: University of Wisconsin Press.

Hirsch, E.D. (1987) Cultural Literacy: What Every American Needs to Know. Boston: Houghton Mifflin.

Hofstadter, R. (1962) Anti-intellectualism in American Life. New York: Random House.

Holmes Group (1986) Tomorrow's Teachers: A Report of the Holmes Group. East Lansing, MI: Holmes Group.

Holmes Group (1990) Tomorrow's Schools: Principles for the Design of Professional Development Schools. East Lansing, MI: Holmes Group.

Houston, W. R. ed. (1990) Handbook of Research on Teacher Education. New York: Macmillan.

Howey, K.R. and Gardner. W.E. eds. (1983) The Education of Teachers. New York: Longman.

Howey, K. R., & Zimpher, N. L. (1989) Profiles of Preservice Teacher Education. Albany: State University of New York Press.

Huberman, M. (1993) The Lives of Teachers. New York: Teachers College Press.

Hughes, R. (1993) Culture of Complaint: The Fraying of America. New York: Oxford University Press.

Jackson, P. (1968) Life in Classrooms. New York: Holt, Rinehard and Winston.

Jackson, P. (1986) The Practice of Teaching. New York: Teachers College Press.

Jencks, C., & Riesman, D. (1968) The Academic Revolution. Garden City, NY: Doubleday.

Johnson, H. C., & Johanningmeier, E. V. (1972) Teachers for the Prairie: The University of Illinois and the Schools, 1868-1945. Urbana: University of Illinois Press.

Johnson, W.R. (1987) Empowering Practitioners: Holmes, Carnegie and the Lessons of History. History of Education Quarterly, 27, 2, pp.221-40.

Judge, H. (1977) American Schooling and History: an English View, Oxford Review of Education, 3, 3, pp.235-46.

Judge, H. (1982) American Graduate Schools of Education: A View from Abroad. New York: Ford Foundation.

Judge, H. (1989) Images and Reflections: The U.S.A., Comparative Education, 25, pp. 333-37.

Kaestle, C.F. (1983) Pillars of the Republic: Common Schools and American Society 1780-1860. New York: Hill and Wang.

Katz, L. and Raths, J. eds. (1984) Advances in Teacher Education. Norwood: Ablex Publishing Corporation.

Kirp, D.L. (1982) Just Schools: The Idea of Racial Equality in American Education. Berkeley: University of California Press.

Kirst, M.W. (1984) Who Controls our Schools? New York: W.H. Freeman and Co.

Koerner, J. D. (1963) The Miseducation of American Teachers. Boston: Houghton Mifflin.

Lanier, J. E., & Little, J. W. (1986) Research on Teacher Education, in Wittrock, M. C. ed. Handbook of Research on Teaching, pp. 527-69. New York: Macmillan.

Little, J.W., & McLaughlin, M.W. eds. (1993) Teachers' Work: Individuals, Colleagues, and Contexts. New York: Teachers College Press.

Lortie, D. C. (1975) Schoolteacher: A Sociological Study. Chicago: University of Chicago Press.

Ludmeren, K. (1985) Learning to Heal: The Development of American Medical Education. New York: Basic Books.

Mattingly, P. H. (1975) The Classless Profession: American Schoolmen in the Nineteenth Century. New York: New York University Press.

McCarty, D.J. & Associates (1973) New Perspectives on Teacher Education. San Francisco: Jossey Bass.

McNeil, L.M. (1985) Contradictions of Control: School Structure and School Knowledge. Boston: Routledge and Kegan Paul.

National Commission for Excellence in Education (1983) A Nation at Risk: The Imperative for Educational Reform. Washington, D.C.: U.S Government Printing Office.

Newman, J. W. (1990) America's Teachers: An Introduction to Education. New York: Longman.

Powell, A. G., Farrar, E., & Cohen, D. (1985) The Shopping Mall High School: Winners and Losers in the Educational Market Place. Boston: Houghton Mifflin.

Powell, A. G. (1980) The Uncertain Profession: Harvard and the Search for Educational Authority. Cambridge: Harvard University Press.

Ravitch, D. (1983) The Troubled Crusade. New York: Basic Books.

Reynolds, M.C. ed. (1989) The Knowledge Base for the Beginnning Teacher. Oxford: Pergamon.

Rothstein, W.G. (1987) American Medical Schools and the Practice of Medicine: A History. New York: Oxford University Press.

Sarason, S. B., Davidson, K. S., & Blatt, B. (1986) The Preparation of Teachers: An Unstudied Problem in Education, revised ed. Cambridge: Brookline Books.

Schlesinger, A.M. (1991) The Disuniting of America: Reflections on a Multicultural Society. New York: W.W. Norton.

Schon, D. (1983) The Reflective Practitioner. New York: Basic Books.

Schon, D. (1987) Educating the Reflective Practitioner: Toward a New Design for Teaching and Learning in the Professions. San Francisco: Jossey-Bass.

Sedlak, M., & Schlossman, S. (1986) Who will Teach? Historical Perspectives on the Changing Appeal of Teaching as a Profession. Santa Monica, CA: Rand Corporation.

Sedlak, M., Wheeler, C., Pullin, D., & Cusick, P. (1986) Selling Students Short: Classroom Bargains and Academic Reform in the American High School. New York: Teachers College Press.

Sizer, T. R. (1984) Horace's Compromise: The Dilemma of the American High School. Boston: Houghton Mifflin.

Smith, B.O. (1980) A Design for a School of Pedagogy. Washington, DC: U.S. Department of Education.

Soltis, J. F. ed. (1987) Reforming Teacher Education: The Impact of the Holmes Group Report. New York: Teachers College Press.

Spring, J. (1990) The American School 1642-1990. New York: Longman.

Sykes, G. (1985) Teacher Education in the United States, in Clark, B. R. ed. The School and the University: An International Perspective. Berkeley: University of California Press.

Taft, P. (1974) United They Teach: The Story of the United Federation of Teachers. Los Angeles: Nash.

Veysey, L. (1965) The Emergence of the American University. Chicago: University of Chicago Press.

Warren, D. (1985) Learning from Experience: History and Teacher Education, Educational Researcher, 14, pp. 5-12.

Warren, D. ed. (1989) American Teachers: Histories of a Profession at Work. New York: Macmillan.

Weiss, L. (1989) Crisis in Teaching: Perspectives on Current Reform. Albany: State University of New York Press.

Wiebe, R. (1975) The Segmented Society: An Introduction to the Meaning of America. New York: Oxford University Press.

Wise, A.E. (1979) Legislated Learning. Berkeley: University of California Press.

Wise, A.E. & Darling-Hammond, L. (1987) Licensing Teachers: Design for a Teaching Profession. Santa Monica: Rand Corporation.

Wisniewski, R., & Ducharme, E. R. eds. (1989) The Professors of Teaching. Albany: State University of New York Press.

Young, K.E. & others. (1983) Understanding Accreditation. San Francisco: Jossey Bass.

ENGLAND

Aldrich, R. (1990) The Evolution of Teacher Education, in Graves, N. J. ed. Initial Teacher Education: Policies and Progress, pp. 12-24. London: Kogan Page with The Institute of Education.

Aldrich, R. (1992) Educational Legislation of the 1980s in England: An Historical Analysis, History of Education, 21, pp. 57-69.

Alexander, R. (1992) Policy and Practice in Primary Education. London: Routledge.

Barrett, E., Barton, L., Furlong, J., Galvin, C., Miles, S., & Whitty, G. (1992a) Initial Teacher Education in England and Wales: A Topography. London: Institute of Education.

Barrett, E., Barton, L., Furlong, J., Galvin, C., Miles, S., & Whitty, G. (1992b) New Routes to Qualified Teacher Status, Cambridge Journal of Education, 22, pp. 323-35.

Barrett, E., & Galvin, C., with Barton, L., Furlong, J., Miles, S., & Whitty, G. (1993) The Licensed Teacher Scheme: A Modes of Teacher Education Project Survey. London: Institute of Education.

Barton, L., Pollard, A., & Whitty, G. (1992) Experiencing CATE: The Impact of Accreditation Upon Initial Training Institutions in England, Journal of Education for Teaching, 18, pp. 41-57.

Bash, L., & Coulby, D. (1989) The Education Reform Act: Competition and Control. London: Cassell Educational Ltd.

Beattie, N. (1990) The Bomber and the Flak: A Personal Response to Recent, Relevant Experience, Cambridge Journal of Education, 20, pp. 105-13.

Becher, T. (1987) British Higher Education. London: Allen and Unwin.

Becher, T., & Kogan, M. (1992) Process and Structure in Higher Education, second ed. London: Routledge.

Bell, R., Fowler, G., & Little, K. (1973) Education in Great Britain and Ireland: A Source Book. London: Routledge.

Bennett, S. N., Wragg, E. C., Carre, C. G., & Carter, D. S. G. (1992). A Longitudinal Study of Primary Teachers' Perceived Competence in, and Concerns About, National Curriculum Implementation, Research Papers in Education, 7, pp. 53-78.

Benton, P. ed. (1990) The Oxford Internship Scheme: Integration and Partnership in Initial Teacher Education. London: Gulbenkian Foundation.

Board of Education (1926) Report of (Hadow) Consultative Committee on The Education of the Adolescent. London: Her Majesty's Stationery Office.

Board of Education (1931) Report of (Hadow) Consultative Committee on The Primary School. London: Her Majesty's Stationery Office.

Board of Education (1933) Report of (Hadow) Consultative Committee on Infant and Nursery Schools. London: Her Majesty's Stationery Office.

Bibliography

Board of Education (1944) Report of (McNair) Departmental Committee on Teachers and Youth Leaders. London: Her Majesty's Stationery Office.

Bolton, E. (1993) Imaginary Gardens with Real Toads, in Chitty, C. & Simon, B. eds. Education Answers Back: Critical Responses to Government Policy, pp. 3-16. London: Lawrence and Wishart Limited.

Bonnett, M., & Doddington, C. (1990) Primary Teaching: What has Philosophy to Offer? Cambridge Journal of Education, 20, pp. 115-21.

Booth, M. B., Furlong, V. J., & Wilkin, M. eds. (1990) Partnership in Initial Teacher Training. London: Cassell Educational Ltd.

Bowe, R., Ball, S. J., & Gold, A. (1992) Reforming Education and Changing Schools: Case Studies in Policy Sociology. London: Routledge.

Broadfoot, P. (1985) Towards Conformity: Educational Control and the Growth of Corporate Management in England and France, in Lauglo, J.& McLean, M. eds., The Control of Education. London: Heinemann.

Broadfoot, P. (1992) Teaching and the Challenge of Change: Educational Research in Relation to Teacher Education, European Journal of Teacher Education, 15, pp. 45-52.

Burton, L. (1992). Becoming a Teacher of Mathematics, Cambridge Journal of Education, 22, pp. 377-86.

Carswell, J. (1985) Government and the Universities in Britain. London: Cambridge University Press.

Centre for Contemporary Cultural Studies (1981) Unpopular Education: Schooling and Social Democracy in England Since 1944. London: Hutchinson.

Chitty, C. (1989) Towards a New Education System: The Victory of the New Right? London: The Falmer Press.

Chitty, C., & Rein, N. (1969) Blackwards, Tribune (14 November).

Chitty, C., & Simon, B. eds. (1993) Education Answers Back: Critical Responses to Government Policy . London: Lawrence and Wishart Ltd.

Clarke, K. (1992) Speech for the North of England Education Conference, 4 January 1992. London: Her Majesty's Stationery Office.

Coulby, D., & Bash, L. (1991) Contradiction and Conflict: The 1988 Education Act in Action. London: Cassell Educational Ltd. Council for the Accreditation of Teacher Education (1990) CATE News.

Cowen, R. (1990) Teacher Education: A Comparative View, in Graves, N. J. ed. Initial Teacher Education: Policies and Politics, pp. 45-57. London: Kogan Page with The Institute of Education.

Crosland, C.A.R. (1956) The Future of Socialism. London: Jonathan Cape.

Crosland, S. (1982) Tony Crosland. London: Cape.

Cross Commission (1888) Report of The Royal Commission on the Elementary Acts. London: Her Majesty's Stationery Office.

Cruickshank, M. (1970) A History of the Training of Teachers in Scotland. Edinburgh: The Scottish Council for Research in Education.

Dart, L. & Drake, P. (1993) School-based Teacher Training: A Conservative Practice, Journal of Education for Teaching, 19, pp. 175-89.

Dearing, R. (1994) The National Curriculum and its Assessment: Final Report. London: School Curriculum and Assessment Authority.

Dent, H. C. (1977) Training of Teachers in England and Wales 1800-1975. London: Hodder and Stoughton.

Department for Education (1992a) Choice and Diversity: A New Framework for Schools. London: Her Majesty's Stationery Office.

Department for Education (1992b) Circular No. 9/92: Initial Teacher Training (Secondary Phase). London: Her Majesty's Stationery Office.

Department for Education (1992c) Reform of Initial Teacher Training: A Consultation Document. London: Her Majesty's Stationery Office.

Department for Education (1993a) Draft Circular: The Initial Training of Primary School Teachers: New Criteria for Course Approval. London: Her Majesty's Stationery Office.

Department for Education (1993b) Circular No.14/93: The Initial Training Training of Primary School Teachers: New Criteria for Courses. London: Her Majesty's Stationery Office.

Department for Education (1993c) The Government's Proposals for the Reform of Initial Teacher Training. London: Her Majesty's Stationery Office.

Department for Education (1993d) News: OFSTED Reports Back School Based Teacher Training, 20.

Department for Education (1993e) News: Patten Opens Up New Options for Primary Teacher Training, 188.

Department of Education and Science (1963) Report of the Robbins Committee on Higher Education. London: Her Majesty's Stationery Office.

Department of Education and Science (1965) Circular No. 10/65 on the Organisation of Secondary Education. London: Her Majesty's Stationery Office.

Department of Education and Science (1967) Report of (Plowden) Central Advisory Council on Children and Their Primary Schools. London: Her Majesty's Stationery Office.

Department of Education and Science (1972) Education: A Framework for Expansion: A White Paper. London: Her Majesty's Stationery Office.

Department of Education and Science (1972) Report of (James) Committee on Teacher Education and Training. London: Her Majesty's Stationery Office.

Department of Education and Science (1973) Circular No. 7/73 on The Development of Higher Education in the Non-University Sector. London: Her Majesty's Stationery Office.

Department of Education and Science (1979) Aspects of Secondary Education in England: A Survey by HM Inspectors of Schools. London: Her Majesty's Stationery Office.

Department of Education and Science (1983) Teaching Quality: A White Paper. London: Her Majesty's Stationery Office.

Department of Education and Science (1984a) Circular No. 3/84: Initial Teacher Training: Approval of Courses. London: Her Majesty's Stationery Office.

Department of Education and Science (1984b) Education Observed 2: A Review of Published Reports by HM Inspectors on Primary Schools and 11-16 and 12-16 Comprehensive Schools. London: Her Majesty's Stationery Office.

Department of Education and Science (1985) The Curriculum from 5 to 16. London: Her Majesty's Stationery Office.

Department of Education and Science (1987) Quality in Schools: The Initial Training of Teachers. London: Her Majesty's Stationery Office.

Department of Education and Science (1988a) Circular No. 7/88: Local Management of Schools. London: Her Majesty's Stationery Office.

Bibliography

Department of Education and Science (1988b) Education Observed: Initial Teacher Training in the Universities in England, Northern Ireland and Wales. London: Her Majesty's Stationery Office.

Department of Education and Science (1988c) The New Teacher in School: A Survey by HM Inspectors in England and Wales. London: Her Majesty's Stationery Office.

Department of Education and Science (1988d) Qualified Teacher Status: Consultation Document. London: Her Majesty's Stationery Office.

Department of Education and Science (1989a) Circular No.12/89: School Teachers' Pay and Conditions of Employment. London: Her Majesty's Stationery Office.

Department of Education and Science (1989b) Circular No. 18/89: The Education (Teachers) Regulations 1989. London: Her Majesty's Stationery Office.

Department of Education and Science (1989c) Circular No. 24/89: Initial Teacher Training: Approval of Courses. London: Her Majesty's Stationery Office.

Department of Education and Science (1989d) Initial Teacher Training in France: The Training of Secondary Teachers in the Academie de Toulouse. London: Her Majesty's Stationery Office.

Department of Education and Science (1989e) Teaching: It's a Vital Profession : The Professional Teacher Program in New Jersey. London: Her Majesty's Stationery Office.

Department of Education and Science (1991) School-based Initial Teacher Training in England and Wales: A Report by H M Inspectorate. London: Her Majesty's Stationery Office.

Dickinson, A. ed. (1992) Perspectives on Change in History Education. London: Institute of Education.

Dowling, P., & Noss, R. eds. (1990) Mathematics Versus the National Curriculum. London: The Falmer Press.

Dunford, J., & Sharp, P. (1990) The Education System in England and Wales. London: Longman Group Ltd.

Edwards, T. (1990) Schools of Education – Their Work and Their Future, in Thomas, J.B. ed. British Universities and Teacher Education: A Century of Change, pp. 180-92. London: The Falmer Press.

Edwards, T. (1992a) Change and Reform in Initial Teacher Education, National Commission on Education Briefing, 9, pp. 1-4.

Edwards, T. (1992b) Issues and Challenges in Initial Teacher Education, Cambridge Journal of Education, 22, pp. 283-91.

Eggleston, J. (1992) The Challenge for Teachers. London: Cassell Educational Ltd.

Ellis, T., Haddow, B., McWhirter, J., & McClogan, D. (1976) William Tyndale: The Teacher's Story. London: Writers and Readers Publishing Cooperative.

Evans, K. (1985) The Development and Structure of the English School System. Kent: Hodder and Stoughton.

Fish, D. (1989) Learning Through Practice in Initial Teacher Training. London: Kogan Page Ltd.

Flude, M., & Hammer, M. eds. (1990) The Education Reform Act-1988: Its Origins and Implications. London: The Falmer Press.

Gilroy, D. P. (1992) The Political Rape of Initial Teacher Education in England and Wales, Journal of Education for Teaching, 18, pp. 5-22.

Gilroy, D. P. & Day, C. (1993) The Erosion of INSET in England and Wales: Analysis and Proposals for a Redefinition, Journal of Education for Teaching, 19, pp. 141-57.

Ginsburg, M., Wallace, G., & Miller, H. (1988) Teachers, Economy and the State: An English Example, Teaching and Teacher Education, 4, pp. 317-37.

Goodlad, S. (1984) Education for the Professions. Surrey: The Society for Research into Higher Education and the National Foundation of Education Research.

Gordon, P., Aldrich, R., & Dean, D. (1991) Education and Policy in England in the Twentieth Century. London: The Woburn Press.

Gore, L., & Mitchell, P. (1992) School-Based Training: A Local Education Authority Perspective, Cambridge Journal of Education, 22, pp. 351-61.

Gosden, P. H. J. H. (1972) The Evolution of a Profession. Oxford: Blackwell.

Graves, N. (1990) Thinking and Research on Teacher Education, in Graves, N. J. ed. Initial Teacher Education: Policies and Progress, pp. 58-73. London: Kogan Page with The Institute of Education.

Graves, N. J. ed. (1990) Initial Teacher Education: Policies and progress. London: Kogan Page with The Institute of Education.

Hake, C. (1993) Partnership in Initial Teacher Training: Talk and Chalk. London: Tufnell Press.

Hansard (1993) House of Lords Official Report, Education Bill (H.L.) – Second Reading, vol. 550, no.11, 7 December 1993, cols. 819-931.

Hansard (1994) House of Lords Official Report, Education Bill (H.L.) – Committee (First Day) , vol. 552, no. 54, 10 March 1994, cols. 1540-1674.

Hencke, D. (1978) Colleges in Crisis: The Reorganization of Teacher Training, 1971-77. New York: Penguin.

Hopkins, D., & Reid, K. eds. (1985) Rethinking Teacher Education. London: Croom Helm.

Jacques, K. (1992) Mentoring in Initial Teacher Education, Cambridge Journal of Education, 22, pp. 337-49.

Jones, M. G. (1938) The Charity School Movement. Cambridge: Cambridge University Press.

Judge, H. (1984) A Generation of Schooling: English Secondary Schools Since 1944. Oxford: Oxford University Press.

Judge, H. (1990) The Education of Teachers in England and Wales, in Gumbert, E. ed. Fit to Teach: Teacher Education in International Perspective, pp. 7-28. Atlanta: Georgia State University Press.

Kelly, A. V. (1993) Education as a Field of Study in a University: Challenge, Critique, Dialogue, Debate, Journal of Education for Teaching, 19, pp. 125-39.

Kelly, T. (1981) For Advancement of Learning: The University of Liverpool, 1881-1981. Liverpool: Liverpool University Press.

Knight, C. (1990) The Making of Tory Education Policy in Post-war Britain: 1950-1986. London: The Falmer Press.

Lancaster, J. (1808) Improvements in Education, Containing a Complete Epitome, of the System of Education, Invented and Practised by the Author. Borough Road, Southwark: J. Lancaster.

Lawlor, S. (1990) Teachers Mistaught: Training in Theories or Education in Subjects? London: G. Donald & Co. Ltd.

Lawn, M., & Ozga, J. (1986) Unequal Partners: Teachers Under Indirect Rule, British Journal of Sociology of Education, 7, pp. 225-38.

Lawton, D. (1989) Education, Culture and the National Curriculum. London: Hodder and Stoughton.

Lawton, D. (1990) The Future of Teacher Education, in Graves, N. J. ed. Initial Teacher Education: Policies and Progress, pp. 144-152. London: Kogan Page with The Institute of Education.

Lawton, D. (1992) Education and Politics in the 1990s: Conflict or Consensus. London: The Falmer Press.

Lawton, D. (1993) Is There Coherence and Purpose in the National Curriculum? in Chitty, C. & Simon, B. ed. Education Answers Back: Critical Responses to Government Policy, pp. 61-69. London: Lawrence and Wishart Ltd.

Lawton, D., & Chitty, C. eds. (1988) The National Curriculum. London: Institute of Education.

Lawton, D., & Gordon, P. (1987) Her Majesty's Inspectorate. London: Routledge.

Lewis, H. D. (1989) Some Aspects of Education in France Relevant to Current Concerns in the UK, Comparative Education, 25, pp. 369-78.

Lowe, R. (1988) Education in the Post-war Years: A Social History. London: Routledge.

Macintyre, G. (1991) Accreditation of Teacher Education: The Story of CATE 1984-1989. London: The Falmer Press.

Maclean, R. (1992) Teachers' Career and Promotion Patterns: A Sociological Analysis. London: The Falmer press.

McClelland, V.A. (1989) Reflections on a Changing Concept of Teacher Education, in McClelland, V.A. & Varma, V. P. ed. Advances in Teacher Education, pp. 19-33. London: Routledge.

McClelland, V. A., & Varma, V. P. eds. (1989). Advances in Teacher Education. London: Routledge.

Maclure, S. (1989) Education Reformed: A Guide to the Education Reform Act, second ed. London: Hodder and Stoughton.

Marsh, C. (1990) Recent Developments in Primary Initial Teacher Training in Wales: An Outsider's Perspective, Journal of Education for Teaching, 16, pp.185-97.

McPherson, A., & Raab, C. D. (1988) Governing Education: A Sociology of Policy Since 1945. Edinburgh: Edinburgh University Press.

Ministry of Education (1957) The Training of Teachers. London: Her Majesty's Stationery Office.

Ministry of Education (1963) Report of (Newsom) Central Advisory Council on Half Our Future. London: Her Majesty's Stationery Office.

Naish, M. (1990) Teacher Education Today, in Graves, N. J. ed. Initial Teacher Education: Policies and Progress, pp. 25-44. London: Kogan Page with The Institute of Education.

National Union of Teachers (1970) Teacher Education: The Way Ahead. London.

National Union of Students (1971) NUS Survey of Student Teacher Opinion. London.

National Union of Students (1971) The Education and Training of Teachers: Perspectives for Change. London.

National Union of Students (1972) Teacher Education After James: An Alternative Perspective. London.

Nias, J. (1989) Primary Teachers Talking: A Study of Teaching as Work. London: Routledge.

Niblett, W. R., Humphreys, D. W., & Fairhurst, J. R. (1975) The University Connection: The Antecedents, Concept and Development of Institutes of Education: 1922-1972. Oxford: National Federation for Education Research.

Noss, R. (1989) Just Testing: A Critical View of Recent Change in the United Kingdom School Mathematics Curriculum, in Ellerton, N. F. ed. School Mathematics: The Challenge to Change. Deakin: Deakin University Press.

Noss, R., Brown, A., Dowling, P., Drake, P., Harris, M., Hoyles, C., & Mellin-Olsen, S. eds. (1990) Political Dimensions of Mathematics Education: Action & Critique. London: Institute of Education.

O'Hear, A. (1988) Who Teaches the Teachers? London: Social Affairs Unit.

O'Hear, A. (1991) Education and Democracy: Against the Educational Establishment. London: The Claridge Press.

O'Keeffe, D. (1990) Equality and Childhood and the Myths of Teacher Training, in Graves, N. J. ed. Initial Teacher Education: Policies and Progress, pp. 74-92. London: Kogan Page with The Institute of Education.

Office of Her Majesty's Chief Inspector of Schools (1993) The Training of Primary School Teachers: March 1991-March 1992. London: Her Majesty's Stationery Office.

Oliver, R. A. C. (1943) The Training of Teachers in Universities. London: University of London Press.

Osborn, M. & Broadfoot, P., with Abbott, D., Croll, P., & Pollard, A. (1992) The Impact of Current Changes in English Primary Schools on Teacher Professionalism, Teachers College Record, 94, pp. 138-51.

Perkin, H. (1969) Key Profession: The History of the Association of University Teachers. London: Routledge.

Perry, P. (1989) Teacher Awareness of the Economic Foundations of a Free Society, in McClelland, V.A. & Varma, V. P. eds. Advances in Teacher Education, pp. 141-57. London: Routledge.

Pollard, A., & Tann, S. (1987) Reflective Teaching in the Primary School: A Handbook for the Classroom. London: Cassell Educational Ltd.

Poppleton, P. & Pullin, R. (1992) Distant Voices: English Teachers' Views on Change in Initial Teacher Education, Journal of Education for Teaching, 18, pp. 115-29.

Pring, R. (1989) The New Curriculum. London: Cassell Educational Ltd.

Robbins, Lord, and Ford, B. (1965) Report on Robbins, Universities Quarterly, 20.

Ross, A. (1990). The Control of Teacher Education: A General Teaching Council for England and Wales, in Graves, N. J. ed. Initial Teacher Education: Policies and Progress, pp. 124-43). London: Kogan Page with The Institute of Education.

Sharp, P. R. (1987) The Creation of the Local Authority Sector of Higher Education. London: Falmer Press.

Shaw, K. E. (1966) Why No Sociology of Schools? Education for Teaching, 69, pp. 61-67.

Shaw, R. (1992a) Teacher Training in Secondary Schools. London: Kogan Page Ltd.

Shaw, R. (1992b) School-based Training: The View From the Schools, Cambridge Journal of Education, 22, pp. 363-75.

Silver, H. (1987) Education and the Research Process: Forming a New Public. Council for National Academic Awards.

Silver, H. (1990) A Higher Education: The Council for National Academic Awards and British Higher Education, 1964-89. London: The Falmer Press.

Simon, B. (1981) Why No Pedagogy in England? In Simon, B. & Taylor, W. eds. Education in the Eighties. London: Batsford.

Simon, B. (1988) Bending the Rules: The Baker 'Reform' of Education. London: Lawrence and Wishart.

Simons, H. (1988) Teacher Professionalism and the National Curriculum, in Lawton, D. & Chitty, C. ed. The National Curriculum, pp. 78-90. London: Institute of Education.

Smith, R. (1992) Theory: An Entitlement to Understanding, Cambridge Journal of Education, 22, pp. 387-98.

Southey, R., & Southey, C. C. (1844) The Life of Dr. Bell. London: John Murray.

Swanwick, K. (1990) The Necessity of Teacher Education, in Graves, N. J. ed. Initial Teacher Education: Policies and Progress, pp. 93-108. London: Kogan Page with The Institute of Education.

Taylor, W. (1968) Towards a Policy for the Teacher Education of Teachers. In Taylor, W. ed. Twentieth Symposium of the Colston Research Society. Bristol: University of Bristol, Archon Books.

Taylor, W. (1990) The Control of Teacher Education: The Council for the Accreditation of Teacher Education, in Graves, N. J. ed. Initial Teacher Education: Policies and Progress, pp. 109-23. London: Kogan Page with The Institute of Education.

Taylor, W. (1991) Ideology, Accountability and Improvement in Teacher Education, Evaluation and Research in Education, 5, pp. 57-66.

Thomas, J. B. (1990a) Day Training College to Department of Education, in Thomas, J. ed. British Universities and Teacher Education: A Century of Change, pp. 19-38. London: The Falmer Press.

Thomas, J. B. ed. (1990b) British Universities and Teacher Education: A Century of Change. London: The Falmer Press.

Troman, G. (1991) Initial Teacher Education and the New Right, Forum, 33, pp. 42-44.

Turner, J. (1990) Universities, Government Policy and the Study of Education in Britain, Journal of Education for Teaching, 16, pp. 73-82.

Universities Council for the Education of Teachers (1983) Bulletin No. 15.

Universities Council for the Education of Teachers (1984) Bulletin No. 16.

Universities Council for the Education of Teachers (1985) Bulletin No. 17.

Universities Council for the Education of Teachers (1986) Bulletin No. 18.

Universities Council for the Education of Teachers (1987a) Bulletin No. 19.

Universities Council for the Education of Teachers (1987b) The Universities Council for the Education of Teachers 1966-1987: Twenty-one Years of Endeavour.

Universities Council for the Education of Teachers (1988) Bulletin No. 20.

Universities Council for the Education of Teachers (1989) Bulletin No. 21.

Universities Council for the Education of Teachers (1990) Annual Report No. 22.

Universities Council for the Education of Teachers (1991) Annual Report No. 23.

Universities Council for the Education of Teachers (1992) Annual Report No. 24.

University of London Institute of Education (1971) An Enquiry into the Education and Training of Teachers in the area of the Institute 1970/1. London: Institute of Education.

Warnock, M. (1988) A Common Policy for Education. Oxford: Oxford University Press.

Warnock, M. (1992) Higher Education: The Concept of Autonomy, Oxford Review of Education, 18, pp. 119-24.

Whitty, G., Barrett, E., Barton, L., Furlong, J., Galvin, C., & Miles, S. (1992) Initial Teacher Education in England and Wales: A Survey of Current Practices and Concerns, Cambridge Journal of Education, 22, pp. 293-306.

Whitty, G., Barton, L., & Pollard, A. (1987) Ideology and Control in Teacher Education: A Review of Recent Experience in England, in Popkewitz, T. ed. Critical Studies in Teacher Education: Its Folklore, Theory, and Practice, pp. 161-83. London: Falmer.

Wilkin, M. (1992) The Challenge of Diversity, Cambridge Journal of Education, 22, pp. 307-21.

Wilkin, M. ed. (1992) Mentoring in Schools. London: Kogan Page Ltd.

Williams, G. (1992) Changing Patterns of Finance in Higher Education. Buckingham: Open University Press.

Young, M. (1990) Bridging the Theory/Practice Divide: An Old Problem in a New Context, Education and Child Psychology, 7, pp. 14-22.

GENERAL

Altbach, P., & others (1986) New Approaches to Comparative Education. Chicago: University of Chicago Press.

Archer, M. (1979) Social Origins of Educational Systems. London: Sage.

Arnove, R., & others (1992) Emergent Issues in Education: Comparative Perspectives. Albany NY: State University of New York Press.

Auba. J., & Leclerq, J.M. (1985) Les enseignants dans les sociétés modernes: une même interrogation. Paris: La Documentation Française.

Baron G., & Tropp, A. (1961) Teachers in England and America, in Halsey A.H., & others eds. Education, Economy and Society. Glencoe, Ill.: Free Press.

Brickman,W.W. (1985) Educational Roots and Routes in Western Europe. Cherry Hill: Emeritus.

Clark, B.R. ed. (1983) The Higher Education System in Cross-National Perspective. Berkeley: University of California Press.

Clark, B.R. ed. (1984) Perspectives on Higher Education: Eight Disciplinary and Comparative Views. Berkeley: University of California Press.

Clark, B.R. ed. (1985) The School and the University: An International Perspective. Berkeley: University of California Press.

Clark, B.R. ed. (1987) The Academic Profession: National, Disciplinary and Institutional Settings. Berkeley: University of California Press.

Clark, B.R., & Neave, G. eds. (1992) The Encyclopedia of Higher Education, 4 vols. Oxford: Pergamon.

Dunkin, M.J. (1988) Comparative Studies in Teaching and Teacher Education, in Postlethwaite, T.N. ed. The Encyclopedia of Comparative Education and National Systems of Education. Oxford: Pergamon, pp. 60-66.

Eurich, N.P. (1981) Systems of Higher Education in Twelve Countries: A Comparative View. New York: Praeger.

Fraser, S.F. ed. (1969) American Education in Foreign Perspectives. New York: John Wiles.

Flexner, A. (1924) Medical Education: A Comparative View. Boston: Merryweather.

Bibliography

Frischer, D. (1990) La France vue d'en face: l'image de la France analysée et jugée par les étrangers. Paris: Robert Laffont.

Gaziel, H.H., & Taub, D. (1992) Teachers Unions and Educational Reform – A Comparative Perspective: the Cases of France and Israel, Educational Policy, 6, 1, pp.72-86.

Gerbod, P. (1991) Voyages au pays des mangeurs de grenouilles: la France vue par les Britanniques du XVIIIe siècle à nos jours. Paris: Albin Michel.

Goodlad, S. ed. (1984) Education for the Professions. Guildford: NFER-Nelson.

Green, A. (1990) Education and State Formation: the Rise of Education Systems in England, France and the U.S.A. New York: St. Martin's Press

Gumbert, E. ed. (1990) Fit to Teach: Teacher Education in International Perspective. Atlanta: Georgia State University Press.

Halls W.D. ed. (1990) Comparative Education: Contemporary Issues and Trends. London: Jessica Kingsley Publications-UNESCO.

Holmes, B. (1981) Comparative Education: Some Considerations of Method. London: George Allen and Unwin.

Holmes, B., & McLean, M. eds. (1989) The Curriculum: A Comparative Perspective. London: Unwin Hyman.

Hoyle, E., & Magarry, J. eds. (1980) The World Yearbook of Education 1980: the Professional Development of Teachers. London: Kogan Page.

Judge, H. (1988) Cross-national Perceptions of Teachers, Comparative Education Review, 32, 2, pp.143-158.

Judge, H. (1991). Schools of Education and Teacher Education, in Phillips, D. ed. Lessons of Cross-national Comparisons in Education. Oxford Studies in Comparative Education series. Wallingford: Triangle Books.

Judge, H. (1992) Teacher Education in Clark, B.R., & Neave, G.R. eds. The Encyclopedia of Higher Education. Oxford: Pergamon.

Kelsall, R.K., & Kelsall, H.M. (1969) The School Teacher in England and the United States. Oxford: Pergamon.

Kerr, C., & others (1978) Twelve Systems of Higher Education: Six Decisive Issues. New York: International Council for Educational Development.

King, E.J. (1970) The Education of Teachers: a Comparative Analysis. London: Holt, Rinehart and Winston.

King. E.J. (1979) Other Schools and Ours (5th. edn.). London: Holt, Rinehart and Winston.

Lauglo, J., & McLean, M. eds.(1985) The Control of Education: International Perspectives. London: Heinemann.

Lawn, M. ed. (1985) The Politics of Teacher Unions. London: Croom Helm.

Leavit, H.B. ed. (1992) Issues and Problems in Teacher Education: an International Handbook. New York: Greenwood Press.

Litt, E. & Parkinson, M. (1979) United States and United Kingdon Educational Policy: A Decade of Reform. New York: Praeger.

Lomax, D.E. (1976) European Perspectives in Teacher Education. London: John Wiley.

Lynch, J., & Plunkett, D. (1973) Teacher Education and Cultural Change: England, France, West Germany. London: George Allen and Unwin.

Mallinson, V. (1975) An Introduction to the Study of Comparative Education (4th. edn.). London: Heinemann.

Maynes, M.J. (1985) Schooling in Western Europe: A Social History. Albany NY: State University of New York Press.

McLean, M. (1990) Britain and a Single Market Europe. London: Kogan Page.

Muller, D. K., Ringer, F., & Simon, B. eds. (1987) The Rise of the Modern Educational System: Structural Change and Social Reproduction 1870-1920. Cambridge: Cambridge University Press.

Musgrave, F. & Taylor, P.H. (1969) Society and the Teacher's Role. London: Routledge and Kegan Paul.

Neave, G. (1987) Les Nouveaux Défis pour les enseignants et leur formation. Strasbourg: Conseil d'Europe.

Neave, G. (1992) The Teaching Nation. Oxford: Pergamon.

Noah, H., & Eckstein, M. (1993) Secondary School Examinations: International Perspectives. New Haven: Yale University Press.

Noah, H. & Eckstein, M. (1973) Metropolitanism and Education: Teachers and Schools in Amsterdam, London, Paris and New York. New York: Institute of Philosophy and Politics of Education, occasional Paper No. 1. Teachers College Columbia University.

Premfors, R. (1980) The Politics of Higher Education in a Comparative Perspective: France, Sweden, the United Kingdom. Stockholm: Stockholm University Press.

Richardson, C.A. (1953) The Education of Teachers in England, France and the U.S.A. Paris: UNESCO.

Ringer, F. (1979) Education and Society in Modern Europe. Bloomington: Indiana University Press.

Rust, V.D. (1987) Teachers in Comparative Perspective, in Lawson, R.E., & others eds. Education and Social Concern. Ann Arbor: Prakken Publications.

Sharpes, D.K. (1988) International Perspectives on Teacher Education. New York: Routledge.

Taylor, W. (1969) Society and the Education of Teachers. London: Faber.

Taylor, W. (1978) Research and Reform in Teacher Education. Slough: National Foundation for Educational Research.

Taylor, W. (1987) Universities under Scrutiny. Paris: OECD.

Thomas, R.M. ed. (1990) International Comparative Education. Oxford: Pergamon.

Tisher, R.P., & Wideen, M.F. eds. (1990) Research in Teacher Education: International Perspectives. London: Falmer Press.

Vaniscotte, F. (1989) 70 millions d'élèves: l'Europe de l'éducation. Paris: Hatier.

de Vroede, M. (1980) La formation des maîtres en Europe jusqu'en 1914, Histoire de l'Education, 6, pp.35-46.

Walford, G. ed. (1989) Private Schools in Ten Countries: Policy and Practice. London: Routledge.

Weiler, H.L. (1989) Education and Power: The Politics of Educational Decentralization in Comparative Perspective, Educational Policy, 3, 4, pp. 31-43.

Wragg, E.C. (1974) Teaching Teaching. Newton Abbot: David and Charles.

Wragg, E.C. (1982) A Review of Research on Teacher Education. Windsor: NFER-Nelson.

Yates, A. ed. (1970) Current Problems of Teacher Education. Hamburg: UNESCO Institute of Education.